Lecture Notes in Computer Science   3279

Commenced Publication in 1973
Founding and Former Series Editors:
Gerhard Goos, Juris Hartmanis, and Jan van Leeuwen

W0235516

Geoffrey M. Voelker Scott Shenker (Eds.)

Peer-to-Peer Systems III

Third International Workshop, IPTPS 2004
La Jolla, CA, USA, February 26-27, 2004
Revised Selected Papers

Volume Editors

Geoffrey M. Voelker
University of California, San Diego
Department of Computer Science and Engineering
9500 Gilman Dr., MC 0114, La Jolla, CA 92093-0114, USA
E-mail: voelker@cs.ucsd.edu

Scott Shenker
University of California, Berkeley
Computer Science Division, EECS Department
683 Soda Hall, 1776, Berkeley, CA 94720, USA
E-mail: shenker@icsi.berkeley.edu

Library of Congress Control Number: Applied for

CR Subject Classification (1998): C.2.4, C.2, H.3, H.4, D.4, F.2.2, E.1, D.2

ISSN 0302-9743
ISBN 3-540-24252-X Springer Berlin Heidelberg New York

Springer is a part of Springer Science+Business Media

springeronline.com

© Springer-Verlag Berlin Heidelberg 2004
Printed in Germany

Typesetting: Camera-ready by author, data conversion by Olgun Computergrafik
Printed on acid-free paper   SPIN: 11361909   06/3142   5 4 3 2 1 0

Preface

On February 26–27, 2004, the 3rd International Workshop on Peer-to-Peer Systems (IPTPS 2004) brought researchers and practitioners together to discuss the latest developments in peer-to-peer technologies, applications, and systems. As the third workshop in the series, IPTPS 2004 continued the success of the previous workshops in pioneering the state of the art in peer-to-peer systems and identifying key research challenges in the area.

The workshop received 145 submissions in the form of five-page position papers. As with previous workshops, submissions went through two rounds of reviews by an international program committee of 14 experts from industry and academia. In the first round each submission received two reviews. In the second round we focused our attention on submissions with either positive reviews, or with reviews that expressed substantially different opinions. In addition to the technical merit, the reviewing process emphasized originality and the potential of the submission to lead to interesting discussions during the workshop.

In the end, the program committee selected a workshop program of 27 papers covering a wide range of topics including new peer-to-peer applications, advances in routing, load balancing, searching, as well as transport, mobility, and other networking topics. Authors revised accepted position papers to six pages for the workshop program, and made a final round of revision for this volume.

The workshop was composed of eight sessions that spanned two days. To focus discussions, attendance was limited to 67 participants and included substantial time for interaction and discussion between sessions and at social events. A hallmark of the IPTPS workshops is that they serve as a crossroads for researchers to gather from many disciplines and communities, including systems, networking, databases, theory, and scientific computing. The workshop this year continued the trend with lively discussions and insight provided by researchers from these many fields.

The workshop would not have been a success without substantial help from a variety of people. First, we thank the program committee for their dedication and effort during an intense reviewing period spanning the winter holidays. The high quality and diversity of the program is due to their insight, experience, and commitment. We would also like to thank Jennifer Anderson for the outstanding local arrangements at the Sea Lodge in La Jolla, Marvin McNett for system administrative support for the IPTPS 2004 Web server, and Michelle Panik for assistance with formatting this volume. And we graciously thank our sponsors, Microsoft Research and Intel, for their continued generous support of the IPTPS workshops.

This volume includes a report on the discussions during the technical sessions. This report conveys the interactions during the workshop beyond the material included in position papers and presented in talks. We thank Sumeet Singh,

Sriram Ramabhadran, and Kiran Tati for diligently taking notes during the workshop and collecting them into this report.

Finally, we thank all authors who submitted papers to the workshop for continuing to make peer-to-peer computing a vibrant research community, the authors of accepted papers for their ideas and contributions to the area, the speakers for spirited and engaging talks, and all participants for making the workshop a success.

March 2004   Geoffrey M. Voelker and Scott Shenker
                                                        Program Co-Chairs
                                                              IPTPS 2004

Workshop Co-Chairs

Scott Shenker   ICSI and UC Berkeley, USA
Geoffrey M. Voelker   UC San Diego, USA

Program Committee

Steve Gribble   University of Washington, USA
John Kubiatowicz   UC Berkeley, USA
Michael Mitzenmacher   Harvard University, USA
Sylvia Ratnasamy   Intel Research, USA
Srini Seshan   CMU, USA
Alex Snoeren   UC San Diego, USA
Robbert van Renesse   Cornell, USA
Dan Wallach   Rice University, USA
Roger Wattenhofer   ETH-Zurich, Switzerland
Alec Wolman   Microsoft Research, USA
Zhichen Xu   HP Labs, USA
Zheng Zhang   Microsoft Research, China

Steering Committee

Peter Druschel   Rice University, USA
Frans Kaashoek   MIT, USA
Antony Rowstron   Microsoft Research, UK
Scott Shenker   ICSI and UC Berkeley, USA
Ion Stoica   UC Berkeley, USA

Administrative Assistant

Jennifer Anderson   UC San Diego, USA

Sponsoring Institutions

Table of Contents

I   Miscellaneous

II   Networking

III   Routing

IV   Load Balancing and Searching

V   Miscellaneous

VI   Applications

VII   Security

VIII   Routing

Workshop Report for the 3rd International Workshop on Peer-to-Peer Systems (IPTPS 2004)

February 26–27, 2004
Sea Lodge Hotel, La Jolla, CA, USA

Sriram Ramabhadran, Sumeet Singh, and Kiran Tati

Department of Computer Science and Engineering
University of California, San Diego
{nramabha,susingh,ktati}@cs.ucsd.edu

1   Miscellaneous

Shiding Lin, Qiao Lian, Ming Chen, and Zheng Zhang, **A Practical Distributed Mutual Exclusion Protocol in Dynamic Peer-to-Peer Systems.** Presented by Zheng Zhang.

C: Some of the ideas are similar to previous work on Byzantine quorum systems.

Q: How is a consistent ordering on client requests obtained? **A:** A logical clock is used to order client requests. Looser semantics result in a quasi-FIFO ordering of requests rather than strictly FIFO.

Q: Mapping between resource and its replicas is non-atomic due to the presence of churn. How does this affect the protocol? **A:** The protocol relies on the DHT to eventually stabilize and present a consistent replica set. Large churn rates could result in no overlap between the previous set of replicas and the new set of replicas, and therefore the protocol performance may degrade (with possible correctness issues).

Q: What kinds of assumptions are made about the DHT and synchrony in the formal proof of correctness? **A:** One assumption is that two nodes do not simultaneous claim ownership of a replica (could arise due to churn).

Nicolas Christin, John Chuang, **On the cost of participating in a peer-to-peer network.** Presented by Nicolas Christin.

Q: Does your analysis extend if you consider maximum load rather than average loads? In particular, does the star topology result in the social optimum? **A:** We need to extend the analysis to other utility functions, such as non-linear functions of load and delay. More general utility functions model cases where maximum rather than average is important.

C: Randomness in choosing node identifiers is a source of asymmetry because a real system will not be perfectly balanced in terms of load, messages routed, etc. It would be interesting to extend the analysis to account for this.

G.M. Voelker and S. Shenker (Eds.): IPTPS 2004, LNCS 3279, pp. 1–10, 2004.

Q: How will hierarchical constructions where small clusters of nodes are tied together using a DHT help, given that most requests will still have to be routed through the DHT? **A:** It depends on how the clusters are constructed, along with the choice of routing algorithm. A desirable construction is where most of the requests are satisfied locally (through a caching mechanism), while only cache misses go through the DHT.

Mema Roussopoulos, Mary Baker, David Rosenthal, TJ Giuli, Petros Maniatis, Jeff Mogul, **2 P2P or Not 2 P2P?** Presented by Mema Roussopoulos.

C: Lack of trust is mentioned as a danger sign but it is also possible that lack of trust among participating entities motivates a distributed design. This is because some applications are too critical to trust any one centralized entity to implement. DNS is one such example.

Q: Peer-to-peer does not necessarily imply nodes are owned by different entities; it may be regarded as a paradigm for designing large-scale distributed systems. Therefore, it is not clear that somebody with a large budget may not want a peer-to-peer solution. **A:** In our model, peer-to-peer is considered to be a system with autonomous nodes rather than a distributed system with a common administration.

C: Mutual trust, accountability and manageability are all important considerations. Therefore it is not important what is the order of things appearing in the decision; they are all things to be considered when evaluating a peer-to-peer solution.

C: A distinction should be made between being able to design a peer-to-peer solution and wanting to use a peer-to-peer solution. In other words, technical issues should be separated from other issues.

Q: Areas where the decision tree indicates trouble spots are all active areas of research; therefore it is conceivable that a peer-to-peer solution will become desirable as the field matures. Is your decision tree predicting future trends with respect to the success of peer-to-peer in these areas? **A:** These areas are potential trouble spots where peer-to-peer solutions must be engineered carefully for them to be successful.

2   Networking

Hung-Yun Hsieh, Raghupathy Sivakumar, **On Transport Layer Support for Peer-to-Peer Networks.** Presented by Hung-Yun Hsieh.

Q: What is the relationship between your work and rate-less codes (IPTPS 2003)? **A:** Rate-less codes are application layer approaches used for file downloads from multiple sources. While the use of rate-less codes does not require the support from the transport layer, it incurs extra processing (for encoding and decoding) and communication (for transmitting redundant data) overheads. In addition, its support for multipoint-to-point communication is application-dependent (e.g., for non-real-time file downloads).

Q: If content is to be downloaded from multiple sources, there must be some way of verifying that the content is the same at all the sources. Shouldn't this be implemented at the application layer rather than at the transport layer? **A:** Yes, we assume that the peer-to-peer lookup service is responsible for providing the list of supplying peers with replicated content to the requesting peer. The validity of the data/content being transferred can be considered higher layer semantics (e.g., presentation or application layer). Note that even in the case of TCP, it does not verify the content being transferred–its functionality is merely to reliably transfer the data given by the application.

Venkata N. Padmanabhan, Helen J. Wang, Philip A. Chou, **Supporting Heterogeneity and Congestion Control in Peer-to-Peer Multicast Streaming.** Presented by Venkat Padmanabhan.

Q: How sensitive is the performance of the system to the accuracy of the dropping decision? **A:** Identifying the source of congestion is important. For example, if congestion is occurring at a parent, it is best to switch to a better parent. If congestion is happening at a peer, the choice of which parent to drop is not absolutely critical. Again, there are considerations of base layer versus enhancement layer, where the base layer is much more important than the enhancement layer.

Ben Y. Zhao, Ling Huang, Anthony D. Joseph, John D. Kubiatowicz, **Rapid Mobility via Type Indirection.** Presented by Ben Zhao.

Q: Where are the Tapestry nodes (wired/wireless)? **A:** Tapestry is used to implement the overlay mobility infrastructure; the mobile end-hosts use a proxy mechanism.

Q: Is the ability to locate a PDA/laptop relevant, considering they are not likely to be content providers? **A:** We are providing the functionality (indirection service), there may be potential applications in the future.

Q: How is group formation done? **A:** Try to predict common mobility patterns, e.g., car-pooling.

Lidong Zhou, Robbert van Renesse, **P6P: A Peer-to-Peer Approach to Internet Infrastructure.** Presented by Lidong Zhou.

Q: Sites may have multiple IPv6 prefixes. How does this affect your architecture? **A:** P6P can easily support sites with multiple IPv6 prefixes. Such a site needs to install one routing table entry for each IPv6 prefix it owns.

Q: How inherent is IPv6 to your architecture; in other words, what features of IPv6 are used by P6P? **A:** P6P is a proposal to separate the network abstraction presented to end sites (hosts) from the core Internet infrastructure. We believe IPv6 is a reasonable abstraction for end applications. In theory, we could have picked any other appropriate abstractions. In practice, because OS support for IPv6 exists on end hosts, adopting IPv6 facilitates the deployment of P6P and is therefore essential for the practicality of P6P.

Q: How is P6P different from I3? **A:** Like I3, P6P also embrace indirection and the separation of identifiers from location. While I3 aims at presenting a general indirection infrastructure, P6P focuses on a concrete and practical proposal that is more likely to be adopted. In particular, unlike I3, which offers an entirely new API to end applications, P6P advocates IPv6, which is already supported in major operating systems.

Q: Can you quantify the routing overhead? **A:** P6P is not yet deployed, so quantifying overhead is difficult. The routing cost consists mainly of routing lookups and packet tunneling. The latter is relatively well understood because it has been widely used.

3   Routing

Jinyang Li, Jeremy Stribling, Thomer M. Gil, Robert Morris, Frans Kaashoek, **Comparing the performance of distributed hash tables under churn.** Presented by Jinyang Li.

Q: Do you take failed operations into consideration? **A:** Yes. All protocols retry failed/incorrect lookups for up to 4 seconds. So a low success rate (e.g., < 90%) would translate into high lookup latency (> 400 ms).

Q: Is the spread of points on your convex hull graph of any importance? **A:** The spread of points depends on the range of values we choose to vary for each parameter and hence is somewhat arbitrary and does not mean anything much. We also acknowledge that the convex hull found is conservative; it is possible that there are "better" parameter value combinations that we have not explored.

Q: How about protocols that adaptively tune the parameters? **A:** We presented convex hulls for different DHTs. However, that does not mean a given DHT can achieve its convex hull performance, as it needs to optimally pick its parameters. A protocol that adaptively tunes its parameters might operate closer to its ideal convex hull.

Q: In a real system with 100's of parameters it is difficult to isolate the effect of any one parameter using the approach used in this paper; for example, Oracle vs. DB2. Is this a limitation with your approach? **A:** We are lucky that the DHTs under study only have a couple of parameters. Even so, we find many parameters are not really meaningful to the DHT cost-performance tradeoff. The current method of varying all parameters simultaneously is not scalable to hundreds of parameters. However, for a real system with hundreds of parameters, it is likely most of them are not critical. It is conceivable to devise some optimizations to quickly identify these non-critical parameters and throw them out.

Q: What is the effect of congestion and queuing on your simulation model? **A:** We do not simulate queuing delays. We believe the load of DHT lookups and maintenance on the network is relatively small compared with application level traffic and will not be a source of congestion. As can be seen from our graphs, the bandwidth usage of DHT level traffic is very small.

Q: What is the impact of data transfer? **A:** Data transfer is not the focus of the work. One might argue that data transfer traffic might dwarf the maintenance/lookup traffic of DHT operations. If so, this would imply we might want to operate DHTs with generous bandwidth costs constraints. And this paper says that all DHTs under study can be tuned to perform similarly to each other when they generate larger amounts of traffic.

Q: How does this DHT perform under different workloads? **A:** We are currently working on extending the model to include different workloads. The analysis in the paper focuses on one type of workload where the lookups are few. One can imagine things becoming different when lookups are abundant; less lookup hops lead to decreased lookup traffic, learning from lookups become more effective, etc.

Sergio Marti, Prasanna Ganesan, Hector Garcia-Molina, **DHT Routing Using Social Links.** Presented by Sergio Marti.

Q: Social networks are not uniformly distributed. This leads to different properties of the DHT, and in particular may lead to overloading of some well-connected nodes. How do you deal with this? **A:** Load-balancing is a problem, but simple strategies can be used to address this. For example, removing the friend links of the most well-connected nodes results in an approximately even distribution of load.

Q: Does trusting a friend translate to trusting a friend's machine? **A:** That is one of purposes of probability rating; trust in a friend is essentially the same as trust in the ability of the friend to manage his machine.

Q: What is the basis of modeling trust as a probability, i.e., what does it mean if you say that you trust someone with probability 0.9? How is the recursive trust effect modeled correctly, if I trust you and you trust somebody, how much do I trust your friend? **A:** One of the things we experimented with is using a step function instead of a multiplicative model for trust. Modeling trust as a probability is not perfect but does capture a lot of intuition.

Q: DHTs are supposed to be distributed, but social links can only be obtained by a centralized database. **A:** The idea is to use existing infrastructure such as AOL and Yahoo Messenger.

Rodrigo Rodrigues, Charles Blake, **When Multi-Hop Peer-to-Peer Routing Matters.** Presented by Rodrigo Rodrigues.

Q: For database sizes of 1TB, is there really a need for P2P? **A:** You do not want to mix technical issues with motivation issues for P2P.

Q: How many stale routing entries are there? And what is the cost incurred in querying stale data? **A:** We target a large fraction of stale entries (1/3 in our concrete example). The per-object availability can remain as high as desired by setting redundancy levels appropriately. Fetch latency can remain low provided we issue several fetch requests in parallel. The main problem would be increased timeouts on synchronous store operations, but we expect stores to be less frequent than fetches, and we think that waiting for all replicas to reply to a store is a bad policy.

C: Although the paper used HDD growth rates as an indicator of future trends, it is not necessarily the case that this is the same as growth in the amount of content available for sharing via P2P.

4   Load Balancing and Searching

Subhash Suri, Csaba Toth, Yunhong Zhou, **Uncoordinated Load Balancing and Congestion Games in P2P Systems.** Presented by Yunhong Zhou.

Q: Why use a bipartite graph to model the network when a node in a P2P system can be both a client and a server? **A:** It does not really matter; if a node is both a client and a server, it can be modeled as two nodes. Therefore a bipartite graph can be derived from the more general graph of the peers.

David R. Karger, Matthias Ruhl, **Simple Efficient Load Balancing Algorithms for Peer-to-Peer Systems.** Presented by Matthias Ruhl.

Q: In a real system, some objects are more popular or bigger in size than others. Therefore uniformity of key-space may not be the critical issue. **A:** The second protocol can handle arbitrary distributions of load and popularity. However, it has the disadvantage that nodes can move to arbitrary locations in the key-space, thereby potentially creating a security problem.

Q: Instead of using log(n) virtual nodes, can we distribute among the log(n) finger nodes to get the same effect? **A:** It is not clear that this would work.

Q: How does the routing work when nodes can move to arbitrary places in the key-space? **A:** See the details in the paper.

Boon Thau Loo, Ryan Huebsch, Ion Stoica, Joseph Hellerstein, **The Case for a Hybrid P2P Search Infrastructure.** Presented by Boon Thau Loo.

Q: How do you handle the fact that some inverted lists may be too big (popular keywords)? **A:** Stop-words need to be filtered. While this step alone is not sufficient to make keyword search feasible on a DHT, it is necessary.

Q: Apart from query, have you considered the effect of downloads? **A:** This is part of future work.

Q: What is the connection between rare items and rare query terms? **A:** On the average, rare items are likely to have rare keywords.

C: What is classified as a rare item is an artifact of your measurement methodology. Just because your search algorithm is not able to find it does not necessarily mean that the object is rare.

Q: Have you considered other hybrid architectures (for example a hierarchy of DHTs)? This may make sense to limit popular search items to a smaller number of nodes while using the global network to search for more rate items. **A:** This is an interesting idea except that building DHTs over smaller sets of nodes does not exploit the scalability of DHTs.

Shuming Shi, Guangwen Yang, Dingxing Wang, Jin Yu, Shaogang Qu, Ming Chen, **Making Peer-to-Peer Keyword Searching Feasible Using Multi-level Partitioning.** Presented by Zheng Zhang.
(No questions, authors unable to attend.)

5 Miscellaneous

Alan Mislove, Peter Druschel, **Providing Administrative Control and Autonomy in Peer-to-Peer Overlays.** Presented by Alan Mislove.
(No questions recorded.)

Robbert van Renesse, Adrian Bozdog, **Willow: DHT, Aggregation, and Publish/Subscribe in One Protocol.** Presented by Robbert van Renesse.

Q: Almost any DHT can provide multicast, why is Willow special? **A:** In our case multicast is used internally to keep the tree together. Willow also supports aggregation and pub/sub routing.

Helen J. Wang, Yih-Chun Hu, Chun Yuan, Zheng Zhang, Yi-Min Wang, **Friends Troubleshooting Network: Towards Privacy-Preserving, Automatic Troubleshooting.** Presented by Helen Wang.

Q: How representative were the 20 troubleshooting cases you looked at? How likely is it that everybody will have the same value for the registry? **A:** We do not know how representative they are, the 20 cases are real-world troubleshooting cases some of which are gathered from our co-workers' troubleshooting experiences, and some of which are obtained from MS customer tech support. For the second question, the PeerPressure troubleshooting algorithm essentially measures the uniqueness of a suspect entry value among the sample set entry values and ranks the uniqueness metric among the suspects. This is effective for most cases. However, for a highly customized computer, its unique configurations would stand out as mis-configurations – and this is one source of false positives of the PeerPressure algorithm.

C: There is a lot of work in statistics that is potentially relevant, especially anonymous census. **A:** However, the existing techniques cannot address the anonymous accumulation of all the parameters that are needed by Friends Troubleshooting Network.

Q: How do you handle multiple entries? **A:** We currently do not handle multiple entries but this is a future avenue of research.

Q: PeerPressure ranks the suspects on their probabilities of being sick. Then what is next? **A:** The key benefit of PeerPressure is that it significantly narrows down the root cause candidate set. The next step is to trial-and-error with each entry from the lowest rank on and to see whether correcting that entry cures the problem. It is true that this could be tricky since there can be rippling configuration changes from a single configuration change.

Q: The configurations may be site-specific, which you do not know ahead of time. How do you handle that? **A:** In this case, search could be scoped within a domain first. Basically such heuristics could be incorporated into search.

Brad Karp, Sylvia Ratnasamy, Sean Rhea, Scott Shenker, **Spurring Adoption of DHTs with OpenHash, a Public DHT Service.** Presented by Brad Karp.

Q: OpenHash supports both Put/Get and ReDir, which do you expect people to use more? **A:** We don't know yet. We expect that both will be heavily used.

Q: Why don't you want desktops to run this infrastructure? **A:** We are hoping to start by limiting the nodes that participate. As the project advances we may allow additional nodes to participate.

Q: Have you looked at the data management issues (for example infrastructure nodes may fail)? **A:** We have not looked at it yet.

Q: Since it is a public infrastructure don't you have to worry about security issues? **A:** These are open issues.

6   Applications

Emil Sit, Frank Dabek, James Robertson, **UsenetDHT: A Low Overhead Usenet Server.** Presented by Emil Sit.

Q: Does your scheme increase the potential for censorship? **A:** The data is fairly well distributed, an attacked would need to control a very large set of nodes.

Q: Existing system exploits geographic locality. Can you do that? **A:** Certainly you can form sub-groups to exploit locality.

Q: How does your approach compare to the alternate suggestion for USENET to use content on demand? **A:** Implementing content on demand in current USENET is technically very difficult, there any many issues to be dealt with.

F. Le Fessant, S. Handurukande, A.-M. Kermarrec, L. Massoulié,, **Clustering in Peer-to-Peer File Sharing Workloads.** Presented by Fabrice Le Fessant.

Q: Have you used your observations to predict how much improvement you can obtain as a result of the locality properties of P2P? **A:** We don't know yet as we have not done the analysis.

Virginia Lo, Daniel Zappala, Dayi Zhou, Yuhong Liu, Shanyu Zhao, **Cluster Computing on the Fly: P2P Scheduling of Idle Cycles in the Internet.** Presented by Virginia Lo.

Q: How do you make the quizzes indistinguishable from actual results? **A:** Sometimes the queries are the real thing.

Q: How do you see these reputation systems play out? **A:** It's a hard problem and we are not exactly interested in a totally secure reputation system.

7 Security

Baruch Awerbuch, Christian Scheideler,, **Robust Distributed Name Service.** Presented by Christian Scheideler.

Q: Does the assumption about join and leave rate apply to bad guys? **A:** You can come up with cryptographic puzzles, for example.

Q: What if the bad guys all behave very well for a while? **A:** The system is acting on a proactive fashion even when the peers are behaving well; the reliability argument is based on statistics.

Q: How much accuracy do you need in estimating N? Could N just be larger than the number of nodes in the system or do you have to get N right? **A:** You have to get N right to within a constant factor.

William K. Josephson, Emin Gün Sirer, Fred B. Schneider,, **Peer-to-Peer Authentication With a Distributed Single Sign-On Service.** Presented by Gün Sirer.

Q: How do you manage names in CorSSO? **A:** Every authentication server has its own namespace. The names from different authentication servers are combined to create a global name for each principal. These global names are associated with a shorter name at each application server. This approach allows CorSSO to separate the management of the name spaces from each other, yet link them to identify principals uniquely. It also allows legacy services to transition to use CorSSO without having to change their existing user names.

Q: Do you need a new public-private key pair to be generated for each service? **A:** We need a key pair for each sub-policy.

Q: Can the identifiers change over time? **A:** The identifier can change over time.

Q: How do you do replication of client certificates? **A:** Certificates are timed.

Antonio Nicolosi, David Mazières, **Secure Acknowledgment of Multicast Messages in Open Peer-to-Peer Networks.** Presented by Antonio Nicolosi.
(No questions recorded.)

8 Routing

Moni Naor, Udi Wieder, **Know thy Neighbor's Neighbor: Better Routing for Skip-Graphs and Small Worlds.** Presented by Udi Wieder.

Q: Why don't we get 50% improvement? **A:** A non-hop is counted as two hops

Jingfeng Hu, Ming Li, Ning Ning, Weimin Zheng, **SmartBoa: Constructing P2P Overlay Network in the Heterogeneous Internet Using Irregular Routing Tables.** Presented by Ming Li.
(No questions.)

David R. Karger, Matthias Ruhl, **Diminished Chord: A Protocol for Heterogeneous Subgroup Formation in Peer-to-Peer Networks.** Presented by David Karger.

Q: Would it be better to have 2 small DHTs as opposed to 1 DHT? **A:** I don't think so, even if the node sets are disjoint, you can get more robustness against failures by attaching the two groups together. When you start building cache tables the lookup hops don't matter.

Q: Are we moving towards a service based model? **A:** OpenHash does have this idea of separating out this layer of service, you can open the OpenDHT layer to trusted nodes, but then who decides who are trusted? On the other hand, you can limit to high bandwidth nodes.

C: One situation where smaller DHTs may be better is when nodes are geographically close together.

Acknowledgements

We thank the authors for their valuable comments and feedback.

A Practical Distributed Mutual Exclusion Protocol in Dynamic Peer-to-Peer Systems

Shi-Ding Lin[1], Qiao Lian[1], Ming Chen[2], and Zheng Zhang[1]

[1] Microsoft Research, Asia
100080 Beijing, China
{i-slin,i-qlian,zzhang}@microsoft.com
[2] Tsinghua University
100084 Beijing, China
cm01@mails.tsinghua.edu.cn

Abstract. Mutual exclusion is one of the well-studied fundamental primitives in distributed systems. However, the emerging P2P systems bring forward several challenges that can't be completely solved by previous approaches. In this paper, we propose the Sigma protocol that is implemented inside a dynamic P2P DHT and circumvents those issues. The basic idea is to adopt queuing and co-operation between clients and replicas so as to enforce quorum consensus scheme. We demonstrate that this protocol is scalable with system size, robust to contention, and resilient to network latency variance and fault-tolerant.

1 Introduction

One of the fundamental primitives to implement more generic systems and applications on top of P2P DHTs [4][13] is mutual exclusion. Such primitive is also a rudimentary service to guard arbitrary resources when necessary. For example, a concurrency control mechanism is obviously needed for a mutable distributed file system.

For the applications and systems we envision to be built and deployed on those P2P DHTs, one can all but rule out the possibility of enforcing concurrency using stable transaction servers, whether they are external or internal to the system. Therefore, such primitives must be implemented *inside* P2P DHT. The protocol is thus by definition distributed, it must be simple and efficient, and yet robust enough to be of practical use.

Our basic idea is simple: utilizing the fact that nodes in the DHT collectively form a logical space that does not have holes, institute a set of *logical replicas* upon which a quorum consensus protocol grants access to critical section (CS). From a client's perspective, these replicas are always online. However, they may suffer from complete memory loss from time to time. Such random reset occurs when the node that acts as a logical replica crashes and gets replaced by one of its logical neighbor in DHT.

The open and dynamic nature of P2P environment brings another serious challenge. Many previous approaches [10] assume a close system with fixed and relatively moderate number of nodes, and nodes communicate among themselves to reach

G.M. Voelker and S. Shenker (Eds.): IPTPS 2004, LNCS 3279, pp. 11–21, 2004.
© Springer-Verlag Berlin Heidelberg 2004

consensus. These solutions are inapplicable in our context where the number of clients is unpredictable and can swing to be very large. The protocols need to be designed for a harsh and open environment such as a wide-area P2P.

The work in this paper presents a few novel contributions:

- We start by investigating a straightforward, ALOHA-like strawman protocol and show that, the high variation of network latency between clients and replicas is responsible for the large performance degradation. We believe this insight is valuable for any wide-area consensus protocols.
- We demonstrate that a cooperative strategy between clients and replicas is necessary to circumvent latency variance and contention, thus achieving scalability and robustness.
- We propose the *informed backoff* mechanism, which intelligently rebuilds replica's state, to handle the random reset problem of replicas.

The resulting protocol, Sigma, is fully implemented, analyzed and evaluated. We present both analytical and experimental results that demonstrate its performance and efficacy.

We discuss the system model in Section II. The strawman protocol and its performance evaluation are presented in Section III. Building on this, we describe the Sigma protocol in Section IV and experiment results in Section V. Related work is in Section VI and we conclude in Section VII.

2 System Model

In its essence, a P2P DHT offers a virtual space populated by participating peers. The space does not have any holes except for a very transient period of time during membership change.

For a given resource R, its associated server $CS(R)$ can be *logical*. For instance, there can be n replicas whose names are "/foo/bar:i" where $i \in [1..n]$ (see Figure 1). We can hash these names to derive the keys, and the hosting node of each key can serve as one replica. This decoupling of naming and actual server means that we are working with a peculiar "server" who is *always* available but may suffer from memory loss at random point of time. Moreover, as we shall see, the introduction of multiple replicas implies that the latencies between a client to these replicas be highly variable, exerting a significant impact on performance.

Formally speaking, our system model is as follows:

- The replicas are always available, but their internal states may be randomly reset. This is also termed as the failure-recovery model in [8].
- The number of clients is unpredictable and can be very large. Clients are not malicious and fail stop.
- Clients and replicas communicate via messages across unreliable channels. Messages could be replicated, lost, but never forged.

In the context of this paper, both clients and replicas are peers in the DHT (in practice, however, it's only the replicas that have to be DHT members). When a replica grants permission (or vote) to a client, the latter is called *owner* of the former. A client who has collected majority permissions is said to be the *winner* of a round.

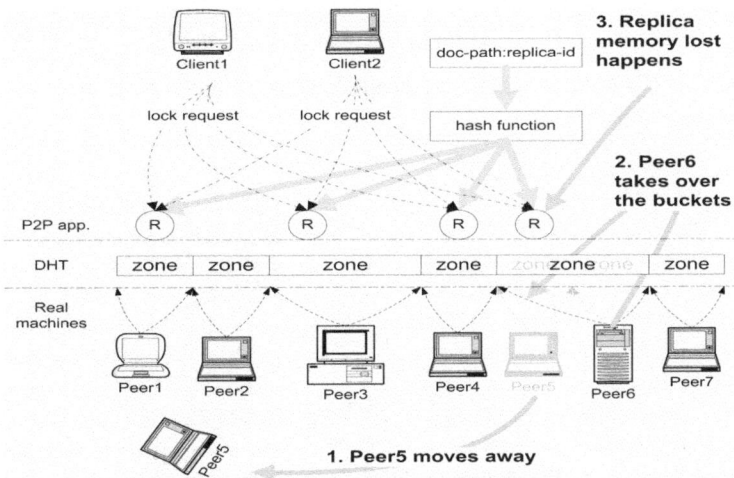

Fig. 1. Majority consensus in a P2P DHT; "bucket" is the unit of DHT and is synonym of "zone", "R" denotes a logical replica. The diagram illustrates that the node crash can be modeled as logical replica reset.

We assume that the typical lifetime of a DHT node is long enough so a client can talk directly to the current node who acts as a logical replica, invoking $O(\log N)$ DHT lookup only after the logical replica takes a reset.

Our primary goal is to derive a set of efficient and highly reliable protocols. We want the protocol to perform as robust as possible, in both low and high contention situation. Finally, it should correct itself rapidly after faults occur.

3   A Strawman Protocol

In this section, we will introduce a strawman protocol which is straightforward to implement, but nevertheless illustrates essential attributes as well as problems of a highly available, majority-based consensus protocol.

The main idea is similar to ALOHA [11] protocol's way of resolving conflicting packets; all clients that want to enter critical section (CS) send requests to each of the replicas and wait for responses. A replica grants a lease if it is not owned by anyone, and otherwise rejects the request but informs the client the current owner. The one who obtains m out of n replicas ($m>n/2$) is the winner at this round. Losers release acquired votes (if any), back-off and retry after a random period. This also guarantees that deadlock will not occur.

The replicas, however, can suffer from random reset after which it forgets about its previous decision and is open to new request. The "change of heart" can cause the mutual exclusion to be broken. Assume that average life of a node is T, the probability that the node may crash in a period of t is t/T. The probability that any k out of m voted replicas resets is $\binom{m}{k}(\frac{t}{T})^k (1 - \frac{t}{T})^{m-k}$. So, the safety will be broken when more than or equal to $2m-n$ resets occur during t, and the probability would be

$\sum_{k=2m-n}^{m} \binom{m}{k}(\frac{t}{T})^{k}(1-\frac{t}{T})^{m-k}$. It turns out that in a given round, to tolerate up to k replica reset $n=3k+1$ and $m=2k+1$ are needed. Thus, as a design choice, we can raise the value of m.

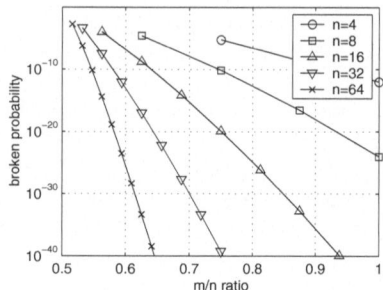

Fig. 2. Probability to break exclusivity.

Figure 2 shows the probability of violating exclusivity, where T is of 10000 seconds, which is the reported average life of a P2P node [12], and t is chosen as 10 seconds, which gives a conservative upper bound of clients staying in the CS. We show the results with different parameters of m/n.

It can be observed that accomplishing robust mutual exclusion with this protocol is realistic. Even with $n=32$ and $m/n=0.75$ (i.e. $m=24$), a very practical setting, the chance of breaking the exclusivity is 10^{-40}. Using this configuration to guard a document whose availability requirement is 15-18 nines is entirely reasonable. The broader point we want to make is that it makes little practical sense to guarantee the conflict probability substantially lower than the availability of the resource to be protected.

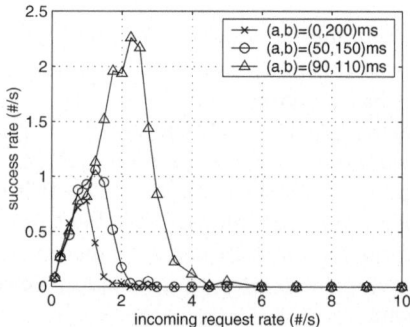

Fig. 3. Performance of strawman protocol, with latency uniformly distributed in (a, b).

The performance of this protocol, however, is an entirely different story. Figure 3 depicts the throughput in various network conditions, where m and n is 24 and 32 respectively. The average network latency of any client to all replicas is fixed at 100ms, but latency of a given client-replica pair is a random variable. This is a reasonable assumption in a wide-area DHT.

The first thing to notice is that the curve looks just like that of ALOHA(see [11]): the throughput increases linearly when contention is low, reaches a peak, and then degrades essentially to zero. It is clear that latency variance has a significant impact: the higher the variance, the worse the throughput.

4   The Sigma Protocol

The main culprit of the strawman protocol's poor performance is the variance of network latency between one client and each replica. Client requests will reach different replicas at different time, so it is hard for all replicas to build a consistent view of competing clients. A second, more subtle issue has to do with the greedy behavior of the clients: they would keep on retrying when collision occurs; therefore nobody can win out. There should be a comprehensive set of techniques to address both problems.

We deal with the first problem by installing a queue at replicas and reshuffle them towards a consistent view in case of high contention. To combat the second issue, we adopt a strategy to enforce clients into a state of *active waiting*. Figure 5 and Figure 6

Figure 6 present pseudo code, described in terms of message handler, for clients and replicas respectively. The two sides exchange messages and the relevant entities and their interactions are depicted in Figure 4.

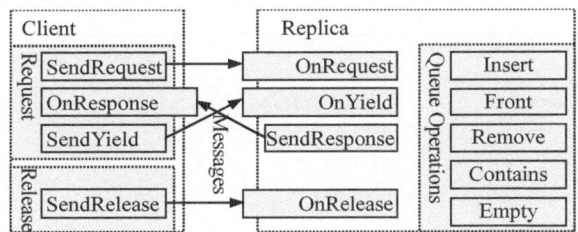

Fig. 4. Architecture of Sigma protocol.

The client states include its id, and an array resp[]. resp[i] records the response from the i-th replica, stating its owner and the associated timestamp. The replica maintains the following: who owns this replica (C_{owner}), and a value of nil indicates this replica has not voted for anyone; T_{owner} stores the timestamp of the request; Queue stores waiting clients in order of their timestamp. We use Lamport's logical clock [7] to generate timestamp.

Client starts by firing REQUEST messages to all replicas (Request in Figure 5). These requests are handled by the OnRequest at the replica, which either grants its vote outright or queue the request up, depending on whether this replica has already voted. Regardless, the id and timestamp of the current owner of the replica (equals to the client's only if the queue is empty) are returned to client by a RESPONSE message.

As the responses arrive at the client (OnResponse in Figure 5), it gradually forms the idea about its place in the race. Suppose m out of n replicas is needed to achieve quorum consensus, there will be all but three outcomes and each can be easily distinguished by examining owner attached in the RESPONSE messages:

```
State Variables:
    id      // the identity of the client
    resp[]  // responses from replica
Request(CS) {
  timestamp := GetLogicalClock();      //lamport's clock
  for each R[i] of CS
    SendRequest(R[i], id, timestamp);
}
OnResponse(R[i], owner, timestamp) {
  resp[i].owner := owner;
  resp[i].timestamp := timestamp;
  if (enough responses received) {
  winner := ComputeWinner();
  if (winner = self)                    // case 1
    return success;
  else if (winner = nil) {    // case 3
    for each resp[i].owner is self {
      SendYield(R[i], id);
      Clear(resp[i]);                   // reset the state
    }
  }
  // case 2: some one else wins, just wait
  }
}
Release(CS) {
  for all R[i] of CS
    SendRelease(R[i], id);
}
```

Fig. 5. Client-side pseudo code.

```
State Variables:
    C_owner          // the client it accepts
    T_owner          // time stamp of C_owner
    Queue            // queue requests up
OnRequest(C, timestamp) {
  if (C_owner = nil) {
    C_owner := C;
    T_owner := timestamp;
  }
  else
    Queue.Insert(C, timestamp);
    SendResponse(C, C_owner, T_owner);
}
OnRelease(C) {
  if (C = C_owner) {
    C_owner := nil;
    if (not Queue.Empty())
      RespQueue();
  }
  else if (Queue.Contains(C))
    Queue.Remove(C);
}
OnYield(C) {
  if (C = C_owner) {
    Queue.Insert(C, T_owner);
    RespQueue();
    if (C != C_owner)
      SendResponse(C, C_owner, T_owner);
  }
}
RespQueue() {            // helper routine
  <C_owner, T_owner> := Queue.Front();
  SendResponse(C_owner, C_owner, T_owner);
  Queue.Remove(C_owner);
}
```

Fig. 6. Replica-side pseudo code.

1. The client is the winner by quorum consensus. It succeeds and gets the permission to enter CS.
2. Some one does win but not this client. The client does nothing because it knows it has been registered on the replicas already. We will detail later when and how it will be notified.
3. *Nobody* has won, and this is the case if $j_{same} + n - j < m$ where j is the number of returned responses and the maximal number of same item in j is j_{same}. The client then sends out a YIELD message to each of the acquired replicas.

The YIELD operation reflects the collaborative nature of Sigma protocol and is a critical performance optimization. The semantic of YIELD is RELEASE+REQUEST. When replica receives a YIELD message, it removes the client from the winning seat and inserts it into the queue, chooses the earliest one and notifies the winner.

The function of the YIELD handling is to reshuffle the queue. The fact that nobody wins indicates that contention has occurred. This, in turn, implies that queues are being built up but the winners are out of place. By issuing the YIELD request, clients are collectively offering the replicas a chance to build a more consistent view and, consequently, choose the right winner. It is important to understand that this will go on until a winner is settled, as such could take multiple rounds of YIELD. Typically, this self-stabilization process will quickly settle, as verified in our experiments [14].

The release operation is straightforward: the client, if is the owner simply relinquishes, or is removed from the queue otherwise. In either case, the next client (if any) is notified by the RESPONSE message.

So far, we have described Sigma in a failure-free environment. In reality, many things may go wrong:

1. After crash, a replica might grant the vote to a new client, despite the fact that it might have already done so to the previous one. We deal with this by raising m/n ratio to reduce the probability of breaking safety. With appropriate parameter, the risk can be negligible in practice (Section III).
2. More seriously, its queue has gone and those waiting clients will get stuck forever. What is called for is a way to rebuild the replica's memory. This is addressed by the *informed backoff* mechanism discussed later.
3. If the client who is currently in the CS crashes before exit, replicas will be stuck. Therefore, replica grants permission to clients with renewable lease [1]. When the lease expires, replica will grant permission to the next client (if any) in the queue.
4. The unreliable communication channel between a client and a replica will cause similar problems as well. In essence, message loss can be mapped to arbitrary crash of clients or replicas, which simplifies the handling.

The combination of informed backoff and lease builds a reliable communication over the unreliable channel and is a variation of failure detector [15] plus timeout. This best-effort approach leverages replica knowledge to achieve better tradeoff between communication cost and system throughput.

Informed backoff is a way to rebuild a restarted replica's state without overloading those healthy replicas. It is extremely simple at its core. Upon a request, replica could predict the expected waiting time T_w and advise it to wait so long before next retry. An empirical calculation of T_w is $T_w = T_{CS} * (P + 1/2)$, where P is the client's position in the queue and T_{CS} is the average CS duration, as observed by the replica of interval between any two consecutive release operations. The 1/2 in the formula is to take current owner of the replica into consideration. Notice that T_w is always updated upon the reception of a retry.

Let's consider the case that the replica has not crashed at all. If the client is notified before its scheduled retry, no harm is done. Otherwise it means that the advised T_w was not accurate (such as some earlier clients take extra time). In this case the client will renew its T_w in its retry. This is of course an overhead, but we are not too far off from the future point when the permission will be granted and thus hopefully this is the only retry that the client will have to endure. If, on the other hand, replica does go through a reset, then the queue is reconstructed with the order similar to the original one, fulfilling our goal.

We now offer a brief analysis of the Sigma protocol:

- **Service policy.** The use of logical clock and the First-Come First-Serve policy at replica does not guarantee FCFS, since client requests can take arbitrarily long to arrive. Thus, Sigma can be best described as quasi-FCFS.
- **Safety.** We guarantee safety with high probability. No known protocols can ensure 100% correctness under failure. We treat replica failure and imprecise failure detector in a uniform manner. As shown in Section III, the probability of violating safety can be practically negligible by setting appropriate m/n.
- **Liveness.** Progress is ensured by using lease.

5   Experimental Results

The Sigma protocol is fully implemented and deployed in a distributed testbed, which can be configured by different network topology models.

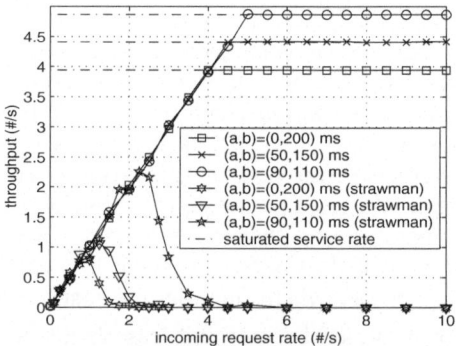

Fig. 7. Throughput versus latency variance and contention, with latency uniformly distributed in (a, b) and average latency being 100ms. The 3-dashed lines correspond to theoretical predictions of saturated throughput, which differ with latency distribution. Data for both the strawman and Sigma are shown. m/n is 24/32.

We assume a pool of infinity clients, and each client will fire request contending for CS according to a Poisson distribution, with λ as the incoming request rate. To focus on the performance aspects of the protocol, we let client exit CS immediately after it enters. After 5 minutes warm-up period we test 10 minutes during which throughput, in terms of the number of serviced requests per second, is measured. This is then repeated for different incoming request rate.

Figure 7 depicts the throughput against different incoming request, varying the latency distribution. One can see that network latency distribution has little impact: the throughput increases linearly when request rate ramps up, until a point when it reaches the saturated rate and then stays flat as predicted by a theoretical model (see [14]). This is the ideal behavior. For comparison purposes, the throughput of the strawman protocol (Figure 3) is also plotted. We can see that the performance improvement is significant.

When replicas suffer from crash and thereafter undergo memory reset, performance will drop. There are many causes contributing to performance degradation and it's difficult to obtain a succinct reasoning. However, in a way a reset has the net effect of enlarging latency variance: a REQUEST, which would otherwise result in a successful RESPONSE, reaches the restarted replica behind those from others who should have been queued.

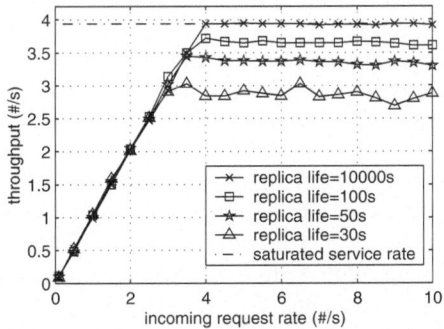

Fig. 8. Throughput versus replica availability, with latency uniformly distributed in (0, 200)ms and m/n being 24/32. The dashed line corresponds to theoretical prediction of saturated throughput. When replica life is 10000 seconds, theoretical throughput can be achieved.

We set the average lifetime of replica to be excessively short. The lifetime is exponentially distributed [2] and different average values are tested. Figure 8 presents our results. The penalty of throughput is perceptible if the replica life is 30 seconds; however, it becomes less and less significant with longer replica life. Given that in a P2P environment, nodes typically will be online for about 10000 seconds [12], we believe that the ideal throughput of Sigma can be achieved in practice.

We have analyzed and measured message cost and show that it is asymptotically bound by $4n$. Due to space limitation, we refer readers to the full technical report [14].

6 Related Work

From the taxonomy of [10], the Sigma protocol would fall into the "permission-based" category. These protocols assume a closed system, in which clients are also the replicas. The context of this work mandates an open system where number of clients is unpredictable.

The more relevant work includes the Byzantine protocols [5][6][9] which also operates in an open-system setting. Obviously, Sigma's idea of virtual replicas is immediately applicable to these protocols to tailor-fit them in a P2P environment. The objectives, however, differ. Sigma is a light-weight synchronization protocol with $O(n)$ message costs and does not attempt to deal with malicious client. Whereas the Byzantine protocols takes a replicated state machine approach with $O(n^2)$ cost and handles malicious client. It is interesting to note that, for a total of $3f+1$ replica, when faults exceed f, both protocols will yield unpredictable results.

Sigma's emphasis is more on the practicality side and pays much attention for performance. In the P2P space, [3] is similar to the strawman protocol, but is augmented with exponential backoff. It is not clear whether its property will hold in face of latency variance, which we believe is the prevailing pattern of a P2P environment.

7   Conclusion and Future Work

The emerging P2P scenario brings forward several challenges to mutually exclusive access of the resource stored in it, such as the huge variance of network latency, unpredictable (and often very large) number of clients and finally high dynamism. These issues are partially addressed in previous works but not completely solved. In this paper, we propose the Sigma: a practical, efficient and fault-tolerant protocol for distributed mutual exclusion inside P2P DHT.

The key points of Sigma protocol are to use logical replicas and quorum consensus to deal with system dynamisms. Quasi-consistency and cooperation between clients and replicas circumvent the large variance of network latency and high contention. Sigma also gracefully deals with failure by two techniques: informed backoff and lease, making protocol fault-tolerant.

We verified that this protocol offers high performance in heterogeneous network condition and various contention rates. In a practical environment, the failure handling mechanism works well with negligible performance penalty and moderate communication overhead. Our detailed technical report [14] includes more extensive empirical and analytical report. The correctness of Sigma protocol is formally proved in [17], in which we extend its applicability to dynamic distributed system in general, not just for P2P.

The concept of logical replica can be further extended [16]. If all quorum members form a DHT and let client request be broadcasted to all of them, each member can vote with their *share* of space (i.e. zone). Thus, a consensus is reached if the client has gathered $f=m/n$ total *fraction* of the total space. The protocol is interesting in that instead of investing in mechanisms to handle membership change, it is designed to cope with non-constant number of members to start with. Furthermore, it brings another level of robustness because the protocol is correct as long as the space owned by good nodes is larger than those owned by compromised/malicious nodes over some threshold. Thus, as a simple defense mechanism, it is possible to continuously institute new members to combat the spread of compromised nodes. While the protocol in [16] was described in terms of the strawman protocol, Sigma can be easily adopted as well as a highly optimized implementation.

Acknowledgement

We thank the anonymous reviewers for their valuable feedbacks. This paper has also benefited from many enlightening discussions with colleagues from other MSR labs including Lidong Zhou, Butler Lampson and Leslie Lamport.

References

1. B. Pawlowski, S. Shepler, et al. The NFS Version 4 Protocol, in Proceedings of the 2nd international system administration and networking conference (SANE2000)
2. D. Liben-Nowell, H. Balakrishnan, and D. Karger, Analysis of the Evolution of Peer-to-Peer Systems, in 21st ACM Symposium on Principles of Distributed Computing (PODC), Monterey, CA, July 2002.
3. G. Chokler, D. Malkhi, and M. Reiter, Backoff Protocols for Distributed Mutual Exclusion and Ordering, in Proceedings of 21st International Conference on Distributed Computing Systems (ICDCS), 2001.
4. I. Stoica, et al, Chord: A Scalable Peer-to-peer Lookup Service for Internet Applications, in Proceedings of ACM SIGCOMM 2001, San Deigo, CA, August 2001.
5. J. Yin, et al. Separating Agreement from execution for Byzantine Fault Tolerant Services, in Proceedings of the 19th ACM Symposium on Operating Systems Principles, Octobor 2003.
6. L. Lamport, R. Shostak and M. Pease, The Byzantine Generals Problem, ACM Transactions on Programming Languages and Systems, 4(3):382-401, July 1982
7. L. Lamport, Time, Clocks and the Ordering of Events in a Distributed System, Communications of the ACM 21, 7 (July 1978), 558-565.
8. M. K. Aguilera, W. Chen, and S. Toueg, Failure detection and consensus in the crash-recovery model. Distributed Computing, Springer-Verlag, 13:2, April 2000, pp. 99-125.
9. M. Castro, B. Liskov, Practical Byzantine Fault Tolerance. in Proceedings of the Third Symposium on Operating Systems Design and Implementation, New Orleans, February 1999.
10. M. G. Velazquez, A Survey of Distributed Mutual Exclusion Algorithms, Colorado State University, Technical Report CS-93-116.
11. N. Abramson, The Aloha System – Another Alternative for Computer Communications. In AFIPS Conference Proceedings, Vol. 36, 1970, pp. 295-298.
12. S. Saroiu, P. Krishna Gummadi, S. D. Gribble, A Measurement Study of Peer-to-Peer File Sharing Systems, in Proceedings of Multimedia Computing and Networking (MMCN) 2002.
13. S. Ratnasamy, P. Francis, M. Handley, R. Karp, and S. Shenker, A Scalable Content-Addressable Network, in Proceedings of ACM SIGCOMM 2001.
14. S. Lin, Q. Lian, M. Chen, and Z. Zhang, A Practical Distributed Mutual Exclusion Protocol in Dynamic Peer-to-Peer Systems, Microsoft Research, Technical Report MSR-TR-2004-13.
15. T. D. Chandra and S. Toueg, Unreliable failure detectors for reliable distributed systems. Journal of the ACM, 43(2):255-267.
16. Z. Zhang, The Power of DHT as a Logical Space. To appear in FTDCS'04.
17. W. Chen, S. Lin, Q. Lian and Z. Zhang. Sigma: A Fast Fault-Tolerant Mutual Exclusion Algorithm in Dynamic Distributed System. Submission in preparation.

On the Cost of Participating
in a Peer-to-Peer Network*

Nicolas Christin and John Chuang

University of California, Berkeley
School of Information Management and Systems
102 South Hall
Berkeley, CA 94720, USA
{christin,chuang}@sims.berkeley.edu

Abstract. In this paper, we model the cost incurred by each peer participating in a peer-to-peer network. Such a cost model allows to gauge potential disincentives for peers to collaborate, and provides a measure of the "total cost" of a network, which is a possible benchmark to distinguish between proposals. We characterize the cost imposed on a node as a function of the experienced load and the node connectivity, and express benefits in terms of cost reduction. We discuss the notion of social optimum with respect to the proposed cost model, and show how our model applies to a few proposed routing geometries for distributed hash tables (DHTs). We further outline a number of open questions this research has raised.

1 Introduction

A key factor in the efficiency of a peer-to-peer overlay network is the level of collaboration provided by each peer. In this paper, we take a first step towards quantifying the level of collaboration that can be expected from each node participating in an overlay, by proposing a model to evaluate the cost each peer incurs as a member of the overlay. We express the benefits of participating in the overlay in terms of a cost reduction.

Such a cost model has several useful applications, among which, (1) providing a benchmark that can be used to compare between different proposals, complementary to recent works comparing topological properties of various overlays [1, 2], (2) allowing for predicting disincentives, and designing mechanisms that ensure a protocol is *strategyproof* [3], and (3) facilitating the design of load balancing primitives.

This work is not the first attempt to characterize the cost of participating in a network. Jackson and Wolinsky [4] proposed cost models to analyze formation strategies in social and economic networks. More recent studies [5, 6] model network formation as a non-cooperative game, where nodes have an incentive to

---

* This work is supported in part by the National Science Foundation through grants ANI-0085879 and ANI-0331659.

G.M. Voelker and S. Shenker (Eds.): IPTPS 2004, LNCS 3279, pp. 22–32, 2004.

participate in the network, but want to minimize the price they pay for doing so. These studies assume that each node has the freedom to choose which links it maintains, whereas we assume that the overlay topology is constrained by a protocol. Moreover, our approach extends previously proposed cost models [4–6], by considering the load imposed on each node in addition to the distance to other nodes and degree of connectivity.

In the remainder of this paper, we first introduce our proposed cost model, before discussing the notion of "social optimum," that is, the geometry that minimizes the sum of all costs over the entire network. We then apply the cost model to several routing geometries used in recently proposed distributed hash table (DHT) algorithms [2, 7–10], and compare the costs incurred by each geometry. We conclude by discussing some open problems this research has uncovered.

2   Proposed Cost Model

The model we propose applies to any peer-to-peer network where nodes request and serve items, or serve requests between other nodes. This includes peer-to-peer file-sharing systems [11], ad-hoc networks [12], distributed lookup services [8, 10], or application-layer multicast overlays [13–15], to name a few examples. Formally, we define an overlay network by a quadruplet (V, E, K, F), where V is the set of nodes in the network, E is the set of directed edges, K is the set of items in the network, and $F : K \rightarrow V$ is the function that assigns items to nodes. Each node $u \in V$ is assigned a unique identifier (integer or string of symbols), which, for the sake of simplicity, we will also denote by u. We define by $K_u = \{k \in K : F(k) = u\}$ the set of items stored at node $u \in V$. We have $K = \bigcup_u K_u$, and we assume, without loss of generality, that the sets K_u are disjoint[1]. We characterize each request with two independent random variables, $X \in V$ and $Y \in K$, which denote the node X making the request, and the item Y being requested, respectively.

Consider a given node $u \in V$. Every time an item $k \in K$ is requested in the entire network, node u is in one of four situations:

1. Node u does not hold or request k, and is not on the routing path of the request. Node u is not subject to any cost.
2. Node u requests item k. In our model, we express the benefits of participating in a peer-to-peer network in terms of latency reduction, similar to related proposals, e.g., [6]. In particular, we assume that the farther the node v holding k is from u (in a topological sense), the costlier the request is. If there is no path between nodes u and v, the request cannot be carried out, which yields an infinite cost. More precisely, we model the cost incurred by node u for requesting k as $l_{u,k}t_{u,v}$, where $t_{u,v}$ is the number of hops between nodes u and v, and $l_{u,k}$ is a (positive) proportional factor. We define the

---

[1] If an item is stored on several nodes (replication), the replicas can be viewed as different items with the exact same probability of being requested.

latency cost experienced by node u, L_u, as the sum of the individual costs $l_{u,k}t_{u,v}$ multiplied by the probability $k \in K_v$ is requested, that is

$$L_u = \sum_{v \in V} \sum_{k \in K_v} l_{u,k} t_{u,v} \Pr[Y = k] , \qquad (1)$$

with $t_{u,v} = \infty$ if there is no path from node u to node v, and $t_{u,u} = 0$ for any u. With this definition, to avoid infinite costs, each node has an incentive to create links such that all other nodes holding items of interest can be reached. An alternative is to store or cache locally all items of interest so that the cost of all requests reduces to $l_{u,k}t_{u,u} = 0$.

3. Node u holds item k, and pays a price $s_{u,k}$ for serving the request. For instance, in a filesharing system, the node uses some of its upload capacity to serve the file. We define the *service cost* S_u incurred by u, as the expected value of $s_{u,k}$ over all possible requests. That is,

$$S_u = \sum_{k \in K_u} s_{u,k} \Pr[Y = k] .$$

4. Node u does not hold or request k, but has to forward the request for k, thereby paying a price $r_{u,k}$. The overall *routing cost* R_u suffered by node u is the average over all possible items k, of the values of $r_{u,k}$ such that u is on the path of the request. That is, for $(u, v, w) \in V^3$, we consider the binary function

$$\chi_{v,w}(u) = \begin{cases} 1 \text{ if } u \text{ is on the path from } v \text{ to } w, \\ \quad \text{excluding } v \text{ and } w \\ 0 \text{ otherwise,} \end{cases}$$

and express R_u as

$$R_u = \sum_{v \in V} \sum_{w \in V} \sum_{k \in K_w} r_{u,k} \Pr[X = v] \Pr[Y = k] \chi_{v,w}(u) . \qquad (2)$$

In addition, each node keeps some state information so that the protocol governing the overlay operates correctly. In most overlay protocols, each node u has to maintain a neighborhood table and to exchange messages with all of its neighbors. The number of neighbors corresponds to the out-degree $\deg(u)$ of the node, resulting in a *maintenance cost* M_u that is characterized by

$$M_u = m_u \deg(u) ,$$

where $m_u \geq 0$ denotes the cost associated with maintaining a link with a given neighbor.

Last, we define the *total cost* C_u imposed on node u as

$$C_u = L_u + S_u + R_u + M_u .$$

We can use C_u to compute the total cost of the network, $C = \sum_{u \in V} C_u$. Note that the expression of C_u only makes sense if S_u, R_u, M_u, and L_u are all expressed using the same unit. Thus, the coefficients $s_{u,k}$, $r_{u,k}$, $l_{u,k}$ and m_u have to be selected appropriately. For instance, $l_{u,k}$ is given in monetary units per hop per item, while m_u is expressed in monetary units per neighbor entry.

3 Social Optimum

The first question we attempt to address is whether we can find a social optimum for the cost model we just proposed, that is, a routing geometry that minimizes the total cost C. We define a routing geometry as in [1], that is, as a collection of edges, or topology, associated with a route selection mechanism. Unless otherwise noted, we assume shortest path routing, and distinguish between different topologies. We discuss a few simplifications useful to facilitate our analysis, before characterizing some possible social optima.

3.1 Assumptions

For the remainder of this paper, we consider a network of $N > 0$ nodes, where, for all $u \in V$ and $k \in K$, $l_{u,k} = l$, $s_{u,k} = s$, $r_{u,k} = r$, and $m_u = m$ [2]. We suppose that the network is in a steady-state regime, i.e., nodes do not join or leave the network, so that the values l, s, r and m are constants. We also suppose that requests are uniformly distributed over the set of nodes, that is, for any node u, $\Pr[X = u] = 1/N$. We make a further simplification by choosing the mapping function F such that all nodes have an equal probability of serving a request. In other words, $\sum_{k \in K_u} \Pr[Y = k] = 1/N$, which implies $S_u = s/N$ regardless of the geometry used. Moreover, if we use $E[x]$ to denote the *expected value* of a variable x, Eqs. (1) and (2) reduce to $L_u = lE[t_{u,v}]$ and $R_u = rE[\chi_{v,w}(u)]$, respectively. Last, we assume that no node is acting maliciously.

3.2 Full Mesh

Consider a full mesh, that is, a network where any pair of nodes is connected by a (bidirectional) edge, i.e., $t_{u,v} = 1$ for any $v \neq u$. Nodes never any route any traffic and $\deg(u) = N - 1$. Thus, for all u, $R_u = 0$, $L_u = l(N-1)/N$, and $M_u = m(N-1)$. With $S_u = s/N$, we get $C_u = s/N + l(N-1)/N + m(N-1)$, and, summing over u,

$$C = s + l(N - 1) + mN(N - 1) .$$

Let us remove a link from the full mesh, for instance the link $0 \to 1$. Because node 0 removes an entry from its neighborhood table, its maintenance cost M_0 decreases by m. However, to access the items held at node 1, node 0 now has to send traffic through another node (e.g., node 2): as a result, L_0 increases by l/N, and the routing cost at node 2, R_2, increases by r/N^2. So, removing the link $0 \to 1$ causes a change in the total cost $\Delta C = -m + l/N + r/N^2$. If $\Delta C \geq 0$, removing a link causes an increase of the total cost, and the full mesh

---

[2] While very crude in general, this simplification is relatively accurate in the case of a network of homogeneous nodes and homogeneous links containing fixed-sized keys such as used in DHTs.

is the social optimum. In particular, the full mesh is the social optimum if the maintenance cost is "small enough," that is, if

$$m \leq l/N + r/N^2 . \tag{3}$$

Note that, as $N \to \infty$, the condition (3) tends to $m = 0$. In fact, we can also express $\Delta C \geq 0$ as a condition on N that reduces to $N \leq \lfloor l/m + r/l \rfloor$ when $m \ll l^2/r$, using a first-order Taylor series expansion.

3.3   Star Network

Suppose now that Eq. (3) does not hold, and consider a star network. Let $u = 0$ denote the center of the star, which routes all traffic between peripheral nodes. That is, $\chi_{v,w}(0) = 1$ for any $v \neq w$ ($v, w > 0$). One can show [16] that $R_0 = r(N-1)(N-2)/N^2$, $L_0 = l(N-1)/N$ and $M_0 = m(N-1)$, so that the cost C_0 incurred by the center of the star is

$$C_0 = m(N-1) + \frac{s}{N} + \frac{l(N-1)}{N} + \frac{r(N-1)(N-2)}{N^2} . \tag{4}$$

Peripheral nodes do not route any traffic, i.e., $R_u = 0$ for all $u > 0$, and are located at a distance of one from the center of the star, and at a distance of two from the $(N-2)$ other nodes, giving $L_u = l(2N-3)/N$. Further, $\deg(u) = 1$ for all peripheral nodes. Hence, $M_u = m$, and the total cost imposed on nodes $u > 0$ is

$$C_u = m + \frac{s + l(2N-3)}{N} . \tag{5}$$

A proof by identification [16] indicates that $C_0 = C_u$ can only hold when N is a constant, or when $l = r = m = 0$. The difference $C_0 - C_u$ quantifies the (dis)incentive to be in the center of the star.

Summing Eqs. (4) and (5), we obtain $C = 2m(N-1) + s + 2l(N-1)^2/N + r(N-1)(N-2)/N^2$. On the one hand, removing any (directed) link from the star either causes a node to be unreachable or prevents a node from contacting any of the other nodes. In either case, $C \to \infty$. On the other hand, adding a link to the star also causes the cost C to increase, when Eq. (3) does not hold. For instance, consider, without loss of generality, adding the link $1 \to 2$: M_1 increases by m, L_1 decreases by l/N (the items held at node 2 can now be reached in one hop), and R_0 decreases by r/N^2 (traffic from 1 to 2 is not routed through 0 anymore). All other costs are unchanged. Hence, the change in the cost C is $\Delta C = m - l/N - r/N^2$, which is positive if Eq. (3) does not hold. Therefore, adding or removing a link to a star when Eq. (3) is not satisfied cannot lead to a social optimum.

From the above study, when Eq. (3) holds (i.e., N or m is small), the social optimum is the full mesh. When Eq. (3) does not hold, repeatedly removing links from the full mesh decreases the cost C until a star topology is reached. Thus, a centralized topology seems to be desirable when N and/or m are significant, while the objective is to minimize the total amount of resources used in the whole network to maintain the overlay. However, we stress that we do not consider robustness against attack, fault-tolerance, or potential performance bottlenecks, all being factors that pose practical challenges in a centralized approach, nor do we offer a mechanism creating an incentive to be in the center of the star. Furthermore, determining under which conditions on l, s, r, m and N the star is the social optimum is an open problem.

4   Case Studies

We next apply the proposed cost model to a few selected routing geometries and compare the results with those obtained in our study of the social optimum. We present the various costs experienced by a node in each geometry, before illustrating the results with numerical examples.

4.1   Analysis

Due to space limitations, we omit here most of the details in the derivations, and instead refer the reader to a companion technical report [16] for complete details.

De Bruijn Graphs. De Bruijn graphs are used in algorithms such as Koorde [7] and ODRI [2], and present very desirable properties, such as short average routing distance and high resiliency to node failures [2]. In a de Bruijn graph, any node u is represented by an identifier string $(u_1, \ldots, u_D)$ of D symbols taken from an alphabet of size Δ. The node represented by $(u_1, \ldots, u_D)$ links to each node represented by $(u_2, \ldots, u_D, x)$ for all possible values of x in the alphabet. The resulting directed graph has a fixed out-degree Δ, and a diameter D.

The maintenance, routing, and latency costs experienced by each node in a De Bruijn graph all depend on the position of the node in the graph [16]. Denote by V' the set of nodes such that the identifier of each node in V' is of the form $(h, h, \ldots, h)$. Nodes in V' link to themselves, and the maintenance cost is $M_u = m(\Delta - 1)$ for $u \in V'$. For nodes $u \notin V'$, we have $M_u = m\Delta$.

For any node $u \in V$, the routing cost R_u is such that $0 \leq R_u \leq r\rho_{\max}/N^2$, where $\rho_{\max}$ denotes the maximum number of routes passing through a given node, or maximum *node loading*, with (see [16]):

$$\rho_{\max} = \frac{(D-1)(\Delta^{D+2} - (\Delta-1)^2) - D\Delta^{D+1} + \Delta^2}{(\Delta - 1)^2}.$$

One can show by contradiction that with shortest-path routing, nodes $u \in V'$ do not route any traffic, so that the lower bound $R_u = 0$ is reached for $u \in V'$. One can also show that $R_u = r\rho_{\max}/N^2$ when $\Delta \geq D$ for the node $(0, 1, 2, \ldots, D-1)$.

We further prove in [16] that the latency cost is bounded by $L_{\min} \leq L_u \leq L_{\max}$ where

$$L_{\min} = \frac{l}{N}\left(D\Delta^D + \frac{D}{\Delta - 1} - \frac{\Delta(\Delta^D - 1)}{(\Delta - 1)^2}\right),$$

and

$$L_{\max} = l \frac{D\Delta^{D+1} - (D+1)\Delta^D + 1}{N(\Delta - 1)} .$$

We have $L_u = L_{\max}$ for nodes $u \in V'$, and $L_u = L_{\min}$ for the node $(0, 1, \ldots, D-1)$ when $\Delta \geq D$. Note that we can simplify the expressions for both $L_{\min}$ and $L_{\max}$ when $N = \Delta^D$, that is, when the identifier space is fully populated.

D-Dimensional Tori. We next consider D-dimensional tori, as in CAN [8], where each node is represented by D Cartesian coordinates, and has $2D$ neighbors, for a maintenance cost of $M_u = 2mD$ for any u.

Routing at each node is implemented by greedy forwarding to the neighbor with the shortest Euclidean distance to the destination. We assume here that each node is in charge of an equal portion of the D-dimensional space. From [8], we know that the average length of a routing path is $(D/4)N^{1/D}$ hops[3]. Because we assume that the D-dimensional torus is equally partitioned, by symmetry, we conclude that for all u,

$$L_u = l \frac{DN^{1/D}}{4} .$$

To determine the routing cost R_u, we compute the node loading as a function $\rho_{u,D}$ of the dimension D. With our assumption that the D-torus is equally partitioned, $\rho_{u,D}$ is the same for all u by symmetry. Using the observation that the coordinates of two consecutive nodes in a path cannot differ in more than one dimension, we can compute $\rho_{u,D}$ by induction on the dimension D [16]:

$$\rho_{u,D} = 1 + N^{\frac{D-1}{D}} \left(-N^{\frac{1}{D}} + D \left(N^{\frac{1}{D}} - 1 + \left(\left\lfloor \frac{N^{\frac{1}{D}}}{2} \right\rfloor - 1 \right) \left(\left\lceil \frac{N^{\frac{1}{D}}}{2} \right\rceil - 1 \right) \right) \right) .$$

For all u, R_u immediately follows from $\rho_{u,D}$ with

$$R_u = r \frac{\rho_{u,D}}{N^2} .$$

PRR Trees. We next consider the variant of PRR trees [17] used in Pastry [9] or Tapestry [18]. Nodes are represented by a string $(u_1, \ldots, u_D)$ of D digits in base Δ. Each node is connected to $D(\Delta - 1)$ distinct neighbors of the form $(u_1, \ldots, u_{p-1}, x, y_{p+1}, \ldots, y_D)$, for $p = 1 \ldots D$, and $x \neq u_p \in \{0, \ldots, \Delta-1\}$. The resulting maintenance cost is $M_u = mD(\Delta - 1)$.

Among the different possibilities for the remaining coordinates $y_{p+1}, \ldots, y_D$, the protocols generally select a node that is nearby according to a proximity metric. We here assume that the spatial distribution of the nodes is uniform, and that the identifier space is fully populated, which enables us to pick $y_{p+1} =$

---

[3] Loguinov et al. [2] refined that result by distinguishing between odd and even values of N.

Table 1. Asymmetry in costs in a de Bruijn graph ($l = 1, r = 1000$)

(Δ, D)	$L_{\min}$	$L_{\max}$	$\frac{L_{\max}}{L_{\min}}$	$R'_{\min}$	$R_{\max}$	$\frac{R_{\max}}{R'_{\min}}$
(2, 9)	7.18	8.00	1.11	3.89	17.53	4.51
(3, 6)	5.26	5.50	1.04	2.05	9.05	4.41
(4, 4)	3.56	3.67	1.03	5.11	13.87	2.71
(5, 4)	3.69	3.75	1.02	1.98	5.50	2.78
(6, 3)	2.76	2.80	1.01	5.38	9.99	1.86

$u_{p+1}, \ldots, y_D = u_D$. Thus, two nodes u and v at a distance of k hops differ in k digits, which, as described in [16], leads to

$$\Pr[t_{u,v} = k] = \frac{\binom{D}{k}(\Delta - 1)^k}{N} . \tag{6}$$

Using Eq. (6) in conjunction with the total probability theorem, leads, after simplification, to

$$R_u = r\frac{\Delta^{D-1}(D(\Delta - 1) - \Delta) + 1}{N^2} . \tag{7}$$

Furthermore, from $L_u = lE[t_{u,v}]$, Eq. (6) gives

$$L_u = l\frac{D\Delta^{D-1}(\Delta - 1)}{N} . \tag{8}$$

Chord Rings. In a Chord ring [10], nodes are represented using a binary string (i.e., $\Delta = 2$). When the ring is fully populated, each node u is connected to a set of D neighbors, with identifiers $((u + 2^p) \mod 2^D)$ for $p = 0 \ldots D - 1$. An analysis similar to that carried out for PRR trees yields R_u and L_u as in Eqs. (7) and (8) for $\Delta = 2$. Simulations confirm this result [10].

4.2   Numerical Results

We illustrate our analysis with a few numerical results. In Table 1, we consider five de Bruijn graphs with different values for Δ and D, and X and Y i.i.d. uniform random variables. Table 1 shows that while the latency costs of all nodes are comparable, the ratio between $R_{\max}$ and the second best case routing cost[4], $R'_{\min}$, is in general significant. Thus, if $r \gg l$, there can be an incentive for the nodes with $R_u = R_{\max}$ to defect. For instance, these nodes may leave the network and immediately come back, hoping to be assigned a different identifier $u' \neq u$ with a lower cost. Additional mechanisms, such as enforcing a cost of entry to the network, may be required to prevent such defections.

Next, we provide an illustration by simulation of the costs in the different geometries. We choose $\Delta = 2$, for which the results for PRR trees and Chord

---

[4] That is, the minimum value for R_u over all nodes but the Δ nodes in V' for which $R_u = 0$.

rings are identical. We choose $D = \{2, 6\}$ for the D-dimensional tori, and $D = \log_\Delta N$ for the other geometries. We point out that selecting a value for D and Δ common to all geometries may inadvertently bias one geometry against another. We emphasize that we only illustrate a specific example here, without making any general comparison between different DHT geometries.

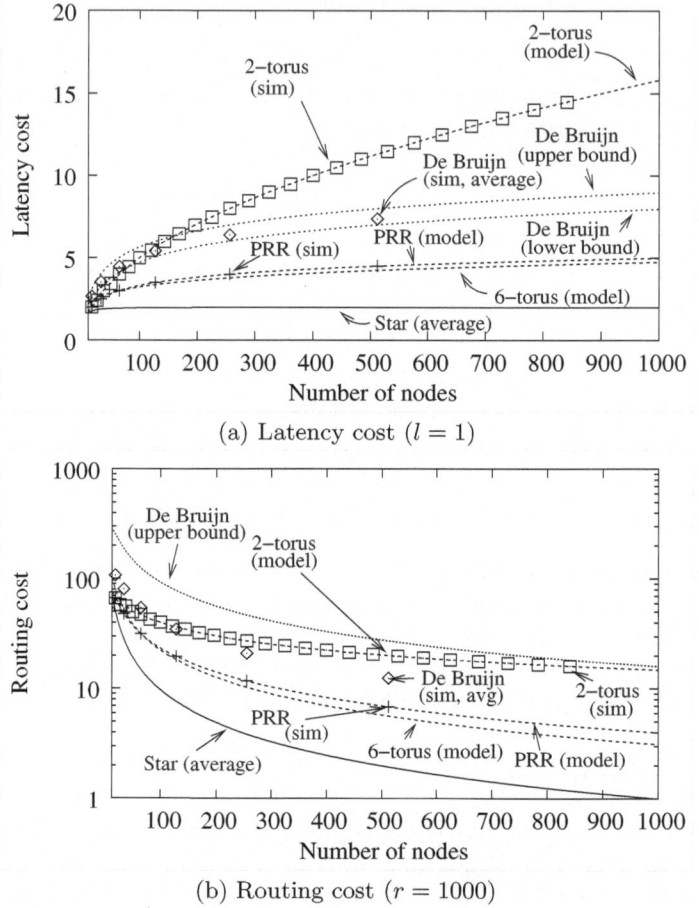

(a) Latency cost ($l = 1$)

(b) Routing cost ($r = 1000$)

Fig. 1. Latency and routing costs. Curves marked "sim" present simulation results.

We vary the number of nodes between $N = 10$ and $N = 1000$, and, for each value of N run ten differently seeded simulations, consisting of 100,000 requests each, with X and Y i.i.d. uniform random variables. We plot the latency and routing costs averaged over all nodes and all requests in Fig. 1. The graphs show that our analysis is validated by simulation, and that the star provides a lower average cost than all the other geometries. In other words, whenever practical, a centralized architecture appears more desirable to the community as a whole than a distributed solution. This relatively counter-intuitive result needs to be taken with a grain of salt, however, given the scalability and resiliency concerns linked to a centralized architecture, and the need for incentive mechanisms to compensate for the asymmetry of a star network.

5 Discussion

We proposed a model, based on experienced load and node connectivity, for the cost incurred by each peer to participate in a peer-to-peer network. We argue such a cost model is a useful complement to topological performance metrics [1, 2], in that it allows to predict disincentives to collaborate (peers refusing to serve requests to reduce their cost), discover possible network instabilities (peers leaving and re-joining in hopes of lowering their cost), identify hot spots (peers with high routing load), and characterize the efficiency of a network as a whole.

We showed that, when the number of nodes is small, fully connected networks are generally the most cost-efficient solution. When the number of nodes is large, star networks may be desirable from the point of view of overall resource usage. This result leads us to conjecture that, when feasible, centralized networks, where the "center" consists of a few fully connected nodes can be an interesting alternative to completely distributed solutions, provided that incentive mechanisms to handle network asymmetries are in place.

We believe however that this paper raises more questions than it provides answers. First, we only analyzed a handful of DHT routing geometries, and even omitted interesting geometries such as the butterfly [19] or geometries based on the XOR metric [20]. Second, applying the proposed cost model to deployed peer-to-peer systems such as KaZaA/FastTrack, which is based on interconnected star networks, could yield some insight regarding user behavior. Third, for the mathematical analysis, we used strong assumptions such as identical popularity of all items, or uniform spatial distribution of all participants, and we assimilated the costs incurred to the actual utility functions of each participant. Relaxing these assumptions is necessary to evaluate the performance of a geometry in a realistic setting. Also, obtaining a meaningful set of values for the parameters (l, s, r, m) for a given class of applications (e.g., file sharing between PCs, ad-hoc routing between energy-constrained sensor motes) remains an open problem. Finally, identifying the minimal amount of knowledge each node should possess to devise a rational strategy, or studying network formation with the proposed cost model are other promising avenues for further research.

References

1. Gummadi, K., Gummadi, R., Gribble, S., Ratnasamy, S., Shenker, S., Stoica, I.: The impact of DHT routing geometry on resilience and proximity. In: Proceedings of ACM SIGCOMM'03, Karlsruhe, Germany (2003) 381–394
2. Loguinov, D., Kumar, A., Rai, V., Ganesh, S.: Graph-theoretic analysis of structured peer-to-peer systems: routing distances and fault resilience. In: Proceedings of ACM SIGCOMM'03, Karlsruhe, Germany (2003) 395–406

3. Ng, C., Parkes, D., Seltzer, M.: Strategyproof computing: Systems infrastructures for self-interested parties. In: Proceedings of the 1st Workshop on the Economics of Peer-to-Peer Systems, Berkeley, CA (2003)

4. Jackson, M., Wolinsky, A.: A strategic model for social and economic networks. Journal of Economic Theory **71** (1996) 44–74

5. Chun, B.G., Fonseca, R., Stoica, I., Kubiatowicz, J.: Characterizing selfishly constructed overlay networks. In: Proceedings of IEEE INFOCOM'04, Hong Kong (2004)

6. Fabrikant, A., Luthra, A., Maneva, E., Papadimitriou, C., Shenker, S.: On a network creation game. In: Proceedings of ACM PODC'03, Boston, MA (2003) 347–351

7. Kaashoek, M.F., Karger, D.: Koorde: A simple degree-optimal distributed hash table. In: Proceedings of IPTPS'03, Berkeley, CA (2003) 323–336

8. Ratnasamy, S., Francis, P., Handley, M., Karp, R., Shenker, S.: A scalable content-addressable network. In: Proceedings of ACM SIGCOMM'01, San Diego, CA (2001) 161–172

9. Rowston, A., Druschel, P.: Pastry: Scalable, decentralized object location and routing for large scale peer-to-peer systems. In: Proceedings of ACM Middleware'01, Heidelberg, Germany (2001) 329–350

10. Stoica, I., Morris, R., Liben-Nowell, D., Karger, D., Kaashoek, M.F., Balakrishnan, H.: Chord: A scalable peer-to-peer lookup protocol for Internet applications. IEEE/ACM Transactions on Networking **11** (2003) 17–32

11. The annotated Gnutella protocol specification v0.4 (2001) http://rfc-gnutella. sourceforge.net/developer/stable/index.html.

12. Perkins, C. (editor): Ad hoc networking. Addison-Wesley, Boston, MA (2000)

13. Banerjee, S., Bhattacharjee, B., Kommareddy, C.: Scalable application layer multicast. In: Proceedings of ACM SIGCOMM'02, Pittsburgh, PA (2002) 205–217

14. Chu, Y.H., Rao, S., Zhang, H.: A case for endsystem multicast. In: Proceedings of ACM SIGMETRICS'00, Santa Clara, CA (2000) 1–12

15. Liebeherr, J., Nahas, M., Si, W.: Application-layer multicast with Delaunay triangulations. IEEE Journal of Selected Areas in Communications **20** (2002) 1472–1488

16. Christin, N., Chuang, J.: On the cost of participating in a peer-to-peer network. Technical report, University of California, Berkeley (2003) http://p2pecon. berkeley.edu/pub/TR-2003-12-CC.pdf. See also: arXiv:cs.NI/0401010.

17. Plaxton, C.G., Rajamaran, R., Richa, A.: Accessing nearby copies of replicated objects in a distributed environment. Theory of Computing Systems **32** (1999) 241–280

18. Zhao, B., Huang, L., Stribling, J., Rhea, S., Joseph, A., Kubiatowicz, J.: Tapestry: A resilient global-scale overlay for service deployment. IEEE Journal on Selected Areas in Communications **22** (2004) 41–53

19. Malkhi, D., Naor, M., Ratajczak, D.: Viceroy: a scalable and dynamic emulation of the butterfly. In: Proceedings of ACM PODC'02, Monterey, CA (2002) 183–192

20. Maymounkov, P., Mazières, D.: Kademlia: A peer-to-peer information system based on the XOR metric. In: Proceedings of IPTPS'02, Cambridge, MA (2002) 53–65

2 P2P or Not 2 P2P?

Mema Roussopoulos[1], Mary Baker[2], David S.H. Rosenthal[3],
Thomas J. Giuli[4], Petros Maniatis[5], and Jeff Mogul[2]

[1] Harvard University, Cambridge, MA
[2] HP Labs, Palo Alto, CA
[3] Stanford University Libraries, Stanford, CA
[4] Stanford University, Stanford, CA
[5] Intel Research, Berkeley, CA

Abstract. In the hope of stimulating discussion, we present a heuristic decision tree that designers can use to judge how suitable a P2P solution might be for a particular problem. It is based on characteristics of a wide range of P2P systems from the literature, both proposed and deployed. These include budget, resource relevance, trust, rate of system change, and criticality.

1 Introduction

Academic research in peer-to-peer (P2P) systems has concentrated largely on algorithms to improve the efficiency [31], scalability [22], robustness [12], and security [33] of query routing in P2P systems, services such as indexing and search [20], dissemination [17], and rendezvous [27] [30] for applications running on top of these systems, or even many of the above [18]. While these improvements may be essential to enhancing the performance of some P2P applications, there has been little focus on what makes a problem "P2P-worthy," or on which other, previously ignored problems may benefit from the application of P2P techniques. What questions should a system designer ask to judge whether a P2P solution is appropriate for his particular problem?

In this position paper, we hope to stimulate discussion by distilling the experience of a broad range of proposed and deployed P2P systems into a methodology for judging how suitable a P2P architecture might be for a particular problem. In Section 2, we identify some salient characteristics axes in typical distributed problems. In Section 3, we describe a spectrum of specific problems for which P2P solutions have been proposed. In Section 4, we propose an arrangement of problem characteristics into a heuristic decision tree. We walk through the tree explaining its choices and why we believe certain paths may lead to successful P2P solutions to important problems, while other paths may encounter difficulties. While any particular set of characteristics axes or fixed decision graph may be inadequate for all purposes, we present the arrangement that has proved most useful in our work so far.

G.M. Voelker and S. Shenker (Eds.): IPTPS 2004, LNCS 3279, pp. 33–43, 2004.

2   Problem Characteristics Axes

In this section, we describe the characteristics we believe are important in assessing the P2P-worthiness of distributed problems. Paraphrasing the call for papers of this workshop, we identify as peer-to-peer those environments that satisfy the following three criteria:

- *Self-organizing:* Nodes organize themselves into a network through a discovery process. There is no global directory of peers or resources.
- *Symmetric communication:* Peers are considered equals; they both request and offer services, rather than being confined to either client or server roles.
- *Decentralized control:* Peers determine their level of participation and their course of action autonomously. There is no central controller that dictates behavior to individual nodes.

Milojičić et al. [26] identify similar criteria.

Our axes are the problem's budget, the relevance of resources to individual peers, the rate of system change, the need for mutual trust, and the criticality of the problem. In more detail:

Budget: If the budget for a centrally controlled solution is ample, a designer is unlikely to consider worthwhile the inefficiencies, latencies and testing problems of a P2P solution. If the budget is limited, a key motivator in the choice of P2P architectures is the lowest possible cost of entry for individual peers, despite increased total system cost. Assembling a system from local, often surplus, components can be justified as a small part of many budgets and may be the only economically feasible approach.

Resource relevance to participants: Relevance is the likelihood that a "unit of service" within a problem (e.g., a single file in a file sharing problem) is interesting to many participants. When resource relevance is high, cooperation in a P2P solution evolves naturally. If relevance is low, cooperation may require artificial or extrinsic incentives to make a possible P2P solution viable.

Trust: The cost to a P2P system of handling mutually distrusting peers is high. Distrust may be a necessary evil of the problem, or it may be desirable as a means of imposing fault isolation throughout a peer community to reduce the risks posed by misbehaving peers.

Rate of system change: Different problems have different requirements for timeliness and consistency. Problems or solutions with high rates of change in the participants, the data or the system parameters make it difficult to meet high requirements for timeliness and consistency.

Criticality: If the problem being solved is critical to the users, they may demand centralized control and accountability irrespective of technical criteria. Even if a P2P solution is not ruled out, the need for expensive fault-tolerance or massive over-provisioning may make it uneconomic.

One question that arises is why we do not consider the physical constraints of a problem along with the budget; some problems have physical constraints such as scale or geographic size that require a distributed solution, regardless of budget. One example is latency due to the speed of light in an interplanetary internet [3]. However, we have found no examples of problems that also require decentralized control or self-organizing peers.

We have excluded other characteristics which, while potentially important, did not enter into this decision tree as far as we have elaborated it. First, it may be important whether resources are public or private; private resources requiring confidentiality may be more difficult to protect and manage in P2P systems, and they may have less relevance to participants. Second, it may be important whether resources are naturally distributed; resources that exist naturally in many places, such as the usage statistics of many individual networks, may be more amenable to a distributed solution, and even a P2P solution.

3   Candidate Problems

We analyze a variety of problems with proposed P2P solutions to determine which of our characteristics they exhibit. These problems come from routing, backup, monitoring, data sharing, data dissemination, and auditing.

3.1   Routing Problems

All distributed systems need a routing layer to get messages to their intended recipients. Routing takes on P2P characteristics when the scale is large enough (e.g., the Internet) or when centralization is ruled out (e.g., wireless ad hoc networks).

Internet Routing. Internet routers must communicate to cope with a dynamically changing network topology to determine how to route outbound packets to their destination. They are arranged into "autonomous systems" which "peer" with each other across organizational boundaries, frequently between competitors.

Routing protocols have historically assumed that economic incentives and legal contracts are sufficient to discourage misbehavior. At the application layer (e.g., Resilient Overlay Networks (RON) [1]) or at the network layer (e.g., BGP [21]), routers trust information from known peers. They cooperate because the information being exchanged is relevant to all peers and important to their function. This cooperation tends to fail if error, misbehavior or usage patterns cause the data to change too fast. To scale to the size of the Internet, BGP tries to limit the rate of change by aggregating routes instead of having ISPs propagate internal routing updates. Aggregation reduces the ability to detect path outages quickly [19]. RON instead gives up scaling to large numbers of nodes in favor of more fine-grained route information exchanges.

Ad hoc Routing in Disaster Recovery. The ad hoc routing problem is to use transient resources, such as the wireless communication devices of a disaster recovery crew, to deploy temporary network infrastructure for a specific purpose. Because each individual node's wireless range does not reach all other nodes, peers in the network forward packets on behalf of each other. The costly alternative is to provide more permanent infrastructure for all possible eventualities in all possible locations. The network is of relevance and critical to all participants, and pre-configured security can give a high level of mutual trust. Once established, the participants (humans in the crew) typically change and move slowly, and do not exchange huge volumes of data.

Metropolitan-Area Cell Phone Forwarding. Ad hoc routing has also been proposed in less critical settings, such as that of public, ad hoc cellular telephony in dense metropolitan areas. The motivation is to reduce the need for base stations, to use the radio spectrum more efficiently, and to avoid payment for air time where traffic does not pass through base stations. Unlike the disaster recovery problem, the participants do not trust each other and they change and move rapidly. In its current state, this problem suffers from the "Tragedy of the Commons" [14]. We doubt that a practical P2P solution to this problem exists, unless either on-going research [2,4] devises strong, "strategy-proof" mechanisms to combat selfishness, or the scope of the problem is limited to close-knit communities with inherent incentives for participation.

3.2 Backup

Backup, the process in which a user replicates his files in different media at different locations to increase data survivability, can benefit greatly from the pooling of otherwise underutilized resources. Unfortunately, the fact that each peer is interested only in its own data opens the way to selfish peer behavior.

Internet Backup. The cost of backup could be reduced if Internet-wide cooperation [9,10] could be fostered and enforced. For example in Samsara [9] peers must hold real or simulated data equivalent to the space other peers hold for them. But there is no guarantee an untrusted node will provide backup data when requested, even if it has passed periodic checks to ensure it still has those data. Such a misbehaving or faulty node may in turn have its backup data elsewhere dropped in retaliation. If misbehaving, it may already have anticipated this reaction and, if faulty, this is exactly why it would participate in a backup scheme in the first place. We believe that data backup is poorly suited for a P2P environment running across trust boundaries.

Corporate Backup. In contrast, when participants enjoy high mutual trust, e.g., within the confines of an enterprise intranet, P2P backup makes sense (Hive-Cache [15] is one such commercial offering). This is because selfish behavior is unlikely when a sense of trusting community or a top-down corporate mandate obviate the need for enforceable compliance incentives.

3.3 Distributed Monitoring

Monitoring is an important task in any large distributed system. It may have simple needs such as "subscribing" to first-order events and expecting notification when those events are "published" (e.g., Scribe [27]); it may involve more complicated, on-line manipulation, for instance via SQL queries, of complex distributed data streams such as network packet traces, CPU loads, virus signatures (as in the on-line network monitoring problem motivating PIER [16]); it may be the basis for an off-line, post mortem longitudinal study of many, high-volume data streams, such as the longitudinal network studies performed by Fomenkov et al. [11].

Although the abstract monitoring problem is characterized by natural distribution of the data sources monitored, specific instances of the problem vary vastly. A longitudinal off-line network study, though important, is not necessarily critical to its recipients, and has low timeliness constraints. In contrast, an ISP may consider the on-line, on-time monitoring of its resources and those of its neighbors extremely critical for its survival. Similarly, the mechanisms for complex network monitoring described by Huebsch et al. [16] may be appropriate for administratively closed, high-trust environments such as PlanetLab [6], and they may be quite inappropriate in environments lacking mutual trust and rife with fraud or subversion. In contrast, an off-line long-term network study affords its investigators more time for validating data against tampering.

3.4   Data Sharing

File Sharing. In file sharing systems, participants offer their local files to other peers and search collections to find interesting files. The cost of deployment is very low since most peers store only items that they are interested in anyway. Resource relevance is high; a great deal of content appeals to a large population of peers. In typical file sharing networks, peer turnover and file addition is high, leading to a high rate of system change. Peers trust each other to deliver the advertised content and most popular file sharing networks do not have the capacity to resist malicious peers. File sharing is mainly used to trade media content, which is not a critical application.

Censorship Resistance. The goal of the FreeNet project [7] is to create an anonymous, censorship-resistant data store. Both publishing and document requests are routed through a mix-net [5] and all content is encrypted by the content's creator. These steps are necessary because peers are mutually suspicious and some peers may be malicious. Peers share their bandwidth as well as disk space, which means that the cost of entry is low, promoting incremental rapid growth; this growth is unstructured, which strengthens the system against legal attacks. FreeNet is intended to provide a medium for material that some group wishes to suppress, thus data are relevant to publishers, readers and attackers alike. Fortunately, censorship-resistance does not require immediate availability, making this a low rate-of-change problem.

Tangler [32] has similar goals. A peer stores a document by encoding it using erasure codes and distributing the resulting fragments throughout the community. To prevent an adversary from biasing where those fragments are distributed, a peer combines its document with pseudo-randomness derived from other peers' documents before erasure coding. To retrieve its own document, a peer must store this randomness (i.e., other peers' documents) locally. Although the problem lacks inherent incentives for participation, this solution ingeniously supplies them.

3.5 Data Dissemination

Data dissemination is akin to data sharing, with the distinction that the problem is not to *store* data indefinitely but merely to *spread* the data for a relatively short amount of time. Often storing is combined with spreading.

Usenet. Usenet, perhaps the oldest and most successful P2P application, is a massively distributed discussion system in which users post messages to "news-groups." These articles are then disseminated to other hosts subscribing to the particular newsgroup, and made available to local users. Usenet has been a staple of the Internet for decades, arguably because of the low cost barrier to peer entry and the high relevance of the content to participating peers. Unfortunately, although the system flourished at a time when mutual trust was assumed, it remains vulnerable to many forms of attack, perhaps jeopardizing its future in less innocent times.

Non-critical Content Distribution. Dissemination of programs, program updates, streaming media [8, 17], and even cooperative web caching [34] are all non-critical content distribution problems.

One successful application is BitTorrent [8], which mitigates the congestion at a download server when relevant (i.e., popular) but non-critical new resources such as programs or updates are posted. Its tit-for-tat policy is effective despite low peer trust.

Cooperative Web caching, although superficially attractive, has not succeeded, for complex and subtle reasons [34]. Although it offered some benefits for large organizations in very low latency environments, and for low-relevance (i.e., unpopular) documents, those benefits were only marginal.

Critical Flash Crowds. Other specific instances of dissemination have been proposed to address flash crowds [28, 29], which could be used to distribute critical data, such as news updates during a major disaster.

3.6 Auditing

Digital Preservation. The *LOCKSS* system preserves academic e-journals in a network of autonomous web caches. Peers each obtain their own complete replicas of the content by crawling the publisher's web site. If the content becomes unavailable from the publisher, the local copy is supplied to local readers. Slowly, in the background, a P2P "opinion poll" protocol [24] provides mutual audit and repairs any damage it detects. Peers trust the consensus of other peers but not any individual peer. Mutual distrust is essential to prevent cascade failures which could destroy every copy of the preserved content. The automatic audit and repair process allows peers to be built from cheap, unreliable hardware with very little need for administration, an important factor given library budgets. Publication of new content and damage to preserved content causes system change; the rates of both are limited. The content preserved is highly relevant to many peers.

Distributed Time Stamping. A secure time stamping service [13] acts as the digital equivalent of a notary public: it maintains a history of the creation and contents of digital documents, allowing clients who trust the service to determine which document was "notarized" first. Correlating the histories of multiple, mutually distrustful secure time stamping services [23] is important, because not everyone doing business in the world can be convinced to trust the same centralized service; being able to map time stamps issued elsewhere to a local trust domain is essential for critical documents (such as contracts) from disparate jurisdictions. Luckily, sensitive documents such as contracts tend to change little or not at all, and high latencies for obtaining or verifying secure time stamps are acceptable, facilitating the development of an *efficient enough* P2P solution to the problem.

4 2 P2P or Not 2 P2P?

Figure 1 is a decision tree organizing our characteristics to determine whether the application of P2P techniques to a particular problem is justified. There are other metrics, other decision trees and other decision graphs than those presented here, but we have found this arrangement particularly useful. We examine our example problems and suggested solutions by traversing the tree in a breadth-first manner.

At the top of the tree we have the "budget" axis. We believe that limited budget is the most important motivator for a P2P solution. With limited budget, the low cost for a peer to join a P2P solution is very appealing. Otherwise, a centralized or centrally controlled distributed solution can provide lower complexity and higher performance for the extra money. Our tree thus continues only along the "limited" budget end of the axis.

Our next most important characteristic is the "relevance" of the resource in question. The more relevant (important to many) the resource, the more motivated peers in a P2P architecture are to participate. Good P2P solutions for problems with low relevance exist but have other mitigating characteristics, as we explain below.

The next axis in the tree is "mutual trust." Successful P2P solutions with trusting peers exist, as do those whose other characteristics justify the performance and complexity cost of measures to cope with mutual distrust. Those problems with low relevance and low trust have the burden of fostering cooperation. While Tangler is a good example, we believe that metropolitan ad hoc wireless networks and Internet backup have not yet succeeded. Motivation for these problems seems inadequate to overcome the low relevance of the resources

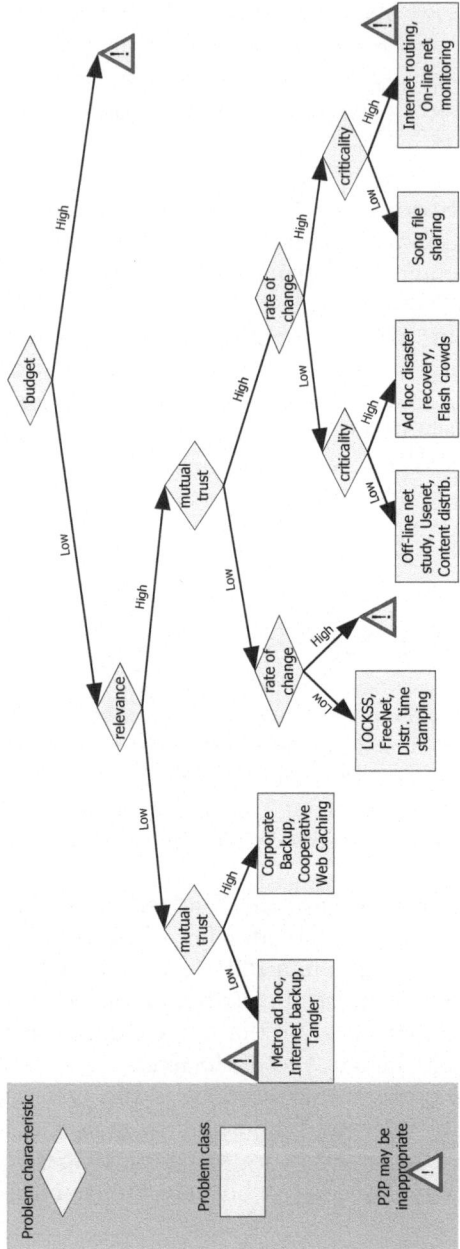

Fig. 1. A decision tree for analyzing the suitability of a P2P solution to a problem. Diamonds indicate decision points. Boxes contain problems or specific P2P solutions to problems. A warning sign over a particular box indicates that the box is a "trouble spot"; a P2P solution for the problems in that box may be inappropriate. In some cases, we include particular P2P solutions (e.g., Tangler) and explain in the text how those solutions overcome the difficulties of their box.

and the overheads of protecting against uncooperative or malicious peers. Where peers are assumed to cooperate, problems such as corporate backup may succeed with P2P solutions, since corporate mandate compensates for low relevance. Similarly with cooperative web caching, proposed solutions [34] indicate that some benefits may be obtainable with P2P techniques; note, however, that actual benefits from cooperative web caching have thus far been only marginal compared to centralized solutions.

Where relevance is high, the required level of trust between peers still has an impact on the suitability of a P2P solution for the problem. Creating artificial economies or "trading" schemes to provide extrinsic incentives for cooperation (as in MojoNation) is generally unsuccessful [25]. The overhead in terms of complexity and performance for managing mutually distrustful peers suggests that solutions will be difficult to implement successfully in a P2P manner, unless other characteristics intercede to simplify the problem.

Such a characteristic is the rate of change in the system. Problems with a low rate of change, such as digital preservation, censorship resistant repositories, and distributed time stamping, may succeed despite mutually distrustful peers. For these problems, mutual distrust among peers is an inherent part of the problem, and thus its cost must be born by any proposed solution. The cost, however, is reduced by the low rate of change, which makes it possible to detect anomalies in the system in time to address them, and reduces the performance impact of the measures to protect against malicious peers. Problems with a high rate of change in untrustworthy environments are unlikely to find successful P2P solutions.

The rate of change in the system remains important even for problems in which peers may trust each other to cooperate. If the rate of peers entering and leaving the system is kept low, then both non-critical problems (such as off-line network studies, Usenet, and content distribution) and critical problems (such as ad hoc wireless network deployment for disaster recovery and flash crowd mitigation) may succeed. If the system moves quickly, we believe that it is easier to deploy non-critical applications such as file sharing that can tolerate inconsistent views among peers. When the problem involves critical information that also changes quickly (as in the case of Internet routing and on-line network monitoring), the designer should consider whether the application benefits sufficiently from other features. To the degree that Internet routing is successful, it is because it is amenable to trading accuracy for scalability through techniques such as aggregation of data. If P2P network monitoring succeeds, it will be because the natural distribution and high volume of the data allow few other architectures.

5   Conclusions

To summarize, the characteristics that motivate a P2P solution are limited budget, high relevance of the resource, high trust between nodes, a low rate of system change, and a low criticality of the solution. We believe that the limited budget requirement is the most important motivator. Relevance is also very important but can be compensated for by "saving graces" such as assumed trust between nodes or strong imposed incentives. Lacking these, we believe that problems with low relevance are not appropriate for P2P solutions. Trust between nodes greatly eases P2P deployment, however there are some applications, such as LOCKSS, FreeNet and distributed time stamping, where deployment across trust domains is a requirement. These applications must pay the overhead of distrust between nodes, but are feasible in a P2P context because a low rate of change makes these costs manageable.

While P2P solutions offer many advantages, they are inherently complex to get right and should not be applied blindly to all problems. In providing a framework in which to analyze the characteristics of a problem, we hope to offer designers some guidance on whether their problem warrants a P2P solution.

Acknowledgments

We would like to thank the following people for their very helpful feedback and suggestions: John Apostolopoulos, Sujata Banerjee, Kevin Lai, Dejan S. Miloji-čić, Mitch Trott, Susie Wee, and Zhichen Xu.

References

1. D. Andersen, H. Balakrishnan, F. Kaashoek, and R. Morris. Resilient Overlay Networks. In *SOSP*, 2001.
2. S. Bansal and M. Baker. Observation-based Cooperation Enforcement in Ad Hoc Networks. Technical report, Stanford University, 2003.
3. S. Burleigh, K. Fall, V. Cerf, R. Durst, K. Scott, H. Weiss, L. Torgerson, and A. Hooke. Delay-Tolernat Networking: An Approach to Interplanetary Internet. *IEEE Communications Magazine*, June 2003.
4. L. Buttyán and J.-P. Hubaux. Stimulating Cooperation in Self-organizing Mobile Ad hoc Networks. *Mobile Networks and Applications*, 2003.
5. D. Chaum. Untraceable electronic mail, return addresses, and digital pseudonyms. *Commun. ACM*, 24(2), 1981.
6. B. Chun, D. Culler, T. Roscoe, A. Bavier, L. Peterson, M. Wawrzoniak, and M. Bowman. PlanetLab: An Overlay Testbed for Broad-Coverage Services. *ACM Computer Communication Review*, 33(3):3–12, July 2003.
7. I. Clarke, O. Sandberg, B. Wiley, and T. W. Hong. Freenet: A Distributed Anonymous Information Storage and Retrieval System. In *Workshop on Design Issues in Anonymity and Unobservability*, 2000.
8. B. Cohen. Incentives Build Robustness in BitTorrent. In *P2P Econ Workshop*, 2003.
9. L. P. Cox and B. D. Noble. Samsara: Honor Among Thieves in Peer-to-Peer Storage. In *SOSP*, 2003.
10. F. Dabek, M. F. Kaashoek, D. Karger, R. Morris, and I. Stoica. Wide-area Cooperative Storage with CFS. In *SOSP*, 2001.
11. M. Fomenkov, K. Keys, D. Moore, and kc claffy. Longitudinal study of Internet traffic from 1998–2003. http://www.caida.org/outreach/papers/2003/nlanr/.
12. K. Gummadi, R. Gummadi, S. Gribble, S. Ratnasamy, S. Shenker, and I. Stoica. The Impact of DHT Routing Geometry on Resilience and Proximity. In *SIGCOMM*, 2003.

13. S. Haber and W. S. Stornetta. How to Time-stamp a Digital Document. *Journal of Cryptology: the Journal of the Intl. Association for Cryptologic Research*, 3(2):99–111, 1991.
14. G. Hardin. The Tragedy of the Commons. *Science*, 162, 1968.
15. HiveCache, Inc. Distributed disk-based backups. Available at http://www.hivecache.com/.
16. R. Huebsch, J. M. Hellerstein, N. Lanham, B. T. Loo, S. Shenker, and I. Stoica. Querying the Internet with PIER. In *VLDB*, 2003.
17. D. Kostić, A. Rodriguez, J. Albrecht, and A. Vahdat. Bullet: High Bandwidth Data Dissemination Using an Overlay Mesh. In *SOSP*, 2003.
18. J. Kubiatowicz, D. Bindel, Y. Chen, S. Czerwinski, P. Eaton, D. Geels, R. Gummadi, S. Rhea, H. Weatherspoon, W. Weimer, C. Wells, and B. Zhao. OceanStore: An Architecture for Global-Scale Persistent Storage. In *ASPLOS*, 2000.
19. C. Labovitz, A. Ahuja, A. Abose, and F. Jahanian. Delayed Internet Routing Convergence. In *SIGCOMM*, 2000.
20. J. Li, B. T. Loo, J. Hellerstein, F. Kaashoek, D. R. Karger, and R. Morris. On the Feasibility of Peer-to-Peer Web Indexing and Search. In *IPTPS*, 2003.
21. K. Lougheed and Y. Rekhter. RFC 1267: Border Gateway Protocol 3, October 1991.
22. D. Malkhi, M. Naor, and D. Ratajczak. Viceroy: A Scalable and Dynamic Emulation of the Butterfly. In *CHI*, 1989.
23. P. Maniatis and M. Baker. Secure History Preservation Through Timeline Entanglement. In *USENIX Security*, 2002.
24. P. Maniatis, M. Roussopoulos, TJ Giuli, D. S. H. Rosenthal, M. Baker, and Y. Muliadi. Preserving Peer Replicas By Rate-Limited Sampled Voting. In *SOSP*, 2003.
25. J. McCoy. Lessons Learned from MojoNation. Personal Communication, April 2002.
26. D. S. Milojičić, V. Kalogeraki, R. Lukose, K. Nagaraja, J. Pruyne, B. Richard, S. Rollins, and Z. Xu. Peer-to-Peer Computing. Technical Report HPL-2002-57, HP Labs, 2002.
27. A. I. T. Rowstron, A.-M. Kermarrec, M. Castro, and P. Druschel. SCRIBE: The design of a large-scale event notification infrastructure. In *Networked Group Communication*, 2001.
28. T. Stading, P. Maniatis, and M. Baker. Peer-to-Peer Caching Schemes to Address Flash Crowds. In *IPTPS*, 2002.
29. A. Stavrou, D. Rubenstein, and S. Sahu. A Lightweight, Robust P2P System to Handle Flash Crowds. In *ICNP*, 2002.
30. I. Stoica, D. Adkins, S. Zhuang, S. Shenker, and S. Surana. Internet Indirection Infrastructure. In *SIGCOMM*, 2002.
31. I. Stoica, R. Morris, D. Karger, M. F. Kaashoek, and H. Balakrishnan. Chord: A Scalable Peer-to-Peer Lookup Service for Internet Applications. In *SIGCOMM*, 2001.
32. M. Waldman and D. Mazières. Tangler: A Censorship-Resistant Publishing System Based On Document Entanglements. In *ACM Conf. on Computer and Communications Security*, 2001.
33. D. Wallach. A Survey of Peer-to-Peer Security Issues. In *Intl. Symposium on Software Security*, 2002.
34. A. Wolman, G. Voelker, N. Sharma, N. Cardwell, A. Karlin, and H. Levy. On the Scale and Performance of Cooperative Web Proxy Caching. In *SOSP*, 1999.

On Transport Layer Support for Peer-to-Peer Networks

Hung-Yun Hsieh and Raghupathy Sivakumar

School of Electrical and Computer Engineering
Georgia Institute of Technology
Atlanta, GA 30332, USA
{hyhsieh,siva}@ece.gatech.edu

Abstract. TCP is the transport protocol used predominantly in the Internet as well as in peer-to-peer networks. However, peer-to-peer networks exhibit very different characteristics from those of conventional client-server networks. In this paper, we argue that the unique characteristics of peer-to-peer networks render TCP inappropriate for effective data transport in such networks. Specifically, we motivate transport layer support for multipoint-to-point connections to address the problem of sources in peer-to-peer networks lacking server-like properties in terms of capacity and availability. We outline several key elements in designing a new transport protocol for supporting effective multipoint-to-point connections. Finally, we present a case study for a multipoint-to-point transport protocol that puts together these design elements in practice. We thus motivate further research along this direction.

1 Introduction

Over the last few years, the area of peer-to-peer networking has attracted considerable attention. The notion of end-users collaborating to create as well as to consume a richer set of services and contents has been quite well received. Resources shared in a peer-to-peer network are distributed in a decentralized fashion, and directly accessible to any host participating in the network.

While existing works in the area of peer-to-peer networking have typically focused on application layer approaches with vertically integrated solutions, the growing scale and diversity of peer-to-peer networks have called for a common platform to facilitate the development and interoperability of peer-to-peer applications. Several research endeavors have gone into building generic architectures, interfaces, and protocols that can support peer-to-peer networks more effectively [1–3].

In this paper, we argue for transport layer support for peer-to-peer networks. TCP (Transmission Control Protocol) has been the predominant transport protocol used in the Internet as well as in peer-to-peer networks. It is designed for a unicast connection between a server and a client. However, peer-to-peer networks exhibit very different characteristics from those of conventional client-server networks. On one hand, the existence of multiple peers with replicated content provides users with multiple potential sources to transfer data from. On the other hand, these peers that act as sources to supply the content typically do not exhibit "server-like" properties due to their limited capacity and transient availability [4]. We argue that using TCP not only prevents the requesting

G.M. Voelker and S. Shenker (Eds.): IPTPS 2004, LNCS 3279, pp. 44–53, 2004.

peer from leveraging the existence of multiple sources for achieving potential performance improvement, but also exposes it to the non-server-like behavior of individual sources thus causing performance degradation.

To this end, we first motivate the benefits of transport layer support for multipoint-to-point connections in peer-to-peer networks[1]. The transport layer plays a defining role in effective data transport between the source and the destination. However, existing transport protocols support only point-to-point and/or point-to-multipoint (multicast) connections. We discuss the performance benefits in enabling multipoint-to-point data transport in Section 2. We then proceed to outline several key components that should be considered in designing new transport layer protocols for supporting multipoint-to-point connections. We discuss these design elements in Section 3. Finally, we present a case study for a multipoint-to-point transport protocol called R^2CP (Radial Reception Control Protocol). We show in Section 4 that R^2CP encompasses the desired transport layer design and allows for further consideration in peer-to-peer networks. We discuss issues for multipoint-to-point transport protocols and summarize the paper in Section 5.

2   Motivation

In this section, we present arguments for supporting multipoint-to-point connections in peer-to-peer networks, from the perspectives of the destination (requesting peer), the source (supplying peer), and the content. While there are several existing applications that can use multiple replicated sources for achieving better performance in terms of faster downloads or resilient streaming at the destination [5–8], we discuss why such application layer approaches cannot effectively support multipoint-to-point communication without any modification at the transport layer. We thus motivate transport layer support for multipoint-to-point connections in peer-to-peer networks.

2.1   The Destination (Requesting Peer)

From the perspective of the peer requesting the content, the benefit of maintaining multipoint-to-point communication is the potential for better resource aggregation and fault tolerance by tapping multiple sources, thus achieving *higher access performance.*

Hosts participating in peer-to-peer networks are typically located at the edges of the Internet. It is reported in [4] that more than 70% hosts in the Napster network measured have asymmetric links via dial-up (V.90), ADSL, or cable modems with the uplink bandwidths significantly lower than the downlink ones. Hence it is conceivable that a majority of connections in peer-to-peer networks is bottlenecked at the source, and the performance of these connections can be improved by using multiple sources with replicated content concurrently. Several peer-to-peer applications [5, 6] have started exploring along this direction to provide the requesting peer with better download or streaming

---

[1] In reference to the TCP/IP protocol model, the transport layer translates the services provided by the network (internet) layer for use by the application. We note, however, that the argument presented in this paper is also applicable to the session layer in the OSI model. The solution proposed thus can build atop conventional transport protocols, with sufficient support from the latter.

performance. Note, however, that a key issue for the destination to support multipoint-to-point connections is the resequencing of data received from multiple sources. Existing approaches have relied on using the hard disk for offline buffering, where data resequencing is performed only after the entire content has been received [7, 8][2]. While such approaches can be used for content downloads, they are not applicable to most other applications that maintain a limited buffer and require the in-sequence delivery service from lower layers. It has been shown in [9] that for such applications the performance achieved can be throttled by the slowest link in the connection if application-layer striping is performed without transport layer support.

Using multipoint-to-point connections is not limited to bandwidth aggregation. It can also allow the requesting peer to mitigate performance degradation due to suboptimal peer selection and transient peer availability. The problem of selecting the "best" source to request data from is non-trivial, especially in peer-to-peer networks where many peers may not be encountered more than once [10] or may not be uniquely identified [11], and they may even provide inaccurate bandwidth information [4]. Similarly, peer transience due to dynamic peer arrivals and departures has been shown in related work to be a serious problem causing disrupted or even aborted communication [4, 11]. The ability to incorporate multiple concurrent sources in a connection thus manifests itself as an ideal solution for these problems, since the performance of a connection is no longer tied to the capacity or availability of individual sources. For example, the departure of any source(s) in the connection will not stall the content delivery at the requesting peer as long as there is still one source available for transmissions. Note that a transport layer protocol supporting multipoint-to-point connections can dynamically maintain the number of sources in the connection, and mask such artifacts in the peer-to-peer network from the application. However, any application layer approach will not be able to address these problems without exposing the same to the application.

2.2   The Source (Supplying Peer)

From the perspective of the peer supplying the content, the benefit of participating in multipoint-to-point communication is the potential for better load balancing in sharing its resource, thus resulting in a *lower average load* on the sources.

It has been reported in [4] that while multiple sources may be available for content supply in peer-to-peer networks, a significant portion of these hosts lacks the high-bandwidth, low-latency profile of a server. For example, in the Napster network measured, 22% of the peers have upstream (outbound) bandwidths that are lower than 100Kbps. Existing systems address this problem by dropping connections or bypassing hosts with low available bandwidths [12]. While such an approach can effectively prevent these low-profile hosts from becoming the bottleneck of the network, it also prevents them from contributing resources (bandwidths) to the network, thus potentially increasing the load on qualified sources. The inefficiency incurred in utilizing low-profile hosts, however, exists only for unicast connections where the performance of

---

[2] We note that although the resequencing delay can potentially be reduced using smaller request blocks [7] with appropriate online scheduling (refer to Section 3.3), the communication overheads incurred that increase with decreasing block sizes can make such an approach undesirable.

the connection is upper-bounded by the bandwidth of the source. A multipoint-to-point connection, on the other hand, can allow low-profile hosts to be aggregated to support a high-bandwidth connection. It hence makes use of all available resources (however small) that every host in the peer-to-peer network can provide, without sacrificing the quality enjoyed by the requesting peer.

Multipoint-to-point support in peer-to-peer networks not only allows low-profile hosts to contribute, but also encourages participation from hosts with relatively high bandwidths. This is because any content search in peer-to-peer networks typically results in the host with the "highest" bandwidth being chosen. Although it can be argued that hosts are willing to share unused resources [13], overloads in the uplink direction can potentially delay the acknowledgment packets sent by the downlink TCP traffic, thus decreasing the maximum utilization achievable in the downlink and increasing the disincentive to share [14]. It has been shown in [4] that hosts tend to *deliberately* misreport their bandwidths, so as not to serve too many requests from other peers. In a system with multipoint-to-point support, however, such "hot spots" can be alleviated, since the requesting peer, by aggregating resources from the runners-up, can achieve the same performance as that by using the best source[3]. Note that a key issue for the source to support multipoint-to-point connections is that no data is redundantly transmitted across multiple sources to the destination. Application layer approaches that perform content coding at the sources have been proposed in content distribution networks [6, 8]. Although these approaches free the requesting peer from involving in coordinating the transmissions of multiple sources, they are not applicable to peer-to-peer networks, since they require the number and distribution (or characteristics) of the sources used to be known a priori for performing content coding or reducing the reception inefficiency. Moreover, it is difficult, if not impossible, to enforce source coding at all autonomous peers. On the other hand, as we discussed in Section 2.1, approaches such as [7] where the receiving application dynamically requests ranges of data from individual sources can suffer from high communication overheads and application complexities without transport layer support.

2.3   The Content

From the perspective of the content itself, the benefit of using multipoint-to-point communication is the ability to *preserve the integrity* of the content better as it is propagated through the peer-to-peer network, which will in turn benefit both the sources and destinations.

Existing transport layer protocols provide a spectrum of reliability services, including unreliable, partially reliable, and fully reliable services, that can be used by different applications. However, an important issue in distributing the content and thus amplifying the capacity of a peer-to-peer network is reliable content replication. Consider a scenario where a video clip is streamed from one host to another, and the requesting

---

[3] We note that load balancing using multipoint-to-point connections is different from that using unicast connections, since the latter uses *only* the "second-best" host and hence can potentially result in decreased performance otherwise enjoyed by the requesting peer without load balancing.

peer later becomes the supplying peer serving other hosts. Since streaming applications typically choose timeliness over reliability, it is possible that the requesting peer has a lossy replication of the original video clip after the streaming is complete. If the lossy copy is streamed to another host without the missing information being restored, the quality of the video will continue to degrade after each replication – eventually rendering the clip unusable. An obvious approach to address this problem is for the application to open a reliable connection after streaming, and retrieves the missing information from the source. However, such an application layer approach increases implementation complexities (the application needs to implement loss detection and recovery) and communication overheads (consider the overheads incurred in TCP when retrieving data in a non-contiguous fashion). While it is non-trivial to design a transport protocol that can support 100% reliability without degrading the application performance otherwise attainable using a partially reliable transport protocol (since the bandwidth used for recovering the lost data may be wasted as far as the application is concerned), such functionality can be easily implemented in the context of multipoint-to-point connections. A transport protocol supporting multipoint-to-point connections can open one more source (in addition to the original data source) dedicated to loss recovery. Such out-of-band loss recovery allows loss recovery to take place without consuming the precious bandwidth available along the data path. In this way, the application can continue to receive data in a timely, partially reliable fashion, but when the connection completes, the data will be reliably replicated to the receiver.

3   Transport Layer Design

We have thus far motivated the benefits of transport layer support for multipoint-to-point connections in peer-to-peer networks. In this section, we discuss several key components in designing a transport layer protocol that can support effective multipoint-to-point connections. We assume that the multipoint-to-point transport protocol needs to provide the application with the same in-sequence data delivery semantics as TCP.

3.1   Multiple States

TCP is designed for point-to-point connections where it assumes a single path between the source and the destination. TCP captures the characteristics of the path it traverses such as bandwidth and latency in the form of TCB (Transmission Control Block) state variables such as congestion window and round-trip time, for determining the send rate of the connection. In a multipoint-to-point connection, packets from different sources traverse different paths to the destination. Since hosts in peer-to-peer networks can exhibit a very high degree of heterogeneity in terms of the connection bandwidth and latency [4], maintaining only one set of TCB variables (single state) in a multipoint-to-point connection can render the send rate and hence the achieved throughput suboptimal. Therefore, a key design in a multipoint-to-point transport protocol is to maintain multiple states in accordance with the number of sources (paths) used in the connection. In the context of TCP, multi-state design allows TCP to maintain one TCB for each path, and hence different sources can use different send rates (depending on the characteristics of the underlying path) for transmitting packets to the destination. Note that out-of-order arrivals at the destination due to packets traversing multiple paths will not trigger unnecessary window cutdown in such a multi-state TCP, since congestion control is performed on a per-path basis. Vanilla TCP with single state, on the other hand, will fail to utilize even the slowest path in the connection when operated over multiple paths.

3.2 Decoupling of Functionalities

To incur minimum overheads resulting from the multi-state design, transport layer functionalities should be divided between those associated with individual paths and those pertaining to the aggregate connection. For example, congestion control estimates the bandwidth of the underlying path, and hence should be performed for each path in the connection. On the other hand, buffer management handles the socket buffer, and hence should not be repetitively implemented across multiple states. While the reliable delivery of data can be considered either as a per-path functionality (packets are reliably delivered along each path) or as a per-connection functionality (packets lost on one path can be recovered through retransmissions on another path), there are several advantages in designing reliability as a functionality of the aggregate connection: (i) Since loss recovery can take place along a path different from the one traversed by the lost packet, path shutdown due to the departure of an active source (e.g. peer transience or failure) does not interfere with the reliable delivery of data. (ii) One path can be dedicated to loss recovery, while the others provide only unreliable (or partially reliable) service. In this way, packets lost along the unreliable paths will be recovered "out-of-band" without stalling the progression of data delivery along these paths.

3.3 Packet Scheduling

Since packets traverse different paths from multiple sources to one destination in a multipoint-to-point connection, a key issue in providing in-sequence data delivery to the receiving application is packet scheduling. Out-of-order arrivals not only call for a large resequencing buffer at the receiver, but can also introduce *head-of-line* blocking. It has been shown in [9] that head-of-line blocking can cause significant performance loss in terms of the maximum aggregate bandwidth achievable. As we mentioned in Section 3.1, different paths in a multipoint-to-point connection can exhibit very different characteristics in terms of bandwidth/latency mismatches and fluctuations. A scheduling algorithm that schedules packets based on a pre-determined bandwidth ratio of individual paths [15] will apparently suffer from bandwidth fluctuations. Moreover, since different paths can exhibit latency mismatches by more than a factor of four [4], a scheduling algorithm based purely on the bandwidth ratio without taking into consideration the latency mismatch will fail to achieve the optimal performance in peer-to-peer networks. Note that the scheduling algorithm should also handle the dynamic arrivals and departures of sources in a multipoint-to-point connection.

3.4 Receiver-Driven Operation

While any data source may come and go, in a multipoint-to-point connection the invariant is the destination (receiver). Moreover, since the receiver is the common point for individual paths in a multipoint-to-point connection, it manifests itself as an ideal location for coordinating packet transmissions of individual sources. Note that the role of the receiver is not limited to performing packet scheduling. The reliability and congestion control functionalities of the transport protocol can also be driven by the receiver. If the receiver is primarily responsible for the reliable delivery of data from the sources, any failure at the source (e.g. due to peer departure) will have minimal impact on the connection. On the other hand, if congestion control is receiver-driven, the receiver will have instant knowledge of the congestion control parameters such as bandwidth and latency that can be used by the packet scheduling algorithm. In this way, the receiver controls *when*, *which*, and *how much* data should be sent from individual sources. Adding or deleting any source from the connection thus has the mere effect of increasing or decreasing the bandwidth available to the connection, without causing any other undesirable disruptions or stalls. Since the intelligence of the transport protocol is primarily located at the receiver, whenever server migration is possible and desirable, the overheads incurred in synchronizing the states maintained (if any) between the old and the new supplying peers will be minimized.

We have thus far identified *multiple states, decoupling of functionalities, packet scheduling, and receiver-driven operation* as the key design elements in a multipoint-to-point transport protocol. We hasten to add that there do exist several additional transport layer elements for which an argument can be made in the context of peer-to-peer networks. Examples of such elements include run-time peer selection, server load distribution, and reliable replication. Consideration of these other elements is part of our ongoing work.

4   Case Study: The R^2CP Protocol

We now present a case study for a multipoint-to-point transport protocol called R^2CP (Radial Reception Control Protocol) that puts together the design elements outlined in Section 3 in practice. R^2CP was originally proposed in [16] for mobile hosts with heterogeneous wireless interfaces (such as 3G and WiFi). In the following, we provide a synopsis of the R^2CP protocol, and show that R^2CP encompasses the desired transport protocol design, allowing it to be considered for peer-to-peer networks.

1. R^2CP is a receiver-driven, multi-state transport protocol that supports multipoint-to-point connections. The R^2CP destination (receiver) maintains multiple states, each of them corresponds to the single state maintained by individual sources (senders) in the connection. Fig. 1 shows the architecture of the R^2CP protocol.
2. R^2CP is built atop a single-state, point-to-point transport protocol called RCP (Reception Control Protocol). RCP is a TCP clone in its general behavior, including the use of the same window-based congestion control mechanism. However, RCP *transposes* the intelligence of TCP from the sender to the receiver such that the RCP receiver is primarily in charge of the congestion control and reliability. The RCP receiver drives the progression of the connection, while the RCP sender merely responds to the instructions sent by the receiver. It is shown in [16] that RCP is indeed TCP-friendly.

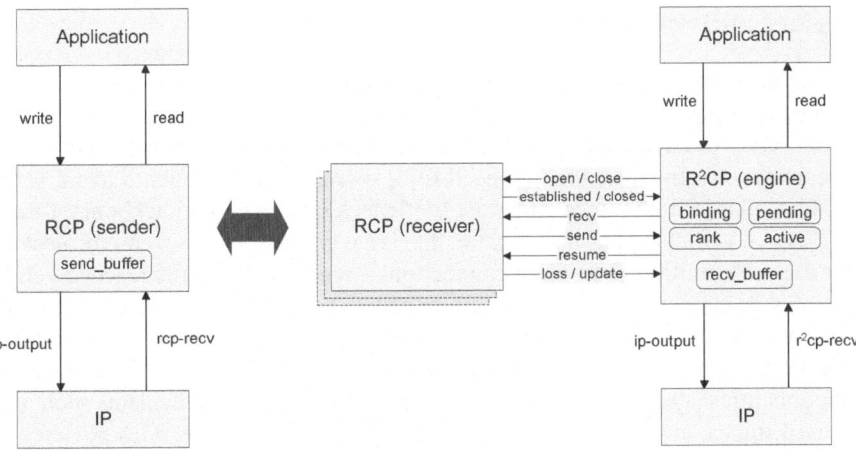

Fig. 1. R^2CP Architecture

3. Multiple RCP pipes in an R^2CP connection are coordinated by the R^2CP engine at the receiver. The R^2CP engine is responsible for buffer management, flow control, and the reliable delivery of data to the application, while individual RCPs implement congestion control. Note that although RCP by itself is a reliable protocol like TCP, R^2CP allows data recovery to occur along the RCP pipe different from the one data was sent. This is achieved in R^2CP through *dynamic binding* of the application data (to be requested) and the RCP packets using the binding data structure (see Fig. 1). Effectively, individual RCPs control *how much* data to request from each sender, while the R^2CP engine control *which* data to request from each sender.

4. The R^2CP engine performs packet scheduling to coordinate packet transmissions along individual RCP pipes. R^2CP uses an RTT-ranked, CWND-based scheduling algorithm to minimize out-of-order arrivals at the receiver. Upon receiving the *send()* call from any RCP pipe that has space in its window for packet requests (note that each RCP pipe is self-clocked like TCP), the R^2CP engine uses the rank data structure to determine *which* data to request from the corresponding source such that the data requested will arrive in sequence. Since R^2CP provides in-sequence data delivery to the application, minimizing out-of-order arrivals can also minimize head-of-line blocking at the receive socket buffer (head-of-line blocking occurs when R^2CP is unable to bind more data to any RCP pipe for requests due to the buffer being filled up). It has been shown in [16] that such a packet scheduling algorithm allows R^2CP to effectively aggregate the bandwidths available along individual paths with bandwidth/latency mismatches and fluctuations.

While we refer interested readers to [16] for a more detailed presentation of the R^2CP protocol and its performance, it is clear from the above discussion that R^2CP follows the design elements outlined in Section 3, allowing it to address the unique characteristics of peer-to-peer networks such as peer heterogeneity and peer transience. Our ongoing work includes developing R^2CP to support load balancing, peer selection, and reliable replication mechanisms for use with peer-to-peer networks.

5   Issues and Summary

While we have made a case for transport layer support for multipoint-to-point connections in peer-to-peer networks, there are several issues that need to be addressed such as potential server overload and network overload due to the greedy use of multipoint-to-point connections. In particular, the need for a sound fairness model to avoid network overload can be of importance when the bottleneck occurs in the backbone of the network. Related work [17] has investigated this issue and proposed several fairness models for use with multipoint-to-point connections – with no consensus reached yet. Note that the design elements outlined in Section 3 allow the fairness model to be seamlessly incorporated in a multipoint-to-point transport protocol. For example, the receiver is the ideal location to enforce the fairness model across multiple pipes. The "decoupling of functionalities" design allows different congestion control mechanisms such as [18] to be used for secondary pipes such that the aggregate connection does not exceed its fair share. We recall from Section 2 that even when the fairness model prevents the requesting peer from enjoying higher throughput than that achievable using a point-to-point connection, a multipoint-to-point transport protocol can still provide significant performance benefits.

In this paper, we argue for transport layer support for peer-to-peer networks. We focus on the benefits of enabling multipoint-to-point communication from the perspectives of requesting peers, supplying peers, and content replication. We first show that existing application layer solutions cannot effectively address the challenges in peer-to-peer networks and support multipoint-to-point communication, whereas a multipoint-to-point transport layer protocol can be a power building block in peer-to-peer networks. We then present several design components for developing a transport layer protocol with multipoint-to-point support. Finally, we present a multipoint-to-point transport protocol called R^2CP that shows potential in addressing the unique characteristics of the peer-to-peer networks. We hence motivate further investigation along this direction.

References

1. Global Grid Forum. (http://www.gridforum.org)
2. Dabek, F., Zhao, B., Druschel, P., Kubiatowicz, J., Stoica, I.: Towards a common API for structured peer-to-peer overlays. In: Proceedings of International Workshop on Peer-to-Peer Systems (IPTPS), Berkeley, CA, USA (2003)
3. Eriksson, J., Faloutsos, M., Krishnamurthy, S.: PeerNet: Pushing peer-to-peer down the stack. In: Proceedings of International Workshop on Peer-to-Peer Systems (IPTPS), Berkeley, CA, USA (2003)
4. Saroiu, S., Gummadi, P., Gribble, S.: A measurement study of peer-to-peer file sharing systems. In: Proceedings of SPIE Conference on Multimedia Computing and Networking (MMCN), San Jose, CA, USA (2002)
5. Kazaa. (http://www.kazaa.com)
6. CenterSpan. (http://www.centerspan.com)
7. Rodriguez, P., Biersack, E.: Dynamic parallel-access to replicated content in the Internet. IEEE/ACM Transactions on Networking 10 (2002) 455–464
8. Byers, J., Luby, M., Mitzenmacher, M.: Accessing multiple mirror sites in parallel: Using Tornado codes to speed up downloads. In: Proceedings of IEEE INFOCOM, New York, NY, USA (1999)

9. Hsieh, H.Y., Sivakumar, R.: A transport layer approach for achieving aggregate bandwidths on multi-homed mobile hosts. In: Proceedings of ACM MOBICOM, Atlanta, GA, USA (2002)
10. Bernstein, D., Feng, Z., Levine, B., Zilberstein, S.: Adaptive peer selection. In: Proceedings of International Workshop on Peer-to-Peer Systems (IPTPS), Berkeley, CA, USA (2003)
11. Bhagwan, R., Savage, S., Voelker, G.: Understanding availability. In: Proceedings of International Workshop on Peer-to-Peer Systems (IPTPS), Berkeley, CA, USA (2003)
12. LimeWire. (http://www.limewire.com)
13. Anderson, D., Cobb, J., Korpela, E., Lebofsky, M., Werthimer, D.: SETI@home: An experiment in public-resource computing. Communications of the ACM **45** (2002) 56–61
14. Feldman, M., Lai, K., Chuang, J., Stoica, I.: Quantifying disincentives in peer-to-peer networks. In: Proceedings of Workshop on Economics of Peer-to-Peer Systems, Berkeley, CA, USA (2003)
15. Xu, D., Hefeeda, M., Hambrusch, S., Bhargava, B.: On peer-to-peer media streaming. In: Proceedings of IEEE ICDCS, Vienna, Austria (2002)
16. Hsieh, H.Y., Kim, K.H., Zhu, Y., Sivakumar, R.: A receiver-centric transport protocol for mobile hosts with heterogeneous wireless interfaces. In: Proceedings of ACM MOBICOM, San Diego, CA, USA (2003)
17. Karbhari, P., Zegura, E., Ammar, M.: Multipoint-to-point session fairness in the Internet. In: Proceedings of IEEE INFOCOM, San Francisco, CA, USA (2003)
18. Kuzmanovic, A., Knightly, E.: TCP-LP: A distributed algorithm for low priority data transfer. In: Proceedings of IEEE INFOCOM, San Francisco, CA, USA (2003)

Supporting Heterogeneity and Congestion Control in Peer-to-Peer Multicast Streaming*

Venkata N. Padmanabhan, Helen J. Wang, and Philip A. Chou

Microsoft Research

Abstract. We consider the problem of supporting bandwidth heterogeneity and congestion control in the context of P2P multicast streaming. We identify several challenges peculiar to the P2P setting including robustness concerns arising from peer unreliability and the ambiguity of packet loss as an indicator of congestion. We propose a hybrid parent- and child-driven bandwidth adaptation protocol that is designed in conjunction with a framework for robustness and that exploits application-level knowledge.

1 Introduction

There has been a growing interest in peer-to-peer, or end host-based, multicast for streaming because of its advantages of being self-scaling, low cost (compared to infrastructure-based approaches), and easy to deploy (compared to IP multicast) (e.g., [4][7][14]). However, a key challenge in P2P multicast is robustness. Unlike routers in IP multicast or dedicated servers in an infrastructure-based content distribution network such as Akamai, peers or end hosts are inherently unreliable due to crashes, disconnections, or shifts in user focus (e.g., a user may hop between streaming sessions or launch other bandwidth-hungry applications). A natural way to achieve robustness is through redundancy, both in network paths and in data. Our work on CoopNet [14][13] has shown that resilient peer-to-peer streaming can be achieved by carefully constructing multiple diverse distribution trees spanning the interested peers, efficiently introducing redundancy in data using multiple description coding (MDC) [8], and striping the descriptions (i.e., substreams) across the diverse set of trees. A key property of MDC, which distinguishes it from traditional layering, is that with *any* subset of the descriptions, a receiver can reconstruct the stream with quality commensurate with the number of descriptions received.

A second key challenge in peer-to-peer multicast (as well as other forms of multicast) is accommodating bandwidth heterogeneity. Heterogeneity in bandwidth can be both static (e.g., due to differences in link speed) and dynamic (e.g., due to congestion). *It is desirable that the framework for congestion control and heterogeneity management build on top of and take advantage of the robustness scheme outlined above.* This then is the focus of the present paper.

A popular approach to supporting bandwidth heterogeneity in the context of unicast as well as multicast streaming is to offer multiple streams, each optimized for a specific

---

* Please visit the CoopNet project page at http://www.research.microsoft.com/projects/CoopNet/ for more information.

G.M. Voelker and S. Shenker (Eds.): IPTPS 2004, LNCS 3279, pp. 54–63, 2004.

bandwidth level. Clients tune in to the stream that best matches their bandwidth. While this approach has the advantage of being simple, it suffers from a number of drawbacks. It is wasteful of bandwidth on links shared by streams of different rates, it typically can only accommodate coarse-grained adaptation, and having clients switch between streams of different bandwidth in response to congestion may be quite disruptive.

An alternative and more elegant approach is the one advocated in the seminal work on Receiver-driven Layered Multicast (RLM) [11]. RLM tackles the heterogeneity and congestion control problems by combining a layered source coding algorithm with a layered transmission system that uses a separate IP multicast group for transmitting each layer of the stream. Receivers specify their level of subscription by joining a subset of the groups; at any point, a receiver's subscription must be a contiguous subset that includes the base layer group. By having receivers drop layers upon congestion and add layers to probe for additional bandwidth, RLM enables scalable and adaptive congestion control in an IP multicast setting.

A significant drawback of RLM, however, is that there is a fundamental mismatch between the ordering of layers based on importance and the lack of widespread support for differentiated treatment of packets in the Internet. In the face of congestion there is no mechanism to ensure that the network preferentially drops enhancement layer packets over the base layer ones[1]. Thus the support for heterogeneity and congestion control has to be coupled with mechanisms to ensure robustness to packet loss.

Furthermore, RLM cannot be readily applied to peer-to-peer multicast because of several differences compared to IP multicast. First, in P2P multicast, the interior nodes as well as the leaves of the multicast tree are receivers. When an interior receiver adapts the bandwidth usage on its incoming link, the effect on its downstream receivers must be taken into account. Second, in P2P multicast, receivers that are interior nodes may also need to adapt bandwidth usage on their outgoing links, as these may be bottlenecks. And finally, in P2P multicast, the interior nodes of the multicast tree are a dynamic set of end hosts rather than a set of dedicated routers. Hence packet loss seen by a receiver arises not only from congestion in the network at large, but also from the unreliability of its peers, tree dynamics, and local congestion. Hence, it is not always possible to reduce packet loss by shedding traffic. In some cases the more appropriate response is to switch from the current parent to a better one.

Motivated by the above considerations, we approach the problem as follows.

1. **Joint design of support for heterogeneity and robustness:** We design our adaptation scheme for heterogeneity in the context of a framework for robustness [14][13] that incorporates redundancy in network paths and in data. We use a *layered MDC* codec [6], which combines the robustness of MDC with the adaptability of layering.

2. **Hybrid parent- and child-driven adaptation:** Parents and children cooperatively determine the appropriate response to packet loss by exploiting path diversity to localize the cause of packet loss.

---

[1] The RLM paper [11] actually argues that the lack of support for preferential dropping is an advantage since it discourages greedy behavior. However, we believe that this point is moot in the context of peer-to-peer multicast since there are more direct opportunities to cheat, for example, by failing to forward packets. Cooperative behavior is inherently assumed in such settings.

3. **Exploiting application-level knowledge for adaptation:** Both parents and children exploit their knowledge of the relative importance of the layered MDC substreams and the structure of the distribution trees to adapt to changing bandwidth in a way that minimizes the impact on the descendant nodes.

The specific novel contributions of this paper are the adaptation protocol and the application of layered MDC in this context. However, we believe that *our paper also makes a more general contribution by drawing attention to two observations.* First, it may often be advantageous to have the "routers" (i.e., the peers) in a P2P system use application-level knowledge to optimize performance, for example, by shedding less important data when there is congestion. There is no reason for the P2P nodes to simply mimic the "dumb" forwarding that IP routers do. Second, while network path diversity has been used in P2P systems for resilience [13] and for bandwidth management [4], it can also be exploited to give the peers greater visibility into the network using techniques such as tomography [3].

Before getting into layered MDC and our adaptation scheme, we briefly review our previous work on CoopNet, which provides the framework we build on.

2   CoopNet Background

As mentioned in Section 1, CoopNet [14][13] employs redundancy in both network paths and in data to make P2P streaming robust to peer unreliability and failures. Rather than use a single distribution tree as in traditional multicast, CoopNet constructs multiple, diverse distribution trees, each spanning the set of interested peers. The trees are diverse in their structures; for instance node *A* could be the parent of *B* in one tree but be its child in another. Our experiments have suggested that having 8 trees works well. To ensure diverse and bushy (i.e., high fanout) trees, each peer is typically made an interior node (i.e., a "fertile" node) in a few trees and a leaf node (i.e., a "sterile" node) in the remaining trees. In the extreme case, a peer may be fertile (and have several children) in just one tree and be sterile in the remaining trees.

Tree management in CoopNet is done by a centralized tree manager. Our discussion here is agnostic of how exactly tree management is done, and we do not discuss the specifics of how nodes join and leave trees, and find themselves new parents.

The stream is encoded using multiple description coding (MDC). The MDC substreams, or descriptions, are all of equal importance and have the property that *any* subset of them can be used to reconstruct a stream of quality commensurate with the size of the subset. This is in contrast to layered coding, which imposes a strict ordering on the layers; for instance, an enhancement layer is useless in the absence of the base layer or a previous enhancement layer. The flexibility of MDC comes at a modest price in terms of bandwidth (typically around 20%). It is important to note, however, that MDC is optimized for the expected packet loss distribution. If few or no losses are expected, then MDC would adapt by cutting down the amount of redundancy and the bandwidth overhead.

The descriptions generated by the MDC codec are striped across the diverse set of trees. This ensures that each peer receives the substreams over a diverse set of paths, which makes it quite likely that it will continue to receive the majority of the descriptions (and hence be able to decode a stream of reasonable quality) even as other peers experience failures.

In our earlier CoopNet work, we assumed that all peers received streams of the same bandwidth. Also, we did not consider how peers might respond to congestion. We turn to these issues next.

3   Key Questions

Our discussion of an adaptation framework for accommodating bandwidth heterogeneity and congestion control is centered around the following key questions:

1. How should the stream data be organized to enable peers to subscribe to just the portion that matches their current available bandwidth?
2. How should peers respond to packet loss?
3. How should RLM-style adding and dropping of layers be done so that the impact on the other peers is minimized?

We discuss these questions in the sections that follow.

4   Layered MDC

A particularly efficient and practical MDC construction uses layered coding and Forward Error Correction (FEC) as building blocks. Layered coding is used to prioritize the data, while FEC, such as Reed-Solomon encoding, is then used to provide different levels of protection for the data units. Determining the protection level for the data units is an optimization procedure that is based on both the importance of the data units and the packet loss distribution across *all* clients.

When the clients' bandwidths are heterogeneous, either due to different link capacities or dynamic network conditions, MDC becomes less efficient. A naive way of supporting heterogeneity is to treat descriptions just as layers are treated in RLM: dropping descriptions upon congestion and adding descriptions to see if additional bandwidth is available. However, this approach is inefficient since the MDC construction is optimized for the entire ensemble of (heterogeneous) clients. For high-bandwidth clients, there is wasteful redundancy in the MDC, which unnecessarily degrades quality. For low-bandwidth clients, the redundancy would typically be insufficient to enable decoding the received stream.

In [6], we have developed a novel *layered MDC* scheme in which the descriptions are partitioned into layers. For our discussion here, we consider two layers, a base layer and an enhancement layer. The base layer descriptions are optimized for just the low-bandwidth clients. The enhancement layer descriptions are optimized for the high-bandwidth clients, while also providing additional protection for the less-protected data units in the base layer. This ensures that the more important data units have a higher probability of being successfully delivered over the best-effort Internet.

This layered MDC construction is clearly optimal for the low-bandwidth clients. Our experiments also indicate that high-bandwidth clients suffer a modest penalty of about 1.4 dB (in terms of distortion) compared to the case where all of the descriptions are optimized exclusively for the high-bandwidth clients. Thus layered MDC combines layering and robustness without sacrificing much in terms of efficiency.

In the context of P2P streaming with heterogeneous clients, the base layer alone is sent to the low-bandwidth clients while both the base and the enhancement layers are sent to the high-bandwidth clients. Clients adapt to dynamic fluctuations in bandwidth by adding/dropping descriptions in their current highest layer (or in the next layer above/below if the current layer is full/empty).

5 Inferring the Location of Congestion

When a node experiences packet loss in its incoming stream, the appropriate response depends on the reason for the packet loss. As discussed in Section 6, if there is congestion near the node's incoming link, then the node should shed some incoming traffic, while if there is congestion near its parent's outgoing link, then the parent should shed some outgoing traffic, possibly destined for another node.

The interesting question then is how a node can determine where congestion is happening. In our framework (Section 2), each node receives substreams from multiple parents. Thus each node is in a position to monitor the packet loss rate of the substream from each parent. *This loss rate information from a diverse set of network paths can be used to infer the likely location of network congestion using techniques akin to network tomography [3].* If a child node experiences significant packet loss in most or all trees, it can reasonably conclude that the congestion is occurring at or close to its incoming link. Likewise, if a parent node receives packet loss indications from most or all of its children, it can reasonably conclude that congestion is occurring at or near its outgoing link.

To evaluate the efficacy of this heuristic, we conducted a simple simulation experiment. We generated a 1000-node topology using the BRITE topology generator [12]. We used the preferential connectivity model provided by BRITE (based on the work of Barabasi et al. [2]), which helps capture the power-law distribution of node degrees observed in practice. The resulting topology had 662 leaves (i.e., nodes with degree 1), which we treat as candidates for peers (parents or children). In each run of the experiment, we pick a child node and 16 parent nodes (corresponding to 16 distribution trees) at random. We compute the shortest path routes from the parent nodes to the child node. Each link contained in one of these shortest paths is independently marked as "congested" with a probability of 10%. The substream from a parent node to the child is assumed to suffer congestion if one or more links along the path is marked as congested; we simply term the parent as "congested" in such a case.

Likewise, the path from a potential parent (i.e., a leaf node in the topology other than the chosen parents and the child) to the child is considered to be congested (and hence prone to packet loss) if it includes a congested link; again, for ease of exposition, we term the potential parent as being "congested" in such a case.

Figure 1 shows the fraction of congested potential parents versus the fraction of congested current parents over 1000 runs of the experiment. The scatter plot shows the results of the individual runs while the solid line shows the mean. It is clear that when a

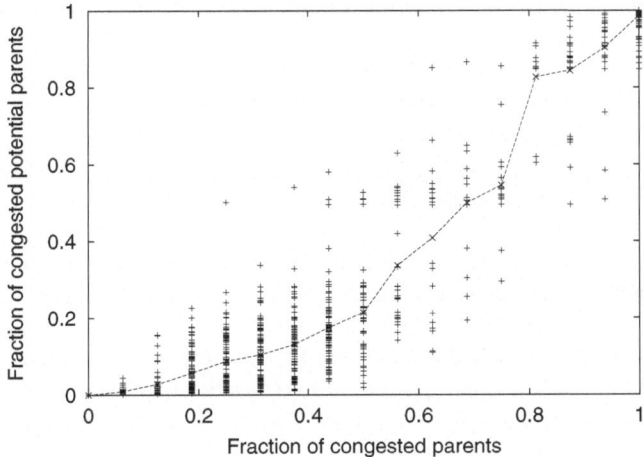

Fig. 1. Fraction of congested parents versus fraction of congested potential parents.

large fraction (say over 75%) of a node's current parents are congested, it is also likely that a large fraction of its potential parents would be congested. This is so because congestion is likely near the node's incoming link. In such a case, the node should shed incoming traffic to alleviate the congestion.

Conversely, the experiment also shows that if we swap the roles of parents and children, then when a large fraction of a node's children are congested, then there is the likelihood of congestion near the node's outgoing link. Thus, when a node receives packet loss indications from most or all of its children, it should shed outgoing traffic to alleviate the congestion.

Furthermore, *sharing of information between parents and children can lead to a more robust inference of the location of congestion.* For instance, consider a child that is unlucky to have several parents with congested uplinks[2]. The child can deduce that this is the case (and search for new parents) based on the knowledge of complaints that its parents are receiving from their other children. In the absence of complaint information from its parents, the child might have incorrectly concluded that the congestion is at its incoming link and hence proceeded to shed incoming traffic.

6   Adaptation Protocol

We now discuss our adaptation protocol. As outlined in Section 4, we assume that the stream has been coded into sets of descriptions corresponding to each of the base layer and one or more enhancement layers; each description is termed a "substream" here.

As in RLM, there are two aspects to the adaptation protocol: shedding traffic when there is congestion, and adding traffic when there isn't congestion. We discuss each of

---

[2] This may happen in practice because congested links may be concentrated in the "last-mile" to/from peers rather than be spread uniformly throughout the network as in our simple experiment described above.

these in turn. Our emphasis is on pointing out the unique opportunities for optimization in a P2P setting.

6.1 Shedding Traffic

When congestion is encountered, the appropriate reaction depends on the location of the congested link(s). We consider three cases:

1. If congestion is at or near the outgoing link of a node, the node sheds outgoing traffic to alleviate the congestion. It does this by shedding children, who then have to look for new parents.
2. If congestion is at or near the incoming link of the node, the node sheds incoming traffic to alleviate the congestion. It does this by shedding parents. This entails also shedding any children that may have been receiving the now-discontinued substream(s).
3. If congestion is in the "middle", then the child node looks for new parents with a view to routing around or avoiding the point(s) of congestion.

We now turn to the interesting questions of how a congested parent picks children to shed and how a congested child picks parents to shed.

A congested parent preferentially sheds children that are receiving descriptions from the highest enhancement layer. Of such children, it preferentially sheds those that have no children or have few descendants in the tree of interest. (Recall from Section 2 that each peer is a leaf node in most of the trees.) The objective is to pick children that will be least affected by being orphaned because they are receiving substreams of the least importance from the congested parent and have few or no descendants dependent on them. Such *parent-driven* selective dropping results in better quality than a policy of randomly dropping packets across all children.

Likewise, a congested child preferentially sheds parents from whom it is receiving descriptions belonging to the highest enhancement layer. Of such parents, it preferentially sheds those that are sending it substreams for which it has no children or has few descendants. Such *child-driven* selective dropping likewise results in better quality than randomly dropping incoming streams.

This hybrid parent- and child-driven congestion control scheme elegantly addresses a key difficulty in using layered coding in today's Internet, viz., the mismatch between the prioritization of the layers and the lack of widespread support for service differentiation in the Internet.

6.2 Adding Traffic

Receivers not only need to adapt to worsening network conditions but also need to probe for newly available bandwidth, if any. When a receiver has not experienced any loss for a threshold period of time, it carries out a *join experiment*, as in RLM, by subscribing to an additional description in the current highest layer or one in the next higher layer if all of the descriptions in the current highest layer are already being received. Subscribing to the new description involves joining the corresponding tree.

There is always the danger that a join experiment "fails" because the additional traffic congests a link that was operating almost at capacity. Such an unsuccessful join experiment could lead to packet loss and quality degradation at the receiver as well as other nodes (in particular, its descendants). A key advantage of using layered MDC over plain layered coding is that its inherent redundancy limits the damaged caused by an unsuccessful join experiments. For our discussion here, we assume that subscribing to an additional description causes the loss of at most one description's worth of data (basically, the additional data can at worst displace an equal amount of data previously subscribed to). If the losses are confined to the same layer as the new description, then we are no worse off than before the join experiment because all descriptions in a layer are equally valuable. Even if losses are suffered in a lower and hence more important layer, the redundancy in layered MDC can typically help recover the affected layer.

In contrast, RLM with plain layered coding is far more susceptible to the deleterious effects of failed join experiments, in addition to the deleterious effects of random packet loss. This is because there is nothing to mask packet loss suffered by a lower and hence more important layer, which can then render all subsequent layers of received data useless and degrade quality significantly.

To evaluate this, we compared the impact of join experiments with plain layered coding (RLM) to those with plain multiple description coding (MDC). We set the total number of substreams to be the same in both cases: 32 (thin) layers with RLM, and 32 descriptions with MDC. We assumed that layers (respectively, descriptions) are independently lost with probability 10%, and that the MDC system is optimized for this loss probability. Figure 2 shows for the RLM system (with circles) and the MDC system (without circles) typical video quality (measured as PSNR in dB[3]) as a function of the number of substreams to which a receiver is subscribed after performing the join in a join experiment. For the RLM system, even if the join succeeds (dotted line with circles), quality does not improve significantly since it is saturated at a low level due to the random packet loss frequently disrupting the more important layers; moreover, if the join fails (solid line with circles), quality falls even further. In contrast, for the MDC system, if the join succeeds (dotted line), quality is good for any number of substreams above 25, while if the join fails (solid line), quality remains the same as before the join. *Thus the loss resilience provided by MDC also enhances the robustness of congestion control.*

7   Related Work

There has been much work following up on and improving on RLM [11]. There has been work on adjusting the rate of each layer dynamically and adding/dropping layers in a manner that is TCP-friendly [15, 10]. In our work, we do not advocate a specific policy in this regard and could leverage this related work. There has also been work on replacing the "thick" RLM layers with "thin" layers (called "thin streams") to enable more fine-grained adaptation [16]. Since in our scheme we add/drop individual descriptions rather than entire layers, we enjoy the same benefits as thin streams and in addition

---

[3] Peak Signal-to-Noise Ratio in decibels is given by $10\log_{10}(255^2/D)$, where D is the mean squared error between the original and reconstructed luminance video pixels.

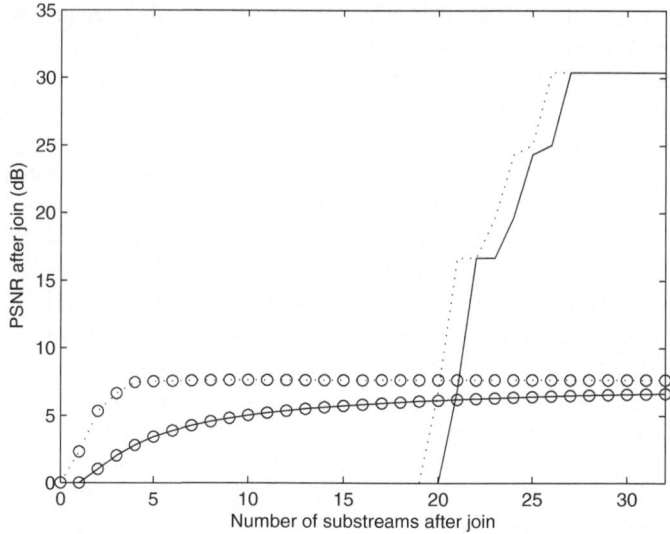

Fig. 2. Join Experiment for RLM vs. MDC: no collateral damage in MDC.

also have the benefit of robustness. An alternative approach for enabling fine-grained adaptation is to use dynamic layers, i.e., layers whose transmission rate changes over time [9].

In term of support for heterogeneity in P2P multicast streaming, we are aware of a couple of different approaches. In end system multicast [1], clients choose between separate (non-layered) low-bandwidth (100 Kbps) and high-bandwidth (300 Kbps) streams. In SplitStream [4], the stream is divided into substreams that are striped across multiple trees. The number of stripes that a host subscribes to is a function of its bandwidth. The focus is on accommodating static bandwidth heterogeneity rather than dynamic fluctuations caused by congestion. There has also been work on exploiting heterogeneity to improve the efficiency and scalability of P2P overlays by assigning a greater share of the work to the more resourceful peers [5]. This is an orthogonal problem to heterogeneity support and congestion control for data transmission over such P2P overlays.

8   Conclusion

In this paper, we have presented the design of a bandwidth adaptation protocol for P2P multicast streaming with several novel features. First, the adaptation protocol is designed jointly with a framework for robustness that incorporates redundancy in network paths and in data. Second, parent and child nodes work in conjunction to determine the appropriate response to packet loss by exploiting tree diversity to localize the cause of packet loss. Third, both parents and children exploit knowledge of the relative importance of layered MDC substreams and the structure of the distribution trees to adapt to changing bandwidth in a way that minimizes the impact on the descendant nodes.

Although our discussion here has focussed on CoopNet for the sake of concreteness, many of the ideas have general applicability to multicast and non-multicast P2P settings. For instance, the robustness of join experiments with layered MDC would be advantageous in any RLM-like setting, even one based on a single distribution tree. Inferring the location of congestion could be useful even in an on-demand (non-multicast) streaming scenario where the receiver requests different substreams from different peers.

References

1. End System Multicast. http://esm.cs.cmu.edu/.
2. BARABASI, A. L., AND ALBERT, R. Emergence of Scaling in Random Networks. *Science*, 286 (Oct. 1999), 509–512.
3. BU, T., DUFFIELD, N., PRESTI, F. L., AND TOWSLEY, D. Network Tomography on General Topologies. In *Proc. ACM SIGMETRICS* (June 2002).
4. CASTRO, M., DRUSCHEL, P., KERMARREC, A.-M., NANDI, A., ROWSTRON, A., AND SINGH, A. SplitStream: High-bandwidth Content Distribution in a Cooperative Environment. In *Proc. SOSP* (Oct. 2003).
5. CHAWATHE, Y., RATNASAMY, S., BRESLAU, L., AND SHENKER, S. Making Gnutella-like P2P Systems Scalable. In *Proc. ACM SIGCOMM* (Aug. 2003).
6. CHOU, P. A., WANG, H. J., AND PADMANABHAN, V. N. Layered Multiple Description Coding. In *Proc. Packet Video Workshop* (Apr. 2003).
7. CHU, Y., RAO, S. G., SESHAN, S., AND ZHANG, H. Enabling Conferencing Applications on the Internet using an Overlay Multicast Architecture. In *Proc. ACM SIGCOMM* (Aug. 2001).
8. GOYAL, V. K. Multiple Description Coding: Compression Meets the Network. *IEEE Signal Processing Mag.* (Sept. 2001), 74–93.
9. KWON, G., AND BYERS, J. Smooth Multirate Multicast Congestion Control. In *IEEE Infocom* (Apr. 2003).
10. LIU, J., LI, B., AND ZHANG, Y. A Hybrid Adaptation Protocol for TCP-friendly Layered Multicast and Its Optimal Rate Allocation. In *IEEE Infocom* (June 2002).
11. MCCANNE, S. R., JACOBSON, V., AND VETTERLI, M. Receiver-driven Layered Multicast. In *Proc. ACM SIGCOMM* (Aug. 1996).
12. MEDINA, A., LAKHINA, A., MATTA, I., AND BYERS, J. BRITE: An Approach to Universal Topology Generation. In *Proc. MASCOTS* (Aug 2001).
13. PADMANABHAN, V. N., WANG, H. J., AND CHOU, P. A. Resilient Peer-to-Peer Streaming. In *Proc. IEEE ICNP* (Nov. 2003).
14. PADMANABHAN, V. N., WANG, H. J., CHOU, P. A., AND SRIPANIDKULCHAI, K. Distributing Streaming Media Content Using Cooperative Networking. In *Proc. NOSSDAV* (May 2002).
15. WIDMER, J., AND HANDLEY, M. Extending Equation-based Congestion Control to Multicast Applications. In *Proc. ACM SIGCOMM* (Aug. 2001).
16. WU, L., SHARMA, R., AND SMITH, B. Thin Streams, An Architecture for Multicasting Layered Video. In *Proc. NOSSDAV* (1997).

Rapid Mobility via Type Indirection

Ben Y. Zhao, Ling Huang, Anthony D. Joseph, and John Kubiatowicz

Computer Science Division, University of California, Berkeley
{ravenben,hling,adj,kubitron}@cs.berkeley.edu

Abstract. Economies of scale and advancements in wide-area wireless networking are leading to the availability of more small, networked mobile devices, placing higher stress on existing mobility infrastructures. This problem is exacerbated by the formation of *mobile crowds* that generate storms of location update traffic as they cross boundaries between base stations. In this paper, we present a novel aggregation technique we call *type indirection* that allows mobile crowds to roam as single mobile entities. We discuss our design in the context of *Warp*, a mobility infrastructure based on a peer-to-peer overlay, and show that its performance approaches that of Mobile IP with optimizations while significantly reducing the effect of handoff storms.

1 Introduction

Economies of scale and advancements in wide-area wireless networking are leading to the widespread availability and use of millions of wirelessly-enabled mobile computers, Personal Digital Assistants (PDAs), and other portable devices. The same trends are also resulting in the large-scale deployment of publically acessible wireless access points in both fixed (*e.g.*, hotel, coffee shop, etc.) and mobile (*e.g.*, train, subway, etc.) environments [1].

We consider two rapid mobility scenarios. The first is rapid individual mobility across network cells (*e.g.*, a mobile user on an inter-city bus travelling on a highway with cell sizes of half a mile). This scenario requires fast handoff handling to maintain connectivity. A second, more problematic scenario is a bullet train with hundreds of mobile users. With cell sizes of half a mile, there are frequent, huge bursts of cell crossings that will overwhelm most mobility and application-level protocols.

The challenge is to provide fast handoff across frequent cell crossings for a large number of users, potentially traveling in clusters (*mobile crowds*). Handled naively, the delay in processing handoffs will be exacerbated by the large volume of users moving in unison, creating congestion and adding scheduling and processing delays and disrupting the timely delivery of packets to the mobile hosts.

A similar problem exists in cellular networks. As mobile crowds travel across the network, cells can "borrow" frequencies from neighbors, but base stations are often overloaded by control traffic and as a result, drop calls [2]. In certain cases, specialized "mobile trunk" base stations can be colocated with mobile crowds to aggregate control traffic. The mobile trunk maintains connectivity with nearby base stations while forwarding traffic from local mobile hosts. Ideally, each provider would place such a base station on each bus or train segment, but the individual component and maintenance costs are prohibitive.

G.M. Voelker and S. Shenker (Eds.): IPTPS 2004, LNCS 3279, pp. 64–74, 2004.

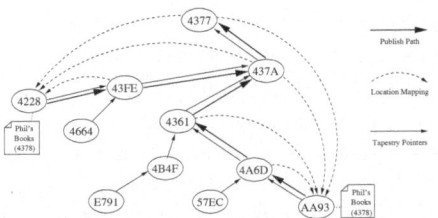

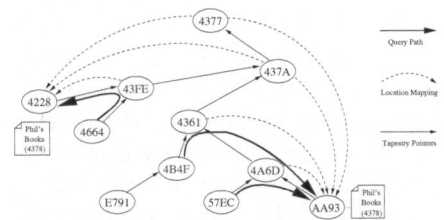

Fig. 1. *Tapestry object publication.* Two copies of an object (4378) are published to its root node at 4377.

Fig. 2. *Tapestry route to object.* Nodes send messages to object 4378.

Previous works propose to minimize handoff delay using incremental route reestablishment and hierarchical foreign agents or switches, or by organizing the wireless infrastructure as a static hierarchy or collection of clusters [3–5]. A proposal also exists for Mobile IP to adopt a simplified version of hierarchical handoff management [6]. These approaches specify separate mechanisms to handle handoffs at different levels of the hierarchy. Also, since they statically define aggregation boundaries in the infrastructure, foreign agents or switches are prone to overloading by spikes in handoff traffic, such as those generated by the movement of large mobile crowds.

To address these issues, we introduce *Warp*, a mobility infrastructure leveraging flexible points of indirection in a peer-to-peer overlay. Warp uses a mobile node's unique name to choose the members of a virtual hierarchy of indirection nodes. These nodes act as hierarchical foreign agents to support fast handover operations. Warp also supports hierarchical types, where mobile crowds can redirect traffic through single indirection points and aggregate handoffs as a single entity. For example, an access point on the train can perform handoffs as a single node while forwarding traffic to local mobile nodes. Although our techniques can be applied by layering the decentralized object location and routing (DOLR) API on several structured peer-to-peer networks [7], we discuss Warp in the context of the Tapestry overlay network.

We begin with a brief overview of the Tapestry [8] protocol. In Section 3, we discuss basic mobility support, followed by a discussion in Section 4 of rapid mobility and hierarchical type mobility. We present simulation results in Section 5, and finish with related work and our conclusions in Section 6.

2 Tapestry Overview

We provide a brief overview of Tapestry [8], a scalable structured peer-to-peer (P2P) infrastructure that routes messages to nodes and objects.

2.1 Routing Layer

Object and node IDs are chosen uniformly at random from the namespace of fixed-length bit sequences with a common base (e.g. Hexadecimal). Each node uses local routing tables to route messages incrementally to the destination ID digit by matching prefixes of increasing length (e.g., $4***\Longrightarrow 45**\Longrightarrow 459*\Longrightarrow 4598$ where $*$'s represent wildcards). A node N has a routing table with multiple levels, where the nth level stores nodes matching at least $n-1$ digits to N. The ith entry in the jth level is the location of the node *closest in network latency* that begins with $prefix_{j-1}(N) + i$.

To forward on a message from its nth hop router, a node examines its $n+1^{th}$ level routing table and forwards the message to the link corresponding to the $n+1^{th}$ digit in the destination ID. This routing substrate provides efficient location-independent routing within a logarithmic number of hops and using compact routing tables.

2.2 Data Location

A server S makes a local object O available to others by routing a "publish" message to the object's "root node," the live node O's identifier maps to. At each hop along the path, a location mapping from O to S is stored. Figure 1 illustrates object publication, where two replicas of an object are published. A client routes queries toward the root node (see Figure 2), querying each hop on the way, and routing towards S when it finds the O to S location mapping. For nearby objects, queries quickly intersect the path taken by publish messages, resulting in low latency routing to objects [8].

The data location layer embeds indirection pointers into the routing framework. This built-in redirection routes messages to their destinations using only location-independent IDs. We leverage this generic mechanism for routing to named endpoints in Warp. We also note that the routing protocol chooses the placement of these indirection points and transparently maintains them across changes in the overlay network.

3   Mobility Support

We now discuss how to layer mobility support on top of a structured peer-to-peer overlay, referring to *mobile nodes* (MN) interacting with *correspondent hosts* (CH).

3.1   Basic Mobility Support

A mobile node roaming outside of its home network connects to a local proxy node as its temporary care-of-addresses. Mobile nodes are client-only nodes that do not route or store data for the overlay. We assume that infrastructure nodes are nodes with relatively fixed positions, giving them the perspective of a relatively stable infrastructure. Nodes join and leave the infrastructure using Tapestry's dynamic membership algorithms [9]. *Node Registration* As with mobile IP, a mobile node MN registers itself with a nearby proxy node P[1]. When a proxy receives a registration from MN, it uses the DOLR interface [7] to publish MN as an endpoint. The infrastructure then routes messages destined for the MN endpoint to the proxy. We call this use of the natural indirection facility to perform redirection of messages (possibly multiple times) *type indirection*. At each node along the path from proxy to MN's root node, a local pointer to the last node on the path is stored. The result is a multi-hop *forwarding path* from MN's root to its proxy.

---

[1] Registrations are encrypted with a node's private key. Node IDs are hashes of public keys and verified by certificates issued by a central certificate authority

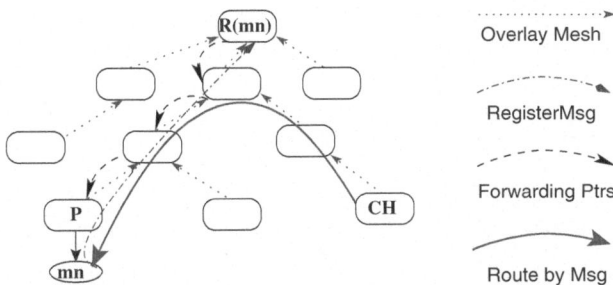

Fig. 3. *Communicating with a mobile host.* Mobile node mn registers with proxy P, and correspondent host CH sends a message to mn.

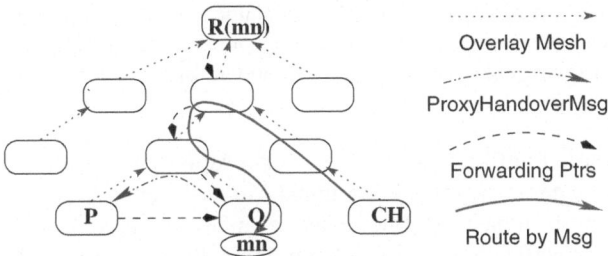

Fig. 4. *Updating a location binding via ProxyHandoverMsg.* Correspondent host CH sends a message to mobile node mn after mn moves from proxy P to Q.

When a correspondent host CH sends a message to MN, Tapestry routes the message towards MN's root. When the message intersects the forwarding path, it follows the path of pointers to the proxy and MN. Figure 3 shows a node CH routing a message to MN. Note that hops in structured overlays such as Tapestry generally increase in physical length (# of IP hops) closer to the destination. Messages avoid the longer hops to the root by intersecting the forwarding path. This is key to reducing routing stretch for communication with closeby CH's.

Unlike other approaches to traffic redirection [10], Tapestry uses the overlay to transport both control and data traffic. By using points inside the network to redirect traffic, we eliminate the need to communicate with the endpoints when routes change. In the case of Warp, it means that as nodes move, proxy handover messages modify the forwarding path between proxies without incurring a roundtrip back to the home agent or correspondent host.

Mobile nodes listen for periodic broadcasts from nearby proxies for discovery, similar to techniques used by Mobile IP. Fast-moving nodes can proactively solicit proxy nodes via expanding ring search multicast to reduce discovery latency.

Proxy Handover. Mobile node MN performs a proxy handover from P to Q by sending a ProxyHandoverMsg to Q, <MN, P, Q> signed with its secret key. Q sets up a forwarding route to MN, and requests that P sets up a forwarding pointer to Q. Q then routes the ProxyHandoverMsg towards MN's root node, and builds a forwarding path to itself. The

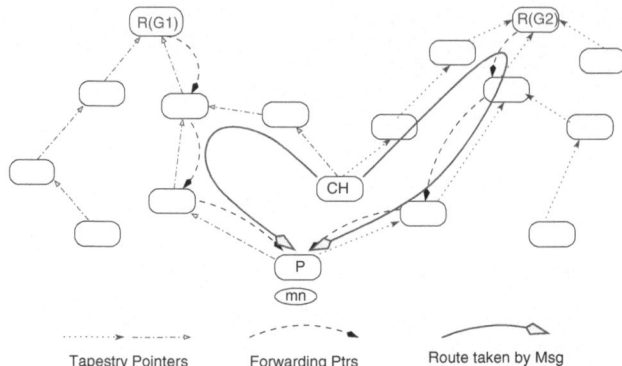

Fig. 5. *Node aliasing with 2 IDs.* This shows CH communicating to a mobile host (MH) using node aliasing. MH registers with two independent pseudorandom IDs mn_{G1} and mn_{G2}. CH measures the end to end latency to MH using both and caches the shorter route for future communication.

message is forwarded until it intersects P's forwarding path. Note the path taken by the handover message is roughly proportional to the distance between P and Q. This is a key distinction from basic Mobile IP, and is analogous to a version of hierarchical handoff [3] with dynamically constructed, topologically-aware hierarchies.

When the message intersects a node A that is on the forwarding path to MN, it redirects the forwarding pointers to point to the new path. A then forwards the message downwards to P. Each node along the way schedules its forwarding pointer for deletion and forwards the message towards P[2]. When the message reaches P, P schedules the forwarding pointer to Q for deletion. Once all deletions are completed, handover is complete. The process is shown in Figure 4.

If the proxies do not overlap in coverage area, then MN will have a window of time after it leaves coverage of P and before it completes handover to Q. In this scenario, P performs a limited amount of buffering for MN, and then forwards the buffer to Q when a forwarding pointer is established [11].

Location Services for Mobile Objects. We also support the routing of messages to objects residing on mobile nodes. An object named O residing on mobile node MN is published in the overlay with the location mapping from O to MN. A message for O routes towards O's root until it finds the location mapping. Recognizing MN's ID as a mobile address[3], the overlay routes the message for O as a normal message addressed to the mobile node MN. The message routes to MN's proxy, MN, then O.

3.2 Node Aliasing

One way to improve resilience and performance is for the mobile node mn to advertise its presence via multiple identities, each mapping to an independent root. We call this

---

[2] A delay in deleting forwarding pointers is required to handle potential reorderings of messages between nodes by the underlying transport layer.

[3] All mobile node IDs share a specialized tag appended to their normal ID

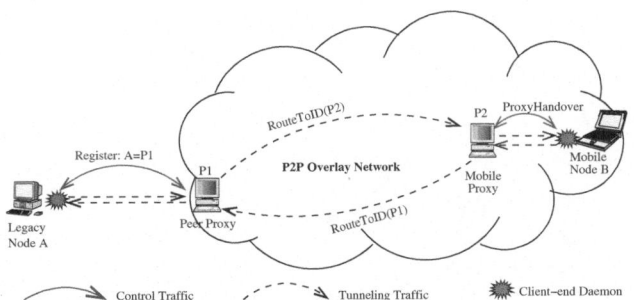

Fig. 6. *Tunneling legacy application traffic through client-end daemons and overlay proxies..* A legacy node A communicates with mobile node B.

node aliasing. Here, mn hashes its original ID concatenated with each of a small set of sequential natural numbers to generate independent pseudorandom IDs, and registers under each ID, creating several forwarding paths to the mobile proxy via independent root nodes.

When establishing a connection, a correspondent host (CH) generates these IDs independently, and sends messages in parallel on all forwarding paths. With feedback from the mobile node, CH chooses the ID that incurs the least latency for their connection, effectively reducing message delivery time to that of the shortest forwarding path. Figure 5 shows how CH begins communication with mn using a node aliasing factor of two. Note that after significant movement across the network, MN can repeat the path selection process to try to reduce end-to-end latency.

Alternatively, the CH can choose to continue to send duplicate messages out to several forwarding paths for additional fault-tolerance. We show in Section 5 that two IDs provide significant reduction in routing latency.

3.3   Supporting Legacy Applications

Warp supports communication between mobile nodes and legacy (non-overlay) nodes using a mechanism similar to those presented in the contexts of the Tapestry and I3 projects ([12, 10]). Mobile nodes are assigned unique DNS names with a specialized suffix, such as .tap. The mobile node stores a mapping from a hash of its DNS name to its overlay ID into the overlay.

Figure 6 shows an example of the connection setup. Legacy node A wants to establish a connection to mobile node B. The local daemon redirects the DNS lookup request, retrieves the mobile node's stored ID using a hash of B, and forwards traffic through the overlay address to B's overlay ID.

4   Supporting Rapid Mobility

Recall that in our approach, routing to mobile nodes uses indirection to translate a mobile ID into an overlay identifier. Routing to a mobile object goes through two levels

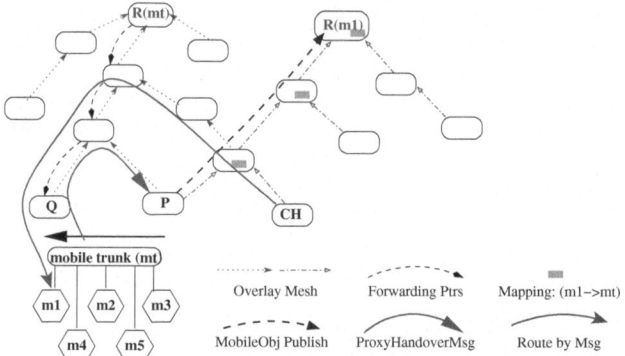

Fig. 7. *Mobile crowds.* Five members (m1..5) of a crowd connected to a mobile trunk (mt). A message routes to m1 as the crowd moves from proxy P to Q.

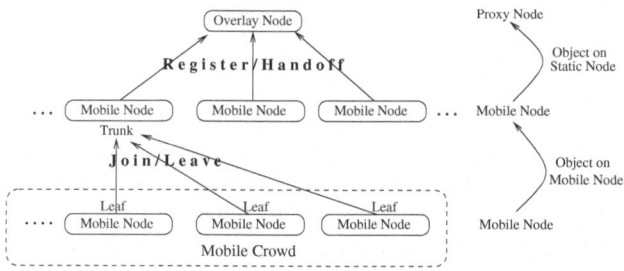

Fig. 8. A figure summarizing levels of *type indirection*. The arrows on right illustrate relative relationships between types.

of this *type indirection*, from object ID to mobile node ID to proxy ID. Here we discuss chaining multiple levels of type indirection to aggregate mobile crowds as single entities, reducing handoff message storms to single handoff messages.

4.1 Mobile Crowds

A *mobile crowd* forms where large groups of mobile users travel together. Examples include a large number of train passengers with wireless laptops and PDAs or tourists wirelessly accessing information on historic sites on a group tour. Such groups cause large bursts of handoff messages as they move in unison across cell boundries.

To minimize the resulting delay and congestion at nearby basestations, we choose a mobile node as the *mobile trunk*, and use it as a secondary proxy for others in the mobile crowd. The trunk advertises each member of the crowd (a *mobile leaf*), as a locally available object. Messages to a mobile leaf routes first to the trunk, then to the leaf. As the crowd moves across cell boundaries, only the trunk needs to update its location with a single handover.

Figure 7 shows an example. When a mobile node joins a mobile trunk in the crowd, the trunk publishes the <m1,mt> "location mapping." A message addressed to m1 routes towards m1's root. When it finds a location mapping, the message is redirected towards node `mt`. It encounters the mapping from `mt` to its proxy `Q`, routes to `Q`, `mt`, then `m1`.

4.2 Discussion

Type indirection reduces handoff messages from one message per node to one message per crowd. For more flexibility, a crowd can choose an unique crowd ID. Any mobile trunk would register with the proxy using the crowd ID instead of its own node ID. This allows multiple trunks to function simultaneously to guard against trunk failures or departures. Furthermore, since the trunk can suffer degraded performance, the responsibility can rotate across crowd members at periodic intervals to provide fairness.

We can further chain together type indirections for more interesting scenarios. For example, multiple bluetooth-enabled devices on a passenger may form a personal mobile crowd. These devices connect to a local mobile trunk, which joins a mobile trunk on the tour bus, which itself acts as a mobile node traveling through the network. Figure 8 shows different types of mobility, and how we leverage type indirection.

5   Measurements and Evaluation

In this section, we evaluate our infrastructure design via simulation. Our performance metric is *routing stretch*, the ratio of routing latency on an overlay to the routing latency of IP. We use the shortest path latency as the IP layer latency. Note that our results do not account for computational overhead at nodes. We believe that processing time will be dominated by network latencies. More comprehensive measurement results are available [13].

We use a packet-level simulator running on transit stub topologies [14] of 5,000 nodes. Each topology has 6 transit domains of 10 nodes each; each transit node has 7 stub domains with an average of 12 nodes each. Our simulator measures network latency, but does not simulate network effects such as congestion, routing policies, or retransmission at lower layers. To reduce variance, we take measurements on 9 different 5,000 node transit stub topologies, each with 3 random overlay assignments.

5.1   Routing Efficiency

We studied the relative routing performance of our system and Mobile IP under different roaming scenarios. Mobile IP performance is a function of the distance from `MN` to `NODECH`, and from `MN` to its `HA`. Our system allows free roaming without a home network, and latency is dependent on the distance between `CH` and `MN`. We compare our system against three Mobile IP scenarios, where the distance between `MN` and its `HA` is (1) $< \frac{1}{3} \cdot D$ (near), (2) $> \frac{2}{3} \cdot D$ (far), and (3) $> \frac{1}{3} \cdot D$ and $< \frac{2}{3} \cdot D$ (mid), where D is network diameter.

Figure 9 shows that for correspondents close to the mobile node (*i.e.*, `MN` near `CH`), basic Mobile IP generally performs quite poorly under scenarios 1 and 3 due to triangle routing. In contrast, Warp's RDP shows some initial variability for short routing paths, but generally performs well with low stretch. Warp with node aliasing of factor 2

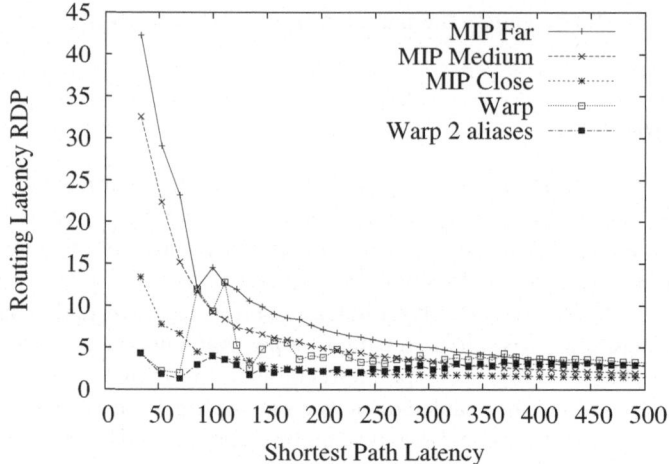

Fig. 9. *Routing stretch.* Routing latency via Warp (with and without node aliasing) and Mobile IP measured as a ratio of shortest path IP latency.

significantly outperforms all others. Note that Mobile IP with route optimization [15] achieves a routing stretch of 1.

5.2 Rapid Mobility

We evaluate Warp's support for rapid mobility by comparing latency to handle cell handovers relative to Mobile IP. Time is measured from the initial request for location binding update to when all forwarding routes are updated and consistent. Figure 10 show that when the mobile node roams far from its home network, it can take between 1-2 seconds for basic Mobile IP to converge after a handoff request. Note that this result is independent of the rate of movement, and is only a function of distance from the home network. In contrast, handoff latency in Warp is linear to the movement rate. Note that the redirection of traffic via convergence points in Tapestry is similar in function to hierarchical foreign agents in Mobile IP [6].

Note that the "jitter" or delay in traffic seen by the application during handoff is not identical to handoff latency. It is the time elapsed before a valid forwarding path is constructed to the new proxy. Warp sets up an immediate forwarding path between the proxies to allow seamless traffic forwarding while updating the full forwarding path, similar to the Mobile IP smooth handoffs scheme [16]. In cellular networks, the jitter, or latency between adjacent proxies, is often less than 50ms and within the tolerable range of most streaming media applications.

Finally, we examine the load placed on network routers by mobile crowds. Specifically, we count the expected number of handoff messages required as mobile crowds cross boundaries between base stations. We consider several scenarios: 1) naive mobility support with no aggregation, 2) using aggregation while assuming uniform distribution of crowd sizes from 1 to 50, 3) using aggregation with exponential distribution of crowd sizes with parameter $p = 0.1$, 4) using aggregation with a binomial distribution

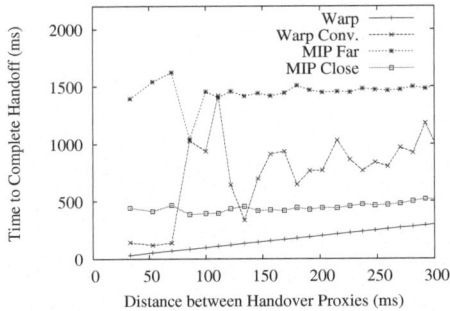

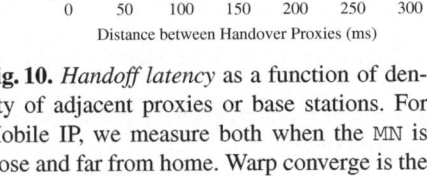

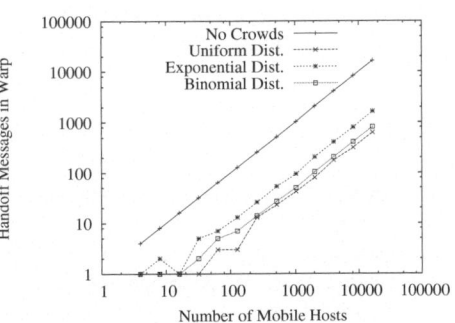

Fig. 10. *Handoff latency* as a function of density of adjacent proxies or base stations. For Mobile IP, we measure both when the MN is close and far from home. Warp converge is the time to full routing state convergence.

Fig. 11. *Handoff load.* Reducing handoff messages of mobile crowds in Warp as a function of population size. Crowd sizes follow uniform, exponential, and binomial distributions.

of crowd sizes centered around 20 with parameter $p = 0.5$. Figure 11 shows the significant reduction in handoff messages. As the overall population increases, the net effect is a linear factor reduction in handoffs based on the mean crowd size. The result means that Warp can support larger and faster mobile crowds while using less bandwidth.

6   Related Work and Conclusion

The Internet Indirection Infrastructure project [10], supports a mobility framework (ROAM [17]) by storing generic triggers in the network infrastructure for traffic redirection. Each trigger maps a mobile node ID to its current IP address. A mobile node chooses an overlay node based on its mobile ID, and sends it trigger location updates to it while roaming. I3 triggers can be used to simulate a variety of mobility mechanisms, including hierarchical mobility and aggregation among mobile crowds. Whereas Tapestry uses the structured routing mesh to form the hierarchies necessary for traffic redirection, ROAM nodes would require input from the mobile nodes to construct them in an ad-hoc fashion.

Previous work has proposed hierarchical management for localizing handoff processing [3, 6]. Also, optimizations similar to our proxy forwarding have been proposed for Mobile IP [16]. In addition to matching these optimizations in performance, the key to our work is the reliance on a self-organizing and adaptive protocol to manage these mechanisms. For example, our analogous mechanism to hierarchical handoff leverages virtual routing paths in the Tapestry routing mesh. Our mechanisms require no explicit management in choosing or maintaining the hierarchy. The Tapestry routing protocol quickly adapts to changes in network topology and unexpected failures. Finally, we also leverage the novel mechanism of type indirection to aggregate mobile crowds into a single mobile entity.

In summary, Warp treats mobile nodes as objects residing on proxies. We propose the use of type indirection to aggregate mobile crowds as single mobile entities to reduce handoff messages. While Warp and the DOLR interface can be deployed on any peer to peer protocol that supports the Key-Based Routing API [7], overlays that utilize proximity neighbor selection will produce better routing performance.

References

1. Brewin, B.: Transportation companies moving to offer Wi-Fi service. In: ComputerWorld. (2003)
2. Katzela, I., Naghshineh, M.: Channel assignment schemes for cellular mobile telecommunication systems: A comprehensive survey. IEEE Personal Communications Magazine **3** (1996)
3. Caceres, R., Padmanabhan, V.N.: Fast and scalable handoffs for wireless internetworks. In: Proceedings of MobiCom, ACM (1996)
4. Toh, C.K.: The design and implementation of a hybrid handover protocol for multi-media wireless LANs. In: Proceedings of MobiCom, ACM (1995)
5. Keeton, K., Mah, B.A., Seshan, S., Katz, R.H., Ferrari, D.: Providing connection-oriented network services to mobile hosts. In: Proceedings of MLIC, USENIX (1993)
6. Perkins, C.E.: Mobile-IP local registration with hierarchical foreign agents. IETF Draft (1996)
7. Dabek, F., Zhao, B., Druschel, P., Kubiatowicz, J., Stoica, I.: Towards a common API for structured P2P overlays. In: Proc. of IPTPS, Berkeley, CA (2003)
8. Zhao, B.Y., Huang, L., Rhea, S.C., Stribling, J., Joseph, A.D., Kubiatowicz, J.D.: Tapestry: A global-scale overlay for rapid service deployment. IEEE JSAC **22** (2003) 41–53
9. Hildrum, K., Kubiatowicz, J.D., Rao, S., Zhao, B.Y.: Distributed object location in a dynamic network. In: Proc. of SPAA, Winnipeg, Canada, ACM (2002)
10. Stoica, I., Adkins, D., Zhuang, S., Shenker, S., Surana, S.: Internet indirection infrastructure. In: Proc. of SIGCOMM, ACM (2002)
11. Balakrishnan, H., et al.: Improving reliable transport and handoff performance in cellular wireless networks. Wireless Networks **1** (1995)
12. Zhao, B.Y., Huang, L., Stribling, J., Joseph, A.D., Kubiatowicz, J.D.: Exploiting routing redundancy via structured peer-to-peer overlays. In: Proc. of ICNP, Atlanta, GA, IEEE (2003)
13. Zhao, B.Y., Joseph, A.D., Kubiatowicz, J.D.: Supporting rapid mobility via locality in an overlay network. Technical Report CSD-02-1216, U. C. Berkeley (2002)
14. Zegura, E.W., Calvert, K., Bhattacharjee, S.: How to model an internetwork. In: Proc. of INFOCOM, IEEE (1996)
15. Perkins, C.E., Johnson, D.B.: Route optimization in Mobile IP. IETF draft. (1997)
16. Perkins, C.E., Wang, K.: Optimized smooth handoffs in Mobile IP. In: Proceedings of ISCC, IEEE (1999)
17. Zhuang, S.Q., Lai, K., Stoica, I., Katz, R.H., Shenker, S.: Host mobility using an internet indirection infrastructure. In: Proceedings of MobiSys. (2003)

P6P: A Peer-to-Peer Approach
to Internet Infrastructure*

Lidong Zhou[1] and Robbert van Renesse[2]

[1] Microsoft Research Silicon Valley, Mountain View, CA 94043
lidongz@microsoft.com
[2] Department of Computer Science, Cornell University, Ithaca, NY 14853
rvr@cs.cornell.edu

Abstract. P6P is a new, incrementally deployable networking infra-structure that resolves the growing tensions between the Internet routing infrastructure and the end sites of the Internet. P6P decouples the two through a P2P overlay network formed by the edge routers. P6P brings the benefits of IPv6 directly to end hosts, solving the major headache of IPv6 deployment as well as those of ISP switching, multihoming, and dynamic addressing.
P6P advocates Internet innovations at the overlay formed by the edge routers, rather than at the core Internet. P2P protocols can be incor-porated into P6P to provide advanced features such as multicast. This opens the door for P2P research to play a central role in shaping the future of the Internet. The paper describes the P6P design and architec-ture, addresses the security and performance concerns, and shows simu-lation results that support its feasibility.

1 Introduction

The current Internet has been torn with tensions between the inertia of the *core Internet*, which forms the public routing infrastructure, and the ever increasing demands from local *end sites*. While IPv6 was proposed to provide end hosts with a large address space for truly end-to-end connectivity and with better support for features such as multicast, anycast, and mobility, the core Internet has been defying the switch to IPv6.

This paper presents P6P, a new networking infrastructure that alleviates the tension between the core Internet and peer end sites. P6P hinges on the de-coupling of addresses as *identifiers* from addresses as *locators* for routing. The decoupling creates a clean separation of end sites from the core Internet routing infrastructure, as well as an isolation of the transport layer from the network layer. More specifically, P6P provides end hosts with IPv6 capabilities, while preserving IPv4 for core Internet routing; the transport layer for end hosts uses IPv6 addresses as end-to-end identifiers, while the core Internet uses IPv4 ad-dresses for routing packets. The use of persistent unique identifiers for end hosts

* This work was funded in part by DARPA/AFRL-IFGA grant F30602-99-1-0532, and by the AFRL/Cornell Information Assurance Institute.

G.M. Voelker and S. Shenker (Eds.): IPTPS 2004, LNCS 3279, pp. 75–86, 2004.
© Springer-Verlag Berlin Heidelberg 2004

restores the end-to-end connectivity, thereby simplifying deployment of IPSec and P2P applications. Perhaps most importantly, P6P can be incrementally deployed and uses the support for IPv6 networking already available in all major operating system platforms.

The mapping from identifiers to locators is accomplished through a P2P overlay network formed by *edge routers* that connect end sites to the core Internet. Persistent identifiers are isolated from any changes to how the site connects to the core Internet through the mapping updates in the overlay. Therefore, P6P shields local sites from ISP switching/multihoming. The overlay can use existing distributed hash table (DHT) protocols (e.g., Chord [1]) to achieve scalability.

P6P is a promising candidate as a P2P killer app. P6P targets concrete and fundamental networking problems in the current Internet and has the potential to shape the future of the Internet. A full deployment of P6P requires the kind of scalability that many P2P protocols are designed to achieve. Because P6P builds upon relatively stable edge routers that maintain a manageable amount of state, P6P circumvents the problem of churn in many P2P protocols and is un-hampered by NATs or firewalls. P6P goes beyond providing IPv6 routing to end sites; we envision P6P to be a unified and constantly evolving framework that incorporates advanced features such as multicast and anycast. This reflects our belief that the innovations on the network services for the end sites should be accomplished at P6P, rather than in the core Internet. With P6P, the evolution of the Internet translates into new challenges to P2P research.

Section 2 presents the architecture of P6P. Section 3 describes P6P tunnel routing protocol, how P6P accommodates ISP switching, and how security can be incorporated into P6P routing. A preliminary performance evaluation through simulation is presented in Sect. 4. Alternative design choices, nested deployment of P6P, and the support for multihoming, multicast, and robustness are the topic of Sect. 5. We discuss related work in Sect. 6 and conclude in Sect. 7.

2 P6P Architecture

P6P assigns IPv6 addresses, referred to as *P6P addresses*, to hosts in each end site, referred to as a *P6P site*. P6P addresses are *identifiers that are permanently assigned to hosts (or interfaces) in IPv6 sites*. Each site has a unique site identifier, which is a common and location-independent 48-bit prefix of the P6P addresses in the site, possibly assigned by IANA (Internet Assigned Numbers Authority), and is distinguishable from the site identifiers within native IPv6 addresses.

Note that P6P is not intended to solve the problems of Mobile IP routing and addressing. The proposed solutions for Mobile IP (e.g., [2]) should work as well with P6P as with native IPv6 and are orthogonal to the work described in this paper. While P6P site identifiers are location-independent, P6P addresses are not, as they are tied to their sites. Having P6P addresses be location-independent would no longer make them aggregatable, severely complicating scalability. Also, it would no longer be possible to use the existing IPv6 protocols available for networking within sites.

Each edge router in P6P consists logically of two types of components: *Internal Gateway* (IG) and *External Gateway* (EG). An IG forwards P6P packets between a P6P site and its EG. The IG has its own P6P address, and hosts in the site use it as their default gateway. Each P6P site has to be connected to at least one IG, but multiple IGs may share a single EG. EG components are attached to the core Internet and exchange encapsulated P6P packets through tunnels set up between them.

When an EG receives a P6P packet from an IG, the EG retrieves the P6P destination address from the packet. For routing, each EG maintains a routing table that maps a site identifier to a set of *address records*, each containing the type of protocol used to tunnel P6P packets and the corresponding protocol address of the peer EG. Such protocols may include IPv4, UDP/IPv4, or even native IPv6—a valid option for sites concerned about IPv6 renumbering. Figure 1 shows an example of P6P configuration. The routing table of each EG is populated and maintained by the overlay formed by the EGs, as described in the next section.

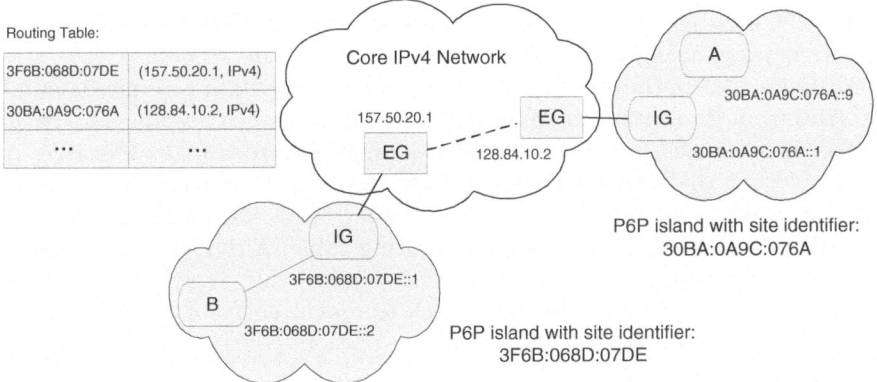

Fig. 1. An example of two P6P sites connected to a core IPv4 network.

3   P6P Routing

The P6P architecture requires a way to map P6P addresses to address records. Unlike site identifiers in standard IPv6 unicast addresses, P6P site identifiers are not location-dependent, and thus a non-hierarchical mapping is necessary between site identifiers and EGs. This section describes one protocol for implementing such a mapping based on a DHT. Alternatives are discussed in Sect. 5.1. Due to space limitation, we omit error handling and other details.

3.1   Basic Protocol

Each EG runs a DHT agent that implements the DHT routing protocol. While in theory it would be possible to use a DHT to find the EG's address records corresponding to a P6P site identifier, doing so for each packet would be too expensive. Instead, each EG maintains a routing table that caches a subset of the mapping. Changes to the mapping are infrequent and are dealt with in Sect. 3.2. The routing table of an EG initially contains only an entry for its own site identifier. The address records in this entry correspond to the set of protocols that this EG supports, and the set of ISPs the EG is connected to. Let $\mathcal{DHT}(x)$ be the EG that the site identifier x maps to in the DHT. The EG then uses the DHT agent to send an INSTALL message containing its local P6P site identifier id and its address records to $\mathcal{DHT}(id)$. On receipt of an INSTALL message, an EG copies the routing entry in the INSTALL message into its local routing table.

When an EG receives a P6P packet from its IG, the EG first checks whether it already has a mapping for the site identifier id of the destination P6P address in its routing table. If so, the EG selects an appropriate address record and sends the packet accordingly. If not, the EG sends a LOOKUP request to $\mathcal{DHT}(id)$ using the DHT. The LOOKUP request contains the site identifier and the set of local address records for returning the response. If the site exists, the receiving EG should have a mapping for the site identifier, and returns the entire entry inside an INSTALL message. This response is not sent using the DHT, but directly over the core network using the return address in the LOOKUP request.

An important optimization is for each EG to piggyback a (limited) number of entries from its routing table on each routing message it sends. The receiver merges these entries into its own routing table. In order to be effective, it is important that the sender selects good entries from its routing table. Random entries are likely not to correspond to popular sites. We currently use the K most recently looked up entries in the routing table. Although it is possible to piggyback on encapsulated data packets as well, we only piggyback on INSTALL and LOOKUP messages. We also piggyback the local entry of the routing table on LOOKUP messages so that P6P response packets can be routed without an additional LOOKUP.

3.2   Updating Address Records

So far we have assumed that the address records of a site do not change. Isolating end sites from the core Internet shields a site from changes in how the site connects to the core Internet (e.g., due to switching ISPs or adding ISPs for multihoming.) In these infrequent cases, address records must be updated. Thus, a routing table in an EG should be considered a *cache* of mappings from P6P to core addresses; P6P must balance freshness and overhead.

Fortunately, it is likely that, when a customer switches ISPs or gets a new address from an ISP to replace its old one, ISPs offer a grace period, during which the customer can continue to receive packets on the old address. Thus out-of-date address records are likely to remain valid for some time, affording P6P some time for updates. We call this time $T_{transition}$.

P6P routing table entries have version numbers for controlling replacement. Routing table entries maintain the time at which a new version of an address record is installed. Each EG increments the version number of its own mapping every $T_{refresh}$ seconds as well as whenever its address record changes, and installs the new mapping (using an INSTALL request). When routing a P6P packet, an EG looks up a mapping as before. If the mapping is older than some constant T_{expire} or does not exist, the EG sends a LOOKUP request using the DHT. If the mapping exists, whether old or new, the EG sends the packet across the core network using the address record in the entry.

The following should hold:

$$T_{refresh} < T_{expire} < T_{transition}$$

$T_{transition}$ is expected to be at least on the order of days, and we are currently using $T_{refresh} = 15\,\text{minutes}$ and $T_{expire} = 30\,\text{minutes}$ in our prototype.

3.3 Security

In the P6P routing protocol, as described this far, it would be easy for an adversary to hijack a P6P site identifier simply by installing a DHT entry for the P6P site identifier with any address records of choice. The problem is resolved through public key cryptography.

Entries in the routing table consist of a pair of X.509 certificates [3]: an *owner certificate* and a *map certificate*. The owner certificate establishes the owner of a P6P site identifier. It contains the P6P site identifier and a public key. The corresponding private key is held only by the owner of the P6P site identifier. We expect the owner certificate to be signed by the provider of P6P site identifiers (i.e., IANA). A site obtains this certificate when applying for a P6P site identifier along with the private key to be used for signing mappings.

The map certificate establishes a mapping of a P6P site identifier to address records. It is signed using the private key of the owner of the P6P site identifier. The map certificate also contains the mapping's version number, which is used for updates but also prevents replay attacks.

INSTALL messages contain these two certificates for each mapping. For each received mapping, an EG should check both certificates in case the mapping was previously unknown, or is an update for a currently installed mapping.

The solution scales well, as each EG only needs to have an owner certificate for its P6P site identifier, the corresponding private key (for signing new map certificates), and the public key of IANA.

An alternative to owner certificates is to apply the idea of *cryptographically generated addresses* [4] to site identifiers, where a P6P site identifier contains the hash of the site owner's public key. This scheme no longer relies on a trusted authority to issue owner certificates because the site's owner public key is verifiable through the site identifier itself. However, by embedding the information of the public key in the site identifier, changes to a site's public key (e.g., due to revocation.) force changes in the site identifier, thereby eliminating an important advantage of P6P that P6P addresses are permanent.

Finally, the DHT itself has to be secure. P6P implements its own integrity through the use of X.509 certificates, but relies on the DHT for its availability.

Note that the reachability of a destination host hinges not only on the connectivity between the source EG and the destination EG, but also on the availability of the mapping from the site identifier of the destination to the address records of the destination EG. The work in [5], for example, offers the needed solutions.

4   Evaluation

We developed a simulation to evaluate the P6P routing protocol. The performance of P6P tunneling in a steady state with no routing table misses is relatively well understood because similar techniques are widely used (e.g., in IPv6 transition mechanisms listed in Sect. 6). So, our evaluation focuses on the cases of routing table misses that necessitate LOOKUP requests before packets are tunneled. In particular, we were interested in the ratio of routing table misses, as well as in the distribution of the P6P routing load across the EGs, as functions of N, the number of P6P sites, and K, the number of piggybacked entries on LOOKUP and INSTALL messages. We ignore DHT churn at this time because we expect the EGs to be fairly stable, although we do intend to study the impact of churn on P6P performance in the near future.

The simulation runs 1000 rounds, and each run has N microrounds, where N is the number of sites. In each microround, a random source site is chosen, as is a random destination site, according to a Zipf distribution (the sites are ranked according to their incoming packet rates.) Next, a packet is sent from a randomly chosen address within the source site to a randomly chosen address within the destination site. Expiration times and failures are not modeled in these simulations.

In the first set of experiments, we fixed K to 8. Figure 2 shows the average *miss ratio* (i.e., the number of routing table misses divided by N), as a function of the round number (time, if you will) for various N. Note that the x-axis has a log scale, and so the average miss ratio appears to decrease approximately logarithmically with time until about 90% of routing requests (including all of the most popular ones) can be filled from the local routing table. After that the decrease slows down, as LOOKUP requests still occur for unpopular sites. In Fig. 3

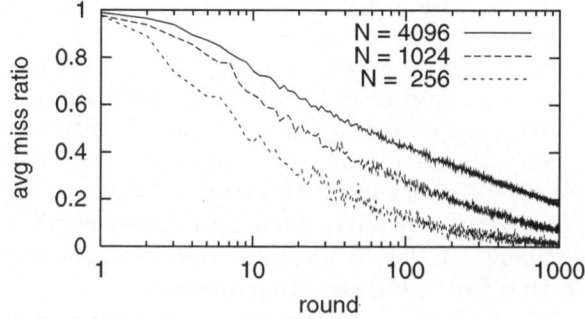

Fig. 2. Average miss ratio as a function of round number for various N. $K = 8$.

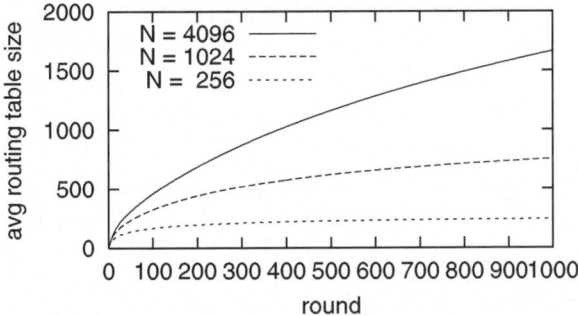

Fig. 3. Average number of entries in the routing table as a function of round number for various N. $K = 8$.

we show the average number of entries in the sites' routing tables as a function of the round number.

In the next set of experiments we used 4096 sites, and varied K, the number of piggybacked routing table entries on routing protocol messages. In Fig. 4 we show the average miss ratio as a function of round number. We see that even if $K = 1$, piggybacking improves the protocol considerably compared to not piggybacking. However, increasing K only gradually improves efficiency.

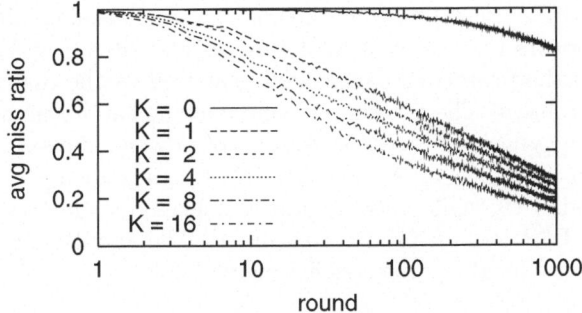

Fig. 4. Average miss ratio as a function of round number for various values of K. $N = 4096$.

To see how load grows as a function of N, we look at the average number of LOOKUP requests received divided by N in the 100th round of the simulation. In Fig. 5, we plot the average load over all sites as a function of N. For $K > 0$, the load appears to grow approximately logarithmically with N, which indicates that the protocol scales well. (For $K = 0$, the load is high while the effectiveness is low.) The load decreases logarithmically with K, and as it comes at the price of larger protocol messages, choosing a large K is not cost-effective. The load is still high in round 100, but as the load reduces in later rounds, the tendencies as a function of N and K appear to remain the same (not shown in this paper).

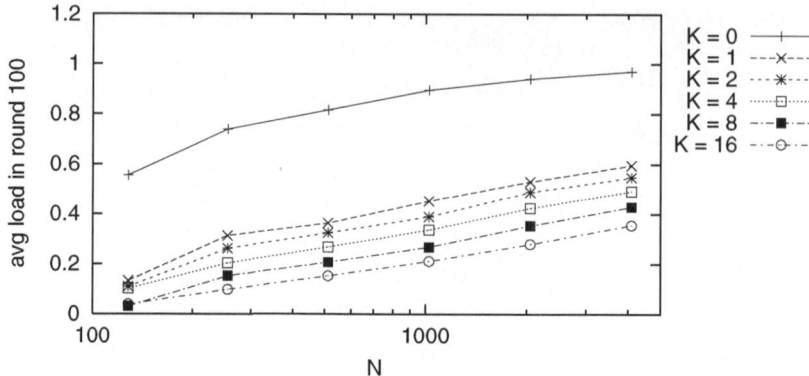

Fig. 5. Average load on EGs in round 100 as a function of N.

We were initially concerned that the P6P routing protocol might place an uneven load on sites because of the highly non-uniform Zipf distribution of site popularity. After all, all LOOKUP requests for the most popular site go to one particular other site (as selected by the DHT.) This concern appears unfounded for $K > 0$. Except for $K = 0$, the variance is low (not shown here), and thus piggybacking ensures that the load is distributed well among the EGs.

The simulation results are synthetic and the number of sites small, and a large-scale deployment will be necessary for further validation and for obtaining realistic latency measurements. Nonetheless, the simulation results indicate that the protocol appears to scale well in the number of sites. Piggybacking significantly improves the protocol's performance, as well as the distribution of load across the P6P routers. The amount of piggybacking can be small, as increasing the amount of piggybacking increases the size of protocol messages linearly while improving the performance of the protocol only logarithmically. Most packets can be routed immediately, while only the initial packets for unpopular sites require waiting for the P6P lookup protocol to finish. The simulation results may be pessimistic because locality of access is not modeled.

5   Discussion

5.1   Alternative Routing Protocols

We choose to present a simple and clean design of P6P because the design is intended to serve as a proof of concept to show the feasibility of this approach. For example, P6P currently adopts a well-known DHT protocol for routing, but such a protocol is certainly not optimal for P6P. It could also be argued that the DHT technology is not yet mature enough, and we only have experience with DHTs on relatively small scales.

Other possibilities for mapping would include the use of a directory service. For example, an EG can retrieve a set of address records by doing a reverse DNS lookup on the P6P site identifier. This would require the introduction of a new record type to DNS, but also some new protocol to replace the piggybacking of P6P routing in order to reduce the load on DNS. For example, the most popular mappings could be gossiped using an epidemic protocol [6].

Relying on and extending the existing DNS infrastructure could cause conflicts because the new functions might demand different system design tradeoffs than the original DNS functions. Alternatively, the overlay formed by the P6P EGs can provide a directory service of its own, making it possible to deploy P6P without relying on another infrastructure and to customize the directory service for P6P only. In fact, we could also imagine that the DNS functionalities be implemented in P6P.

5.2   Nested Deployment

P6P can be deployed within a site as well as on the Internet, resulting in a nested deployment of P6P. Within the site, IPv6 sub-sites would be connected through the site's private IPv4 network. A private DHT (or a simpler mapping mechanism such as a directory) would tie the sub-sites together into a P6P network. The site's IG would serve as the site's IPv6 exit router. This IG has to be connected to an internal P6P relay router that the sub-sites can tunnel to.

Two small modifications to P6P are necessary to make this work. First, instead of using the 48-bit site identifier, the key for the site's internal DHT would be made up from all or part of the subnet identifier in order to distinguish the various sub-sites. Secondly, internal EGs should route packets destined for local sub-sites using its DHT-managed routing tables, but packets destined for remote P6P sites, as well as native IPv6 addresses, should be routed to the site's exit router.

5.3   Multihoming, Multicast, and Robustness

P6P does not require cooperation of the core routers or of the ISPs to take advantage of multihoming. A site can simply attach its EG to multiple ISPs and list all connections in its set of address records. The address records can be extended to contain policies for indicating a primary link or for traffic engineering.

P6P can incorporate application-level multicast (e.g., Narada [7] and Overcast [8]) to provide applications with the illusion of IPv6 multicast. P6P can also adapt ideas from RON [9] and Detour [10] for routing robustness.

6   Related Work

The general idea of using P2P for implementing IPv6 appeared in [11], where the IPv6 addresses for the end hosts are not aggregated. P6P instead trades off generality for scalability by aggregating IPv6 addresses for each site. P6P further improves the scalability using piggybacking and addresses the security concern.

In [12], the advantages and disadvantages of separating identifiers and locators, two roles currently overloaded on IP addresses, are discussed in the context of the GSE proposal [13]. GSE proposes to split an IPv6 address into two parts, the first containing the locator, and the second the identifier. GSE routers rewrite the locator part of the IPv6 address as they forward a packet. The essential difference between GSE and P6P is that GSE is a header-rewriting technology (like NAT), while P6P is a layering technology. Therefore, in P6P the locators are not visible to hosts. Clean separation between the network and transport layers in P6P provides end hosts with truly end-to-end connectivity.

UIP (Unmanaged Internet Protocol) [14] also advocates the separation of naming and routing. However, UIP aims to facilitate ubiquitous network computing by designing a new Internet-independent routing infrastructure. As a consequence, it has to build up a DHT when nodes join, while P6P can use the existing Internet infrastructure for the construction of the DHT.

HIP (Host Identity Payload) is yet another proposal that supports the decoupling of internetworking from transport layer. The deployment of HIP requires a new protocol number assigned by IANA and changes to DNS for maintaining the mapping. In contrast, P6P does not require such dramatic changes to the current Internet infrastructure and can be incrementally deployed.

IPNL (IP Next Layer) [15] is an alternative proposal to IPv6. IPNL is layered on top of IPv4 with NAT-boxes, and uses DNS domain names as addresses, while using the structure of domain names as a way to route packets. IPNL achieves many of the same properties as P6P, but requires a large software development commitment. PeerNet [16] goes a step further and proposes to replace the IP layer with a P2P protocol that separates identifiers from addresses. The main objective is routing in wireless networks. Compared to IPNL and PeerNet, P6P deployment is relatively cheap because most operating systems support IPv6 stacks and many important applications have been ported.

I3 (Internet Indirection Infrastructure) [17] shares many of the same objectives with P6P, and also uses a DHT in order to separate identifiers from addresses and to support a wide variety of end-to-end communication options. I3 is an overlay, and with it comes a new API. P6P provides a standard IPv6 API, requires no changes to end hosts, and is unencumbered by churn.

The architecture of P6P is related to transitioning mechanisms such as ISATAP [18], 6to4 [19], and Teredo [20]. None of these provide a separation of identifiers and locators, nor the ability to add new communication services.

7   Conclusion

P6P is an overlay routing architecture that, transparently to end-hosts, implements the IPv6 routing abstraction. P6P simplifies transition to IPv6, but also provides features that have value even in a core IPv6 network. These derive from the fact that P6P allows end-host addresses to be administered separately from the addresses used in the core routing infrastructure. Such features include the ability to renumber the core Internet, to switch ISPs, and to support multihoming, without reconfiguring entire sites, breaking connections, updating DNS records, mutual cooperation of ISPs, or increased load on core routers. P6P can be extended to support multicast and robust routing.

P6P is easy to deploy as it interoperates with the IPv6 stacks supported by all major operating systems. Moreover, P6P can be deployed incrementally without any changes to existing IPv6 routing protocols.

We present the key elements of a preliminary design and evaluation to demonstrate the feasibility of the approach. Various alternative design choices, optimizations, and other engineering/deployment details are yet to be explored fully. Even so, P6P has already shown promises as a killer-app for P2P protocols.

Acknowledgments

We are grateful to Piyoosh Jalan, Adrian Bozdog, and Michael A. Marsh for their early contributions to this work, and to Yih-Chun Hu for the discussion on cryptographically generated addresses. We would also like to thank the anonymous reviewers for their comments and suggestions that helped improve the paper.

References

1. Stoica, I., Morris, R., Karger, D., Kaashoek, M.: Chord: A scalable peer-to-peer lookup service for Internet applications. [21]
2. Perkins, C.: IP mobility support (1996) RFC 2002.
3. CCITT: Recommendation X.509: The Directory Authentication Framework (1988)
4. O'Shea, G., Roe, M.: Child-proof authentication for MIPv6 (CAM). ACM Computer Communications Review **31** (2001)
5. Castro, M., Druschel, P., Ganesh, A., Rowstron, A., Wallach, D.: Secure routing for structured peer-to-peer overlay networks. In: Proceedings of the 5th Symposium on Operating System Design and Implementation (OSDI'02), Boston, MA (2002)
6. Demers, A., Greene, D., Hauser, C., Irish, W., Larson, J., Shenker, S., Sturgis, H., Swinehart, D., Terry, D.: Epidemic algorithms for replicated database maintenance. In: Proc. of the 6th ACM Symp. on Principles of Distributed Computing, Vancouver, BC (1987) 1–12
7. Chu, Y., Rao, S., Seshan, S., Zhang, H.: Enabling conferencing applications on the Internet using an overlay multicast architecture. [21]
8. Jannotti, J., Gifford, D., K.L., J., M.F., K., O'Toole Jr., J.: Overcast: Reliable multicasting with an overlay network. In: Proceedings of the 4th Symposium on Operating System Design and Implementation (OSDI'00), San Diego, CA (2000)
9. Andersen, D., Balakrishnan, H., Kaashoek, M., Morris, R.: Resilient Overlay Networks. In: Proc. of the 18th ACM Symp. on Operating Systems Principles, Banff, Canada (2001) 131–145
10. Collins, A.: The Detour framework for packet rerouting. Master's thesis, University of Washington, Seattle (1998)
11. Zhou, L., van Renesse, R., Marsh, M.: Implementing IPv6 as a peer-to-peer overlay network. In: Workshop on Reliable Peer-to-Peer Distributed Systems, Proc. 21st IEEE Symposium on Reliable Distributed Systems, Suita, Japan (2002)
12. Crawford, M., Mankin, A., Narten, T., Stewart, J., Zhang, L.: Separating identifiers and locators in addresses: An analysis of the GSE proposal for IPv6 (1999) Internet Draft, draft-ietf-ipngwg-esd-analysis-05.txt.
13. O'Dell, M.: GSE–an alternate addressing architecture for IPv6 (1997) Internet Draft, draft-ietf-ipngwg-gseaddr-00.txt.

14. Ford, B.: Unmanaged Internet Protocol: Taming the edge network management crisis. In: 2nd Workshop on Hot Topics in Networks (HotNets-II). (2003)
15. Francis, P., Gummadi, R.: IPNL: A NAT-extended Internet architecture. [21]
16. Eriksson, J., Faloutsos, M., Krishnamurthy, S.: PeerNet: Pushing Peer-to-Peer down the stack. In: Peer-to-Peer Systems—Second International Workshop (IPTPS'03). Volume 2735 of Lecture Notes on Computer Science., Cambridge, MA, Springer-Verlag (2003) 268–277
17. Stoica, I., Adkins, D., Zhuang, S., Shenker, S., Surana, S.: Internet Indirection Infrastructure. In: Proc. of ACM SIGCOMM'02, Pittsburgh, PA (2002)
18. Templin, F.: Intra-Site Automatic Tunnel Addressing Protocol (ISATAP) (2001) Internet Draft, draft-ietf-ngtrans-isatap-00.txt.
19. Holdrege, M., Srisuresh, P.: Connection of IPv6 domains via IPv4 clouds (2001) RFC 3056.
20. Huitema, J.: Teredo: Tunneling IPv6 over UDP through NATs (2002) Internet Draft, draft-ietf-ngtrans-shipworm-08.txt.
21. ACM SIGCOMM: Proc. of the '01 Symp. on Communications Architectures & Protocols. In: Proc. of the '01 Symp. on Communications Architectures & Protocols, San Diego, CA, ACM SIGCOMM (2001)

Comparing the Performance
of Distributed Hash Tables Under Churn*

Jinyang Li, Jeremy Stribling, Thomer M. Gil,
Robert Morris, and M. Frans Kaashoek

MIT Computer Science and Artificial Intelligence Laboratory, Cambridge, MA
{jinyang,strib,thomer,rtm,kaashoek}@csail.mit.edu
http://pdos.lcs.mit.edu/

Abstract. A protocol for a distributed hash table (DHT) incurs communication costs to keep up with churn – changes in membership – in order to maintain its ability to route lookups efficiently. This paper formulates a unified framework for evaluating cost and performance. Communication costs are combined into a single cost measure (bytes), and performance benefits are reduced to a single latency measure. This approach correctly accounts for background maintenance traffic and timeouts during lookup due to stale routing data, and also correctly leaves open the possibility of different preferences in the tradeoff of lookup time versus communication cost. Using the unified framework, this paper analyzes the effects of DHT parameters on the performance of four protocols under churn.

1 Introduction

The design space of DHT protocols is large. While all designs are similar in that nodes forward lookups for keys through routing tables that point to other nodes, algorithms differ in the amount of state they keep: from $O(1)$ with respect to a network size of size n [7,9] to $O(\log n)$ [10,13,14,16] to $O(\sqrt{n})$ [6] to $O(n)$ [5]. They also differ in the techniques used to find low latency routes, in the way they find alternate paths after encountering dead intermediate nodes, in the expected number of hops per lookup, and in choice of parameters such as the frequency with which they check other nodes for liveness.

How is one to compare these protocols in a way that separates incidental details from more fundamental differences? Most evaluations and comparisons of DHTs have focused on lookup hopcount latency, or routing table size in unchanging networks [2,12,15]. Static analysis, however, may unfairly favor protocols that keep large amounts of state, since they pay no penalty to keep the state up to date, and more state usually results in lower lookup hopcounts and latencies.

---

* This research was conducted as part of the IRIS project (http://project-iris.net/), supported by the National Science Foundation under Cooperative Agreement No. ANI-0225660.

This paper presents a framework for evaluating DHT algorithms in the face of joining and leaving nodes, in a way that makes it easy to compare tradeoffs between state maintenance costs and lookup performance. The paper compares the Tapestry [16], Chord [14], Kelips [6], and Kademlia [10] lookup algorithms within this framework. These four reflect a wide range of design choices for DHTs.

We have implemented a simple simulator that models inter-node latencies using the King method [3]. This model ignores effects due to congestion. We compare the performance of the DHTs using a single workload consisting of lookup operations and a particular model of churn. With these restrictions, we find that with the right parameter settings all four DHTs have similar overall performance. Furthermore, we isolate and analyze the effects of individual parameters on DHT performance, and conclude that common parameters such as base and stabilization interval can behave differently in DHTs that make different design decisions.

2   A Cost Versus Performance Framework

DHTs have multiple measures for both *cost* and *performance*. Cost has often been measured as the amount of per-node state. However, an analysis should also include the cost of keeping that state up to date (which avoids timeouts), and the cost of exploring the network to search for nearby neighbors (which allows low-latency lookup). A unified cost metric should indicate consumption of the most valuable system resource; in our framework it is the number of bytes of messages sent. This choice reflects a judgment that network capacity is a more limiting resource to DHTs than memory or CPU time.

Lookup performance has often been measured with hopcount, latency, success rate, and probability of timeouts. Our framework uses lookup latency as the unified performance metric relevant to applications. Lookup hopcount can be ignored except to the extent that it contributes to latency. The framework accounts for the cost of trying to contact a dead node during a lookup as a latency penalty equal to a small constant multiple of the round trip time to the dead node, an optimistic simulation of the cost of a timeout before the node pursues the lookup through an alternate route. DHTs retry alternate routes for lookups that return failed or incorrectly for up to four seconds, which effectively converts failed lookups into high latencies.

Protocol parameters tend to obscure differences in cost and performance among protocols, since the parameters may be tuned for different workloads. A key challenge is to understand differences solely due to parameter choices. We evaluate each protocol over a range of parameter values, outlining a performance envelope from which we can extrapolate an optimal cost-performance tradeoff curve.

3   Protocol Overviews

This paper evaluates the performance of four existing DHT protocols (Tapestry [16], Chord [14], Kelips [6], and Kademlia [10]) using the above framework. This

Table 1. Tapestry parameters.

Parameter	Range
Base	$2 - 128$
Stabilization interval	36 sec $-$ 19 min
Number of backup nodes	$1 - 4$
Number of nodes contacted during repair	$1 - 20$

section provides brief overviews of each DHT, identifying the tunable parameters in each.

3.1 Tapestry

The ID space in Tapestry is structured as a tree. A Tapestry node ID can be viewed as a sequence of l base-b digits. A routing table has l levels, each with b entries. Nodes in the mth level share a prefix of length $m - 1$ digits, but differ in the mth digit. Each entry may contain up to c nodes, sorted by latency. The closest of these nodes is the entry's *primary neighbor*; the others serve as *backup neighbors*.

Nodes forward a lookup message for a key by resolving successive digits in the key (*prefix-based routing*). When no more digits can be resolved, an algorithm known as *surrogate routing* determines exactly which node is responsible for the key [16]. Routing in Tapestry is recursive.

For lookups to be correct, at least one neighbor in each routing table entry must be alive. Tapestry periodically checks the liveness of each primary neighbor, and if the node is found to be dead, the next closest backup in that entry (if one exists) becomes the primary. When a node declares a primary neighbor dead, it contacts some number of other neighbors asking for a replacement; the number of neighbors used in this way is configurable. Table 1 lists Tapestry's parameters for the simulations.

3.2 Chord

Chord identifiers are structured in an identifier circle. A key k is assigned to k's successor (i.e., the first node whose ID is equal to k, or follows k in the ID space). In this paper's variant of Chord, a lookup for a key visits the key's *predecessor*, the node whose ID most closely precedes the key. The predecessor tells the query originator the identity of the key's successor node, but the lookup does not visit the successor. The base b of the ID space is a parameter: a node with ID x keeps $(b - 1) \log_b(n)$ fingers whose IDs lie at exponentially increasing fractions of the ID space away from itself. Any node whose ID lies within the range $x + (\frac{b-1}{b})^{i+1} * 2^{64}$ and $x + (\frac{b-1}{b})^i * 2^{64}$, modulo 2^{64}, can be used as the ith finger of x. Chord leverages this flexibility to obtain Proximity Neighbor Selection [2, 13]. Each node also keeps a *successor list* of s nodes. Chord can route either iteratively or recursively [14]; this paper presents results for the latter.

Table 2. Chord parameters.

Parameter	Range
Number of successors	4 − 32
Finger base	2 − 128
Finger stabilization interval	40 sec − 19 min
Successor stabilization interval	4 sec − 19 min

Table 3. Kelips parameters.

Parameter	Range
Gossip interval	18 sec − 19 min
Group ration	8, 16, 32
Contact ration	8, 16, 32
Contacts per group	2, 8, 16
Times a new item is gossiped	2, 8
Routing entry timeout	30 min

A Chord node x periodically pings all its fingers to check their liveness. If a finger i does not respond, x issues a lookup request for the key $x + (\frac{b-1}{b})^i * 2^{64}$, yielding node f. Node x retrieves f's successor list, and uses the successor with the lowest latency as the level i finger. A node separately stabilizes its successor list by periodically retrieving and merging its successor's successor list; successor stabilization is separate because it is critical for correctness but is much cheaper than finger stabilization. Table 2 lists the Chord parameters that are varied in the simulations.

3.3 Kelips

Kelips divides the identifier space into k groups, where k is a constant roughly equal to the square root of the number of nodes. A node's group is its ID mod k. Each node's routing table contains an entry for each other node in its group, and "contact" entries for a few nodes from each of the other groups. Thus a node's routing table size is a small constant times $\sqrt{n}$, in a network with n nodes.

The variant of Kelips in this paper defines lookups only for node IDs. The originating node executes a lookup for a key by asking a contact in the key's group for the IP address of the target key's node, and then (iteratively) contacting that node. If that fails, the originator tries routing the lookup through other contacts for that group, and then through randomly chosen routing table entries.

Nodes periodically gossip to discover new members of the network, and may also learn about other nodes due to lookup communication. Routing table entries that have not been refreshed for a certain period of time expire. Nodes learn RTTs and liveness information from each RPC, and preferentially route lookups through low RTT contacts.

Table 4. Kademlia parameters.

Parameter	Range
Nodes per entry (k)	4, 8, 16, 32
Parallel lookups (α)	1 – 10
Stabilization interval	20 min – 1 hour

Table 3 lists the parameters we use for Kelips. Rations are the number of nodes mentioned in the gossip messages. Contacts per group is the maximum number of contact entries per group in a node's routing table; if it has value c, then the size of each node's routing table is $\sqrt{n} + c(\sqrt{n} - 1)$.

3.4   Kademlia

Kademlia structures its ID space as a tree. The distance between two keys in ID space is their exclusive or, interpreted as an integer. The k nodes whose IDs are closest to a key y store a replica of y. The routing table of a node x has 64 buckets b_i ($0 \leq i < 64$) that each store up to k node IDs with a distance to x between 2^i and 2^{i+1}.

Kademlia performs iterative lookups: a node x starts a lookup for key y by sending parallel lookup RPCs to the α nodes in x's routing table whose IDs are closest to y. A node replies to a lookup RPC by sending back a list of the k nodes it believes are closest to y in ID space. Each time node x receives a reply, it sends a new RPC to the next-closest node to y that it knows about, trying at all times to keep α outstanding RPCs. This continues until some node replies with key y, or until k nodes whose IDs are closest to y (according to x) did not return any new node ID closer to y. The simulated workloads look up node IDs, and the last step in a lookup is an RPC to the target node. Our Kademlia implementation favors proximate nodes. Like Kelips, Kademlia learns existence and liveness information from each lookup. Table 4 summarizes the parameters varied in the Kademlia simulations.

4   Evaluation

We implemented these four DHTs in a discrete-event packet-level simulator, p2psim[1]. The simulated network consists of 1,024 nodes with inter-node latencies derived from measuring the pairwise latencies of 1,024 DNS servers using the King method [3]. The average round-trip delay is 152 milliseconds, which serves as a lower bound for the average DHT lookup time for random keys. The simulator does not simulate link transmission rate or queuing delay. All experiments involve only key lookup, as opposed to data retrieval.

Nodes issue lookups for random keys at intervals exponentially distributed with a mean of ten minutes, and nodes crash and rejoin at exponentially distributed intervals with a mean of one hour. This choice of mean session time

---

[1] http://pdos.lcs.mit.edu/p2psim

is consistent with past studies [4], while the lookup rate guarantees that nodes perform several lookups per session. Each experiment runs for six hours of simulated time, and nodes keep their IP address and ID for the duration of the experiment.

For each of the graphs below, the x-axis shows the communication cost: the average number of bytes sent per second sent by live nodes. The communication cost includes lookup, join, and routing table maintenance traffic. The size in bytes of each message is counted as 20 bytes for headers plus 4 bytes for each node mentioned in the message. The y-axis shows performance: the average lookup latency, including timeout penalties (three times the round trip time) and lookup retries (up to a maximum of four seconds).

4.1   Protocol Comparisons

Each protocol has a number of parameters that affect cost and performance. As an example, Figure 1 shows Tapestry's cost and performance for several hundred parameter combinations. There is no single best combination of parameter values. Instead, there is a set of best achievable cost-performance combinations: for each given cost, there is a least achievable latency, and for each latency, there is a least achievable cost. These best points are on the *convex hull* of the full set of points, a segment of which is shown by the line in Figure 1. Points not on the convex hull represent inefficient parameter settings which waste bandwidth.

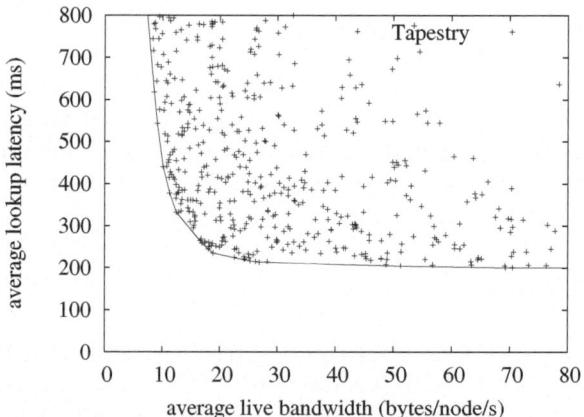

Fig. 1. Cost versus performance under churn in Tapestry. Each point represents the average lookup latency and communication cost achieved for a unique set of parameter values. The convex hull represents the best achievable cost-performance combinations.

Figure 2 compares the convex hulls of Tapestry, Chord, Kademlia and Kelips. Any of the protocols can be tuned to achieve a latency less than 250 ms if it is allowed enough bandwidth. The small difference in latency (20 ms) between Chord and Tapestry when bandwidth is plentiful is because Tapestry achieves

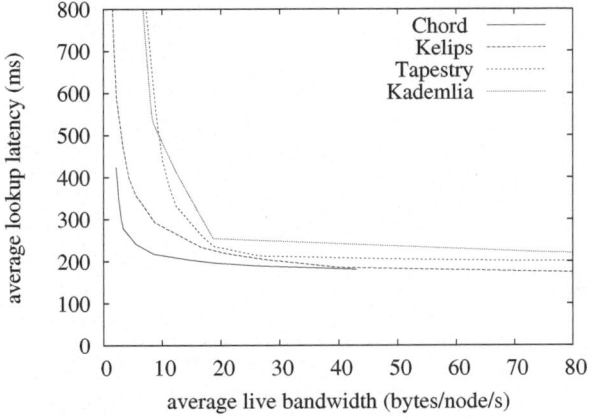

Fig. 2. The convex hulls for all four protocols.

a success rate of only 99.5%, compared to 100% in Chord, due to a slower join process that causes inconsistent views on which node is responsible for a given key. Kademlia uses iterative routing, which we observe to be slower than recursive routing when hopcounts are similar. When bandwidth is limited, the protocols differ significantly in performance. Chord in particular uses its bandwidth quite efficiently and can achieve low lookup latencies at little cost. This behavior appears to be due to Chord giving priority to stabilizing successors over fingers when bandwidth is limited, since correct successors are all that is needed to ensure correct lookups. By focusing its limited stabilization traffic on this small, constant amount of state (as opposed to its full $O(\log n)$ state), Chord is able to maintain correctness. The other protocols do not have a simple way to ensure correct lookups, and so their lookup times are increased by the need to retry lookups that return incorrect responses.

4.2   Parameter Exploration

Figure 1 shows that some parameter settings are much more efficient than others. This result raises the question of which parameter settings cause performance to be on the convex hull; more specifically,

- What is the relative importance of different parameters on the performance tradeoff for a single protocol?
- Do similar parameters have similar effects on the performance tradeoffs of different protocols?

These questions are not straightforward to answer, since different parameters can interact with one another, as we will see below. To isolate the effect of a single parameter, we calculate the convex hull segment for each fixed value of that parameter while varying all the other parameter values. The convex hull of these segments should trace the full convex hull as shown in Figure 2.

Tapestry: Figure 3 shows the effect of identifier base on the performance of Tapestry. Each line on the figure represents the convex hull segment for a specific

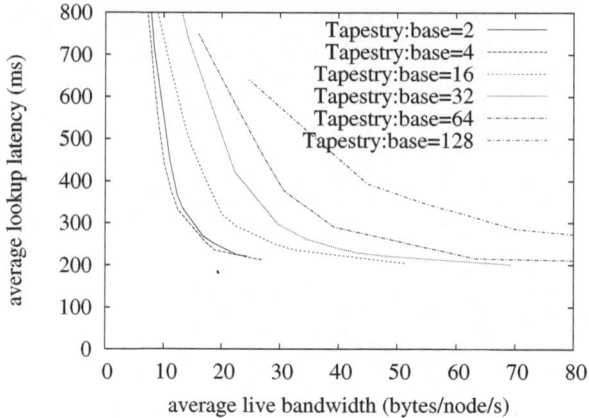

Fig. 3. The effect of base in Tapestry.

value of base. With respect to bandwidth, these results are not surprising; as we decrease base, each node has fewer entries in its routing table[2], and thus needs to contact fewer nodes during stabilization, using less bandwidth. For bases 2 and 4 nodes keep exactly the same amount of state, but base 4 lowers the hopcount leading to slightly improved latencies.

The latency results, however, are a bit counter-intuitive: every value of base is able to achieve the same lookup performance, even though a smaller base results in more hops per lookup on average. This behavior is due to Tapestry's proximity routing. The first few hops in every lookup tend to be to nearby neighbors, and so the time for the lookup becomes dominated by the last hop, which is essentially to a random node in the network. Therefore, in a protocol with proximity routing, the base can be configured as a small value in order to save bandwidth costs due to stabilization.

Figure 4 illustrates the effect of stabilization interval on the performance of Tapestry. As nodes stabilize more often, they achieve lower latencies by avoiding more timeouts on the critical path of a lookup. Although this improvement comes at the cost of bandwidth, the results show that the cost in bandwidth is marginal when compared to the savings in lookup latency. Thus, not only can the base be set low, but stabilization also can happen frequently to keep routing state up to date under churn. For this workload, a reasonable value is 72 seconds.

Other experiments (not shown here) indicate that best performance is largely insensitive to number of backup nodes (as long as there are more than 1) and numbers of nodes contacted during repair.

Chord: Chord separately stabilizes finger and successors. While the relevant graphs are not shown for reasons of space, a 72 second successor stabilization interval is enough to ensure a high success rate (above 99%); faster rates result

---

[2] If identifiers have base b in a network with n nodes, routing tables contain $b * \log_b n$ entries on average [16].

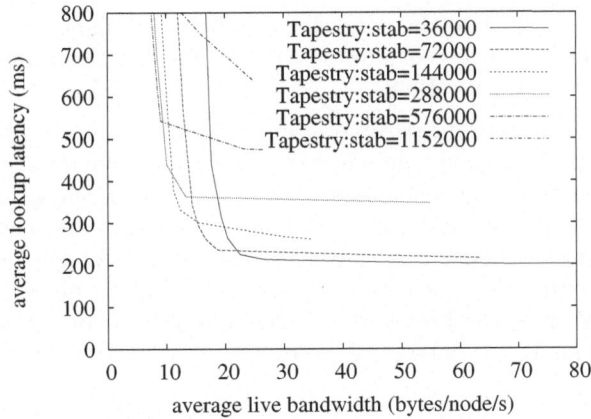

Fig. 4. The effect of stabilization interval in Tapestry (values are in milliseconds).

in wasted bandwidth while slower rates result in a greater number of timeouts during lookups. The finger stabilization interval affects performance without affecting success rate, so its value must be varied to achieve the best tradeoff. Faster finger stabilization results in lower lookup latency due to fewer timeouts, but at a higher communication cost.

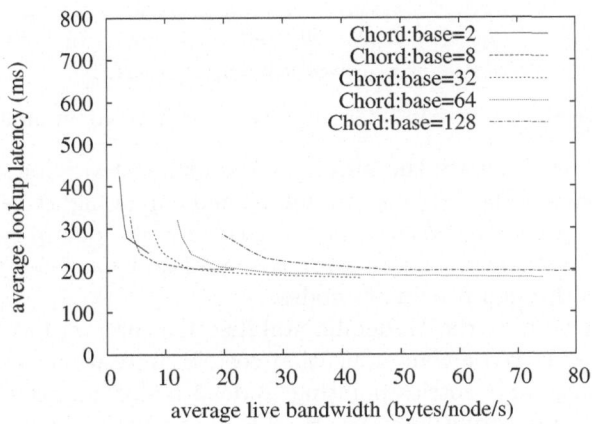

Fig. 5. The effect of base in Chord.

Unlike Tapestry, there is no single best base value for Chord. Figure 5 shows the convex hulls for different base values. The final convex hull is essentially made up of two base values (2 and 8). Changing the base from 2 to 8 causes the best achieved lookup latency to drop from 240 milliseconds to 203 milliseconds due to decreased hopcount from 3.3 to 2.5. In comparison, small bases in Tapestry (see Figure 3) can achieve the same low latencies as higher bases; we believe this is due to a more involved join algorithm that samples a larger number of candidate neighbors during PNS.

Kelips: The most important parameter in Kelips in the gossip interval. Figure 6 shows that its value has a strong effect on the cost versus performance tradeoff. The other parameters improve performance without increasing cost, and thus are simple to set. For example, more contacts per group are always preferable, since that results in a more robust routing table and a higher probability that a lookup will complete in just one hop, at only slightly higher cost. With 16 contacts, for instance, the best lookup latency is 180 ms in 1.2 average hops as opposed to 280 ms in 1.9 hops for 2 contacts.

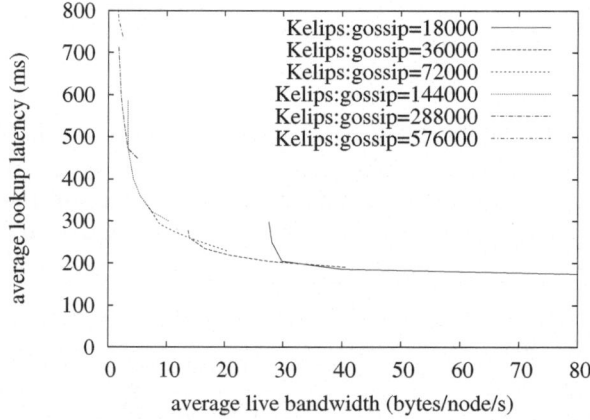

Fig. 6. The effect of gossip interval in Kelips (values are in milliseconds).

Kademlia: Figure 7 shows the effect on Kademlia of varying the number of parallel lookups (α). The final convex hull is made up of higher values of α, with bigger α resulting in lower latency at the cost of more lookup traffic. A bigger α decreases the time spent waiting for timeouts and increases the chances of routing lookups through proximate nodes.

Figure 8 shows that the Kademlia stabilization interval has little effect on latency, but does increase communication cost. Stabilization does decrease the number of routing table entries pointing to dead nodes, and thus decreases the number of timeouts during lookups. However, parallel lookups already ensure that these timeouts are not on the critical path for lookups, so their elimination does not decrease lookup latency.

4.3   Discussion

Base and stabilization interval have the most effect on DHT performance under churn, although they affect different protocols in different ways. These results are tied to our choice of workload: the effect of base depends on the size of the

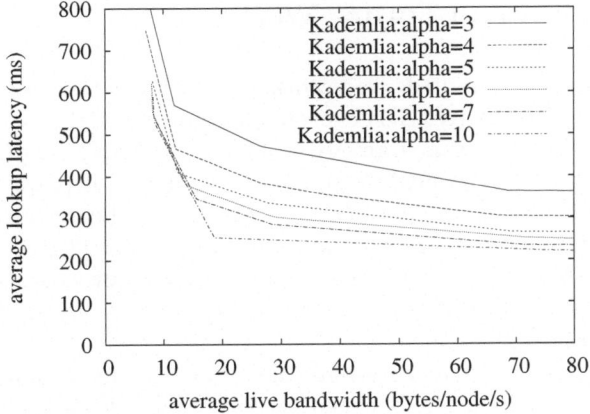

Fig. 7. The effect of parallel lookups in Kademlia. Values of 1 and 2 are not shown, and perform considerably worse than $\alpha = 3$.

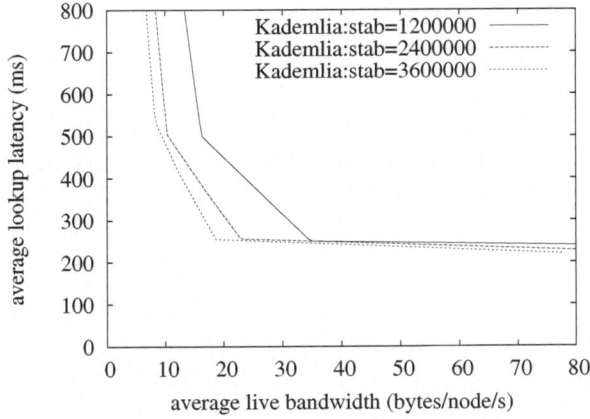

Fig. 8. The effect of stabilization interval in Kademlia (values are in milliseconds).

network, while the effect of stabilization depends on the average session time of churning nodes.

5   Related Work

This paper's contribution is a unified framework for comparing DHTs under churn and the effects of their parameters on performance under churn. Liben-Nowell et al. [8] focus only on the asymptotic communication cost due to Chord stabilization traffic. Rhea et al. [11] present Bamboo, a DHT protocol designed to handle networks with high churn efficiently and gracefully. In a similar vein, Castro et al. [1] describe how they optimize their Pastry implementation, MSPastry, to handle consistent routing under churn with low overhead. The implementation of the protocols described here include similar optimizations.

6   Conclusions and Future Work

This paper presents a unified framework for studying the cost versus lookup latency tradeoffs in different DHT protocols, and evaluates Tapestry, Chord, Kelips, and Kademlia in that framework. Given the workload described in Section 4, these protocols can achieve similar performance if parameters are sufficiently well-tuned. However, parameter tuning is a delicate business; not only can different parameters interact within a protocol to affect the cost versus performance tradeoff, but similar parameters in different protocols, such as base and stabilization interval, can behave differently. We also identify several parameters that are irrelevant under churn.

As future work, we plan to isolate and evaluate the design decisions that cause performance deviations between the protocols. We will also explore how varying the workload affects the cost versus performance tradeoff. We hope that understanding the tradeoffs inherent in different design decisions, as well as in parameter tuning, will lead to more robust and efficient DHT designs.

Acknowledgments

We thank Russ Cox for his help writing the simulator, Frank Dabek for numerous useful discussions as well as the King dataset measurements, and the anonymous reviewers for their helpful comments.

References

1. CASTRO, M., COSTA, M., AND ROWSTRON, A. Performance and dependability of structured peer-to-peer overlays. Tech. Rep. MSR-TR-2003-94, Microsoft Research, Dec. 2003.
2. GUMMADI, K. P., GUMMADI, R., GRIBBLE, S., RATNASAMY, S., SHENKER, S., AND STOICA, I. The impact of DHT routing geometry on resilience and proximity. In *Proceedings of the 2003 ACM SIGCOMM* (Karlsruhe, Germany, Aug. 2003).
3. GUMMADI, K. P., SAROIU, S., AND GRIBBLE, S. D. King: Estimating latency between arbitrary Internet end hosts. In *Proceedings of the 2002 SIGCOMM Internet Measurement Workshop* (Marseille, France, Nov. 2002).
4. GUMMADI, P. K., SAROIU, S., AND GRIBBLE, S. A measurement study of Napster and Gnutella as examples of peer-to-peer file sharing systems. *Multimedia Systems Journal 9*, 2 (Aug. 2003), 170–184.
5. GUPTA, A., LISKOV, B., AND RODRIGUES, R. One hop lookups for peer-to-peer overlays. In *Proceedings of the Ninth Workshop on Hot Topics in Operating Systems* (May 2003).
6. GUPTA, I., BIRMAN, K., LINGA, P., DEMERS, A., AND VAN RENESSE, R. Kelips: Building an efficient and stable P2P DHT through increased memory and background overhead. In *Proceedings of the Second IPTPS* (2003).
7. KAASHOEK, M. F., AND KARGER, D. R. Koorde: A simple degree-optimal hash table. In *Proceedings of the Second IPTPS* (2003).

8. LIBEN-NOWELL, D., BALAKRISHNAN, H., AND KARGER, D. R. Analysis of the evolution of peer-to-peer systems. In *Proceedings of the 2002 ACM Symposium on Principles of Distributed Computing* (Aug. 2002).

9. MALKHI, D., NAOR, M., AND RATAJCZAK, D. Viceroy: A scalable dynamic emulation of the butterfly. In *Proceedings of the 2002 ACM Symposium on Principles of Distributed Computing* (Aug. 2002).

10. MAYMOUNKOV, P., AND MAZIERES, D. Kademlia: A peer-to-peer information system based on the XOR metric. In *Proceedings of the First IPTPS* (Mar. 2002).

11. RHEA, S., GEELS, D., ROSCOE, T., AND KUBIATOWICZ, J. Handling churn in a DHT. Tech. Rep. UCB/CSD-3-1299, UC Berkeley, Computer Science Division, Dec. 2003.

12. RHEA, S., ROSCOE, T., AND KUBIATOWICZ, J. Structured peer-to-peer overlays need application-driven benchmarks. In *Proceedings of the Second IPTPS* (2003).

13. ROWSTRON, A., AND DRUSCHEL, P. Pastry: Scalable, distributed object location and routing for large-scale peer-to-peer systems. In *Proceedings of the 18th IFIP/ACM International Conference on Distr ibuted Systems Platforms (Middleware 2001)* (Nov. 2001).

14. STOICA, I., MORRIS, R., LIBEN-NOWELL, D., KARGER, D. R., KAASHOEK, M. F., DABEK, F., AND BALAKRISHNAN, H. Chord: A scalable peer-to-peer lookup protocol for Internet applications. *IEEE/ACM Transactions on Networking* (2002), 149–160.

15. XU, J. On the fundamental tradeoffs between routing table size and network diameter in peer-to-peer networks. In *Proceedings of the IEEE Infocom* (Mar. 2003).

16. ZHAO, B. Y., HUANG, L., STRIBLING, J., RHEA, S. C., JOSEPH, A. D., AND KUBIATOWICZ, J. D. Tapestry: A resilient global-scale overlay for service deployment. *IEEE Journal on Selected Areas in Communications 22*, 1 (Jan. 2004), 41–53.

DHT Routing Using Social Links[*]

Sergio Marti, Prasanna Ganesan, and Hector Garcia-Molina

Stanford University
{smarti,prasanna,hector}@cs.stanford.edu

Abstract. The equality and anonymity of peer-to-peer networks makes them vulnerable to routing denial of service attacks from misbehaving nodes. In this paper, we investigate how existing social networks can benefit P2P networks by leveraging the inherent trust associated with social links. We present a trust model that lets us compare routing algorithms for P2P networks overlaying social networks. We propose SPROUT, a DHT routing algorithm that significantly increases the probability of successful routing by using social links. Finally, we discuss further optimization and design choices for both the model and the routing algorithm.

1 Introduction

Because of the anonymity of peers and the lack of a centralized enforcement agency, P2P systems are especially vulnerable to a category of attacks we call misrouting attacks. We use the term *misrouting* to refer to any failure by a node to forward a message to the appropriate peer according to the correct routing algorithm. This includes dropping the message or forwarding the message to other colluding nodes instead of the correct peer, perhaps in an attempt to control the results of a query. A malicious node may wish to masquerade as the index owner of the key being queried for in order to disseminate bad information and suppress content shared by other peers.

In addition, malicious users can acquire several valid network identifiers and thus control multiple distinct nodes in the network. This is referred to as the Sybil attack and has been studied by various groups (e.g. [3] [?] [6]). This implies that a small number of malicious users can control a large fraction of the network nodes, increasing the probability that they participate in any given message route.

To avoid routing messages through possibly malicious nodes, we would prefer forwarding our messages through nodes controlled by people we know personally, perhaps from a real life social context. We could most likely assume our friends would not purposefully misroute our messages[1]. Likewise, our friends could try and forward our message through their friends' nodes. This would require a mechanism to identify who our social contacts are and locate them in the network when they are online.

---

[*] This research is supported in part by NSF Grant (IIS-9817799).
[1] We assume a slim, but nonzero, chance that a virus or trojan has infected their machine, causing it to act maliciously.

Fortunately, this mechanism already exists in the form of various social network services. AOL, Microsoft, and Yahoo! all provide instant messaging services to millions of users, alerting them when their friends log on. Many websites, like Friendster, specialize in creating and utilizing social networks. We propose building peer-to-peer networks which leverage these existing social network services to establish additional, highly trusted, links at little additional cost. To determine the value of such a system we need a new way of modelling social trust and how it translates to the chance of misrouting. We present such a trust model in Section 2.

Adopting social links in an unstructured P2P network is relatively simple, since nodes are free to connect to any peers. However, using them in structured networks (e.g. DHTs) is more challenging because peer connections are typically determined algorithmically. In Section 3 we present SPROUT, a routing algorithm that takes advantage of social links in structured networks, and compare it to current standard routing techniques in Section 4. Social networks can be exploited by P2P systems for a variety of other reasons. In Section 5 we discuss application scenarios where our model is useful, as well as other related and future work. Finally, we conclude in Section 6.

2   Trust Model

The basic assumption of this paper is that computers managed by friends are not likely to be selfish or malicious and deny us service or misroute our messages. Similarly, friends of friends are also unlikely to be malicious. We assume the likelihood of a node B purposefully misrouting a message from node A is proportional to the distance from A's owner to B's owner in the social network.

2.1   Trust Function

We express the trust that a node A has in node B as $T(A, B)$. Based on our assumption, this value is dependent only on the distance (in hops) d from A to B in the social network. To quantify this measure of trust we use the expected probability that node B will correctly route a message from node A. The reason for this choice will become apparent shortly.

One simple trust function would be to assume our friends' nodes are very likely to correctly route our messages, say with probability $f = 0.95$. But their friends are less likely (0.90), and their friends even less so (0.85). A node's trustworthiness decreases linearly with respect to its distance from us in the social network. This would level off when we hit the probability that any random node will successfully route a message, say $r = 0.6$. In large networks probability r represents the fraction of the network expected to be good nodes willing to correctly route messages. Thus, $r = 0.6$ indicates that we expect that 40% of the network nodes (or more accurately network node identifiers) will purposefully misroute messages. In smaller networks, r is the probability that a peer at a large social distance from us will route correctly. Here we have presented a linear trust function. We consider others in Section 4.3.

We do not claim any of these functions with any specific parameter values is an accurate trust representation of any or all social networks, but they do serve to express the relation we believe exists between social structure and the probability of intentional routing misbehavior.

2.2 Path Rating

We need to compare the likelihood that a message will reach its destination given the path selected by a routing algorithm. For this reliability metric we calculate a *path trust rating*, denoted by P, by multiplying the separate node trust ratings for each node along the routing path from the source to destination. For example, assume source node S wishes to route a message to destination node D. In order to do so a routing algorithm calls for the message to hop from S to A, then B, then C, and finally D. Then the path rating will be $P = T(S, A) * T(S, B) * T(S, C) * T(S, D)$. Given that $T(X, Y)$ is interpreted as the actual probability node Y correctly routes node X's message, then P is the probability that the message is received and properly handled by D. Note that $T(X, Y)$ is dependent only on the shortest path in the social network between X and Y and thus independent of whether Y was the first, second, or nth node along the path.

Including the final destination's trust rating is optional and dependent on what we are measuring. If we wish to account for the fact that the destination may be malicious and ignore a message, we include it. Since we are using path rating to compare routing algorithms going to the same destination, both paths will include this factor, making the issue irrelevant.

3   Social Path Routing Algorithm

We wish to leverage the assumed correlation between routing reliability and social distance by creating a peer-to-peer system that utilizes social information from a service such as a community website or instant messenger service. Though there are many ways to exploit social links, for this paper, we focus on building a distributed hash table (DHT) routing algorithm. Specifically, we build on the basic Chord routing algorithm [10]. Our technique is equally applicable to other DHT designs, such as CAN [8] or Pastry [9].

When a user first joins the Chord network, it is randomly assigned a network identifier from 0 to 1. It then establishes links to its *sequential neighbors* in idspace, forming a ring of nodes. It also makes $O(\log n)$ *long links* to nodes halfway around the ring, a quarter of the way, an eighth, etc. When a node inserts or looks up an item, it hashes the item's key to a value between 0 and 1. Using greedy clockwise routing it can locate the peer whose id is closest to the key, and is thus responsible for indexing the item, in $O(\log n)$ hops.

Our Social Path ROUTing (SPROUT) algorithm adds to Chord additional links to any friends that are online. All popular instant messenger services keep a user aware of when their friends enter or leave the network. Using this existing mechanism a node can maintain links to their friends in the DHT as well. This provides them with several highly trusted links to use for routing messages. When a node needs to route to key k SPROUT works as follows:

1. Locate the friend node whose id is closest to, but not greater than, k.
2. If such a friend node exists, forward the message to it. That node repeats the procedure from step 1.
3. If no friend node is closer to the destination, then use the regular Chord algorithm to continue forwarding to the destination.

3.1   Optimizations

Here we present two techniques to improve the performance of our routing algorithm. We evaluate them in Section 4.2.

Lookahead. With the above procedure, when we choose the friend node closest to the destination we do not know if it has a friend to take us closer to the destination. Thus, we may have to resort to regular Chord routing after the first hop. To improve our chances of finding social hops to the destination we can employ a *lookahead* cache of 1 or 2 levels. Each node may share with its friends a list of its friends and, in 2-level lookahead, its friends-of-friends. A node can then consider all nodes within 2 or 3 social hops away when looking for the node closest to the destination. We still require that the message be forwarded over the established social links.

Minimum Hop Distance. Though SPROUT guarantees forward progress towards the destination with each hop, it may happen that at each hop SPROUT finds the sequential neighbor is the closest friend to the target. Thus, in the worst case, routing is $O(n)$.

To prevent this we use a *minimum hop distance (MHD)* to ensure that the following friend hop covers at least *MHD* fraction of the remaining distance (in idspace) to the destination. For example, if *MHD* = 0.25, then the next friend hop must be at least a quarter of the distance from the current node to the destination. If not then we resort to Chord routing, where each hop covers approximately half of the distance. This optimization guarantees us $O(\log n)$ hops to any destination but causes us to give up on using social links earlier in the routing process. When planning multiple hops at once, due to lookahead, we require the path to cover $\frac{MHD}{k}$ additional distance for each additional hop, for some appropriate k.

4   Results

In this section we evaluate our friend-routing algorithm as well as present optimizations. We also discuss the trust model and compare the different trust functions.

4.1   Simulation Details

To try out our SPROUT algorithm for DHTs we decided to compare it to Chord. We use two sources for social network data for our simulations. The first is data taken from the Club Nexus community website established at Stanford University. This dataset consists of over 2200 users and their links to each other as determined by their Buddy Lists. The second source was a synthetic social network generator based on the Small World topology algorithm presented in [7]. Both the Club Nexus data and the Small World data created social networks with an average of approximately 8 links per node. We assigned each social network node a random id in Chord.

   We also ran experiments using a trace of a social network based on 130,000 AOL Instant Messenger users and their Buddy Lists provided by BuddyZoo [2]. Because of the size of this dataset, we have only used the data to verify results of our other experiments.

   For each experiment we chose 1000 random nodes and, for each node, 1000 random keys to search for (uniformly from 0 to 1). We computed a path using each routing algorithm and gathered statistics on path length and trust rating. Each data point presented below is the average of all 1,000,000 paths.

   In Section 4.2 we use the linear trust function described in Section 2 with $f = 0.95$ and $r = 0.6$, which corresponds to 40% of the nodes misbehaving. We feel such a large fraction of bad nodes is reasonable because of the threat of Sybil attacks. We evaluate different trust functions and parameter values in Section 4.3.

4.2   Algorithm Evaluation

We first evaluate SPROUT, using a lookahead of 1 and $MHD = 0.5$, to Chord using the Club Nexus social network data. The first and third rows of Table 1 give the measured values for both the average path length and average path rating (or path *reliability*) of both regular Chord routing and SPROUT. With an average path length of 5.343 and average rating per path of 0.3080, Chord performed much worse in both metrics than SPROUT, which attained values of 4.569 and 0.4661, respectively. In fact, a path is over 1.5 times as likely to succeed using standard SPROUT as with regular Chord.

Table 1. SPROUT vs. Chord

	Avg. Path Length	Avg. Reliability
Regular Chord	5.343	0.3080
Augmented Chord	4.532	0.3649
SPROUT(1,0.5)	4.569	0.4661

   But this difference in performance may be simply due to SPROUT having additional links available for routing, and the fact that they are friend links may have no effect on performance. To even the comparison we augmented Chord by giving each node an equal number of random links for Chord to use as it has friend links. The performance of the augmented Chord (AC) is given in the second row of Table 1. As expected, with more links to choose from AC performs significantly better than regular Chord, especially in terms of path length. But SPROUT is still 1.3 times as likely to route successfully. In the following sections we compare SPROUT only to the augmented Chord algorithm.

How were the lookahead and *MHD* values used above chosen? Table 2 shows the results of our experiments in varying both parameters in the same scenario. As we see, the largest increase in reliability comes from using a 2-level lookahead. But this comes at a slight cost in average path length, due to the fact that more lookahead allows us to route along friend links for more of the path. For example, for *MHD* = 0.5, no lookahead averaged 0.977 social links per path, while 1-level lookahead averaged 2.533 and 2-level averaged 3.491. Friend links tend to not be as efficient as Chord links, so forward progress may require 2 or 3 hops, depending on the lookahead depth. But friend links are more likely to reach nodes closer to the sending node on the social network.

Table 2. Evaluating lookahead and *MHD*

MHD	Lookahead					
	None		1-level		2-level	
	Length	Rating	Length	Rating	Length	Rating
0	4.875	0.4068	5.101	0.4420	5.378	0.4421
0.125	4.805	0.4070	5.003	0.4464	5.258	0.4478
0.25	4.765	0.4068	4.872	0.4525	5.114	0.4551
0.5	4.656	0.4033	4.569	0.4661	4.757	0.4730

Increasing *MHD* limits the choices in forward progressing friend hops, causing the algorithm to switch to Chord earlier than otherwise, but mitigates inefficient progress. A large *MHD* seems to be most effective at both shortening path lengths and increasing path rating. This is not very surprising. Since our reliability function is multiplicative each additional link appreciably drops the path reliability.

From these results we chose to use a 1-level lookahead and an *MHD* of 0.5 for our standard SPROUT procedure. Though 2-level lookahead produced slightly better path ratings we did not feel it warranted the longer route paths and exponentially increased node state propagation and management. Our available social network data indicates that a user has on average between 8 and 9 friends. Thus, we would expect the average node's level-1 lookahead cache to hold less than 100 entries.

The path ratings presented above were relatively small, indicating a low, but perhaps acceptable, probability of successfully routing to a destination in the DHT. If the number of friends a user has remains relatively constant but the total number of network nodes increases we would expect performance to drop. But by how much? To study this we ran our experiment using our synthetic

Small World model for networks of different sizes with a maximum peer social degree proportional to $O(\log n)$. We present these results in Figure 1.

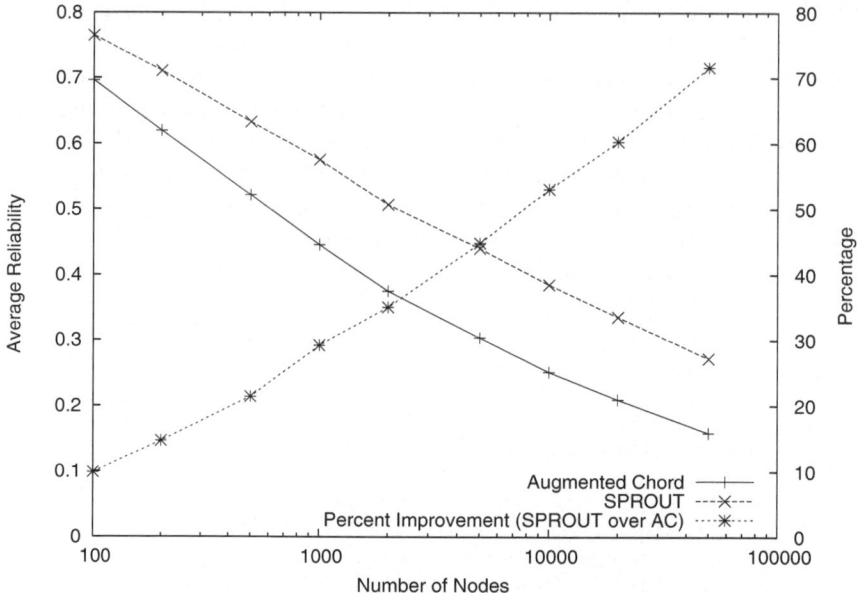

Fig. 1. Performance of SPROUT and AC in different size Small World networks. The third curve shows the relative performance of SPROUT with respect to AC, plotted on the right-hand y-axis. Note that the x-axis is logscale

As expected, for larger networks the path length increases, thus decreasing overall reliability. Because the average path length is $\Theta(\log n)$ as in Chord and we are using a multiplicative path rating, the reliability drops exponentially with respect to $\log n$. The range of network sizes tested is insufficiently large to properly illustrate an exponential curve, giving it a misguiding linear appearance. Notice that the relative performance gain of SPROUT over AC increases as the network grows. At 10,000 nodes SPROUT performs over 50% better than AC. As the network grows, the average number of social links increases slightly. The benefit SPROUT derives from additional friend links is greater than the benefit AC derives from additional random links.

4.3   Calculating Trust

All of our previous results used a linear trust function with $f = 0.95$. Of course other trust functions or parameter values may be more appropriate for different scenarios. $T(A, B)$, using the linear trust function LT we previously described, is defined in Equation 1 as a function of d, the distance from A to B in the social network.

$$LT(d) = \max(1 - (1-f)d, r) \tag{1}$$

Instead of a linear drop in trust, we may want to model an exponential drop at each additional hop. For this we use an exponential trust function ET, shown in Equation 2.

$$ET(d) = \max(f^d, r) \tag{2}$$

Another simple function we call the step trust function $ST(d)$ assigns an equal high trustworthiness of f to all nodes within h hops of us and the standard rating of r to the rest. Equation 3 defines the step trust function.

$$ST(d) = \mathbf{if}\ (d < h)\ \mathbf{then}\ f\ \mathbf{else}\ r \tag{3}$$

In our experiments we set h, the *social horizon*, to 5.

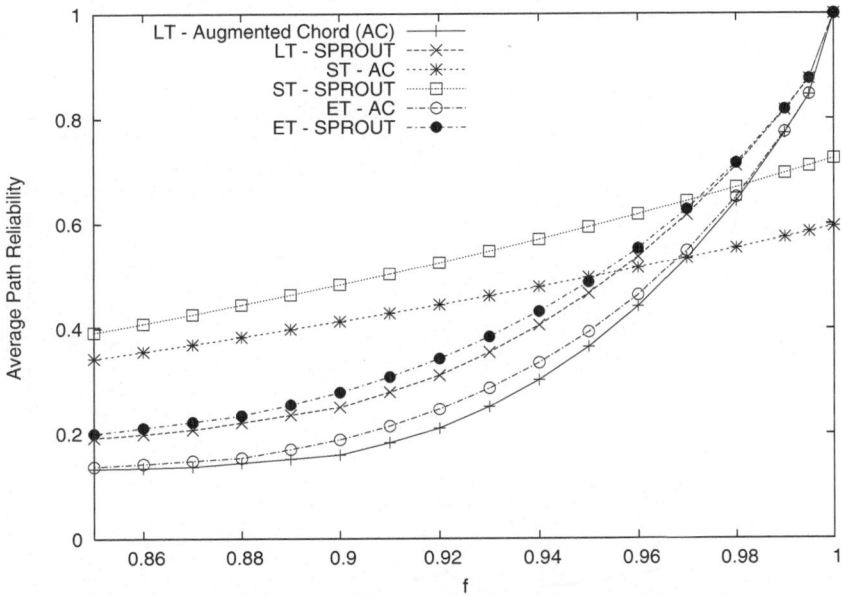

Fig. 2. Performance of SPROUT and AC for different trust functions and varying f. Higher value is better

All three functions are expressed so that f is the rating assigned to nodes one hop away in the social network, the direct friends. In Figure 2 we graph both routing algorithms under all three trust functions as a function of the parameter f.

We see here that both the linear (LT) and exponential (ET) trust functions perform equivalently while the step trust function (ST) gives less performance difference for varying f. For all trust functions SPROUT demonstrates a clear improvement over augmented Chord for $f > 0.85$. For example, at $f = 0.96$

using the exponential function SPROUT succeeds in routing 55% of the time, while AC only 46%.

We also varied r, the expected fraction of good nodes in the network. We found that for values of $r < 0.75$ performance remained almost constant. Above 0.75 both algorithms steadily increased.

4.4   Message Load

One problem SPROUT faces is uneven load distribution due to the widely varying social connectivity of the nodes. Peers with more social links are expected to forward messages for friends at a higher rate than weakly socially connected peers. To study this issue we measure the number of messages forwarded by each node over all 1,000,000 paths for both SPROUT(1,0.5) and augmented Chord. The resulting load on each node, in decreasing order, is given by the first two curves in Figure 3. The load is calculated as the fraction of all messages a node participated in routing.

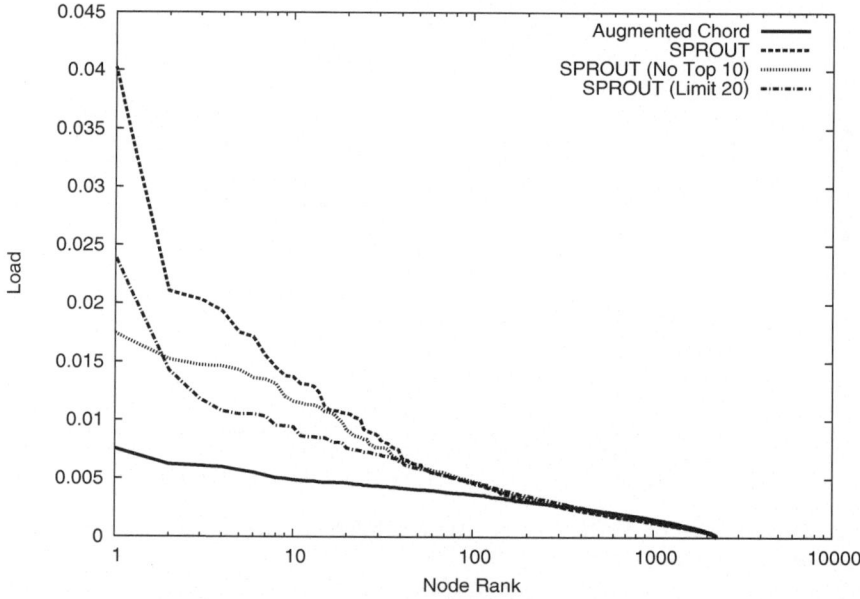

Fig. 3. Distribution of load (in fraction of routes) for augmented Chord and SPROUT. Lower is better. Social links were removed for the top 10 highest connected nodes for the *No Top 10* curve. All nodes were limited to at most 20 social links for the *Limit 20* curve. Note the logscale x-axis

The highest loaded node in the SPROUT experiment was very heavily loaded in comparison to AC (4% vs 0.75%). As expected, a peer's social degree is proportional to its load, with the most connected peers forwarding the most messages.

Though the top 200 nodes suffer substantially more load with SPROUT than AC, the remaining nodes report equal or less load. Because the average path length for SPROUT is slightly higher than for AC, the total load is greater in the SPROUT scenario. Yet the median load is slightly lower for SPROUT, further indicating an imbalanced load distribution.

To analyze the importance of the highly connected nodes we removed the social links from the top 10 most connected nodes, but kept their regular Chord links and reran the experiment. As the third curve in Figure 3 shows, the load has lowered for the most heavily weighted nodes, yet remains well above AC. Surprisingly the reliability was barely affected, dropping by 2% to 0.4569. If highly connected nodes were to stop forwarding for friends due to too much traffic, the load would shift to other nodes and the overall system performance would not be greatly affected.

Instead of reacting to high load, nodes may wish to only provide a limited number of social links for routing from the start. We limited all nodes to using only at most 20 social links for SPROUT. As we can see from the *Limit 20* curve in Figure 3, the load on the highly-loaded peers (excluding the most loaded peer) has fallen further, but not significantly from the *No Top 10* scenario. The average path reliability has dropped only an additional 1.5% to 0.4500.

In the end, it is the system architect who must decide whether the load skew is acceptable. For weakly connected homogeneous systems, fair load distribution may be critical. For other systems, improved reliability may be more important. In fact, one could take advantage of this skew. Adding one highly-connected large-capacity node to the network would increase reliability while significantly decreasing all other nodes' load.

5   Related and Future Work

In [1], Castro et al propose using stricter network identifier assignment and density checks to detect misrouting attacks in DHTs. They suggest using constrained routing tables and redundant routing to circumvent malicious nodes and provide more secure routing. SPROUT is complementary to their approach, simply increasing the probability that the message will be routed correctly the first time. One technique of theirs that would be especially useful in our system was their route failure test based on measuring the density of network ids around oneself and the purported destination. Not only can this technique be used to determine when a route has failed, but it can be used to evaluate the trustworthiness of a node's sequential neighbors by comparing local density to that at random locations in idspace or around friends.

One open question is whether node ids can be assigned more intelligently to improve trustworthiness. That is, if identifiers were assigned to nodes based on the current ids of their connected friends, what algorithm or distribution for id assignment would optimize our ability to route over social links?

We would like to evaluate SPROUT in a system using replication. To illustrate, assume we use k replicas, and node A attempts to insert an item in the

DHT and B searches for that item's key. If a message has an expected probability p of reaching its destination, then the probability of B discovering A's item is $1 - (1 - p^2)^k$. Using the values in Table 1 for p and $k = 3$, SPROUT would succeed 52% of the time compared to only 35% for AC.

Users may be willing to declare more friends if it would improve their performance. How many social links would each user need to maintain to reach a target average path rating?

With few modifications our model can be used to evaluate other issues, such as Quality of Service. If peers prioritized message forwarding based on service agreements and/or social connections we may want to use latency to compare routing algorithms. Using functions that give expected delay at each node in place of trust functions, and using an additive, instead of multiplicative, path rating function, we could express this appropriately. In [5] we explore this and other issues and demonstrate that SPROUT performs even better with respect to Chord in such systems.

6   Conclusion

We have presented a method for leveraging the trust relationships gained by marrying a peer-to-peer system with a social network, and applied it to the problem of mitigating misrouting attacks. We described a model for evaluating routing algorithms is such a system and proposed SPROUT, demonstrating how it can improve successful routing in a system where a large fraction of the nodes are malicious.

Acknowledgements

The authors would like to thank Orkut Buyukkokten for providing us with the Club Nexus data and Adam D'Angelo for providing us with the BuddyZoo data.

References

1. Castro, M., Drushel, P., Ganesh, A., Rowstron, A., and Wallach, D. Secure routing for structured peer-to-peer overlay networks. In *OSDI '02* (2002).
2. D'Angelo, A. BuddyZoo. http://www.buddyzoo.com.
3. Friedman, E., and Resnick, P. The social cost of cheap pseudonyms. *Journal of Economics and Management Strategy 10*, 2 (1998), 173–199.
4. Gummadi, K., Gummadi, R., Gribble, S., Ratnasamy, S., Shenker, S., and Stoica, I. The impact of DHT routing geometry on resilience and proximity. In *Proc. ACM SIGCOMM* (2003).
5. Marti, S., Ganesan, P., and Garcia-Molina, H. SPROUT: P2P Routing with Social Networks. Tech. rep., 2004. dbpubs.stanford.edu/pub/2004-5.
6. Marti, S., and Garcia-Molina, H. Identity crisis: Anonymity vs. reputation in p2p systems. In *IEEE 3rd International Conference on Peer-to-Peer Computing (P2P 2003)*.

7. Puniyani, A. R., Lukose, R. M., and Huberman, B. A. Intentional Walks on Scale Free Small Worlds. *ArXiv Condensed Matter e-prints* (July 2001). http://aps.arxiv.org/abs/cond-mat/0107212.
8. Ratnasamy, S., Francis, P., Handley, M., Karp, R., and Shenker, S. A scalable content addressable network. Tech. Rep. TR-00-010, Berkeley, CA, 2000.
9. Rowstron, A., and Druschel, P. Pastry: Scalable, decentralized object location, and routing for large-scale peer-to-peer systems. *IFIP/ACM International Conference on Distributed Systems Platforms* (2001), 329–350.
10. Stoica, I., Morris, R., Liben-Nowell, D., Karger, D. R., Kaashoek, M. F., Dabek, F., and Balakrishnan, H. Chord: a scalable peer-to-peer lookup protocol for internet applications. *IEEE/ACM Trans. Netw. 11*, 1 (2003), 17–32.

When Multi-hop Peer-to-Peer Lookup Matters

Rodrigo Rodrigues and Charles Blake

MIT Computer Science and Artificial Intelligence Laboratory
rodrigo@csail.mit.edu, cb@mit.edu

Abstract. Distributed hash tables have been around for a long time [1, 2]. A number of recent projects propose peer-to-peer DHTs, based on multi-hop lookup optimizations. Some of these systems also require data permanence. This paper presents an analysis of when these optimizations are useful. We conclude that the multi-hop optimizations make sense only for truly vast and very dynamic peer networks. We also observe that resource trends indicate this scale is on the rise.

1 Introduction

Distributed hash tables (DHTs) propose a logically centralized, physically distributed, hash table abstraction that can be shared simultaneously by many applications [1, 2].

Recently, DHTs have been proposed as a basic interface for building peer-to-peer systems [3–6]. These peer-to-peer DHTs share, in their design, the fact that they are divided into a *lookup* layer, which locates nodes responsible for objects in the system, and a *storage* layer that provides the DHT abstraction.

Most work on peer-to-peer DHTs takes the necessity of routing in a flat address space as a given. In particular, peer-to-peer DHTs (with a single exception [7]) employ small lookup state optimizations that lead to multiple routing hops, typically $O(log\ N)$. While often not explicit, we can speculate that the designers of these DHTs fear that the bandwidth or memory requirements of an approach where every node maintains complete system membership information are overwhelming for a "large scale" membership.

Since levels of routing indirection complicate several aspects of the system (e.g., security, server selection, operation latency) we believe it is useful to quantify what "large scale" means. Our thesis is that, in realistic deployment scenarios for peer-to-peer DHTs, maintaining complete membership information is both possible and beneficial.

The main contribution of this paper is to present an analytic model that allows us to determine when indirection is desirable. To answer this question we need to take into account several variables of the system. The most obvious ones are the membership durations and the size of the system, since these affect the size of the membership state and the bandwidth needed to maintain up-to-date membership information. Other variables are also important, though more implicitly, such as the total amount of data stored in the DHT (assuming that the DHT provides a reliable mapping – other assumptions, along with

G.M. Voelker and S. Shenker (Eds.): IPTPS 2004, LNCS 3279, pp. 112–122, 2004.

applications other than DHTs, are discussed in section 6). This will influence how large and dynamic the membership can be – if the membership is too dynamic, the bandwidth required to maintain data redundancy will overwhelm the peers' capacity [8].

Our analysis allows us to conclude that routing only matters for peer networks in excess of a few tens of millions of nodes. For smaller networks, the feasibility of maintaining *data* requires membership to be stable enough that maintaining full membership is cheap. With such stable membership, lookup indirection is an unnecessary complexity that can even hurt overall performance (e.g., by increasing lookup latency or impeding server selection).

The remainder of the paper is organized as follows. Section 2 presents the model for redundancy maintenance in a peer-to-peer DHT. Section 3 presents the model for the bandwidth cost of maintaining full membership information. Section 4 analyzes when routing needs optimizing, and this analysis is generalized to produce a result independent of churn in Section 5. In Section 6 we discuss possible applications of multi-hop routing schemes (other than peer-to-peer DHTs), and we conclude in Section 7.

2   DHT Data Maintenance

In this section we consider the bandwidth necessary for maintaining data in a peer-to-peer DHT. As mentioned, the bandwidth constrains are going to limit the amount of data in the system, the membership dynamics, and the number of nodes in the system, hence it will also influence the need for a routing substrate. We present a simple analytic model for bandwidth usage that attempts to provide broad intuition and still applies in some approximation to currently proposed systems. A more detailed version of this analysis is presented in a previous publication [8].

2.1   Assumptions

We assume a simple redundancy maintenance algorithm: whenever a node leaves or joins the system, the data that node either held or will hold must be downloaded from somewhere. Note that by *join* and *leave* we mean really joining the system for the first time or leaving forever. We do not refer to transient failures, but rather the intentional or accidental loss of the contributed data. Transient failures are masked by the use of appropriate redundancy techniques. We also assume there is a static data placement strategy (i.e., a function from the current membership to the set of replicas of each block).

We make a number of simplifying assumptions. Each one is *conservative* – increased realism would increase the bandwidth required. The fact that we perform an average case analysis also makes it conservative, since it does not consider the worst-case accidents of data distribution and other variations.

We assume identical per-node space and bandwidth contributions. In practice, nodes may store different amounts of data and have different bandwidth capabilities. Maintaining redundancy may require in certain cases more bandwidth than the average bandwidth. Creating more capable nodes from a set of less capable nodes might take more time. Average space and bandwidth therefore conservatively bound the worst case – the relevant bound for a guarantee.

We assume a constant rate of joining and leaving. Here also, the worst case is the appropriate figure to use for any probabilistic bound. The average rate is therefore conservative. We also assume independence of leave events. Since failures of networks and machines are not truly independent, more redundancy would be required in practice to provide better guarantees.

We assume a constant steady-state number of nodes and total data size. A decreasing population requires more bandwidth while an increasing one cannot be sustained indefinitely. It would also be more realistic to assume data increases with time or changes which would again require more bandwidth.

2.2   Data Maintenance Model

Consider a set of N identical hosts which cooperatively provide guaranteed storage over the network. Nodes are added to the set at rate α and leave at rate λ, but the average system size is constant, i.e. $\alpha = \lambda$. On average, a node stays a member for $T = N/\lambda$.

Our data model is that the system reliably stores a total of D bytes of unique data stored with a redundancy expansion factor k, for a total of $S = kD$ bytes of contributed storage. One may think of k as either the replication factor or the expansion due to coding. The desired value of k depends on both the storage guarantees and redundant encoding scheme [8].

We now consider the data maintenance bandwidth required to maintain this redundancy in the presence of a dynamic membership. Note that the model does not consider the bandwidth consumed by queries.

Each node *joining* the overlay must download all the data which it must later serve, however that subset of data might be mapped to it. The average size of this transfer is S/N. Join events happen every $1/\alpha$ time units. So the aggregate bandwidth to deal with nodes joining the overlay is $\frac{\alpha S}{N}$, or S/T.

When a node *leaves* the overlay, all the data it housed must be copied over to new nodes, otherwise redundancy would be lost. Thus, each leave event also leads to the transfer of S/N bytes of data. Leaves therefore also require an aggregate bandwidth of $\frac{\lambda S}{N}$, or S/T. The total bandwidth usage for all data maintenance is then $\frac{2S}{T}$, or a per node average of:

$$B/N = 2\frac{S/N}{T}, \quad \text{or} \quad BW/node = 2\frac{space/node}{lifetime} \tag{1}$$

Figure 1 plots some example "threshold curves" in the lifetime-membership plane. These assume a cable modem connection (limited by its 200 kbps upstream connection) and that 25% of the upstream bandwidth is used for data redundancy maintenance. They assume the redundancy factor is $k = 8$. This is an appropriate encoding rate if availability is over about 75% and we use replication [8].

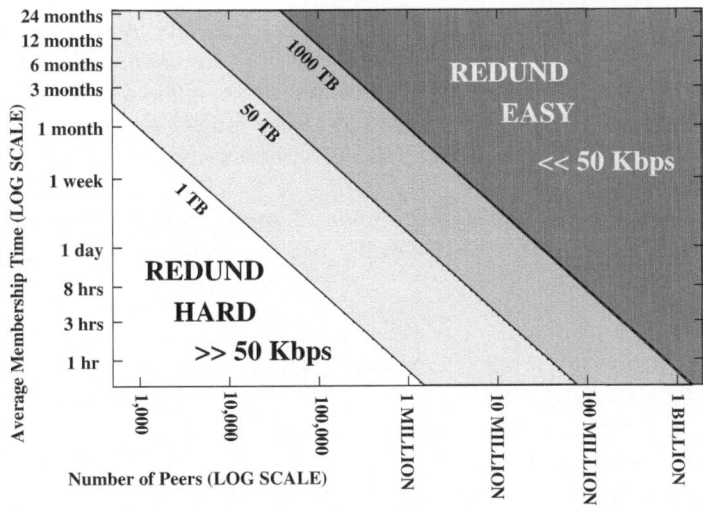

Fig. 1. Log-Log plots for the participation requirements of a cable modem network. Plotted are regions below which various amounts of unique data will incur over 25% link saturation just to maintain the data. These use a redundancy $k = 8$.

This figure shows that for a million nodes to cooperatively store a petabyte of data in a DHT, nodes must remain in the system for about one month on average (albeit with possible temporary disconnections [8]).

3   Full Information Lookup

Now we turn to the cost of maintaining complete membership information at each node. The storage cost of maintaining these data structures is negligible. For instance, 10 million IPv4 addresses occupy only 57 MB. What is important are the bandwidth costs which we now analyze.

3.1   Trivial Join Protocol

To bound bandwidth needs, we present a simple protocol for the cost of maintaining full membership information in a peer-to-peer system. The point of this protocol is not to constitute a "complete" system implementation. Instead, we use it for its ostensible simplicity of description, implementation, and analysis. Such analysis will afford us a rough estimate for the main bandwidth costs of membership maintenance, neglecting less costly details such as TCP-layer retransmits.

Our join algorithm is simply this: the joining node downloads the entire member list from anyone and then notifies everyone he is a member. Join notifications are sent continuously until acknowledged from each node. To avoid exorbitant retransmits, the retry time scale is exponentially backed off to some upper limit related to the session time distribution.

This protocol is intentionally simple to ease analysis. A more sophisticated multicast protocol might lower the cost of distributing membership information. The bound we generate is hence quite conservative, since a larger point of this paper is that good system design introduces such fancier protocols and complexity only when required, not proactively for systems of scales which are unlikely to be relevant any time soon.

Assuming that a fraction u of the nodes is unreachable during each notification attempt, this generates the following per-join bandwidth consumption.

- *outbound*:
  $N \times 48 \times (1 + u + u^2 + ...) = \frac{48N}{1-u}$,
  where $48 = 20$ byte node id $+28$ byte UDP header.
- *inbound*:
  acks: $N \times 28$ bytes. (neglecting IP packet loss)
  member list: $N \times 26$ bytes,
  where $26 = 20$ byte id $+6$ byte IPv4 address/port.

The average per-node upload or download bandwidth to handle node joins is given by:

$$(outbound + inbound)\frac{\lambda}{N} = (54 + \frac{48}{1-u})N\frac{\lambda}{N} = (54 + \frac{48}{1-u})N/T \qquad (2)$$

3.2   Trivial Leave Protocol

As protocols go, doing nothing at all is fairly simple. All that matters is all remaining nodes to individually notice when a host has been persistently down. This is most naturally done by some staggered or random probing of hosts stretched out over a period of time, τ. Taking partial availability into account, suppose a host must be non-responsive m times – say 4 times to yield a false eviction rate of about $1/256$ for unavailability $u = 1/4$. The expected fraction of stale entries is then $P_{stale} = 1 - T/(T + m\tau)$. E.g., $P_{stale} = 1/3$ and $m = 4$ implies that $\tau = T/8$.

A plausible timescale of *true* membership dynamics in data sharing peer-to-peer systems, T, is one-to-several weeks [9]. So, $\tau = 1$ *day* is a plausible target. The bandwidth costs of such a staggered, retrying host eviction is modest. E.g., for $N = 8,640,000$ a refresh time of 1 *day* only costs 100 *probes/s* or roughly 20 kbps with 28 byte probe packets.

If N is a bit smaller and queries are randomly distributed then query traffic itself can act as a passive probe at no cost of additional bandwidth. E.g. if the system size is $N = 100,000$ nodes and 64 kbps are used for uploading 8 kB blocks then $\tau \approx 1$ *day*.

3.3   Stale Membership Issues

The principal consequence of the existence of a small fraction of stale membership data is in slightly longer timeouts on *synchronous* "store" operations. When storing data on new nodes the system must timeout store requests that fail, creating a higher operation latency, perhaps ten times the worst case network round-trip – a few seconds of real time. In replica-oriented redundancy, the first few replicas are likely to be stored very quickly yielding some immediate data reliability and availability. Synchronously waiting for the slowest few peers to store provides diminishing returns on the reliability of a data block.

Additionally, reads dominate writes in most applications. It is often a very desirable tradeoff for writes to be a highly concurrent background operation if reads can be made faster. Engineering an entire system around an optimized write latency with no particular application in mind seems off track. E.g., writes to a backup system which occur at off hours to maximize the "user-level" data coherency can take almost as long as one likes while having the particular backup recovery block one wants as soon as possible is more important. Since full-information lookups can surely do at least somewhat better dynamic server selection for "get" operations, the end to end performance of user-relevant operations could be faster.

4 When Indirection Helps

Now we move on to the main question of this paper: When do DHTs profit from multi-hop lookup?

4.1 Combining Our Bounds

To answer this question we combine the results of the two previous sections, first graphically and then algebraically. Figure 2 shows, in the lifetime-membership plane, the intersection between Figure 1 and the region bounded by equation 2. In other words, it shows, on the one hand, when is a peer-to-peer DHT feasible in terms of redundancy maintenance bandwidth (i.e., the region above the dashed lines of Figure 1). On the other hand, it also shows when it is not feasible to maintain complete membership information (i.e., the region below the lines defined by equation 2). For the latter region, we plotted two curves. The solid curve assumes that the average membership maintenance bandwidth for node joins saturated 25% of a cable modem uplink speed (50 Kbps), and fixed $u = 0.25$ in equation 2. We may argue that in some scenarios we would like to start optimizing this cost even earlier, so we plotted another curve (marked "$<< 1$ Kbps") corresponding to an average membership maintenance bandwidth of 1 Kbps. This ignores the costs of handling node departures, as we have shown that this cost is small.

The intersection of these two lines delineates the interesting region where small lookup state DHTs may be an adequate solution, since it is required to avoid the large bandwidth consumption of maintaining full membership information (the shaded quadrant marked "multi-hop matters"). The quadrant above the dashed lines and also above the solid line defines when a peer-to-peer DHT is feasible, but multi-hop lookup is not required (marked "lookup easy").

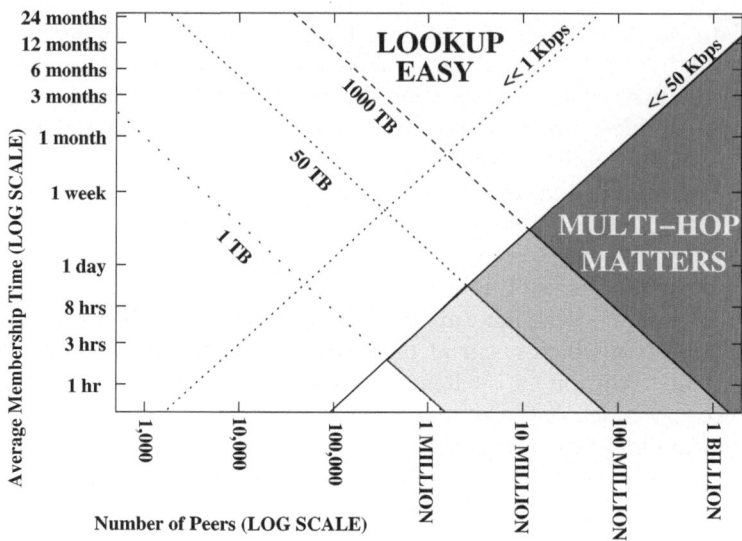

Fig. 2. Putting it all together. The dashed lines from Figure 1 border the feasibility of a peer-to-peer DHT. The lines marked "<< 1 Kbps" and "<< 50 Kbps" border the need for multi-hop lookup. The shaded region corresponds to the deployment scenarios where peer-to-peer DHTs are feasible and multi-hop optimizations may be required.

4.2   Data, Pointers, and All That

Figure 2 shows that, for a petabyte of data, DHT feasibility needing multi-hop lookup requires over 10 million participants. Further, for 10 million hosts to store 1 petabyte of unique data, each node will only contribute merely 100 megabytes of unique data, or 800 megabytes of total data (recall we used $k = 8$). This seems like a modest contribution, only 1% of a small disk in a standard PC sold today. More meaningful contributions would require a more stable membership, and thus lessen the need for multi-hop routing.

For a smaller DHT (50 TB), multi-hop DHTs may be interesting if we have to employ a few million nodes to serve the data. To store only *pointers* to a few petabytes of data might require only 1 TB to be stored in the DHT. While storing only pointers does lower the membership scale at which multi-hop optimizations matter, as Figure 2 shows, it only does so for extremely volatile memberships. This then raises the question about how the data itself is being maintained (see Figure 1). If the data is being maintained then a fairly reliable pool of peers is available and could also be used for the lookup service without multi-hop schemes. (The lookup service adds negligible load since looking up a block uses much less bandwidth than serving a block.) If the data is *not* reliable, then it seems strange to have an indexing service that is much more reliable and available. For the scenario of unreliable data or distributed caching, one of the approaches in Section 6 is more appropriate.

4.3   Hardware Trends

The discussion so far suggests that for systems with the many millions of nodes needed for multi-hop lookup to be a relevant optimization, data maintenance bandwidth constraints prevent using more than a few hundred MB/node. A quick reflection of hardware trends, recapped by Table 1, suggest that multi-hop optimizations will be even less interesting in the future. This table shows how long it would take to upload your hard disk through your network connection for a "typical" user, and how this figure has evolved.

Table 1. Disk increased by 8000-fold while bandwidth increased only 50-fold.

Year	Disk	Home access		Academic access	
		Speed (Kbps)	Days to send	Speed (Mbps)	Time to send
1990	60 MB	9.6	0.6	10	48 sec
1995	1 GB	33.6	3	43	3 min
2000	80 GB	128	60	155	1 hour
2005	0.5 TB	384	120	622	2 hour

Table 1 suggests that disk upload time is getting larger quickly. This implies that if peers are to contribute substantial fractions of their disks then their participation must become more and more stable. This additional stability makes a multi-hop indirection infrastructure even less necessary. This supports the point that multi-hop lookups will not be necessary if one wishes to build a DHT from a large peer population: the more you move "up" on the graph in Figure 2, the less likely it is that multi-hop will matter.

5   Factoring Out Churn

The idea of Section 4 can be generalized to a simple algebraic result *independent of membership turnover*. Equation 1 and Equation 2 can be equated to discover when membership maintenance overhead is about as large as data maintenance overhead:

$$\frac{2S/N}{T} = \frac{(54 + \frac{48}{1-u})N}{T} \approx \frac{118N}{T} \Rightarrow N \approx \frac{S/N}{60 \text{ bytes}}$$

This gives the rough scale at which small-state (i.e., multi-hop) lookup optimizations matter. Per node contributions in the gigabytes implies multi-hop importance scales in the tens of millions. E.g., if $S/N = 3$ GB, then one only needs multi-hop lookup when $N > 50$ *million*.

While it is hard to know for sure, the current Internet is very unlikely to have more than 50 million hosts simultaneously running the distributed service 75% of the time. At the same time it seems very likely that many if not most computers in the current Internet have 3 GB of disk space to contribute.

The hardware trends mentioned in Section 4 are therefore quite indicative. As the disk-bandwidth disparity grows, multi-hop lookup systems will become less relevant.

Even if our model is imprecise, estimating only the order of magnitude of membership maintenance, it still seems unavoidable to conclude that current multi-hop DHTs seem relevant, forward-looking designs only when one has either an enormous system scale supporting a small amount of data or draconian membership freshness guarantees.

6   Whither Peer-to-Peer Routing?

The analysis of the paper seems to imply that peer-to-peer routing is only useful in a limited number of situations with very high membership, moderate peer dynamics, and small total data state. However, our analysis is limited to *robust* peer-to-peer DHTs, i.e., DHTs that provide a consistent and reliable mapping from keys to values. Peer-to-peer routing may be extremely useful for other classes of applications. In this section we highlight some relevant examples.

One example are DHTs that do not try to provide a consistent and reliable mapping or do not place replicas randomly. An example of a DHT that falls into this category is Coral [10]. This DHT only stores soft-state – thus it does not require lookups to always retrieve the latest data that was stored under that key – and it uses clustering techniques to create nearby copies of the data. For both reasons, Coral does not incur in the DHT data maintenance costs of Section 2, as the model in question does not apply to it.

The second example is the class of applications, other than DHTs, that take advantage of the peer-to-peer routing topology. An example of such an application is implementing a cooperative multicast infrastructure [11–13], but other applications exist. These applications do not necessarily store data, and therefore do not incur in the costs of Section 2. Furthermore these applications may find peer-to-peer routing useful for reasons other than saving bandwidth, since they take advantage of the topology that is automatically formed by the routing layer. Therefore the analysis in Section 4 does not apply here, and multi-hop routing can be useful independently of system churn.

Some peer-to-peer storage systems exploit indirection to perform dynamic volatile replica creation along the lookup path. Such caching spreads the load for popular content at the cost of substantial additional bandwidth usage. Effectively, the curves in Figure 1 are shifted away from the origin. While this is a possibly interesting application of multi-hop lookups, only one level of indirection (i.e., two total routing hops) seems necessary to support this.

7   Conclusion

This paper argues that the feasibility of a peer-to-peer DHT may imply either a relatively stable membership, or an extremely large participation in the system. If the membership is somewhat stable, then the utility of multi-hop lookup optimizations must be questioned.

Our analysis tries to quantitatively bound when multi-hop lookups may be needed. The main conclusion is that this optimization is required only if the system is comprised of more than tens of millions of nodes (under conservative assumptions).

Further, hardware trends indicate that, if peers are to donate significant fractions of the their free storage space to the DHT, then multi-hop lookup optimizations are even less likely to be required in the future.

Acknowledgements

We would like to thank Nick Feamster, Sean Rhea, and Mike Walfish for helpful comments on drafts of this paper.

This research is supported by DARPA under contract F30602-98-1-0237 and by the NSF under Cooperative Agreement ANI-0225660 (http://project-iris.net). Rodrigo Rodrigues was supported by a fellowship from the Calouste Gulbenkian Foundation, and was previously supported by a Praxis XXI fellowship.

References

1. Gribble, S., Brewer, E., Hellerstein, J., Culler, D.: Scalable, distributed data structures for internet service construction. In: Proceedings of the 4th USENIX Symposium on Operating Systems Design and Implementation (OSDI 2000). (2000)
2. Litwin, W., Neimat, M.A., Schneider, D.A.: LH* - linear hashing for distributed files. In: Proceedings of the 1993 ACM SIGMOD International Conference on Management of Data. (1993)
3. Ratnasamy, S., Francis, P., Handley, M., Karp, R., Shenker, S.: A scalable content-addressable network. In: Proc. ACM SIGCOMM. (2001)
4. Rowstron, A., Druschel, P.: Pastry: Scalable, distributed object location and routing for large-s cale peer-to-peer systems. In: Proc. IFIP/ACM International Conference on Distributed Systems Platforms (Middleware 2001). (2001)
5. Stoica, I., Morris, R., Karger, D., Kaashoek, M.F., Balakrishnan, H.: Chord: A scalable peer-to-peer lookup service for internet applications. In: Proc. ACM SIGCOMM. (2001)
6. Zhao, B., Kubiatowicz, J., Joseph, A.: Tapestry: An infrastructure for fault-tolerant wide-area location and routing. Technical Report UCB/CSD-01-1141, UC Berkeley (2001)
7. Gupta, A., Liskov, B., Rodrigues, R.: Efficient routing for peer-to-peer overlays. In: Proc. First Symposium on Networked Systems Design and Implementation (NSDI '04). (2004)
8. Blake, C., Rodrigues, R.: High availability, scalable storage, dynamic peer networks: Pick two. In: Proc. 9th Workshop on Hot Topics in Operating Systems. (2003)
9. Bhagwan, R., Savage, S., Voelker, G.: Understanding availability. In: Proc. 2nd International Workshop on Peer-to-Peer Systems (IPTPS '03). (2003)
10. Freedman, M., Mazières, D.: Sloppy hashing and self-organizing clusters. In: Proceedings of the 2nd International Workshop on Peer-to-Peer Systems (IPTPS '03). (2003)

11. Castro, M., Druschel, P., Kermarrec, A.M., Rowstron, A.: SCRIBE: A large-scale and decentralised application-level multicast infrastructure. IEEE Journal on Selected Areas in Communications (2002)
12. Ratnasamy, S., Handley, M., Karp, R., Shenker, S.: Application-level multicast using content-addressable networks. In: 3rd International Workshop on Networked Group Communication (NGC'01). (2001)
13. Zhuang, S., Zhao, B., Joseph, A., Katz, R., Kubiatowicz, J.: Bayeux: An architecture for scalable and fault-tolerant wide-area data dissemination. In: Network and Operating System Support for Digital Audio and Video (NOSSDAV'01). (2001)

Uncoordinated Load Balancing and Congestion Games in P2P Systems*

Subhash Suri[1], Csaba D. Tóth[1], and Yunhong Zhou[2]

[1] Department of Computer Science, University of California, Santa Barbara, CA 93106
{suri,toth}@cs.ucsb.edu
[2] Hewlett-Packard Laboratories, 1501 Page Mill Road, Palo Alto, CA 94304
yunhong.zhou@hp.com

Abstract. In P2P systems, users often have many choices of peers from whom to download their data. Each user cares primarily about its own response time, which depends on how many other users also choose that same peer. This interaction is best modeled as a game among self-interested agents, which we call *uncoordinated load balancing*. The players in this game are the rational and strategic users who are free to act in their own self-interest. We describe some of our recent work on this problem, and propose several new research directions, including analyzing Nash equilibria under general latency functions, a cost to switch servers, settings where user groups are dynamic, as well as the complexity of finding Nash solutions, and incentives for peers to be truthful in revealing their load.

1 Introduction

In Peer-to-peer (P2P) systems, data are often replicated to enable a high level of availability and fault tolerance. As a result, users typically have choice of many hosts from whom to download their data. Each user is selfish and strategic, and wants to minimize its response time. On the other hand, when serving data to multiple users, a host must share its limited bandwidth among those users. Therefore, the latency (response time) experienced by a user when downloading data from a host depends on *how many other users are connected to that host*. Different hosts may have different speeds. We assume that the response time is inversely proportional to the speed of the host, but *grows linearly* with the total number of users connected to a host. (All our results generalize to the case where the response time grows as the pth power of the load.)

Each user independently trying to maximize its utility is essentially engaged in a game with other users, which we call *uncoordinated load balancing*. Unlike traditional load balancing, however, users are not interested in optimizing the social welfare (e.g., *total* response time). Instead, each user has its own private objective. The stable outcomes of these interactions are the Nash equilibria – outcomes in which no user can improve its utility by switching unilaterally. In general, Nash equilibrium solutions can be much worse than the centralized outcomes, and Papadimitriou [8] has coined the term "price of anarchy" to denote the *worst-case ratio between a Nash outcome and the*

---

* Research of the first two authors was partially supported by NSF grants CCR-0049093 and IIS-0121562.

G.M. Voelker and S. Shenker (Eds.): IPTPS 2004, LNCS 3279, pp. 123–130, 2004.
© Springer-Verlag Berlin Heidelberg 2004

social optimum. We describe several problems and results concerning the price of anarchy for uncoordinated load balancing, and explore many associated algorithmic and structural questions. We begin by describing our model for the load balancing game.

2   Model and Results

An instance of the load balancing game is modeled as a bipartite graph G between a set U of n users (data requesting peers) and a set V of m hosts (data hosting peers). An edge (i, j) indicates that user i can obtain its data from node j. A *peer matching* is a (many to one) mapping $M : U \rightarrow V$ that assigns each user to a host[1]. That is, each user is matched to exactly one host, but a host can be matched to multiple users (or none).

Different hosts can have different speeds. Suppose a host j has speed σ_j and is matched to d_j users, then we assume that the *response time*, or *latency*, to each user i connected to this host is $\lambda_i = f(d_j)/\sigma_j$, where $f()$ is an increasing function of the load d_j. In general, the response time has two components, one host dependent and one network dependent. In our simplified model, we consider just the host-related latency, and treat network latency to be a constant. Under the *linear model*, the latency is simply d_j/σ_j. (More generally, we consider latency functions of the form d_j^{p-1}/σ_j, for $p \geq 1$.) The cost of a peer matching M is the total latency of all the users:

$$\text{cost}(M) = \sum_{i=1}^{n} \lambda_i.$$

A matching is a *Nash equilibrium* if no user can improve its latency by unilaterally switching to another host. Let M_{nash} be a Nash solution, and let M_{opt} be the (coordinated) social optimum. The *price of anarchy* $\rho(G)$ is the worst-case bound on the ratio between the costs of M_{nash} and M_{opt} for the problem instance G.

We have been able to prove that if all hosts have equal speed, then the price of anarchy is

$$\rho(G) \leq (1 + 2/\sqrt{3}) \approx 2.15$$

A more revealing way to express the price of anarchy is the following: we show that $\rho(G) \leq 1 + \frac{2m}{n}$, which tends to one as the ratio between the number of users to hosts grows. We also exhibit an instance G for which $\rho(G) \geq 2.001$, even with linear latency and equal speed for all the servers.

With arbitrary speed hosts, we can prove a general bound of 2.5 on the price of anarchy. If the latency function grows as the L_p norm of the host loads, we show that the price of anarchy is bounded by $\frac{p}{\log p}(1 + o(1))$. The matching cost turns out to be related to the *sum of the squares of the server loads*. Thus, our techniques also lead to improved bounds for a natural online greedy scheme for load balancing [1]. In this short paper, we give a brief overview of some of our key results, so that we can formulate the research problems we wish to propose; full papers describing our mathematical results are in preparation [5, 13].

---

[1] To avoid trivialities, we assume that for each client, there is at least one server that can provide the data.

3   Related Work

Several algorithms have been proposed recently for peer selection, such as "controlled update propagation" [12]," adaptive peer selection" [2], among others. While these papers do acknowledge the fact that users selfishly want to choose peers with the best response time, they fail to model the game theoretic interaction among the users.

Our uncoordinated load balancing game belongs to the general class of *congestion games* introduced by Rosenthal [9] in game theory. In computer science, perhaps the best known congestion game is the network routing, studied by Koutsoupias and Papadimitriou [6], Czumaj and Vöcking [3], Roughgarden [10], and Roughgarden and Tardos [11], among others.

The load balancing game differs from these routing games in one important and fundamental respect: load balancing is *atomic*, while the routing games are *non-atomic*. In the latter, a user's task (flow) can be split arbitrarily (across multiple paths). By contrast, in atomic games, one user is wholly assigned to a single host[2]. In routing games, one also assumes that each user puts only a *negligible* traffic load on a network link. We do not require such an assumption – a user can own an arbitrarily large fraction of a host.

The more traditional *coordinated or centralized* load balancing has a long history in distributed systems. Our peer matching problem has connections with the load balancing variant in which we wish to minimize the L_2 norm of the server loads. The best known result on this problem is by Awerbuch et al. [1], who show that the online greedy algorithm achieves a constant factor *competitive ratio*. Using our techniques, we are able obtain an improved upper bound for the greedy's performance.

4   Bounding the Price of Anarchy

It is well-known that Nash equilibria do not always optimize the social welfare, with the Prisoner's Dilemma being one of the best-known examples. Our peer matching problem is no exception: an equilibrium matching does not necessarily have minimum cost. See Figure 1 for examples.

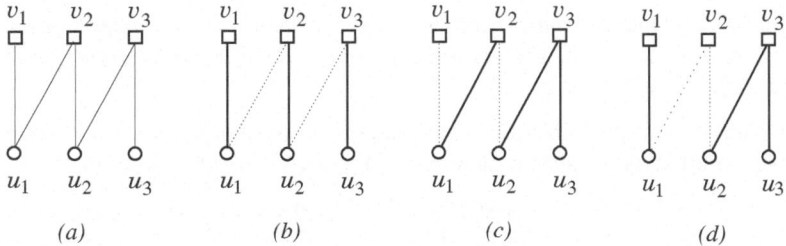

Fig. 1. (a) A client-server graph. (b) An optimal matching of cost 3. (c) A Nash but sub-optimal matching of cost 5. (d) A non-equilibrium matching.

---

[2] Indeed, for the the non-atomic version of the uncoordinated load balancing, we can show the price of anarchy is one; that is, Nash is always optimal.

Fortunately, it can be shown that the price of anarchy (the worst-case ratio between a Nash solution and the social optimum) for the peer matching game is quite modest. We begin with some preliminary facts relating the optimal and the Nash matchings.

Upper Bounds

We have n clients, labeled $1, 2, \ldots, n$, and m servers, labeled $1, 2, \ldots, m$. The term *server load* denotes the *number* of clients assigned to that server in a given matching. We first observe that the cost of a matching (sum of clients' latency) is related to the sum of the *squared* server loads. That is, if M is a matching, in which client i has latency λ_i and server j has load ℓ_j and speed σ_j, then

$$\text{cost}(M) = \sum_{i=1}^{n} \lambda_i = \sum_{j=1}^{m} \frac{\ell_j^2}{\sigma_j}. \tag{1}$$

This follows because each of the ℓ_j clients matched to server j suffers latency ℓ_j/σ_j. Given a problem instance, let M_{opt} denote an optimal peer matching, and let M_{nash} denote a Nash matching. Let O_j and N_j denote the set of clients assigned to server j in M_{opt} and M_{nash}, respectively. We use the shorthand notation $o_j = |O_j|$ and $n_j = |N_j|$ for the cardinalities of these sets. If a client is assigned to server j in the Nash but to server k in the optimal, then the following **Nash Condition** must hold, where σ_j and σ_k denote the speeds of these servers:

$$\frac{n_j}{\sigma_j} \leq \frac{n_k + 1}{\sigma_k}, \quad \text{if} \quad N_j \cap O_k \neq \emptyset.$$

This condition basically expresses the fact the client could not have improved its latency by switching. This innocent looking condition is powerful enough to give us the following important **Nash Inequality**: *If M_{opt} is an optimal matching and M_{nash} is a Nash matching, then*

$$\sum_{j=1}^{m} \frac{n_j^2}{\sigma_j} \leq \sum_{j=1}^{m} \frac{(n_j + 1)o_j}{\sigma_j}.$$

This fundamental inequality allows us to prove the following upper bounds on the price of anarchy.

Theorem 1. *With linear latency functions and arbitrary server speeds, the price of anarchy is at most 2.5. If all servers have the same speed, then the price of anarchy is at most $1 + 2/\sqrt{3} \approx 2.15$.*

There are several specializations and generalizations of this main result. We mention a few. First, if all servers have an identical and linear latency function, then

$$\frac{\text{cost}(M_{\text{nash}})}{\text{cost}(M_{\text{opt}})} \leq 1 + \frac{2m}{n}.$$

Thus, as the ratio (number of clients)/(number of servers) grows, *every Nash solution approaches the social optimum*. Second, if the server latency grows as the pth power of the server load, then we can measure the total latency using the L_p norm. In this case, the price of anarchy turns out to be $\frac{p}{\log p}(1 + o(1))$.

A Lower Bound

Figure 1(c) shows an example where the Nash solution is $5/3$ times the optimal. A more involved construction shows that the price of anarchy is at least 2.001, even with identical and linear latency functions.

5   Greedy Matching: A Myopic Strategy

Nash equilibrium is a compelling solution concept for distributed systems with self-interested players. Unfortunately, the concept is descriptive, not prescriptive: it does not suggest algorithms for computing an equilibrium and finding (distributed) algorithms for Nash equilibria remains a topic of current research.

We are therefore motivated to investigate the following simple *greedy* strategy: clients arrive in the system online in an arbitrary order; upon arrival, each client selects a permissible server with the smallest current latency, and *this selection is irrevocable*. The greedy is a myopic strategy – each client makes the best choice available to it at the moment, although future choices by *other clients* may make it regret its selection. While greedy does not generally lead to Nash solutions, it may well be a strategy most commonly used in practice. Thus, a natural question to ask is: *how bad is the greedy matching in the worst case?*

Surprisingly, even greedy has a modest price of anarchy: we show that with linear latency and arbitrary server speeds, the worst-case ratio $\text{cost}(M_{\text{greedy}})/\text{cost}(M_{\text{opt}})$ is less than $17/3 \approx 5.67$. If all servers have equal speed, then the ratio improves to $2 + \sqrt{5} \approx 4.24$. These results imply improved bounds on the competitive ratio of the (coordinated) greedy solution for L_2 norm server load balancing [1].

6   Optimal, Nash, and Greedy: Some Structural Results

The price of anarchy focuses on the worst-case equilibrium solution. A more optimistic analysis could consider the *best case* Nash solution and ask how close to the social optimum can one get? In this section, we consider some questions like this and provide a few partial answers.

Theorem 2. *Assuming that every server has the same latency function $\lambda(x)$ and $x \cdot \lambda(x)$ is convex, then every optimal matching is also a Nash matching.*

Thus, for instance, if all servers have linear and identical latency functions, then the best-case Nash achieves social optimum. The following theorem, on the other hand, gives general conditions under which *no Nash solution is optimal*.

Theorem 3. *Assuming non-identical but linear latency functions, there are instances of the peer matching game where no Nash equilibrium matching is optimal. Assuming that every server has the same latency function $\lambda(x)$ and $x \cdot \lambda(x)$ is non-convex, there are instances where no Nash equilibrium matching is optimal.*

On the other hand, the following general result shows that under a broad class of latency functions, every Nash solution can be generated by the greedy strategy (with an appropriate order of client arrival).

Theorem 4. *If servers have monotone increasing (though not necessarily identical) latency functions, then every Nash matching can be generated by the greedy scheme.*

Finally, if the clients' job is allowed to be split across multiple servers, then it turns out that *every Nash solution is optimal*. That is, the price of anarchy equals 1. A non-atomic model of service is actually used in practice by the KaZaa system.

7   Research Directions

Our model and results suggest several natural and intriguing research problems, which should be of interest to distributed systems in general and peer to peer networks in particular. We mention some of the most promising such directions.

7.1   Computing Nash Matchings

The Nash equilibrium is a celebrated result in game theory. Unfortunately, there is no polynomial time algorithm known for computing a Nash solution in *general games*. The peer matching game, however, is not a general game. In fact, with identical and linear latency (or more generally, the latency functions with convex $x \cdot \lambda(x)$), even the *best case* Nash can be computed in polynomial time, by using graph matching ideas [5, 4]. However, these algorithms require that the entire client-server graph be known to all the clients. It will be interesting to explore algorithms that are distributed and require only *local information* (i.e. each client knows only about its permissible servers).

7.2   From Greedy to Nash

The matching determined by the online greedy scheme is within a constant factor of the social optimum, but it may not be stable – some of the users may want to switch to a different server. It may be interesting to investigate how to transform a greedy matching into a Nash. Suppose that users get one chance to switch their server in each round. How many rounds are needed before a stable solution is found?

7.3   The Cost of Switching Servers

In the greedy scheme, a client is not allowed to switch after its initial selection – in effect, the cost for switching servers is *infinite*. On the other hand, Nash solutions assume that a user can switch servers at zero cost. Thus, Nash and greedy can be viewed as two extremes in this cost spectrum. A natural question to ask is this: suppose a user incurs a cost α whenever he switches its server; what is the price of anarchy?

The server cost model may also have interesting algorithmic implications. With the infinite switching cost, we have a simple, distributed, online algorithm for computing the equilibrium matching (i.e. the greedy). With zero switching cost, no such (distributed) algorithm is known. Is it possible that adding switching cost improves the algorithmic complexity of finding a stable solution?

7.4   Coping with a Dynamic Client Set

We have assumed a static client group. In practice, new clients constantly arrive and old ones leave. Little is know about the loss of efficiency in such a *dynamic* setting – it involves *both the lack of information about future arrivals as well as the lack of co-ordination*. One basic problem is to investigate the price of anarchy where we compare centralized optimum to a solution in which clients are always at Nash – that is, when-ever a new client arrives or an old one leaves, the remaining set recomputes a Nash matching. Next, it would be more realistic to consider this problem with a fixed switch-ing cost. Still more realistic would be the model where the cost of switching depends on the *state of the client* – e.g., the cost may monotonically increase with time for each client, reflecting its unwillingness to switch as its job nears completion.

7.5   Effect of Server Speeds

Our upper bound for the price of anarchy is worse when servers can have arbitrary speeds (i.e. the ratio bound is 2.5 vs. 2.15 for equal speed servers). Intriguingly, we know of no lower bound that shows that price of anarchy should be worse with hetero-geneous servers. It would be an interesting result to show that the price of anarchy with arbitrary speeds servers is never worse than with equal speed servers.

7.6   General Latency Functions

We have considered mostly linear or monomial latency functions. It would be worth investigating more general latency functions. In Section 6, we mentioned a few basic, isolated results in this direction, but much remains unknown. One very useful class to consider is the *piecewise linear* latency functions. We do not know of any non-trivial results for this class.

7.7   The Optimistic Nash

We have primarily considered the worst-case (pessimistic) Nash, except for the singular result of Theorem 2. The best-case Nash solutions are also compelling objects of study. With linear latency functions, perhaps the price of anarchy is modest enough to not worry about the best case. However, with higher order latency functions, the worst-case Nash may be too unattractive a solution, and it would be interesting to obtain bounds for the best-case Nash. It seems like a challenging problem.

7.8   Advertising Server Loads

The greedy matching, as perhaps any reasonable algorithm, requires the knowledge of current server loads. How should the load information be kept up-to-date and propa-gated to the clients? One simple idea is for each client to *probe* its permissible servers; the schemes in [2, 12] assume that the server either announces its load, or the client in-fers it through a test download. When there are many potential servers, this can be quite expensive. A possible direction to explore is to maintain either historical or current server load information in the system.

7.9   Truthfulness and Mechanism Design

Because P2P participants are assumed to be selfish, and there is no central authority, how can one ensure that players are truthful? In our context, what incentive does a server have to truthfully declare its load? It can lie both ways – if he benefits from serving many clients (e.g. through goodwill or ranking in the system), he may under-report, hoping to attract more clients; if he does not benefit, then he can over-report. Nisan and Ronen [7] have advocated using the VCG (Vickrey-Clarke-Grove) mechanism to compensate servers in a scheduling application. Ours is another natural setting where further research of this kind is needed.

References

1. A. Awerbuch, A. Azar, E. F. Grove, P. Krishnan, M. Y. Kao, and J. S. Vitter. Load balancing in the L_p norm. *Proc. 36th FOCS*, 1995, pp. 383–391.
2. D. Bernstein, Z. Feng, B. Levine, S. Zilberstein. Adaptive peer selection. *Proc. 2nd IPTPS*, 2003, pp. 237–246.
3. A. Czumaj and B. Vöcking. Tight bounds for worst-case equilibria. *Proc. 13th SODA*, 2002, pp. 413–420.
4. N. Harvey, R. Ladner, L. Lovász, and T. Tamir. Semi-matchings for bipartite graphs and load balancing. *Proc. 8th WADS*, 2003, pp. 294–306.
5. A. Kothari, S. Suri, C. D. Tóth, and Y. Zhou. On a server selection game among selfish clients. In preparation.
6. E. Koutsoupias and C. Papadimitriou. Worst-case equilibria. *Proc. 16th STACS*, 1999, pp. 404–413.
7. N. Nisan and A. Ronen. Computationally feasible VCG mechanisms. *Proc. 2nd Conf. on EC*, 2000, pp. 242–252.
8. C. Papadimitriou. Algorithms, games, and the Internet. *Proc. 33rd STOC*, 2001, pp. 749–753.
9. R. W. Rosenthal. A class of games possessing pure-strategy Nash equilibria. *Int. J. of Game Theory* 2:65–67, 1973.
10. T. Roughgarden. *Selfish Routing*. PhD thesis, Cornell University, 2002.
11. T. Roughgarden and E. Tardos. How Bad is Selfish Routing? *Journal of ACM* 49 (2):235–259, 2002.
12. M. Roussopoulos and M. Baker. CUP: Controlled Update Propagation in Peer-to-Peer networks. *USENIX Annual Technical Conference*, 2003, pp. 167–180.
13. S. Suri, C. D. Tóth, and Y. Zhou. Selfish load balancing and atomic congestion games. *Proc. 20th SoCG*, 2004, to appear.

Simple Efficient Load Balancing Algorithms for Peer-to-Peer Systems

David R. Karger[1] and Matthias Ruhl[2]

[1] MIT Computer Science and Artificial Intelligence Laboratory
Cambridge, MA 02139, USA
karger@csail.mit.edu
[2] IBM Almaden Research Center
San Jose, CA 95120, USA
ruhl@almaden.ibm.com

Abstract. Load balancing is a critical issue for the efficient operation of peer-to-peer networks. We give two new load-balancing protocols whose provable performance guarantees are within a constant factor of optimal. Our protocols refine the *consistent hashing* data structure that underlies the Chord (and Koorde) P2P network. Both preserve Chord's logarithmic query time and near-optimal data migration cost.

Our first protocol balances the distribution of *the key address space* to nodes, which yields a load-balanced system when the DHT maps items "randomly" into the address space. To our knowledge, this yields the first P2P scheme simultaneously achieving $O(\log n)$ degree, $O(\log n)$ look-up cost, and constant-factor load balance (previous schemes settled for any two of the three).

Our second protocol aims to directly balance the distribution of *items* among the nodes. This is useful when the distribution of items in the address space cannot be randomized – for example, if we wish to support range-searches on "ordered" keys. We give a simple protocol that balances load by moving nodes to arbitrary locations "where they are needed." As an application, we use the last protocol to give an optimal implementation of a distributed data structure for range searches on ordered data.

1 Introduction

A core problem in peer to peer systems is the distribution of items to be stored or computations to be carried out to the nodes that make up the system. A particular paradigm for such allocation, known as the *distributed hash table (DHT)*, has become the standard approach to this problem in research on peer-to-peer systems [1–4].

An important issue in DHTs is load-balance – the even distribution of items (or other load measures) to nodes in the DHT. All DHTs make some effort to load-balance, generally by (i) randomizing the DHT address associated with each item with a "good enough" hash function and (ii) making each DHT node

G.M. Voelker and S. Shenker (Eds.): IPTPS 2004, LNCS 3279, pp. 131–140, 2004.

responsible for a balanced portion of the DHT address space. Chord is a proto-typical example of this approach: its "random" hashing of nodes to a ring means that each node is responsible for only a small interval of the ring address space, while the random mapping of items means that only a limited number of items land in the (small) ring interval owned by any node.

This attempt to load-balance can fail in two ways. First, the typical "random" partition of the address space among nodes is not completely balanced. Some nodes end up with a larger portion of the addresses and thus receive a larger portion of the randomly distributed items. Second, some applications may preclude the randomization of data items' addresses. For example, to support range searching in a database application the items may need to be placed in a specific order, or even at specific addresses, on the ring. In such cases, we may find the items unevenly distributed in address space, meaning that balancing the address space among nodes is not adequate to balance the distribution of items among nodes. We give protocols to solve both of the load balancing challenges just described.

Address-Space Balancing. Current distributed hash tables do *not* evenly parti-tion the address space into which keys get mapped; some machines get a larger portion of it. Thus, even if keys are numerous and random, some machines re-ceive more than their fair share, by as much as a factor of $O(\log n)$ times the average.

To cope with this problem, many DHTs use *virtual nodes*: each real machine pretends to be several distinct machines, each participating independently in the DHT protocol. The machine's load is thus determined by summing over several virtual nodes', creating a tight concentration of (total) load near the average. As an example, the Chord DHT is based upon consistent hashing [5], which requires $O(\log n)$ virtual copies to be operated for every node.

Virtual nodes have drawbacks. Besides increased storage requirements, they demand network bandwidth. In general, to maintain connectivity of the network, every (virtual) node must frequently ping its neighbors, make sure they are still alive, and replace them with new neighbors if not. Running multiple virtual nodes creates a multiplicative increase in the (very valuable) network bandwidth consumed for maintenance.

Below, we will solve this problem by arranging for each node to activate *only one* of its $O(\log n)$ virtual nodes at any given time. The node will occasionally check its inactive virtual nodes, and may migrate to one of them if the distri-bution of load in the system has changed. Since only one virtual node is active, the real node need not pay the original Chord protocol's multiplicative increase in space and bandwidth costs. As in the original Chord protocol, our scheme gives each real node only a small number of "legitimate" addresses on the Chord ring, preserving Chord's (limited) protection against address spoofing by mali-cious nodes trying to disrupt the routing layer. (If each node could choose an arbitrary address, then a malicious node aiming to erase a particular item could take responsibility for that item's key and then refuse to serve the item.)

Another nice property of this protocol is that the "appropriate" state of the system (i.e., which virtual nodes are active), although random, is *independent* of the history of item and node arrivals and departures. This Markovian property means that the system can be analyzed as if it were static, with a fixed set of nodes and items; such analysis is generally much simpler than a dynamic, history-dependent analysis.

Combining our load-balancing scheme with the Koorde routing protocol [1], we get a protocol that simultaneously offers (i) $O(\log n)$ degree per real node, (ii) $O(\log n / \log \log n)$ lookup hops, and (iii) constant factor load balance. Previous protocols could achieve any two of these but not all 3 – generally speaking, achieving (iii) required operating $O(\log n)$ virtual nodes, which pushed the degree to $O(\log^2 n)$ and failed to achieve (i).

Item Balancing. A second load-balancing problem arises from certain database applications. A hash table randomizes the order of keys. This is problematic in domains for which order matters – for example, if one wishes to perform range searches over the data. This is one of the reasons binary trees are useful despite the faster lookup performance of hash tables. An order-preserving dictionary structure cannot apply a randomized (and therefore load balancing) hash function to its keys; it must take them as they are. Thus, even if the address space is evenly distributed among the nodes, an uneven distribution of the keys (e.g., all keys near 0) may lead to all load being placed on one machine.

In our work, we develop a load balancing solution for this problem. Unfortunately, the "limited assignments" approach discussed for key-space load balancing does not work in this case – it is easy to prove that if nodes can only choose from a few addresses, then certain load balancing tasks are beyond them. Our solution to this problem therefore allows nodes to move to arbitrary addresses; with this freedom we show that we can load-balance an arbitrary distribution of items, without expending much cost in maintaining the load balance.

Our scheme works through a kind of "work stealing" in which underloaded nodes migrate to portions of the address space occupied by too many items. The protocol is simple and practical, with all the complexity in its performance analysis.

Extensions of our protocol can also balance weighted items, where the weight of an item can for example reflect its storage size, or its popularity and the resulting bandwidth requirements.

Preliminaries. We design our solutions in the context of the Chord DHT [4] but our ideas seem applicable to a broader range of DHT solutions. Chord uses Consistent Hashing to assign items to nodes, achieving key-space load balance using $O(\log n)$ virtual nodes per real node. On top of Consistent Hashing, Chord layers a routing protocol in which each node maintains a set of $O(\log n)$ carefully chosen "neighbors" that it uses to route lookups in $O(\log n)$ hops. Our modifications of Chord are essentially modifications of the Consistent Hashing protocol assigning items to nodes; we can inherit unchanged Chord's neighbor structure and routing protocol. Thus, for the remainder of this paper, we ignore issues of routing and focus on the address assignment problem.

In this paper, we will use the following notation.

n is the number of nodes in system

N is the number of items stored in system (usually $N \gg n$)

ℓ_i is the number of items stored at node i

$L = N/n$ is the average (desired) load in the system

As discussed above, Chord maps items and nodes to a ring. We represent this space by the unit interval $[0, 1)$ with the addresses 0 and 1 are identified, so all addresses are a number between 0 and 1.

2   Address-Space Balancing

We will now give a protocol that improves consistent hashing in that every node is responsible for a $O(1/n)$ fraction of the address space with high probability (whp), without use of virtual nodes. This improves space and bandwidth usage by a logarithmic factor over traditional consistent hashing. The protocol is dynamic, with an insertion or deletion causing $O(\log \log n)$ other nodes to change their positions. Each node has a fixed set of $O(\log n)$ possible positions (called "virtual nodes"); it chooses exactly one of those virtual nodes to become *active* at any time – this is the only node that it actually operates. A node's set of virtual nodes depends only on the node itself (computed e.g. as hashes $h(i, 1), h(i, 2), \ldots, h(i, c \log n)$ of the node-id i), making malicious attacks on the network difficult.

We denote the address $(2b + 1)2^{-a}$ by $\langle a, b \rangle$, where a and b are integers satisfying $0 \leq a$ and $0 \leq b < 2^{a-1}$. This yields an unambiguous notation for all addresses with finite binary representation. We impose an ordering $\prec$ on these addresses according to the *length* of their binary representation (breaking ties by magnitude of the address). More formally, we set $\langle a, b \rangle \prec \langle a', b' \rangle$ iff $a < a'$ or $(a = a'$ and $b < b')$. This yields the following ordering:

$$0 = 1 \prec \frac{1}{2} \prec \frac{1}{4} \prec \frac{3}{4} \prec \frac{1}{8} \prec \frac{3}{8} \prec \frac{5}{8} \prec \frac{7}{8} \prec \frac{1}{16} \prec \cdots$$

We describe our protocol in terms of an ideal "locally optimal" state it wants to achieve.

Ideal State: Given any set of active virtual nodes, each (possibly inactive) virtual node "spans" a certain range of addresses between itself and the succeeding active virtual node. Each real node has activated the virtual node that spans the minimal possible (under the ordering just defined) address.

Note that the address space spanned by one virtual node depends on which other virtual nodes are active; that is why the above is a local optimality condition. Our protocol consists of the simple update rule that any node for which the local optimality condition is not satisfied, instead activates the virtual node that satisfies the condition. In other words, each node occasionally determines which of its $O(\log n)$ virtual nodes spans the smallest address (according to $\prec$), and activates that particular virtual node. Note that computing the "succeeding active node" for each of the virtual nodes can be done using standard Chord lookups.

Theorem 1. *The following statements are true for the above protocol, if every node has $c \log n$ virtual addresses that are chosen $\Omega(\log n)$-independently at random.*

(i) *For any set of nodes there is a unique ideal state.*

(ii) *Given any starting state, the local improvements will eventually lead to this ideal state.*

(iii) *In the ideal state of a network of n nodes, whp all neighboring pairs of active nodes will be at most $(4 + \varepsilon)/n$ apart, when $\varepsilon \leq 1/2$ and $c \geq 1/\varepsilon^2$. (This bound improves to $(2 + \varepsilon)/n$ for very small ε.)*

(iv) *Upon inserting or deleting a node into an ideal state, in expectation at most $O(\log \log n)$ nodes have to change their addresses for the system to again reach the ideal state.*

Proof Sketch: The unique ideal state can be constructed as follows. The virtual node immediately preceding address 1 will be active, since its real-node owner has no better choice and cannot be blocked by any other active node from spanning address 1. That real node's other virtual nodes will then be out of the running for activation. Of the remaining virtual nodes, the one most closely preceding $1/2$ will become active for the same reason, etc. We continue in this way down the ordered list of addresses. This greedy process clearly defines the unique ideal state, showing (i).

Claim (ii) can be shown by arguing that every local improvement reduces the "distance" of the current state to the ideal state (in an appropriately chosen metric). We defer the details to the full version of this paper (cf [6, Lemma 4.5]), where we also discuss the rate at which local improvements have to be performed in order to guarantee load balance.

For the following, we will assume that virtual addresses are chosen independently at random. As with to the original consistent hashing scheme [7], this requirement can be relaxed to $\Omega(\log n)$-independence by applying results of [8]

To prove (iii), recall how we constructed the ideal state for claim (i) above by successively assigning nodes to increasing addresses. In this process, suppose we are considering one of the first $(1 - \varepsilon)n$ addresses. Consider the interval I of length ε/n preceding this address. At least εn of the real nodes have not yet been given a place on the ring. Among the possible $c\varepsilon n \log n$ possible virtual positions of these nodes, with high probability one will land in the length-ε/n interval I under consideration. So whp, for each of the first $(1 - \varepsilon)n$ addresses in the order, the virtual node spanning that address will land within distance ε/n preceding the address. Since these first $(1 - \varepsilon)n$ addresses break up the unit circle into intervals of size at most $4/n$, claim (iii) follows. Note that for very small ε, the first $(1 - \varepsilon)n$ addresses actually break up the unit circle in intervals of size $2/n$, which explains the additional claim.

For (iv), it suffices to consider a deletion since the system is Markovian, i.e. the deletion and addition of a given node are symmetric and cause the same number of changes. Whenever a node claiming an address is deleted, its disappearance may reveal an address that some other node decides to claim, sacrificing its current spot, which may recursively trigger some other node to move. But each such migration means that the moving node has left behind no address as good as the one it is moving to claim. Note also that only a few nodes are close enough to any vacated address to claim it (distant ones will be shielded by some closer active node), and thus, as the address being vacated gets higher and higher in the order, it become less and less likely that any node that can take it will want it. We can show that after $O(\log \log n)$ such moves, no node assigned to a higher address is likely to have a virtual node close to the vacated address, so the movements stop. $\square$

We note that the above scheme is highly efficient to implement in the Chord P2P protocol, since one has direct access to the address of a successor. Moreover, the protocol can also function when nodes disappear without invoking a proper deletion protocol. By having every node occasionally check whether they should move, the system will eventually converge towards the ideal state. This can be done with insignificant overhead as part of the general maintenance protocols that have to run anyway to update the routing information of the Chord protocol.

One possibly undesirable aspect of the above scheme is that $O(\log \log n)$ nodes change their address upon the insertion or deletion of a node, because this will cause a $O(\log \log n/n)$ fraction of all items to be moved. However, since every node has only $O(\log n)$ possible positions, it can cache the items stored at previous active positions, and will eventually incur little data migration cost: when returning to a previous location, it already knows about the items stored there. Alternatively, if every real node activates $O(\log \log n)$ virtual nodes instead of just 1, we can reduce the fraction of items moved to $O(1/n)$ per node insertion, which is optimal within a constant factor. All other performance characteristics are carried over from the original scheme. It remains open to achieve $O(1/n)$ data migration *and* $O(1)$ virtual nodes while attaining all the other metrics we have achieved here.

Related Work. Two protocols that achieve near-optimal address-space load-balancing without the use of virtual nodes have recently been given [9, 10]. Our scheme improves upon them in three respects. First, in those protocols the address assigned to a node depends on the rest of the network, i.e. the address is *not* selected from a list of possible addresses that only depend on the node itself. This makes the protocols more vulnerable to malicious attacks. Second, in those protocols the address assignments depend on the construction history, making them harder to analyze. Third, their load-balancing guarantees are only shown for the "insertions only" case, while we also handle deletions of nodes and items.

3   Item Balancing

We have shown how to balance the address space, but sometimes this is not enough. Some applications, such as those aiming to support range-searching operations, need to specify a particular, non-random mapping of items into the address space. In this section, we consider a dynamic protocol that aims to balance load for *arbitrary* item distributions. To do so, we must sacrifice the previous protocol's restriction of each node to a small number of virtual node locations – instead, each node is free to migrate anywhere. This is unavoidable: if each node is limited to a bounded number of possible locations, then for any n nodes we can enumerate all the addresses they might possibly occupy, take two adjacent ones, and address all the items in between them: this assigns all the items to one unfortunate node.

Our protocol is randomized, and relies on the underlying P2P routing framework only insofar as it has to be able to contact "random" nodes in the system (in the full paper we show that this can be done even when the node distribution is skewed by the load balancing protocol). The protocol is the following (where ε is any constant, $0 < \varepsilon < 1$). Recall that each node stores the items whose addresses fall between the node's address and its predecessor's address, and that ℓ_j denotes the load on node j. Here, the index j runs from $1, 2, \ldots, n$ in the order of the nodes in the address space.

Item Balancing: Each node i occasionally contacts another node j at random. If $\ell_i \le \varepsilon \ell_j$ or $\ell_j \le \varepsilon \ell_i$ then the nodes perform a load balancing operation (assume wlog that $\ell_i > \ell_j$), distinguishing two cases:

Case 1: $i = j + 1$: In this case, i is the successor of j and the two nodes handle address intervals next to each other. Node j increases its address so that the $(\ell_i - \ell_j)/2$ items with lowest addresses get reassigned from node i to node j. Both nodes end up with load $(\ell_i + \ell_j)/2$.

Case 2: $i \ne j + 1$: If $\ell_{j+1} > \ell_i$, then we set $i := j + 1$ and go to case 1. Otherwise, node j moves between nodes $i - 1$ and i to capture half of node i's items. This means that node j's items are now handled by its former successor, node $j + 1$.

To state the performance of the protocol, we need the concept of a *half-life* [11], which is the time it takes for half the nodes or half the items in the system to arrive or depart.

Theorem 2. *If each node contacts $\Omega(\log n)$ other random nodes per half-life as well as whenever its own load doubles, then the above protocol has the following properties.*

(i) *With high probability, the load of all nodes is between $\frac{\varepsilon}{8} L$ and $\frac{16}{\varepsilon} L$.*

(ii) *The amortized number of items moved due to load balancing is $O(1)$ per item insertion or deletion, and $O(N/n)$ per node insertion or deletion.* $\square$

The proof of this theorem relies on the use of a potential function (some constant minus the entropy of the load distribution) that is large when the load is unbalanced. We show that item insertions and node departures cause only limited increases in the potential, while our balancing operation above causes a significant decrease in the potential if it is large.

The traffic caused by the update queries necessary for the protocol is sufficiently small that it can be buried within the maintenance traffic necessary to keep the P2P network alive. (Contacting a random node for load information only uses a tiny message, and does not result in any data transfers per se.) Of greater importance for practical use is the number of items transferred, which is optimal to within constants in an amortized sense.

Extensions and Applications. The protocol can also be used if items are replicated to improve fault-tolerance, e.g. when an item is stored not only on the node primarily responsible for it, but also on the $O(\log n)$ following nodes. In that setting, the load ℓ_j refers only to the number of items for which a node j is *primarily* responsible. Since the item movement cost of our protocol as well as the optimum increase by a factor of $O(\log n)$, our scheme remains optimal within a constant factor.

Our protocol can be adapted for the case when items have weights, and the load of a node is the sum of the weights of the items stored at the node. The weight of an item can reflect its size, or its bandwidth consumption, in case of items with different popularity. The analysis is similar; we can show that the insertion or deletion of an item of weight w causes an amortized weight of $O(w)$ to be moved. There is however, one restriction: the protocol can only balance the load upto what the items allow locally. For example, consider two nodes, one node storing a single item with weight 1, the other node a single item with weight 100. If these two nodes enter in a load exchange, then there is no exchange of items what will equalize the two loads.

The above protocol can provide load balance even for data that cannot be hashed. In particular, given an ordered data set, we may wish to map it to the $[0, 1)$ interval in an order-preserving fashion. Our protocol then supports the implementation of a range search data structure. Given a query key, we can use Chord's standard lookup function to find the first item following that key *in the keys' defined order*. Furthermore, given items a and b, the data structure can follow node successor pointers to return all items x stored in the system that satisfy $a \leq x \leq b$. We give the first such protocol that achieves an $O(\log n + Kn/N)$ query time (where K is the size of the output).

Related Work. Randomized protocols for load balancing by moving items have received much attention in the research community. A P2P algorithm similar to ours was studied in [12]. However, their algorithm only works when the set of nodes and items are fixed (i.e. without insertions or deletions), and they give no provable performance guarantees, only experimental evaluations.

A theoretical analysis of a similar protocol was given by Anagnostopoulos, Kirsch and Upfal [13], who also provide several further references. In their setting, however, items are assumed to be jobs that are executed at a fixed rate, i.e. items disappear from nodes at a fixed rate. Moreover, they analyze the average wait time for jobs, while we are more interested in the total number of items moved to achieve load balance.

In recent independent work, Ganesan and Bawa [14] consider a load balancing scheme similar to ours and point out applications to range searches. However, their scheme relies on being able to quickly find the least and most loaded nodes in the system. It is not clear how to support this operation efficiently without creating heavy network traffic for these nodes with extreme load.

Complex queries such as range searches are also an emerging research topic for P2P systems [15, 16]. An efficient range search data structure was recently given [17]. However, that work does not address the issue of load balancing the number of items per node, making the simplifying assumption that each node stores only one item. In that setting, the lookup times are $O(\log N)$ in terms of the number of items N, and not in terms of the number of nodes n. Also, $O(\log N)$ storage is used per data item, meaning a total storage of $O(N \log N)$, which is typically much worse than $O(N + n \log n)$.

4   Conclusion

We have given several provably efficient load balancing protocols for distributed data storage in P2P systems. (More details and analysis can be found in a thesis [6].) Our algorithms are simple, and easy to implement, so an obvious next research step should be a practical evaluation of these schemes.

In addition, several concrete open problems follow from our work. First, it might be possible to further improve the consistent hashing scheme as discussed at the end of section 2. Second, our range search data structure does not easily generalize to more than one order. For example when storing music files, one might want to index them by both artist and year, allowing range queries according to both orderings. Since our protocol rearranges the items according to the ordering, doing this for two orderings at the same time seems difficult. A simple solution is to rearrange not the items themselves, but just store pointers to them on the nodes. This requires far less storage, and makes it possible to maintain two or more orderings at once. The drawback is that it requires another level of indirection, which might be undesirable for fault-tolerance reasons. Lastly, permitting nodes to choose arbitrary addresses in our item balancing protocol makes it easier for malicious nodes to disrupt the operation of the P2P network. It would be interesting to find counter-measures for this problem.

Acknowledgments

We would like to thank the anonymous reviewers for their helpful comments.

References

1. Kaashoek, F., Karger, D.R.: Koorde: A Simple Degree-optimal Hash Table. In: Proceedings IPTPS. (2003)
2. Malkhi, D., Naor, M., Ratajczak, D.: Viceroy: A Scalable and Dynamic Emulation of the Butterfly. In: Proceedings PODC. (2002) 183–192
3. Ratnasamy, S., Francis, P., Handley, M., Karp, R., Shenker, S.: A Scalable Content-Addressable Network. In: Proceedings ACM SIGCOMM. (2001) 161–172

4. Stoica, I., Morris, R., Karger, D., Kaashoek, F., Balakrishnan, H.: Chord: A Scalable Peer-to-peer Lookup Service for Internet Applications. In: Proceedings ACM SIGCOMM. (2001) 149–160
5. Karger, D., Lehman, E., Leighton, T., Levine, M., Lewin, D., Panigrahy, R.: Consistent Hashing and Random Trees: Tools for Relieving Hot Spots on the World Wide Web. In: Proceedings STOC. (1997) 654–663
6. Ruhl, M.: Efficient Algorithms for New Computational Models. PhD thesis, Massachusetts Institute of Technology (2003)
7. Lewin, D.M.: Consistent Hashing and Random Trees: Algorithms for Caching in Distributed Networks. Master's thesis, Massachusetts Institute of Technology (1998)
8. Schmidt, J.P., Siegel, A., Srinivasan, A.: Chernoff-Hoeffding bounds for applications with limited independence. In: Proceedings SODA. (1993) 331–340
9. Adler, M., Halperin, E., Karp, R.M., Vazirani, V.V.: A Stochastic Process on the Hypercube with Applications to Peer-to-Peer Networks. In: Proceedings STOC. (2003) 575–584
10. Naor, M., Wieder, U.: Novel Architectures for P2P Applications: the Continuous-Discrete Approach. In: Proceedings SPAA. (2003) 50–59
11. Liben-Nowell, D., Balakrishnan, H., Karger, D.: Analysis of the Evolution of Peer-to-Peer Systems. In: Proceedings PODC. (2002) 233–242
12. Rao, A., Lakshminarayanan, K., Surana, S., Karp, R., Stoica, I.: Load Balancing in Structured P2P Systems. In: Proceedings IPTPS. (2003)
13. Anagnostopoulos, A., Kirsch, A., Upfal, E.: Stability and Efficiency of a Random Local Load Balancing Protocol. In: Proceedings FOCS. (2003) 472–481
14. Ganesan, P., Bawa, M.: Distributed Balanced Tables: Not Making a Hash of it all. Technical Report 2003-71, Stanford University, Database Group (2003)
15. Harren, M., Hellerstein, J.M., Huebsch, R., Loo, B.T., Shenker, S., Stoica, I.: Complex Queries in DHT-based Peer-to-Peer Networks. In: Proceedings IPTPS. (2002) 242–250
16. Huebsch, R., Hellerstein, J.M., Lanham, N., Loo, B.T., Shenker, S., Stoica, I.: Querying the Internet with PIER. In: Proceedings VLDB. (2003) 321–332
17. Aspnes, J., Shah, G.: Skip Graphs. In: Proceedings SODA. (2003) 384–393

The Case for a Hybrid P2P Search Infrastructure

Boon Thau Loo[1], Ryan Huebsch[1], Ion Stoica[1], and Joseph M. Hellerstein[1,2]

[1] UC Berkeley, Berkeley CA 94720, USA
{boonloo,huebsch,istoica}@cs.berkeley.edu
[2] Intel Research Berkeley
jmh@cs.berkeley.edu

Abstract. Popular P2P file-sharing systems like Gnutella and Kazaa use unstructured network designs. These networks typically adopt flooding-based search techniques to locate files. While flooding-based techniques are effective for locating highly replicated items, they are poorly suited for locating rare items. As an alternative, a wide variety of structured P2P networks such as distributed hash tables (DHTs) have been recently proposed. Structured networks can efficiently locate rare items, but they incur significantly higher overheads than unstructured P2P networks for popular files. Through extensive measurements of the Gnutella network from multiple vantage points, we argue for a hybrid search solution, where structured search techniques are used to index and locate rare items, and flooding techniques are used for locating highly replicated content. To illustrate, we present experimental results of a prototype implementation that runs at multiple sites on PlanetLab and participates live on the Gnutella network.

1 Introduction

Unstructured networks such as Gnutella [1] and Kazaa [4] have been widely used in file-sharing applications. These networks are organized in an ad-hoc fashion and queries are flooded in the network for a bounded number of hops (TTL). While these networks are effective for locating highly replicated items, they are less so for rare items[1].

As an alternative, there have been proposals for using inverted indexes on distributed hash tables (DHTs) [8]. In the absence of network failures, DHTs guarantee perfect recall, and are able to locate matches within a small number of hops (usually $log(n)$ hops, where n is the number of nodes). However, DHTs may incur significant bandwidth for publishing the content, and for executing more complicated search queries such as multiple-attribute queries. Despite significant research efforts to address the limitations of both flooding and DHT search techniques, there is still no consensus on the best P2P design for searching,

In this paper, we measure the traffic characteristics of the Gnutella network from multiple vantage points located on PlanetLab [6]. Our findings confirm that while Gnutella is effective for locating highly replicated items, it is less suited for locating rare items. In particular, queries for rare items have a low recall rate (i.e., the queries fail to return files even though the files are actually stored in the network). In addition, these queries have poor response times. While these observations have been made before, to

---

[1] In this paper, we will use the terms "files" and "items" interchangeably.

G.M. Voelker and S. Shenker (Eds.): IPTPS 2004, LNCS 3279, pp. 141–150, 2004.

the best of our knowledge, our study is the first to quantify them in a real network. For example, we show that as many as 18% of all queries return no results, despite the fact that for two thirds of these queries, there are results available in the network.

We use extensive measurements to analyze the traffic characteristics of Gnutella, and based on our observations, we propose a simple hybrid design that aims to combine the best of both worlds: use flooding techniques for locating popular items, and structured (DHT) search techniques for locating rare items.

We find that such a design is particularly appropriate for existing P2P file-sharing systems in which the number of replicas follow a long tailed distributions: flooding-based techniques work best for the files at the head of the distribution, while DHT techniques work best for the files at the tail of the distribution.

To evaluate our proposal, we present experimental results of a hybrid file-sharing implementation that combines Gnutella with PIER, a DHT-based relational query engine [11]. Our prototype runs at multiple sites on the PlanetLab testbed, and participates live on the Gnutella network.

2   Setting and Methodology

To analyze the Gnutella network, we have instrumented the LimeWire client software [5]. Our client can participate in the Gnutella network either as an ultrapeer or leaf node, and can log all incoming and outgoing Gnutella messages. In addition, our client has the ability to inject queries into the network and gather the incoming results.

The current Gnutella network uses several optimizations to improve the performance over the original flat flooding design. Some of the most notable optimizations include the use of *ultrapeers* [3] and *dynamic querying* [2] techniques. Ultrapeers perform query processing on the behalf of their *leaf nodes*. When a node joins the network as a leaf, it selects a number of ultrapeers, and then it publishes its file list to those ultrapeers.

A query for a leaf node is sent to an ultrapeer which floods the query to its ultrapeer neighbors up to a limited number of hops. Our crawl reveals that most ultrapeers today support either 30 or 75 leaf nodes[2]. Dynamic querying is a search technique whereby queries that return fewer results are re-flooded deeper into the network. Our modified client supports both of these optimizations.

2.1   Gnutella Search Quality

To estimate the size of the Gnutella network, we began our study by performing a crawl of Gnutella. To increase the accuracy of our estimation, the crawl was performed in

---

[2] This is confirmed by the development history of the LimeWire software: newer LimeWire ultrapeers support 30 leaf nodes and maintain 32 ultrapeer neighbors, while the older ultrapeers support 75 leaf nodes and 6 ultrapeer neighbors. As a side note, in newer versions of the LimeWire client, leaf nodes publish Bloom filters of the keywords in their files to ultrapeers [7, 2]. There have also been proposals to cache these Bloom filters at neighboring nodes. Bloom filters reduce publishing and searching costs in Gnutella, but preclude substring and wildcard searching (which are similarly unsupported in DHT-based search schemes.)

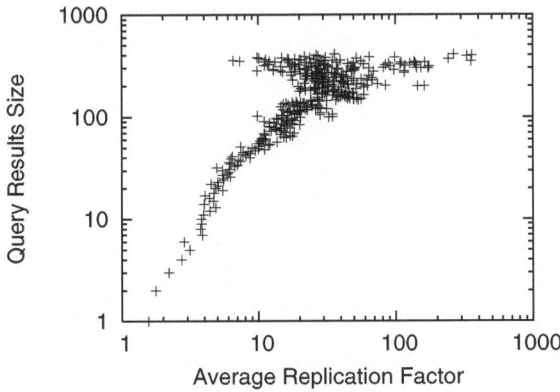

Fig. 1. Correlating Query Results Size vs. Average Replication Factor.

parallel from 30 ultrapeers for about 45 minutes. This parallel crawl was carried out on 11 Oct 2003 at around noon (Pacific time). The network size of Gnutella at the time of the crawl was around 100,000 nodes, and there were roughly 20 million files in the system.

Next, we turn our attention to analyzing the search quality of Gnutella, both in terms of *recall* and *response time*. The recall of a query is defined as the number of results returned divided by the number of results actually available in the network. Results are distinguished by filename, host, and filesize. Thus, each replica of a file is counted as a distinct result. Given the difficulty of taking a snapshot of all files in the network at the time the query is issued, we approximate the total number of results available in the system by issuing the same query simultaneously from all 30 PlanetLab ultrapeers, and taking the union of the results. This approximation is appropriate for the following two reasons. First, as the number of PlanetLab ultrapeers exceeds 15, there is little increase in the total number of results (see Fig. 3). This suggests that the number of results returned by all 30 ultrapeers is a reasonable approximation of the total number of results available in the network. Second, because this approximation underestimates the number of total results in the network, the recall value that we compute is an overestimation of the actual value.

We obtained Gnutella query traces, and chose 700 distinct queries from these traces to replay at each of the PlanetLab ultrapeers. To factor out the effects of workload fluctuations, we replayed queries at three different times. In total, we generated 63,000 queries ($700 \times 30 \times 3$). We make three observations based on the results returned by these queries.

First, as expected, there is a strong correlation between the number of results returned for a given query, and the number of replicas in the network for each item in the query result set. The *replication factor* of an item is defined as the total number of identical copies of the item in the network. Again, to approximate this number, we count the number of items with the same filename in the union of the query results obtained by the 30 ultrapeers for the same query. We then compute the average replication factor of a query by averaging the replication factors across all distinct filenames in the query result set. Figure 1 summarizes our results, where the Y-axis shows query results set

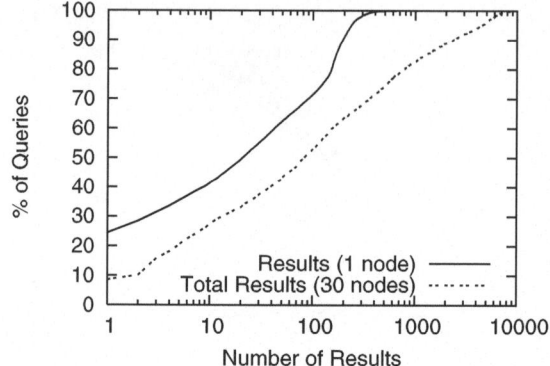

Fig. 2. Result size CDF of Queries issued from 30 Ultrapeers.

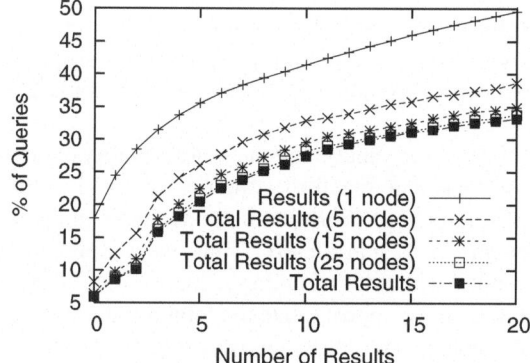

Fig. 3. Result size CDF for Queries $\leq$ 20 results.

size, and the X-axis shows the average replication factor averaged across all queries for each results set size. In general, queries with small result sets return mostly rare items, while queries with large result sets return both rare and popular items, with the bias towards popular items.

Second, our results demonstrate the effectiveness of Gnutella in finding highly replicated content. Figure 2 plots the CDF of the number of results returned by all queries (the *Results* curve), and a lower bound on the total number of matching items per query (the *Total Results* curve). We compute this lower bound by taking the union of all result sets obtained by the 30 ultrapeers for each query. Note that there are queries returning as many as 1,500 results, which would seem more than sufficient for most file-sharing uses. In addition, Fig. 4 shows that the queries with large result sets also have good response times. For queries that return more than 150 results, we obtain the first result in 6 seconds on average.

Third, our results show the *ineffectiveness* of Gnutella in locating rare items. Figure 4 shows that the average response time of queries that return few results is poor. For queries that return a single result, 73 seconds elapsed on average before receiving the first result.

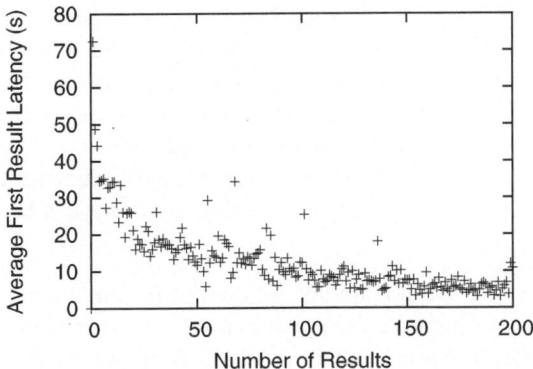

Fig. 4. Correlating Result Size vs. First Result Latency.

An important point to note is that queries that return few items are quite prevalent. Figure 3 shows the results of the same experiment as Fig. 2, limited to queries that return at most 20 results for 5, 15 and 25 ultrapeers. Note that while 29% of queries receive more than 100 results, and 9% receive more than 200 results, there are 41% of queries that receive 10 or fewer results, and 18% of queries that receive *no* results. For a large fraction of queries that receive no results, matching results are in fact available in the network at the time of the query. Taking the union of results from all 30 ultrapeers for each query, the results improve considerably: only 27% of queries receive 10 or fewer results, and only 6% of queries receive no results. This means that there is an opportunity to reduce the percentage of queries that receive no results from 18% to at least 6%, or equivalently to reduce the number of queries that receive no results by at least 66%. We say "at least" because the union of results is an underestimation of the total number of results available in the network.

2.2   Increase the Search Horizon?

An obvious technique to locate more rare items in Gnutella would be to increase the search horizon using larger TTLs. While this would not help search latency, it could improve query recall. As the search horizon increases, the number of query messages sent will increase almost exponentially. Given that queries that return few results are fairly common, such aggressive flooding to locate rare items is unlikely to scale. In future work, we plan to quantify the impact of increasing the search horizon on the overall system load.

2.3   Summary

Our Gnutella measurements reveal the following findings:

– Gnutella is highly effective for locating popular items. Not only are these items retrieved in large quantities, the queries also have good response times.

- Gnutella is less effective for locating rare items: 41% of all queries receive 10 or fewer results, and 18% of queries receive *no* results. Furthermore, the results have poor response times. For queries that return a single result, the first result arrives after 73 seconds on average. For queries that return 10 or fewer results, 50 seconds elapsed on average before receiving the first result.
- There is a significant opportunity to increase the query recall for locating rare items. For instance, the number of queries that return no results can be reduced from 18% to at least 6%.

Thus, there are a considerable number of queries for rare items, and there is a considerable opportunity to improve the recall and response times of these queries. Furthermore, we note that flooding more aggressively is not an answer to this problem, as flooding with a higher TTL will not necessarily decrease the response time, and will significantly increase the system load.

3   The Case for Hybrid

Various research efforts have proposed DHTs as an alternative to unstructured networks like Gnutella, arguing that DHTs can improve query performance. In this section, we explore the feasibility of a DHT-based query system. In a flooding scheme, *queries are moved towards the data*. In contrast, DHT-based search schemes move *both queries and data*, causing them to rendezvous in the network. This movement typically consists of two phases. First, a *content publishing* phase moves copies of data into traditional inverted files which are then indexed by keyword in a DHTs. They are also known as inverted indexes. Each inverted file comprises a set of unique file identifiers (a *posting list*) for a distinct keyword. Secondly, a *query execution* phase performs boolean search by routing the query via the DHT to all sites that host a keyword in the query, and executing a distributed join of the postings list entries of matching items.

While DHT-based search provides perfect recall in the absence of network failures, a full-fledged DHT implementation has its own drawbacks. The content publishing phase can consume large amounts of bandwidth compared to queries that retrieve sufficient results via flooding in an unstructured network. Consider the query "Britney Spears" that requests all songs from this popular artist. "Britney" and "Spears" are popular keywords with large posting lists. The publishing costs of building the inverted indexes for these two keywords are high. A "Britney Spears" query also requires shipping large posting lists to perform the distributed join. Recent back-of-the-envelope calculations [12] suggest that shipping large posting lists over DHTs is bandwidth-expensive. While compression techniques and Bloom filters would reduce the bandwidth requirements of publishing, a flooding scheme that does not incur any publishing overheads is both simpler and more efficient for such queries.

On the other hand, queries over rare items are less bandwidth-intensive to compute, since fewer posting list entries are involved. To validate the latter claim, we replayed 70,000 Gnutella queries over a sample of 700,000 files[3] using a distributed join algorithm over DHTs [11]. We observed that on average, queries that return 10 or fewer

---

[3] These queries and files were collected from 30 ultrapeers as described in Section 2.1.

results require shipping 7 times fewer posting list entries compared to the average across all queries. This motivates a *hybrid search infrastructure*, where the DHT is used to locate rare items, and flooding techniques are used for searching highly replicated items.

3.1 Hybrid Techniques

The hybrid search infrastructure utilizes *selective publishing* techniques that identify and publish only rare items into the DHT. Different heuristics can be used to identify which items are rare. One simple heuristic is based on our initial observation in Section 2.1: rare files are those that are seen in small result sets. In essence, the DHT is used to cache elements of small result sets. This scheme is simple, but suffers from the fact that many rare items may not have been previously queried and found, and hence will not be published via a caching scheme. For these items, other techniques must be used to determine that they are rare. For example, publishing could be based on well-known term frequencies, and/or by maintaining and possibly gossiping historical summary statistics on file replicas.

This hybrid infrastructure can easily be implemented if all the ultrapeers are organized into the DHT overlay. Each ultrapeer is responsible for identifying and publishing rare files from its leaf nodes. Search is first performed via conventional flooding techniques of the overlay neighbors. If not enough results are returned within a predefined time, the query is reissued as a DHT query.

3.2 Network Churn

A practical concern of using DHTs is the network churn. A high network churn rate would increase the DHT maintenance overhead to manage publishing (and unpublishing). To understand the impact of churn, we measure the connection lifetimes of ultrapeer and leaf neighbors from two leaf nodes and two ultrapeers over 72 hours. The connection lifetimes we measure are a lower bound on the session lifetime as nodes may change their neighbor sets during the course of their Gnutella session. We make the following two observations.

First, the measured average connection lifetimes of leaf and ultrapeer nodes are 58 minutes and 93 minutes respectively. Ultrapeers have 1.5 times longer lifetimes than leaf nodes. To reduce the overheads of DHT maintenance, only stable ultrapeers with more resources should be used as DHT nodes.

Second, the measured *median* connection lifetimes of leaf and ultrapeer nodes are only 13 minutes and 16 minutes respectively. Since the median lifetime is much lower than the mean, by discounting the short-lived nodes we have a fairly stable network. For instance, if we eliminate all leaf nodes whose lifetimes exceed 10 minutes, the average lifetime of the remaining nodes is 106 minutes[4]. In general, the longer a node is up, the longer one can expect a node to stay up. Hence, to address the issue of stale data in the DHT, file information of short-lived nodes should simply not be indexed. These short-lived nodes are not useful sources of data anyway since they are likely to disconnect before others can download their content.

---

[4] This is consistent with the results reported by LimeWire's measurements of 300 connections over several days[7].

4   Preliminary Experimental Results

To evaluate our hybrid design, we deploy a number of *hybrid* clients on PlanetLab that participate on the Gnutella network as ultrapeers. In addition, these clients are plugged into a DHT-based search engine built on top of PIER [11], a P2P relational query engine over DHTs. Our deployment should be seen as a strawman; a fully-deployed hybrid infrastructure would require an upgrade of all existing clients.

In addition to the traditional distributed join algorithm discussed earlier for searching, the PIER search engine also utilizes *Join Indexes*, by storing the *full text* (i.e. the filename) redundantly with each posting list entry. The search query is hence sent only to a single node hosting any one of the search terms, and the remaining search terms are filtered locally. This technique incurs extra publishing overheads, which are prohibitive for text document search, but tolerable for indexing short filenames.

Each hybrid ultrapeer monitors query results from its regular Gnutella traffic. These query results are responses to queries forwarded by the ultrapeer. Query results that belong to queries with fewer than 20 results are then published into the DHT. The publishing rate is approximately one file per 2-3 seconds per node. Each published file and corresponding posting list entries incurs a bandwidth overhead of 3.5 KB per file. Join Indexes increase the publishing overhead to 4 KB per file. A large part of the bandwidth consumption is due to the overheads of Java serialization and self-describing tuples in PIER, both of which could in principle be eliminated.

We test the hybrid search technique in PlanetLab on leaf queries of the hybrid ultrapeers. Leaf queries that return no results within 30 seconds via Gnutella are re-queried using the PIER search engine. PIER returns the first result within 10-12 seconds, with and without Join Indexes respectively. While decreasing the timeout to invoke PIER would improve the aggregate latency, this would also increase the likelihood of issuing extra queries. As part of our future work, we plan to study the tradeoffs between the timeout and query workload. Note that the average latency for these queries to return their first result in Gnutella is 65 seconds (see Fig. 4). Hence, the hybrid approach would reduce the latency by about 25 seconds.

In addition, the hybrid solution reduces the number of queries that receive no results in Gnutella by 18%. This reduction serves as a lower bound of the potential benefits of the hybrid system. The reason why this value is significantly lower than the potential 66% reduction in the number of queries that receive no results is two fold:

– Unlike Gnutella measurements reported in Section 2.1 where queries are proactively flooded from many ultrapeers, in our experiment, we consider only the files that are returned as results to previous queries. Thus, this scheme will not return the rare items that were not queried during our experiments. Employing simple optimizations in which peers publish proactively their list of rare items should considerably boost the benefits of our scheme.

– As the number of clients that implement our scheme increase, we expect the coverage to improve as well. The coverage would be even better in a full-fledged implementation in which each ultrapeer would be responsible for a set of leaf nodes from which they would identify and publish rare items.

Using Join Indexes, each query needs to be sent to only one node. The cost of each query is hence dominated by shipping the PIER query itself, which is approximately 850 B. The distributed join algorithm incurs a 20 KB overhead for each query. These results indicate that the benefits of reducing per-query bandwidth might outweigh the publishing overheads of storing the filename redundantly, which makes Join Indexes a more attractive option.

5   Related Studies

A recent study [9] has shown that most file downloads are for highly replicated items. One might think that their findings contradict our analysis in Section 2.1 that shows that queries for rare items are substantial. However, the two studies focus on different aspects of Gnutella's workload. First, we measure result set sizes of queries, while their study measures download requests. Downloads only reflect successful queries, in instances when users have identified matching items from the result set that satisfied their search queries. This approach excludes queries that failed to find matching rare items even when they exist somewhere in the network, or return too few results that are of relevance to the search query. Second, both studies correctly reflect different aspects of the Zipfian distributions. Their study shows the *head* of the Zipfian popularity distribution, and hence they measure the download requests based on the items that match the top 50 query requests seen. In contrast, our study focuses on the long *tail* of the distribution as well. While individual rare items in the tail may not be requested frequently, these queries represents a substantial fraction of the workload, and are worth optimizing.

A separate study [10] has shown that the popularity distribution of a file-sharing workload is flatter than what we would expect from a Zipfian distribution. The most popular items were found to be significantly less popular than a Zipfian distribution would predict. Our proposed hybrid infrastructure would still apply here, utilizing flooding-based schemes for items in the "flattened head" region, and DHTs for indexing and searching for items in the tail of the distribution.

6   Conclusion

In this paper, we have presented the case for a hybrid search infrastructure that utilizes flooding for popular items and the DHT for searching rare items. To support our case, we have performed live measurements of the Gnutella workload from different vantage points in the Internet. We found that a substantial fraction of queries returned very few or no results at all, despite the fact that the results were available in the network. Preliminary experimental results from deploying 50 ultrapeers on Gnutella showed that our hybrid scheme has the potential to improve the recall and response times when searching for rare items, while incurring low bandwidth overheads.

Acknowledgements

The authors would like to thank Shawn Jeffery, Karthik Lakshminarayanan, Sylvia Ratnasamy, Sean Rhea, Timothy Roscoe, Scott Shenker, Lakshminarayanan Subramanian and Shelley Zhuang for their insights and suggestions. We thank the anonymous reviewers for their comments. This research was funded by NSF grants IIS-0205647, IIS-0208588, IIS-0209108 and Intel Research Berkeley.

References

1. Gnutella. http://gnutella.wego.com.
2. Gnutella Proposals for Dynamic Querying.
   http://www9.limewire.com/developer/dynamic_query.html.
3. Gnutella Ultrapeers. http://rfc-gnutella.sourceforge.net/Proposals/
   Ultrapeer/Ultrapeers.htm.
4. Kazaa. http://www.kazza.com.
5. Limewire.org. http://www.limewire.org/.
6. PlanetLab. http://www.planet-lab.org/.
7. Query Routing for the Gnutella Network. http://www.limewire.com/developer/
   query_routing/keyword_routing.htm/.
8. BALAKRISHNAN, H., KAASHOEK, M. F., KARGER, D., MORRIS, R., AND STOICA, I.
   Looking Up Data in P2P Systems. *Communications of the ACM, Vol. 46, No. 2* (Feb. 2003).
9. CHAWATHE, Y., RATNASAMY, S., BRESLAU, L., LANHAM, N., AND SHENKER, S. Making Gnutella-like P2P Systems Scalable. In *Proceedings of ACM SIGCOMM 2003*.
10. GUMMADI, K. P., DUNN, R. J., SAROIU, S., GRIBBLE, S. D., LEVY, H. M., AND ZAHORJAN, J. Measurement, Modeling and Analysis of a Peer-to-Peer File-Sharing Workload.
    In *Proceedings of the 19th ACM Symposium of Operating Systems Principles (SOSP-19)*
    (Bolton Landing, New York, October 2003).
11. HUEBSCH, R., HELLERSTEIN, J. M., LANHAM, N., LOO, B. T., SHENKER, S., AND STOICA, I. Querying the Internet with PIER. In *Proceedings of 19th International Conference
    on Very Large Databases (VLDB)* (Sep 2003).
12. LI, J., LOO, B. T., HELLERSTEIN, J., KAASHOEK, F., KARGER, D., AND MORRIS, R. On
    the Feasibility of Peer-to-Peer Web Indexing and Search. In *Proceedings of 2nd International
    Workshop on Peer-to-Peer Systems (IPTPS '03)*.

Making Peer-to-Peer Keyword Searching Feasible Using Multi-level Partitioning

Shuming Shi, Guangwen Yang, Dingxing Wang,
Jin Yu, Shaogang Qu, and Ming Chen

Department of Computer Science and Technology, Tsinghua University
Beijing, P.R. China
{ssm01,yujin,qsg02,cm01}@mails.tsinghua.edu.cn,
{ygw,dxwang}@mail.tsinghua.edu.cn

Abstract. This paper discusses large scale keyword searching on top of peer-to-peer (P2P) networks. The state-of-the-art keyword searching techniques for unstructured and structured P2P systems are query flooding and inverted list intersection respectively. However, it has been demonstrated that P2P-based large scale full-text searching is not feasible by using either of the two techniques. We propose in this paper a new index partitioning and building scheme, multi-level partitioning (MLP), and discuss its implementation on top of P2P networks. MLP can dramatically reduce bisection bandwidth consumption and end-user latency compared with the partition-by-keyword scheme. And comparing with partition-by-document, it need only broadcast a query to moderate number of peers to generate precise results.

1 Introduction

It still remains a challenge to perform full-text keyword searching on top of P2P networks. Although dedicated search engines (like Google [5]) can be used to index P2P contents, there are potentially several advantages (e.g. data freshness, scalability, and availability) for P2P systems to support full-text search by themselves.

Two classes of techniques have been proposed for keyword searching in P2P networks: query flooding and inverted list intersection. Unstructured P2P systems, such as Gnutella [4] and KaZaA [9], naturally support keyword searching by flooding queries to some or all peers. Another kind of P2P networks (structured P2P systems), such as CAN [13], Chord [17], Pastry [15], Tapestry [23], and SkipNet [12], don't support full text searching directly. Since they implement distributed hash tables (DHTs), keyword searching can be easily realized via distributing inverted indices among DHT hosts by keywords. A query with k keywords can then be answered by at most k hosts through the intersection of inverted lists. This approach is adopted by some recent proposals [14][18][2][6][7] to add full text searching functionality to structured P2P systems.

However, it has been demonstrated in [10] that the above two techniques and their existing optimizations are not feasible to perform large scale keyword search. The reason is that the bandwidth consumed exceeds the internet's capacity. The large bandwidth consumption translate to high end user latency, which is another critical performance requirement. Furthermore, if a node hosting the reverse index of a popular keyword is down, the high-availability of searching is lost.

G.M. Voelker and S. Shenker (Eds.): IPTPS 2004, LNCS 3279, pp. 151–161, 2004.

From the viewpoint of index partitioning, the above two techniques partition indices by document and keyword, respectively. Both of the two partitioning schemes have their merits and drawbacks. Although there have been several hybrid index organization and partitioning schemes [1][16], but they are not directly applicable to large scale, self organized, and dynamic P2P systems.

In this paper, we propose a hybrid index partitioning scheme, multi-level partitioning (MLP), which is adaptive and can achieve a good tradeoff between partition-by-keyword and partition-by-document. We describe in this paper the design of MLP on top of SkipNet [12]. MLP can dramatically reduce bisection backbone bandwidth consumption and communication latency comparing with the partition-by-keyword scheme. And, comparing with partition-by-document, it needs only to send a query to moderate number of peers to generate precise results.

The rest of the paper is organized as follows. In section 2, we introduce briefly SkipNet and index partitioning as the background. Section 3 presents multi-level partitioning and illustrates how to implement it on top of structured P2P networks. Section 4 describes the experiment results. Related works are discussed in section 5, and we conclude in section 6.

2   Background

MLP is designed and implemented on top of SkipNet [12], to which we will first give a brief introduction. We will also briefly describe index building and partitioning techniques used in existing P2P keyword searching systems.

2.1   SkipNet

SkipNet organizes nodes into a circular distributed data structure. Any node in Skip-Net has a lexicographic ID together with a numeric ID. SkipNet contains multiple levels of rings where ring members are lexicographically ordered according to node's lexicographic ID.

One of the most important features of SkipNet is its supporting for CLB (constrained load balancing), that is, data can be uniformly distributed across a well-defined subset of the nodes in the system. The ID of any data object in SkipNet has the format of "domain!nid". The "domain" part is actually a lexicographic prefix that specifies the set of nodes over which DHT load balance should be performed. The "nid" part determines the specific node on which the data object should be located. Please refer to [12] for more details of SkipNet.

2.2   Index Building and Partitioning

Inverted index is the most widely used indexing structure in full-text searching systems. It comprises many *inverted lists*, one for each word. An inverted list for a word contains all the identifiers of documents in which the word appears.

There are two common P2P index partitioning strategies: *partition-by-document* and *partition-by-keyword*. With partition-by-document, each host maintains a local inverted index of the documents for which it is responsible. Using this strategy, each query must be flooded to all peers. The partition-by-keyword strategy assigns each keyword undivided to a single node, and each node maintains the inverted lists of some keywords. For a query that contains k keywords, at most k nodes are needed to be contacted, avoiding flooding. However, as keyword intersection requires that one or more inverted lists be sent over the network, bandwidth consumption and transmission time can be substantial.

3 Multi-level Partitioning

Multi-level partitioning (MLP) is a P2P-based hybrid partition strategy with two features: uniformity and latency locality. In this section, we describe the main idea of MLP (in section 3.1) and its implementation on top of P2P networks (in section 3.2).

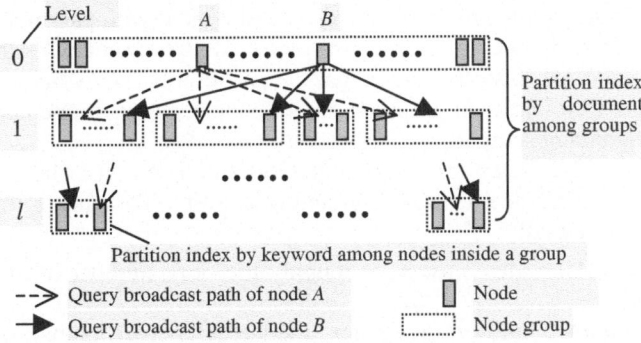

Fig. 1. Node group hierarchy and multi-level partitioning

3.1 Multi-level Partitioning

The definition of MLP relies on a node group hierarchy. In the hierarchy, all nodes are logically divided into k groups (not necessarily to be equal size), and nodes of each group are further divided as k sub-groups. Repeat this process to obtain a node hierarchy with l levels, as shown Figure-1.

Given the hierarchical node groups, the global inverted index is partitioned by document among groups, that is, each group maintains the local inverted index for all documents belonging to this group. Now consider how to maintain the index for a group on level l and how to process a query.

Group index maintenance. For each group on level l, the index is partitioned among nodes according to the partition-by-keyword scheme, that is, each node in the group is responsible for the inverted lists of some keywords. As a result, the group index is distributed among all nodes in the group. When building the index, all nodes must have roughly the same number of inverted lists on them to guarantee the balance of storage utilization. We will illustrate, in Section 3.2, how to achieve this on top of P2P networks.

Query processing. Take a query (initiated from node A) containing keyword w_1 and w_2 as an example. The query is broadcasted from node A to all groups of level 1 (see Figure 1), and down to all groups of next levels, until level l is reached. For each group in level l, the two nodes which contain the inverted lists of keyword w_1 and w_2 are responsible for answering the query. In each group, the two inverted lists are intersected to generate the search results of the group. And then, the search results from all groups are combined level by level and sent back to node A. We can learn from the query processing process that, if all nodes have roughly the same number of inverted lists on them, then they have equal chance to answer a query request. As a result, no node will be overloaded and load balance is guaranteed.

Compared with partition-by-document, MLP avoids flooding a query to all nodes by having only a few nodes in each group to process the query. Note that the node groups from 0 to l-1 are virtual groups and the root group contains all nodes. So the root group should not become a single point of failure.

We call parameter l the *partition interface*, and a MLP with parameter l is called l-MLP. The partition-by-document and partition-by-keyword schemes can both be seen as special cases of MLP. With l=0, we get the partition-by-keyword scheme; and if l is large enough such that each group on level l contains at most one node, we get the partition-by-document scheme.

The goal of MLP is to achieve a good tradeoff among end-user latency, bandwidth consumption, load balance, availability, and scalability. To achieve this, some constrains must be satisfied:

1. **Uniformity.** All nodes must have roughly the same number of inverted lists on them.
2. **Latency locality.** Intra-group latency (the latency between a pair of nodes in the same group) should be smaller than inter-group latency (the latency between nodes of different groups) on each level of the node hierarchy.

Uniformity is required for the balance of load and storage among peers in the system. Latency locality is needed for reducing end-user latency and bisection bandwidth consumption. With latency locality, all nodes in a group are roughly in the same sub-network. Therefore, bisection backbone bandwidth is saved by confining inverted list intersection inside each sub-network.

In the following section we will illustrate how to implement MLP on top of P2P networks to satisfy the above two constrains.

3.2 SkipNet-Based Multi-level Partitioning

In this sub-section, we choose SkipNet as the substrate, on top of which the MLP operates.

3.2.1 Lexicographic ID Generation

Each node in the SkipNet has a lexicographic ID (LexID for abbreviation) and a numeric ID (abbreviated as NumID). The NumID can be generated by computing a cryptographic hash of the node's public key or its IP address, as existing DHTs have done. The generation of LexID is not straightforward. Although [12] suggests using a node's DNS name as its LexID, it is not appropriate to be used here for several reasons. For instance some peers in the system may not have DNS names. The more important reason is, as we shall see, that the LexIDs of nodes must satisfy *latency locality*.

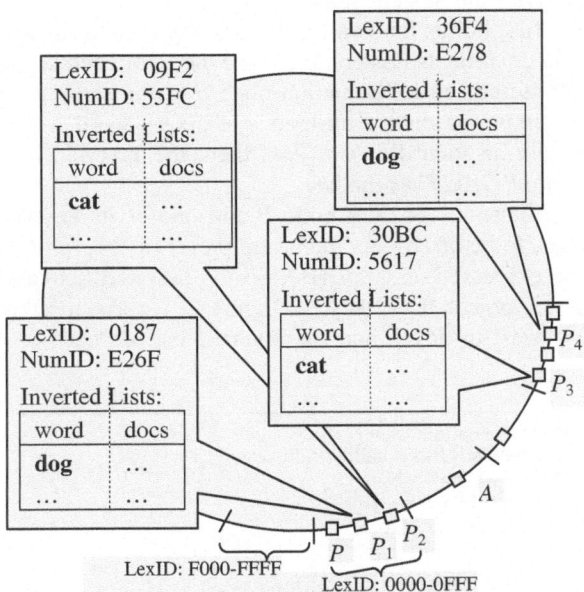

Fig. 2. Index publishing on SkipNet using 1-MLP. The hash code of "dog" and "cat" are E23D and 561B respectively. Only the root ring of SkipNet and the level-0 of the hierarchy are displayed here.

We use a two-step approach to generate LexID for each node. In the first step, we model the internet as a geometric space and compute the coordinates of nodes in a d-dimensional Cartesian space, using GNP [3] or other techniques [20][11]. Then in the second step, the LexID of each node is generated by mapping its coordinates to a circular ID space. Id-mapping can be performed using space-filling curves. Xu et al. [19] demonstrated using space-filling curves to map points in the domain R_d into R_1 such that the closeness relationship among the points is preserved. We adopt a similar but slightly different strategy to do id-mapping. Space limitation prevents us from giving more details. Please refer to our technical report [24] for more details.

3.2.2 Building Hierarchical Groups

To perform MLP, a node group hierarchy is first built as follows. Firstly, all nodes are divided into groups according to the first digits of their LexIDs, as is shown in Figure 2. That is, all nodes with the same first digit in their LexIDs belong to the same group. Secondly, each group is further divided into some sub-groups according to the second digit of LexID. Repeat this process until we reach level l. In a word, the node group hierarchy is built by dividing LexID digit by digit.

From the above process, we can easily see that latency locality is guaranteed.

3.2.3 Index Building

According to the group hierarchy building process, all nodes in the same group G have a common LexID prefix, defined as *domain(G)*. To build index, each node (say node A in domain G) in the system runs the algorithm described in Figure-3. In the algorithm, a node A first builds its own local index (by calling function *buildLocalIndex*) based on all the documents hosted on it. And then, for each keyword, its inverted list is published (or stored) on a destination node B in the same group. B is selected according to the group prefix and the hash code of the keyword, as follows: First hash the keyword to obtain an identifier *kid*. And then, the inverted list is inserted into SkipNet using "*domain(G)!kid*" as the key.

For instance, in Figure-2, consider node P and one of its keyword "cat" (whose hash code is assumed to be *561B*). As the group prefix of P is 0, the object ID for the inverted list can be expressed as "0!561B". So the inverted list can be inserted into SkipNet by using this object ID as key. In Figure-2, we assume that node P_2 is the one with NumID closest to *561B*, and the inverted list of "cat" should be stored to node P_2.

```
SkipNetNode.buildIndex() {
    InvertedList[] lists = buildLocalIndex();
    for i = 1 to lists.length {
        publishInvertedList(lists[i]);
    }
}

SkipNetNode.publishInvertedList(InvertedList list) {
    domain = this.LexID.prefix(l);   // l: the partition interface
    kid = list.keyword.hashcode();
    SkipNetNode node = route(domain + "!" + kid);
    store(node, list);  //store list on node
}
```

Fig. 3. Pseudocode for index building on SkipNet with *l*-MLP

From the above index building process, we can see that, because of the constrained load balance (CBL) property of SkipNet, all nodes in a group have roughly the same number of inverted lists on them. That is, the uniformity condition in Section 3.1 is satisfied.

3.2.4 Query Processing

When receiving a query request, the node runs the algorithm described in Figure-4 to process it. Each query has a "level" field indicating which hierarchical level the query is on. If the query's level is smaller than the partition interface l, the query is broadcasted further to all child subgroups along the hierarchy (see the *broadcastQuery()* function in the pseudocode). This process is repeated until level l is reached. Then, for all keywords in the query, some query messages are sent to the nodes which contain the inverted lists for them.

3.2.5 Discussion

From the above index building and query processing process, we can understand why MLP can achieve high performance. For multi-term queries, MLP reduces end-user latency (comparing with the partition-by-keyword scheme) by parallelizing the inverted list intersection process. Because of latency locality, nodes in the same group are more likely to be in the same sub-network. As a result, the intersection of inverted lists spends less bisection bandwidth. Compared with partition-by-document, MLP avoids flooding a query to all nodes by having only a few nodes in each group to process the query: assuming M node groups at level l, then at most $2M$ nodes are involved to answer a two-term query.

```
SkipNetNode.processQuery (Query q) {
    if(q.level < l)   // l: the partition interface
        broadcastQuery(q);
    else intersectQuery (q);
}

SkipNetNode.broadcastQuery(Query q) {
    q.level++;
    for s = '0' to LexID.max_digit {
        dom = this.LexID.prefix(q.level - 1) + s
        Send q to any of the nodes in domain dom
    }
}

SkipNetNode.intersectQuery(Query q) {
    domain = this.LexID.prefix(q.level);

    String words[] = q.keywords();
    for i = 1 to words.length {
        kid = words[i].hashcode();
        SkipNetNode nd = route(domain + "!" + kid);
        Send q to node nd;
    }
}
```

Fig. 4. Pseudocode for query processing on SkipNet with l-MLP

4   Experiments

We developed a simulated P2P searching system to test the feasibility and efficiency of MLP. In this section, we describe our experimental methodology and results briefly.

4.1   Data Source and Experimental Methodology

We use several network configuration profiles in the experiments. The profiles are all based on Transit-Stub topology [22]. All experimental results displayed in this section are generated by using a configuration profile called NET1. NET1 contains 3 transit domains and 15 stub domains, and all nodes have the upstream and downstream bandwidth of 800*KB*. We assign link latencies of 20ms, 5ms, and 2ms for inter-transit, stub-transit and inter-stub links respectively. We also have tried some other profiles and got similar results.

For a network message of size s to be sent from host A to host B, the time spent is computed by the following formula (the same as in [14]):

$$Time = l(A, B) + s / min(usbw(A), dsbw(B)) \tag{1}$$

Where $l(A, B)$ means the latency between host A and B; and $usbw(A)$, $dsbw(B)$ represent the upstream bandwidth of A and downstream bandwidth of B respectively.

The data used for experiments are from Google programming contest data [5] which includes a selection of 900,000 HTML web pages from 100 different sites in the "edu" domain.

In experiments, we found that the performance of each partitioning scheme depends heavily on data size and query patterns. To test the effect of data size, we vary the number of documents indexed from 10^6 to $3*10^9$ (Google index $3*10^9$ documents [5]). Note that we have only roughly 10^6 documents in hand. We adopt *document scaling* to achieve our goal. That is, to simulate N documents, we actually build a system containing M documents and build the inverted index accordingly. While in searching, the size of inverted list for each keyword is multiplied by a ratio N/M. In the following experiments, the results for more than 10^6 documents are generated by document scaling.

To test the effect of query patterns on search efficiency, nine types of queries are generated as follows: Firstly, all keywords are divided into three categories (popular, medium popular, rare) according to their appearance popularity. Out of the nine query types, there are three one-term query types which are characterized by carrying one popular, medium popular, or rare term respectively. The remaining six types are double-term queries with different combination of keyword categories. Given the nine query types, we can generate a query distribution by assigning *weights* to each query type. We use in the experiments two query distributions, called *ALL1* and *ALL2* respectively. The first distribution (*ALL1*) is generated from the Heaven Web [8] query log. The second distribution (*ALL2*) is generated by giving all the nine query types the same probability.

Due to space limitations, other experimental setups are omitted here (details see [24]).

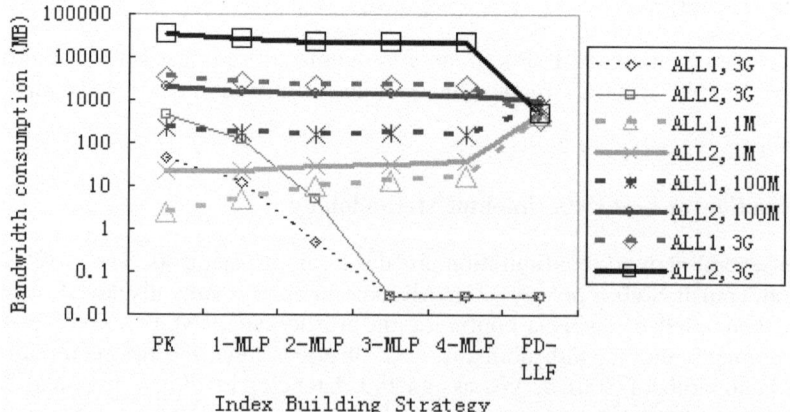

Fig. 5. The aggregate bandwidth (represented by the thick lines) and bisection bandwidth (thin lines) consumption of different strategies, for various amounts of documents in the system (16384 nodes)

4.2 Experimental Results

Figure-5 shows the aggregate bandwidth and bisection bandwidth consumption. In the figure, '3G' means that $3*10^9$ documents are indexed in the system. PK and PD mean partition-by-keyword and partition-by-document respectively. By letting the parameter l of MLP to be large enough, we actually get an optimized partition-by-document strategy, called PD-LLF (Partition-by-Document with Latency Locality Flooding). PD-LLF inherits the latency locality property from MLP and therefore consumes much less bisection bandwidth than ordinary flooding. We can see that, 2-MLP and 3-MLP achieve more than 80 and 1700 times of bisection bandwidth reduction respectively (although spend slightly more aggregate bandwidth when the number of documents indexed is small). This is much more than the bisection improvement needed in [10]. So, by combining MLP with the optimization techniques in [10], the bisection bandwidth is not a bottleneck any more.

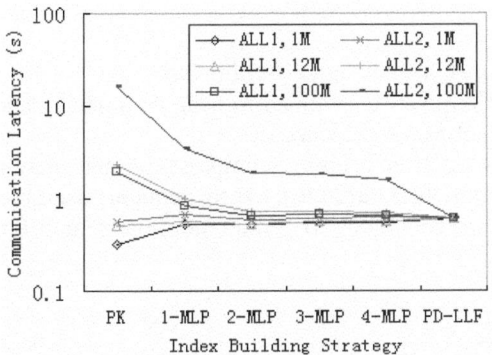

Fig. 6. Communication latency of different strategies, for various amounts of documents in the system (16384 nodes)

Figure-6 exhibits the end-user latency for different data sizes. We can see that, small amounts of documents per node see the benefits of using partition-by-keyword. While for medium or large amount of documents per node, the partition-by-keyword strategy becomes unusable because of too large communication latency. Fortunately, MLP can be used to reduce communication latency effectively in this case. MLP reduces the latency for multiple popular word queries remarkably with the cost of slightly more latency for single word queries.

5 Related Work

There have been recent proposals for keyword search and its optimizations [14][2][6][7] over structured P2P networks. Reynolds and Vahdat [14] design a distributed search engine based on DHT (distributed hash tables) and propose some boosting techniques. Bhattacharjee etc. discusses how to perform result-caching on top of DHTs [2]. They use a data structure called view tree to efficiently store and retrieve prior results. These proposals are all based on the partition-by-keyword strategy, and thus share its merits and drawbacks. KSS (Keyword-Set Search System) in [6] partitions the index by sets of keywords to reduce intersection overhead. However, with KSS, much more storage space is needed, and the bandwidth overhead for index building may also be large.

Efficient searching techniques on unstructured P2P systems are summarized and discussed in [21]. These techniques try to improve efficiency by limiting searches to a fraction of nodes. Although improving search efficiency, they may fail to retrieve important documents.

There have been some publications [1][16] studying hybrid index partitioning among multiple machines in *parallel* or *small scale distributed systems*. Although our MLP is also "hybrid", it bears several distinct features (see section 3) which make it fit to large scale, self-organized and dynamic P2P environments. In contrast, the existing hybrid index partitioning strategies can't be directly applied to P2P networks.

6   Conclusions

We present in this paper a new index building strategy by leveraging multi-level partitioning on top of SkipNet. It is aimed to achieve a good tradeoff between partition-by-keyword and partition-by-document.

Some optimizations, such as caching, compression, and incremental intersection, have been presented in the literature [10][14] for reducing search overhead. MLP can be combined with these techniques to further improve search efficiency. We leave this as future work.

Acknowledgments

We thank Zheng Zhang at Microsoft Research Asia for useful discussions. We also appreciate the anonymous reviewers for their valuable comments.

References

1. C. Badue, R. Baeza-Yates, B. Ribeiro-Neto, and N. Ziviani. Distributed query processing using partitioned inverted files. In Proc. of the 9th String Processing and Information Retrieval Symposium (SPIRE), September 2002.
2. Bobby Bhattacharjee, Sudarshan Chawathe, Vijay Gopalakrishnan, Pete Keleher and Bujor Silaghi. Efficient Peer-To-Peer Searches Using Result-Caching. IPTPS 2003.
3. S. Eugene Ng and Hui Zhang. Predicting Internet Network Distance with Coordinates-Based Approaches. In IEEE INFOCOM'02, 2002.
4. Gnutella. http://gnutella.wego.com.
5. Google. http://www.google.com.
6. O. D. Gnawali. A Keyword Set Search System for Peer-to-Peer Networks. Master's thesis, Massachusetts Institute of Technology, June 2002. UCB/CSD-01-1141, UC Berkeley, Apr. 2001.
7. M. Harren, J. M. Hellerstein, etc. Complex Queries in DHT-based Peer-to-Peer Networks. IPTPS'02.
8. http://e.pku.edu.cn.

9. KaZaA. http://kazaa.com.
10. Jinyang Li, Boon Thau Loo, etc. On the Feasibility of Peer-to-Peer Web Indexing and Search. IPTPS 2003.
11. Marcelo Pias, Jon Crowcroft, Steve Wilbur, Tim Harris, and Saleem Bhatti. Lighthouse for Scalable Distributed Location. IPTPS 2003.
12. Nicholas J. A. Harvey, Michael B. Jones, Stefan Saroiu, Marvin Theimer and Alec Wolman. SkipNet: A Scalable Overlay Network with Practical Locality Properties. USITS'03, 2003.
13. S. Ratnasamy, et al. A Scalable Content-Addressable Network. in ACM SIGCOMM' 2001. San Diego, CA, USA.
14. P. Reynolds and A. Vahdat. Efficient Peer-to-Peer Keyword Searching. Middleware'03, 2003.
15. Rowstron, A. and P. Druschel. Pastry: Scalable, distributed object location and routing for largescale peer-to-peer systems. in IFIP/ACM Middleware. 2001. Heidelberg, Germany.
16. O. Sornil and E. A. Fox. Hybrid partitioned inverted indices for large-scale digital libraries. In Proceedings of the 4th International Conference of Asian Digital Libraries, Bangalore, India, 2001.
17. Stoica, I., et al. Chord: A scalable peer-to-peer lookup service for Internet applications. in ACM SIGCOMM. 2001. San Diego, CA, USA.
18. C. Tang, Z. Xu and M. Mahalingam. Peersearch: Efficient information retrieval in peer-to-peer networks. In Proceedings of HotNets-I, ACM SIGCOMM, 2002.
19. Zhichen Xu, Mallik Mahalingam and Magnus Karlsson. Turning Heterogeneity into an Advantage in Overlay Routing. Infocom'03, 2003.
20. Zhichen Xu, Chunqiang Tang, Zheng Zhang. Building Topology-Aware Overlays Using Global Soft-State. ICDCS 2003.
21. Beverly Yang and Hector Garcia-Molina. Efficient Search in Peer-to-peer Networks. ICDCS'02, 2002.
22. E. Zegura, K. Calvert, and S. Bhattacharjee. How to Model an Internetwork. In Proc. of IEEE Infocom'96, CA, May 1996.
23. Zhao, B. Y,. Kubiatowicz, J.D., and Josep, A.D. Tapestry: An infrastructure for fault-tolerant wide-area location and routing. Tech. Rep. UCB/CSD-01-1141, UC Berkeley, EECS, 2001.
24. Shuming Shi, Guangwen Yang, Dingxing Wang, Jin Yu, Shaogang Qu, Ming Chen. Peer-to-Peer Index Partitioning for Large Scale Keyword Searching. Technique report, Tsinghua University, 2003. http://hpc.cs.tsinghua.edu.cn/clairvoyant/index.htm.

Providing Administrative Control and Autonomy in Structured Peer-to-Peer Overlays

Alan Mislove and Peter Druschel

Rice University

Abstract. Structured peer-to-peer (p2p) overlay networks provide a decentralized, self-organizing substrate for distributed applications and support powerful abstractions such as distributed hash tables (DHTs) and group communication. However, in most of these systems, lack of control over key placement and routing paths raises concerns over autonomy, administrative control and accountability of participating organizations. Additionally, structured p2p overlays tend to assume global connectivity while in reality, network address translation and firewalls limit connectivity among hosts in different organizations. In this paper, we present a general technique that ensures content/path locality and administrative autonomy for participating organizations, and provides natural support for NATs and firewalls. Instances of conventional structured overlays are configured to form a hierarchy of identifier spaces that reflects administrative boundaries and respects connectivity constraints among networks.

1 Introduction

Structured peer-to-peer (p2p) overlay networks provide a decentralized, self-organizing substrate for distributed applications and support powerful abstractions such as distributed hash tables (DHTs) and group communication [13, 18–20, 22, 15]. Most of these systems use randomized object keys and node identifiers, which yields good load balancing and robustness to failures. However, in such overlays, applications cannot ensure that a key is stored in the inserter's own organization, a property known as *content locality*. Likewise, one cannot ensure that a routing path stays entirely within an organization when possible, a property known as *path locality*. In an open system where participating organizations have conflicting interests, this lack of control can raise concerns about autonomy and accountability [13].

Moreover, participants in a conventional overlay must agree on a set of protocols and parameter settings like the routing base, the size of the neighbor set, failure detection intervals and replication strategy. Optimal settings for these parameters depend on factors like the expected churn rate, node failure probabilities and failure correlation. These factors may not be uniform across different organizations and may be difficult to assess or estimate in a large system. The choice of parameters also depends on the required availability and durability of data, which is likely to differ between participating organizations. Yet, conventional overlays require global agreement on protocols and parameter settings among all participants.

Additionally, most structured p2p overlay protocols assume that the underlying network is fully connected. In the real Internet, however, communication among host in different organizations is often constrained. Security firewalls and network address trans-

G.M. Voelker and S. Shenker (Eds.): IPTPS 2004, LNCS 3279, pp. 162–172, 2004.

lation (NAT) often prevent nodes exterior to an organization from contacting interior ones.

In this paper, we present a general technique to configure structured p2p overlay networks into a hierarchy of overlay instances with separate identifier spaces. The hierarchy reflects administrative and organizational domains, and naturally respects connectivity constraints. Our technique leaves participating organizations in control over local resources, choice of protocols and parameters, and provides content and path locality. Each organization can run a different overlay protocol and use parameter settings appropriate for the organization's network characteristics and requirements. Our solution generalizes existing protocols with a single id space, thus leveraging prior work on all aspects of structured p2p overlays, including secure routing [2].

The rest of this paper is organized as follows. Section 2 describes in detail the design of our system and explains how messages are routed across multiple rings. Section 3 discusses the costs, benefits and limitations of our technique. Section 4 details related work and Section 5 concludes.

2 Design

In this section, we describe a hierarchical configuration of overlays that reflects organizational structure and connectivity constraints. For convenience, we will refer to an instance of a structured overlay as a "ring", because the identifier spaces of protocols like Chord and Pastry form a ring. However, we emphasize that our design can be equally applied to structured overlay protocols whose identifier spaces do not form a ring, including CAN, Tapestry, and Kademlia [17, 22, 15].

A *multi-ring* protocol stitches together the rings and implements global routing and lookup. To applications, the entire hierarchy appears as a single instance of a structured overlay network that spans multiple organizations and networks. The rings can use any structured overlay protocol that supports the key-based routing (KBR) API defined in Dabek et al. [7].

Our design relies on a group anycast mechanism, such as Scribe [5, 6]. Scribe maintains spanning trees consisting of the overlay routes from group member nodes towards the overlay node that is responsible for the group's identifier. These trees are then used to implement multicast and anycast. Scribe can be implemented on top of any structured overlay that supports the KBR API. If the underlying overlay protocol uses a technique like proximity neighbor selection [3, 12], then the Scribe trees are efficient in terms of network proximity and anycast messages are delivered to a nearby group member [6].

Figure 1 shows how our multi-ring protocol is layered above the KBR API of the overlay protocols that implement the individual rings. Shown at the right is a node that acts as a gateway between the rings. The instances of structured overlays that run in each ring are completely independent. In fact, different protocols can run in the different rings, as long as they support the KBR API.

2.1 Ring Structure

The system forms a tree of rings. Typically, the tree consists of just two layers, namely a *global ring* as the root and *organizational rings* at the lower level. Each ring has a

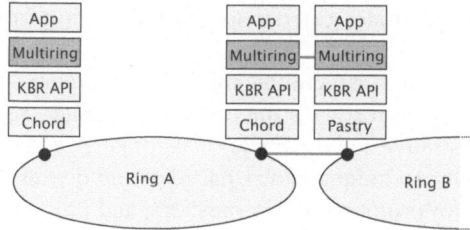

Fig. 1. Diagram of application layers. The two nodes on the right are actually instances of the same node in two different rings.

globally unique *ringId*, which is known to all members of the ring. The global ring has a well-known ringId consisting of all zeroes. It is assumed that all members of a given ring are fully connected in the physical network, i.e., they are not separated by firewalls or NAT boxes.

All nodes in the entire system join the global ring, unless they are connected behind a firewall or a NAT. In addition, each node joins a ring consisting of all the nodes that belong to a given organization. A node is permitted to route messages and perform other operations only in rings in which it is a member.

The global ring is used primarily to route inter-organizational queries and to enable global lookup of keys, while application keys are stored in the organizational rings. Each organizational ring defines a set of nodes that use a common set of protocols and parameter settings; they enjoy content and path locality for keys that they insert into the overlay. In addition, a organizational ring may also define a set of nodes that are connected to the Internet through a firewall or NAT box.

An example configuration is shown in Figure 2. The nodes connected by lines are actually instances of the same node, running in different rings. Ring A7 consists of nodes in an organization that are fully connected to the Internet. Thus, each node is also a member of the global ring. Ring 77 represents a set of nodes behind a firewall. Here, only two nodes can join the global ring, namely the firewall gateway nodes.

2.2   Gateway Nodes

A node that is a member of more than one ring is a *gateway node*. Such a node supports multiple virtual overlay nodes, one in each ring, but uses the same node identifier (id)

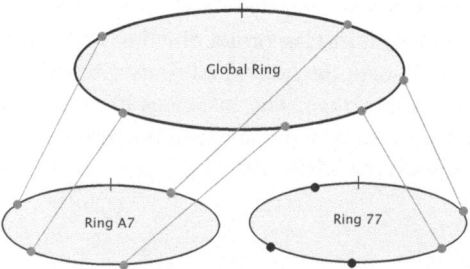

Fig. 2. Example of a ring structure. Nodes shown in gray are instances of the same node in multiple rings, and nodes in black are only in a single ring due to a firewall.

in each ring. Gateway nodes can forward messages between rings, as described in the next section. In Figure 2 above, all of the nodes in ring *A7* are gateway nodes between the global ring and ring *A7*. To maximize load balance and fault tolerance, all nodes are expected to serve as gateway nodes, unless connectivity limitations (firewalls and NAT boxes) prevent it.

Gateway nodes announce themselves to other members of the rings in which they participate by subscribing to an anycast (Scribe) group in each of the rings. The group identifiers of these groups are the ringIds of the associated rings. In Figure 2 for instance, a node *M* that is a member of both the global ring and *A7*, joins the Scribe groups:

Scribe group *A700...0* in the global ring
Scribe group *0000...0* in ringId *A7*

2.3   Routing

Next, we describe how messages are routed in the system. We assume that each message carries, in addition to a target key, the ringId of the ring in which the key is stored. In the subsequent section, we will show how to obtain these ringIds.

Recall that each node knows the ringIds of all rings in which it is a member. If the target ringId of a message equals one of these ringIds, the node simply forwards the message to the corresponding ring. From that point on, the message is routed according to the structured overlay protocol within that target ring.

Otherwise, the node needs to locate a gateway node to the target ring, which is accomplished via anycast. If the node is a member of the global ring, then it forwards the message via anycast in the global ring to the group that corresponds to the desired ringId. The message will be delivered to a gateway node for the target ring that is close in the physical network, among all such gateway nodes. This gateway node then forwards the data into the target ring, and routing proceeds as before.

If the node is not a member of the global ring, then it forwards the message into the global ring via a gateway node by anycasting to the group whose identifier corresponds to the ringId of the global ring. Routing then proceeds as described above.

As an optimization, it is possible for nodes to cache the IP addresses of gateway nodes they have previously obtained. Should the cached information prove stale, a new gateway node can be located via anycast. This optimization drastically reduces the need for anycast messages during routing.

2.4   Global Lookup

In the previous discussion, we assumed that messages carry both a key and the ringId of the ring in which the key is stored. In practice, however, applications often wish to look up a key without knowledge of where the key is stored. For instance, keys are often derived from the hash of a textual name provided by a human user. In this case, the ring in which the key is stored may be unknown.

The following mechanism is designed to enable the global lookup of keys. When a key is inserted into a organizational ring and that key should be visible at global scope, a special indirection record is inserted into the global ring that associates the key with the ringId(s) of the organizational ring(s) where (replicas of) the key is(are) stored. The ringId(s) of a key can now be looked up in the global ring. Note that indirection records are the only data that should be stored in the global ring. Only legitimate indirection records are accepted by members of the global ring to prevent space-filling attacks.

2.5   Multi-level Ring Hierarchies

We believe that a two-level ring hierarchy is sufficient in the majority of cases. Nevertheless, there may be situations where more levels of hierarchy are useful. For instance, a world-wide organization with multiple campuses may wish to create multiple rings for each of its locations in order to achieve more fine-grained content locality. In these cases, it may be advantageous to group these machines into subrings of the organization's ring, further scoping content and path locality.

In order to provide for such extensions, the ring hierarchy described above can be naturally extended. To do so, we view ringIds as a sequence of digits in a configurable base b, and each level of ring hierarchy will append an extra digit onto the parent ring's ringId. Thus, organizations which own a given ringId can dynamically create new rings by appending digits to their ringId.

The routing algorithm can be generalized to work in a multi-level hierarchy as follows. When routing to a remote ring R, the node first checks to see if it is a member of R. If so, it simply routes the message in R using the normal overlay routing.

If the node is not a member of R, it must forward the message to a gateway. If the node is a member of multiple rings, it must choose one of these rings in which to forward the message. This is done by comparing the shared prefix length of each local ringId and R and picking the ring with the longest shared prefix. In the case of multiple ringIds with the longest prefix, the node should pick the shortest one in total length. This process guarantees that the node picks the local ring which is "closest" to the destination ring R.

Once the node has chosen in which local ring L to send the message, it the must determine if it should route the message up (towards the global ring), or down. This is an easy computation, as it is dependent only upon the length of the shared prefix of L and R. If R has L as a prefix, the node should route the message downwards since R is "below" this ring. Thus, the node should forward the message via an anycast to the Scribe group rooted at $substring(R, length(L) + 1)$. The gateway node which receives the message can then use the routing algorithm again in the other ring.

If R does not have L as a prefix, the node should route the message upwards, towards the global ring. This is done by routing the message to the parent ring, or to a ring with ringId $substring(L, length(L) - 1)$. Clearly, messages are routed efficiently by forwarding the message until a ring is found whose id is a prefix of the destination ring, and then routing the message downwards towards the destination ring.

The pseudo-code for routing a message *msg* to the ringId *dst* at a node in ringId *local* is shown in Figure 3. Figure 4, below, shows an example a node in ring *D1A8* routing to a location in the ring *63*.

3   Discussion

In this section, we discuss the costs, benefits and limitations of our proposed technique.

```
(1)   route(dst, msg) {
(2)     if (local == dst) {
(3)       route_normally(msg)
(4)     } else {
(5)       len = length(local)
(6)
(7)       if (dst.hasPrefix(local))
(8)         forward(substring(dst, len+1), msg)
(9)       else
(10)        forward(substring(local, len-1), msg)
(11)   }
(12) }
```

Fig. 3. The pseudocode for routing between rings, which is executed at each node along the route.

3.1 Robustness

Partitioning an overlay network into organizational rings affords content/path locality as well as autonomy over organizations' resources, protocols and parameter choices. However, the partitioning may also reduce the diversity among the set of nodes that store a given object. On the other hand, organizations can assess the churn, failure rate and failure correlation of its own nodes with much greater accuracy than in a global ring. This allows less conservative replication strategies and greater confidence in the resulting object availability and durability.

If the diversity of nodes in an organizational ring is not sufficient to provide the desired durability of objects, then replicas must be stored in different organizations' rings via an appropriate replica placement strategy. The lookup of objects replicated in this manner proceeds by first looking up the object in the local ring and should that fail, looking up the object's indirection record in the global ring, which refers to other rings containing the object.

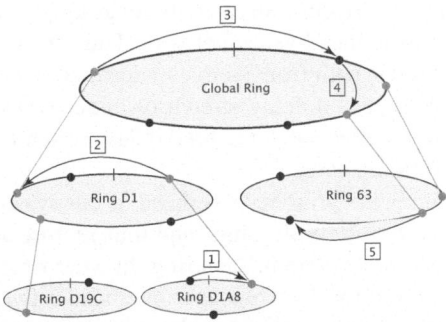

Fig. 4. Diagram of a the routing process with multiple levels of hierarchy. Gray nodes are gateways, which exist in multiple rings and route between them. Numbers 1-5 denote the steps in routing.

When adding a participant node, one must choose the set of rings in which the node should participate. When making this decision, organizations need to strike the right balance between content locality and diversity. For instance, an organizational ring should be large enough to contain nodes with different physical network links to the Internet, independent power sources and locations in different buildings if not cities.

To retain the robustness of a single global overlay network, all nodes without connectivity constraints should join the global ring. All such nodes act as gateway nodes among the rings, thus ensuring load balancing, efficient routing across rings, and fault tolerance. In the case of rings behind firewalls, some loss of these properties is unavoidable due to the limitations of the physical network.

In an organizational ring, objects can be inserted only by a member of the same ring, providing organizations with authority over their resources. This enables organizations to more easily provision storage space. Likewise, it eliminates the threat of denial-of-service attacks from outsiders that aim at filling up the storage, which is a problem in open rings. Nodes that participate in the global ring must store indirection records and forward routing request on behalf of arbitrary other organizations. This is unavoidable as some resource sharing is central to the idea of a cooperative overlay network. However, our system limits data stored in the global ring to legitimate indirection records. This makes space-filling attacks more difficult to mount.

3.2 Performance

The cost of routing a message within a given ring depends on the overlay protocol used within the ring, typically $O(log \text{ N})$ routing hops and, if proximity neighbor selection is used, a delay stretch below two.

In the common case of a two-level hierarchy, routing a message between two organizational rings requires in the worst case three intra-ring routes plus two anycast transmissions. However, caching of gateway nodes eliminates the two anycasts in most cases. Also, all nodes in organizational rings without connectivity constraints are gateways to the global ring, thus eliminating the need for one anycast and one overlay route if the source is such a node.

With proximity neighbor selection used in the overlay protocols, the gateways located via anycast are nearby in the physical network. Thus, the gateway nodes are likely to lie along or near the shortest path from source to destination node in the physical network. Combined with an expected delay stretch of under two for the route segments between the gateways, this suggests that the total delay stretch for an inter-ring route is also around two in the common case.

In terms of maintenance, the principal overhead of our system results from the fact that gateways nodes must join multiple rings, and thus require additional control messages for maintaining the routing state in each ring. In what we consider the most common case of a two-level hierarchy, the worst case overhead is twice that of a single ring. The overhead is lower when many nodes are behind firewalls or NAT boxes. Moreover, a large fraction of the additional control traffic for maintaining organizational rings remains internal to a given organization. Since the basic maintenance overhead of the most efficient structured overlays has been reduced to less than half a message per second and node [1], we believe that the overhead imposed by hierarchical rings is not a concern.

In addition, various optimizations are possible that exploit overlap among the routing state of a given node in the different rings. For instance, the size of the neighbor set (e.g., leaf set in Pastry, successor set in Chord) can be reduced in organizational rings, as the global ring can be used to repair a organizational ring that has become disconnected due to many simultaneous node failures. Since the details depend on the specific overlay protocols used in each ring, we don't discuss them here.

3.3 Security

Our system does not require the use of a specific, new structured overlay protocol. This allows us to leverage existing work, for instance on secure routing in the presence of malicious participants [2]. The nodeId certificates used in this work can be extended to bind a node's IP address to both its nodeId and ringId. When a node joins an anycast group or offers to forward a request into a different ring, it presents its certificate demonstrating that it is actually a member of the ring in question. With both nodeId and ringIds certified, the techniques described in Castro et al. [2] can then be applied to our hierarchical ring structure. A full analysis, however, remains the subject of ongoing work.

3.4 Status

The system as described is actively used within POST, a serverless infrastructure for collaborative applications including email, instant messaging, and shared whiteboards [16]. Users' desktops are collectively hosting the service, and organizational rings provide content/path locality and organizational autonomy.

An implementation of our technique will be available as part of the upcoming FreePastry 1.4 release. The implementation is designed using only the KBR API [7], and can be used with any structured overlay protocol supporting this API. The release is open source and can be downloaded from http://freepastry.rice.edu.

4   Related Work

The use of multiple coexisting rings has been described before, most notably in the context of Coral [9] and SkipNet [13]. In Coral, multiple rings are used to provide data locality, and are configured dynamically based on measured ping delays among participating nodes. The system does not provide organizational autonomy nor data/content locality at the organizational level.

Harvey et al. have first articulated the case for content and path locality [13]. SkipNet uses location-based id assignment in order to provide content and path locality. It employs a skiplist-based search structure to ensure robustness and load balancing despite the inherently uneven population of the identifier space. However, the system is more vulnerable to certain types of attacks that place malicious node near the boundaries of an organization's segment in the namespace [13]. Moreover, SkipNet still requires global agreement on protocols and parameterization. Our multi-ring approach offers greater organizational autonomy and can leverage work on existing protocols at the expense of a somewhat higher overhead for maintaining multiple rings.

An extension of the Chord protocol provides support for multiple virtual rings, each consisting of a subset of the overlay participants [14]. The multiple rings are based on a single overlay instance and a novel routing mechanisms delivers messages to the nearest live node to a given key within a given subset. This technique has lower overlay maintenance overhead than our hierarchical rings approach, but it provides less organizational autonomy and no path locality.

The use of multiple physical rings has been suggested in order to provide universal service discovery and code maintenance [4]. Such work is complementary to this paper.

The Brocade [21] system, based on Tapestry, provides more efficient routing and path locality by using a secondary network of supernodes. Each administrative domain chooses a supernode, and inter-domain routing is accomplished via DHT lookups and landmark routing. This system is complementary to our work as it focuses on routing efficiency and provides neither content/path locality nor organizational autonomy.

Hierarchical peer-to-peer systems have also been explored in Garces-Erce et al. [10], but only with the goal of improving performance of the overlay network routing. A system of hierarchal rings was mentioned in the SkipNet paper as a design alternative, but was rejected due to the overhead of multiple rings. We believe that in our system, this overhead is small enough to provide a practical alternative that can leverage existing work on structured overlays and provides greater organizational autonomy.

Additionally, none of the projects described above address the problem of deploying peer-to-peer overlays over networks with connectivity constraints. Many unstructured peer-to-peer overlays [11] solve this problem through network engineering, including push requests and rendezvous points, but these approaches add complexity and may not scale. Bryan Ford [8] has attempted to solve this problem in general with the use of a new network-layer protocol, the Unmanaged Internet Protocol (UIP). However, the deployment of such technology or IPv6 is still, at best, years away.

5   Conclusions

Structured p2p overlay networks provide a decentralized, self-organizing substrate for large-scale distributed applications. However, most existing overlays provide neither content/path locality nor organizational autonomy. We have presented a hierarchical configuration of structured overlays that provides content/path locality, organizational autonomy and respects connectivity constraints while maintaining global connectivity. A multi-ring protocol stitches together organizational overlays that can run different overlay protocols with different parameter choices. To applications, the entire system appears like a single structured overlay. Since our solution works with any structured overlay protocol, it is able to leverage existing work, e.g., on secure overlay routing.

Acknowledgments

This work was supported in part by NSF (ANI-0225660), by Texas ATP (003604-0079-2001) and by Intel Research. We thank Miguel Castro and Antony Rowstron for discussions that lead to the ideas presented. We would also like to thank the anonymous IPTPS reviewers for their comments.

References

1. M. Castro, M. Costa, and A. Rowstron. Performance and dependability of structured peer-to-peer overlays, 2003. Technical report MSR-TR-2003-94.
2. M. Castro, P. Druschel, A. Ganesh, A. Rowstron, and D. Wallach. Security for structured peer-to-peer overlay networks. In *Proc. of the Fifth Symposium on Operating System Design and Implementation (OSDI 2002)*, Boston, MA, December 2002.
3. M. Castro, P. Druschel, Y. C. Hu, and A. Rowstron. Proximity neighbor selection in tree-based structured peer-to-peer overlays, 2003. Technical report MSR-TR-2003-52.
4. M. Castro, P. Druschel, A.-M. Kermarrec, and A. Rowstron. One ring to rule them all: Service discovery and binding in structured peer-to-peer overlay networks. In *Proceedings of the SIGOPS European Workshop*, Saint-Emilion, France, 2002.
5. M. Castro, P. Druschel, A.-M. Kermarrec, and A. Rowstron. SCRIBE: A large-scale and decentralized application-level multicast infrastructure. *IEEE JSAC*, 20(8), Oct. 2002.
6. M. Castro, P. Druschel, A.-M. Kermarrec, and A. Rowstron. Scalable application-level anycast for highly dynamic groups. In *Proc. NGC 2003*, Munich, Germany, 2003.
7. F. Dabek, B. Zhao, P. Druschel, J. Kubiatowicz, and I. Stoica. Towards a common API for structured peer-to-peer overlays. In *Proc. IPTPS 2003*, Berkeley, California, 2003.
8. B. Ford. Unmanaged internet protocol: Taming the edge network management crisis. In *In Proceedings of the 2nd Workshop on Hot Topics in Networks (HotNets-II)*, Cambridge, MA, 2003.
9. M. Freedman and D. Mazieres. Sloppy hashing and self-organizing clusters. In *In Proceedings of the 2nd International Workshop on Peer-to-Peer Systems (IPTPS '03)*, Berkeley, CA, 2003.
10. L. Garces-Erce, E. Biersack, P. Felber, K. Ross, and G. Urvoy-Keller. Hierarchical peer-to-peer systems. In *Proc. Euro-Par 2003*, Klagenfurt, Austria, 2003.
11. The Gnutella protocol specification, 2000.
    http://dss.clip2.com/GnutellaProtocol04.pdf.
12. R. Gummadi, S. Gribble, S. Ratnasamy, S. Shenker, and I. Stoica. The impact of DHT routing geometry on resilience and proximity. In *Proc. ACM SIGCOMM'03*, Karlsruhe, Germany, 2003.
13. N. Harvey, M. Jones, S. Saroiu, M. Theimer, and A. Wolman. Skipnet: A scalable overlay network with practical locality properties. In *Proc. USITS 2003*, Seattle, WA, 2003.
14. D. Karger and M. Ruhl. An augmented Chord protocol supporting heterogeneous subgroup formation in peer-to-peer networks. In *Proceedings of the 3nd International Workshop on Peer-to-Peer Systems (IPTPS'04)*, San Diego, CA, 2004.
15. P. Maymounkov and D. Mazieres. Kademlia: A peer-to-peer information system based on the xor metric. In *In Proceedings of the 2nd International Workshop on Peer-to-Peer Systems (IPTPS'03)*, Berkeley, CA, 2003.
16. A. Mislove, A. Post, C. Reis, P. Willmann, P. Druschel, D. Wallach, X. Bonnaire, P. Sens, J. Busca, and L. Arantes-Bezerra. Post: A secure, resilient, cooperative messaging system. In *Proceedings of the Ninth Workshop on Hot Topics in Operating Systems (HotOS '03)*, Lihue, HI, 2003.
17. S. Ratnasamy, P. Francis, M. Handley, R. Karp, and S. Shenker. A scalable content-addressable network. In *Proc. ACM SIGCOMM'01*, San Diego, CA, Aug. 2001.

18. S. Ratnasamy, M. Handley, R. Karp, and S. Shenker. Application-level multicast using content-addressable networks. In *NGC*, Nov. 2001.
19. A. Rowstron and P. Druschel. Pastry: Scalable, distributed object location and routing for large-scale peer-to-peer systems. In *IFIP/ACM Middleware 2001*, Heidelberg, Germany, Nov. 2001.
20. I. Stoica, R. Morris, D. Karger, M. F. Kaashoek, and H. Balakrishnan. Chord: A scalable peer-to-peer lookup service for Internet applications. In *Proc. ACM SIGCOMM'01*, San Diego, CA, Aug. 2001.
21. B. Zhao, Y. Duan, L. Huang, A. Joseph, and J. Kubiatowicz. Brocade: Landmark routing on overlay networks. In *Proceedings of the 1st International Workshop on Peer-to-Peer Systems (IPTPS'02)*, Cambridge, MA, 2002.
22. B. Zhao, J. Kubiatowicz, and A. Joseph. Tapestry: An infrastructure for fault-resilient wide-area location and routing. Technical Report UCB//CSD-01-1141, U. C. Berkeley, April 2001.

Willow: DHT, Aggregation,
and Publish/Subscribe in One Protocol*

Robbert van Renesse and Adrian Bozdog

Dept. of Computer Science,
Cornell University Ithaca, NY 14850
{rvr,adrianb}@cs.cornell.edu

Abstract. This paper describes a new peer-to-peer protocol that integrates DHT routing, aggregation, all-to-all multicast, as well as both topic- and content-based publish/subscribe. In spite of this extensive set of features, the Willow protocol is simple, scalable, balances the load well across the members, is proximity-aware, adapts to network conditions, and recovers quickly and gracefully from network partitions and subsequent repairs.

1 Introduction

In recent years, many application-level protocols have been designed for resource location, point-to-point and multicast routing, publish/subscribe, and aggregation. This paper introduces a new protocol, Willow, that provides all of these features. More specifically, Willow supports DHT-based routing, standing SQL aggregation queries on attributes of the nodes, Application-Level Multicast (ALM), and multicast filtering capabilities strong enough to support topic- and content-based pub/sub and more.

As with previous protocols, memory requirements on the nodes grow $O(\log N)$, while latency grows $O(\log N)$ ($O(\log^2 N)$ for aggregation). Willow is proximity-aware, and prefers short hops over long ones. Other than many previous proximity-aware protocols, Willow adapts to link latencies changing over time. A particularly important feature in the Willow protocol is its *zippering* mechanism by which separate Willow instances can be merged efficiently (in $O(\log N)$ parallel steps) into a single instance. The zippering mechanism is an important factor to Willow's stability both in the face of network partitions and in the face of churn.

Willow borrows some of its design from Astrolabe [1, 2]. While Astrolabe was intended to do aggregation only, Astrolabe can in fact be configured to function as a DHT as follows. Rather than manually assigning the Astrolabe domain names, they would be generated by concatenating, say, 32 4-bit digits. DHT routing can then be performed by walking the Astrolabe hierarchy in a

---

* This work was funded in part by DARPA/AFRL-IFGA grant F30602-99-1-0532, and by the AFRL/Cornell Information Assurance Institute.

G.M. Voelker and S. Shenker (Eds.): IPTPS 2004, LNCS 3279, pp. 173–183, 2004.

straightforward manner. Using the SelectCast protocol [3] that runs on Astrolabe, pub/sub can be supported on this infrastructure as well.

Willow, however, is closer in design to a traditional DHT. At the heart of the Willow protocol is a standard Plaxton-routing [4] infrastructure much like that of Kademlia [5]. But where other Plaxton-based DHTs hide aggregation facilities such as supported by Plaxton's original design, Willow exposes them. Compared to Astrolabe, Willow can support more queries, and answers them more quickly. Most importantly, Willow spreads load evenly across the members.

In this overview of the Willow protocol, we discuss related work in Sect. 2, the Willow model in Sect. 3, and the implementation in Sect. 4. A short look at results from simulation experiments are presented in Sect. 5, and Sect. 6 concludes.

2 Related Work

Due to space limitations, we limit ourselves to discussing only the most closely related projects.

Aggregation is important for supporting queries more complex than DHT lookup operations, as well as for scalable monitoring applications. In the area of peer-to-peer aggregation protocols, the most closely related projects besides Astrolabe are DASIS [6], Cone [7], SDIMS [8], SOMO [9], and PIER [10]. DASIS uses a Kademlia-like structure and aggregates information about the members in a way quite similar to Willow. In DASIS, information thus collected is used in the join algorithm to balance the P2P topology better than is typically achieved through random placement.

Cone augments a ring-based DHT with a trie, one for each attribute and aggregation operation. Cone can then support range queries over those attributes.

The SDIMS design exploits the fact that each key in Plaxton-based DHT identifies a tree consisting of the routes from each other node to the root node for that key. In SDIMS, each attribute and aggregation operation is hashed onto a key and then the aggregation is performed along the corresponding tree. The SDIMS implementation extends the Pastry protocol. In order to allow for an administrative hierarchy as in Astrolabe, Pastry was modified to have a leaf set for each administrative domain, rather than a single one.

Rather than augmenting a DHT, SOMO layers over a DHT. Even though Willow is an augmented DHT, SOMO aggregates information up a tree and then multicasts the results back down using the same tree much like in Willow. While Willow uses only a single tree, SOMO has a tree per key like in SDIMS.

In PIER, a DHT is used as a database index, and maps database keys to nodes that store the corresponding tuples. The DHT is augmented in order to allow for enumeration of tuples at nodes so that selection queries can be implemented. Most of the work in PIER so far has focussed on distributed joins rather than on how to support aggregation queries efficiently.

All DHT-based multicast protocols that we are aware of, such as Bayeux [11] and SplitStream [12], are layered on top of a DHT. In those systems, a key is associated with each multicast group, and one or more trees are build on a per-key basis, and these trees follow the DHT routes for those keys. Willow, in contrast, does not associate any keys with groups, but uses filtering in order to send messages to particular subsets of members. This leads to two advantages. Willow has many more routing options for multicast than do previous DHT-based multicast schemes, potentially resulting in better performance and load balancing, and more addressing options, strong enough to support even content-based publish/subscribe.

3   Willow Model

Before we show how the Willow protocol is implemented, we will first describe what Willow looks like once deployed.

3.1   Willow Tree

Each agent chooses a random 128-bit identifier. For the remainder of this paper, we assume that this results in each agent having a unique identifier, although agents can easily detect if their identifiers conflict and resolve this situation by choosing a new random identifier. The identifier determines a path in a virtual binary tree of 129 levels. Starting at the first bit of the identifier and the root of the tree, a 0 bit determines the left child, and a 1 bit the right child, and so on. Vice versa, each node in the tree can be named using a bit string. For example, the root is named by the empty bit string, and its right child is named "1". We call each node in the tree a *domain*, and all the agents whose identifiers start with the domain's identifier are considered members of that domain. In particular, all agents are members of the root domain, and each agent is a member of the leaf domain consisting of only the agent.

Each domain has attributes in addition to its identifier. In the case of a leaf domain, these attributes and their values are written directly by its corresponding agent. In the case of non-leaf domains (aka. *internal domains*), the attributes are determined by the two child domains. If both the left and right child domains are empty (contain no agents), then the set of attributes of the parent domain is empty as well. If only one of the child domains is empty, the attributes are the same as those of the non-empty child domain.

The interesting case is when a domain has two non-empty child domains. We call such domains *branching domains*. The attributes of the parent domain are then determined by an aggregation function over the attributes of the child domains. In Willow this is done using SQL. Imagine the two sets of attributes forming two rows in a relational table. One or more SQL aggregation queries over the table are used to compute the attributes of the parent domain. For example, the aggregation query might be "SELECT MAX(maxload) AS maxload." This specifies that the parent domain will have an attribute *maxload* which is computed by taking the maximum of the *maxload* attributes of both child domains. All nodes share the same aggregation functions, and therefore the root domain

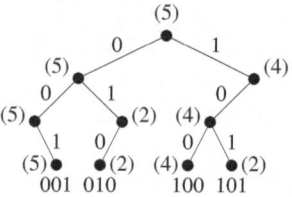

Fig. 1. Willow tree with four agents using three bit identifiers. The maximum load in each domain is indicated between braces.

will have an attribute *maxload* containing the global maximum load. Figure 1 shows an example Willow tree.

Each time the attributes of a leaf domain change, all the attributes of domains on the path up from the leaf domain to the root are recalculated automatically, much like in dependent cells in a spreadsheet. The aggregates are also recalculated in case of membership changes, or when aggregation functions are installed, updated, or removed, all of which can be done on the fly. We note that such updates are not instantaneous, in that there is a latency involved in the dissemination of queries and attribute updates to the various agents. Willow also does not guarantee consistency between the attributes that different agents observe, but all converge quickly to the same state in the absence of updates.

3.2   Willow Operations

Willow supports the following operations:

- *DHT Routing*: route a message to an agent with an identifier nearest to a specified key in terms of the XOR metric [5];
- *Monitoring*: using a JDBC query, specify what data needs to be reported by the agents into the Willow tree, and using an SQL query, how the data should be aggregated;
- *Publish/Subscribe*: route a message down the (logical!) Willow tree to all domains satisfying an SQL predicate specified within the header.

Monitoring is guided by two queries. (Both are installed and aggregated themselves as "executable attributes" within the Willow tree.) Once an agent installs such queries, it will take some time for them to propagate to all agents, and then some time before all the necessary information has been retrieved, reported, and aggregated. In order to determine when a query has completed, Willow has a permanent query installed that reports the total number of members of a domain in the *nmembers* attribute.

For example, say a user wants to determine which machine has the least load. Rather than reporting just the identifier and load of an agent, the user's query would really report (*agent, load, count*), where *agent* and *load* are the least loaded agent for the corresponding domain, and *count* is total number of agents that have reported their load for this query. The user waits until *count* approaches *nmembers*. (Note that unless continuous updates are required, he or she should also remove the query at this time.)

There are queries that do not lend themselves well to aggregation. For example, the agent with the median load would be impossible to determine in the way described above. Such queries will require more than one pass to answer. Any query may be answered simply by collecting all the necessary information of all agents, but often more efficient approaches exist. In the example above, the agent with the median load can be determined using a binary search.

Willow also supports multicast and publish/subscribe. Given any domain, Willow supports a mechanism to forward a message to both child domains. When applied recursively, this mechanism multicast the message to all agents in the domain. The message may contain an SQL condition which is applied to the attributes of each child domain in order to determine whether to forward the message to the child domain or not. For example, it would be possible to send a message to all agents with a load less than 3, as long as a query is installed that reports the minimum load in each domain. Using a Bloom filter, traditional topic-based publish/subscribe can be efficiently supported this way, but the Willow mechanism is quite powerful and can support content-based publish/subscribe as well (both are based on the work in [3] and described in detail there).

For this, each agent would specify a query as one of its attributes which is applied to attributes of messages. The queries are aggregated using logical OR. The Willow SQL query engine supports an EVAL function that allows such queries to be evaluated. In order for this to scale, the queries have to be conservatively simplified. For example, if there are too many terms in an aggregated query, the query can be replaced with TRUE. This has the effect that the message is broadcast in the higher levels of the Willow tree, and filtered in the lower levels. (Note that the same thing happens with Bloom filters, which also conservatively simplify the membership, leading to harmless false positives in the higher levels of the tree.)

4 Willow Implementation

The internal architecture used by Willow is close to that of Kademlia [5], even though the tree maintenance is very different. As the Willow tree itself is virtual, each Willow agent maintains domain information for each of the 128 domains that it is a member of. Given a particular domain $\langle d \rangle$ (a prefix of the agent's identifier of length d bits), the domain information for $\langle d \rangle$ contains the following:

- a small (possibly empty) set of *friends*, which are the "fingers" or "neighbors" used for P2P routing. The friends are members of $\langle d \rangle 0$ if the agent is in $\langle d \rangle 1$, or $\langle d \rangle 1$ if the agent is in $\langle d \rangle 0$;
- the attributes of both the left and right child domains, $\langle d \rangle 0$ and $\langle d \rangle 1$ respectively, one of which (the one that the agent is not in) may be empty;

Figure 2 shows the data maintained by agent 001 in the example of Fig. 1.

DHT routing uses friends for DHT routing exactly as in Kademlia. But in Willow, friends are also used for multicast routing as follows. Multicast messages contain an integer specifying in which domain they need to be forwarded. Initially, this integer is zero. To forward a multicast message with integer d, an

level	friend	child	contact	candidate	maxload
0	101	0	001	010	5
(root)		1	100	101	4
1	010	0	001	001	5
		1	010	010	2
2		0			
		1	001	001	5

Fig. 2. Data maintained by agent 001 in Fig. 1. In actuality, not the identifiers of other agents are stored, but their IP addresses and boot times.

agent considers all the branching domains that it is a member of with a name of d bits or longer. For each such domain, it forwards the message to one of the friends in the corresponding peer child domain (assuming they satisfy the SQL condition attached to the message), replacing the integer to contain the length of the child domain's identifier.

Note that in spite of there being only one logical tree, there is a different physical multicast tree from every agent, and this contributes to good load balancing. Most importantly, if agents are connected to the Internet with only a single link, and can only send one message at a time, the approach can be shown to maximize parallelism for relatively long messages.

4.1   Attribute Propagation

Consider an agent and some domain $\langle d \rangle$. The agent is either in the left or right child domain, say $\langle d \rangle 0$. In that case, the agent derives the attributes of $\langle d \rangle 0$ from the attributes in the domain information of $\langle d+1 \rangle$, while it learns the attributes of $\langle d \rangle 1$ through communication with other agents. This proceeds as follows.

Each domain elects one of its agents to be the *contact* of its domain. The default election strategy favors older, presumably more stable, agents to represent larger domains. This is done using the Willow aggregation facility, which elects both a contact and a *candidate* for each domain. The contact of a branching domain is the younger one of the candidates of its child domains, while the candidate of a domain is the older of the candidates of its child domains. The contact and candidate of leaf domains are both the agent itself. Note that all agents are contacts of exactly one internal domain, except for the oldest agent which is contact only of its leaf domain. The election strategy can be changed as needed simply by installing another aggregation query.

The contact of a domain is responsible for sending the attributes of the domain to the corresponding peer domain. That is, the contact of domain $\langle d \rangle 0$ sends updates of its corresponding attributes to a friend in $\langle d \rangle 1$, which then disseminates the update in its domain through multicast. Although higher level contacts have usually more attributes to aggregate and disseminate, the variance of higher level attributes tends to be low and so updates are often significantly less common than those of lower level domains. This depends of course on the choice of aggregation queries, but in practice we have seen relatively little load on higher level contacts.

4.2   Efficiency

An important aspect of the Willow protocol is how friends are determined, as these determine how well Willow exploits network locality. Currently, Willow maintains only a single friend per peer domain. At regular intervals (currently, once a minute), each agent probes a random agent in each peer domain (determined using a DHT lookup to a random key in that domain). If the random agent exhibits better latency than the current friend, the friend is replaced with the new agent. In Sect. 5 we show that this is an effective strategy.

In the Willow implementation, all communication is through TCP. As TCP connections do not lose any data, only diffs need to be exchanged over these pipes, which reduces communication overhead. TCP takes care of congestion control. Willow further limits the rate of sending updates in order to control load on the network. If a TCP pipe is full or the maximum rate has been exceeded, diffs can be "saved up." Newer updates will typically overwrite parts of older updates, and therefore the amount of backlog that builds up this way is limited. Note that each agent only has to maintain one TCP connection per friend, plus at most two for each of the domains the agent is contact of. Thus the total number of TCP connections per agent is $O(\log N)$.

4.3   Tree Maintenance

So far we have tacitly assumed that there are no membership changes. Willow supports a Tree Maintenance Protocol (TMP) to maintain a single instance of the Willow tree in which all agents have a consistent view of this tree. The TMP is a recursive protocol in which left and right child branches of a domain are repaired in parallel. Even disjoint trees merge quickly once communication between any two agents in the respective trees is established. Such initial contact between separated trees can be established through a rendez-vous host, IP multicast or broadcast. This is also how new agents join the Willow tree. Most other DHTs use DHT routing in order to add new agents, but this does not work efficiently when merging trees or fixing broken DHT structures.

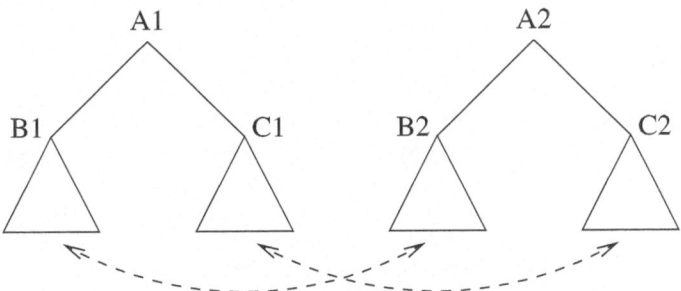

Fig. 3. Two distinct Willow trees are merged recursively and in parallel.

In Fig. 3 we show two disjoint Willow trees (or subtrees). In order to merge domains $A1$ and $A2$, we first recursively merge $B1$ and $B2$ first in parallel with $C1$ and $C2$, and then fix the top-level domains. The TMP uses two types of messages. A sync message contains the name of a (non-leaf) domain and the attributes of both child domains as known by the sender of the message (which is an agent in that domain). It is used when one agent discovers another agent with a different top-level contact. A conflict message contains the level of a domain and the address of a contact, and is used to repair inconsistencies.

On receipt of a sync message, agent R determines if it is in the specified domain. If not, R returns to the sender a normal update message containing the attributes of the smallest common domain. If R is in the domain, it compares both the attributes of the left child domain and the right child domain with those of its own. Both cases are handled in the same way, so we look at just the left child domain. If the attributes of the left child domain were null, or if the existing attributes share the same contact, then R adopts the attributes into its corresponding domain information. If the contact in the domain information is different from the contact in the message, R sends a conflict message to one of the two contacts, containing the address of the other one. On receipt of a conflict message, the agent determines the branching domain from which the contact was calculated, and sends a sync message for that domain to the conflicting contact.

For example, in Fig. 4, $A1$'s contact sends a sync message to $A2$'s contact. Then, after comparing the attributes of its child domains with those of $A1$'s child domains, $A2$'s contact detects conflicts in both child domains. It then sends a conflict message to the contacts of both $B1$ and $C2$, starting two parallel merges. The message to $B1$'s contact contains $B2$'s contact, and on receipt $B1$'s contact transmits to $B2$'s contact the attributes of $E1$ using another sync message. On the receipt of the sync message, $B2$'s contact adopts $E1$ as its right child domain. In parallel with all this, $C1$'s contact adopts $G2$ as its right child. After this, the normal update protocol fixes all attributes for all the agents involved.

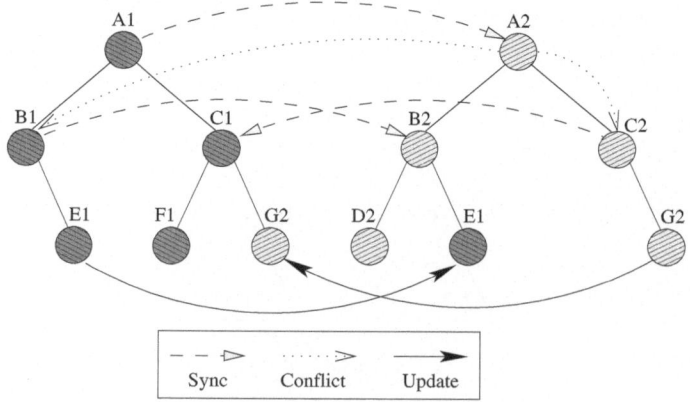

Fig. 4. Example of the zippering protocol.

When applied to two separate Willow trees, the TMP protocol *zippers* both trees together in $O(\log N)$ parallel steps. But the TMP protocol also fixes internal inconsistencies between agents. In particular, when an update message arrives from a peer domain with a conflicting contact, the TMP protocol is started to fix the inconsistency.

Not all inconsistencies can be detected this way. For example, it is possible for an agent in a domain X to know about a peer domain Y, while the contact for X does not. The agents in the peer domain may not know about X, or even if they did, the contact for Y may not. Thus there is no communication between domains X and Y.

The problem is resolved as follows. The Willow attribute update protocol periodically sends update messages at configured intervals, even in the absence of updates (in which case the message will have an empty set of diffs). Currently, Willow is configured to do so every 10 seconds. If an agent in X has not received an update (either directly from an agent in Y, or through multicast in the local domain) for more than 20 seconds, it sends an update for X to a friend in Y. This friend will multicast the attributes in Y, and so the contact for Y will learn about X. That contact in turn will send an update to the contact of X, which will then multicast the attributes of Y within X. After this, all agents in X and Y will know about each other.

An agent that has not received an update for more than 20 seconds will continue to sends updates to the peer domain every 10 seconds. However, if more than 60 seconds have passed, the agent will remove the attributes for the peer domain, and considers it failed.

5   Evaluation

A fully operating Java implementation of Willow is currently available. In order to investigate the scaling issues of Willow, we conducted a study of Willow on a simulated network. In each experiment we placed nodes uniformly at random on a 250x250 millisecond Euclidean plane. The network latency between any two nodes is determined by their Euclidean distance. In these simulations we assume that the bandwidth is constant across the network.

In Fig. 5 we show the maximum end-to-end delay of multicasting a small message from a random node to all other nodes, which we expect to grow $O(\log N)$. We used five different strategies for agents selecting friends in peer domains. They are

- *Random*: use a random agent in the peer domain.
- *Best/2*: use the closest of two random agents.
- *Best/5*: use the closest of five random agents.
- *Optimal*: use the closest agent in the peer domain.

The *optimal* friend selection strategy is not practical, as there is no cost-effective way for all agents to determine their nearest-by peer agent, but serves as a base line. (In fact, the simulation study was limited by investigating this

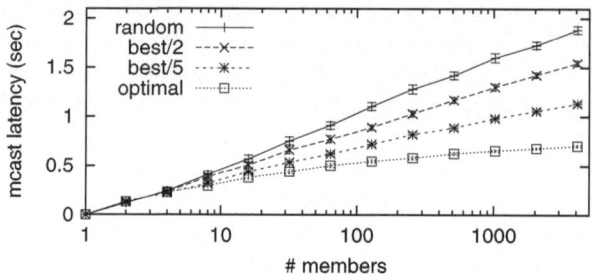

Fig. 5. Multicast latency as a function of the number of agents for different friend selection strategies. The error bars denote 99% confidence intervals.

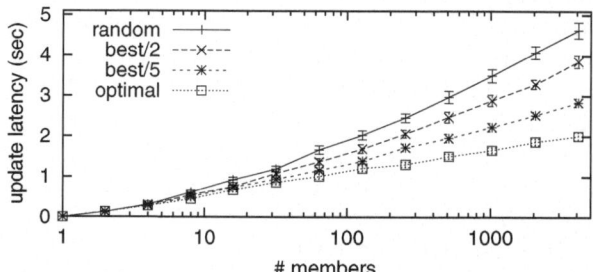

Fig. 6. Update latency as a function of the number of agents for different friend selection strategies.

aspect.) We can see, however, that trying random peer agents over time and maintaining the one with the lowest latency converges fairly quickly to an optimal latency.

In Fig. 6 we show the end-to-end delay of updates, that is, how long it takes between the time that an update is made at a random agent and the time at which all other agents have learned the new root-level aggregate. We simulate a worst-case scenario in which the root-level aggregate indeed changes. Depending on the application this can in fact be a rare event. From a complexity analysis study we expect the latency to grow $O(\log^2 N)$. Load studies omitted here show that load is well balanced across the agents.

6   Conclusion

The Willow protocol represents two contributions over previous work. First, Willow supports all of DHT routing, multicast, publish/subscribe, and aggregation in one simple, location-aware protocol. The aggregation facilities allow for a wide range of queries over the data. Second, Willow includes an efficient tree merging protocol that allows disjoint trees to merge in $O(\log N)$ parallel steps, and also repairs Willow trees efficiently when damaged by churn.

Willow is implemented in 2300 lines of Java code, excluding the SQL parser and engine (representing close to 10,000 lines of Java). Initial experience and simulation results indicate that Willow scales well.

Acknowledgements

We would like to thank Ken Birman, Werner Vogels, Dan Dumitriu, and Vidhyashankar Venkatraman for many useful discussions that have led to the design of Willow, and the anonymous reviewers for their comments and suggestions.

References

1. van Renesse, R.: Scalable and secure resource location. In: Proc. of the Thirty-Third Annual Hawaii Int. Conf. on System Sciences, Los Alamitos, CA, IEEE, IEEE Computer Society Press (2000)
2. van Renesse, R., Birman, K., Vogels, W.: Astrolabe: A robust and scalable technology for distributed system monitoring, management and data mining. ACM Transactions on Computer Systems **21** (2003)
3. Bozdog, A., van Renesse, R., Dumitriu, D.: SelectCast: A scalable and self-repairing multicast overlay routing facility. In: Proc. of the First ACM Workshop on Survivable and Self-Regenerative Systems, Fairfax, VA (2003)
4. Plaxton, C.G., Rajaraman, R., Richa, A.W.: Accessing nearby copies of replicated objects in a distributed environment. In: ACM Symposium on Parallel Algorithms and Architectures. (1997) 311–320
5. Maymounkov, P., Mazieres, D.: Kademlia: A peer-to-peer information system based on the XOR metric. In: Proc. of the First International Workshop on Peer-to-Peer Systems (IPTPS'02), Cambridge, MA (2002)
6. Albrecht, K., Arnold, R., Wattenhofer, R.: Join and leave in peer-to-peer systems: The DASIS approach. Technical Report 427, Dept. of Computer Science, ETH Zurich (2003)
7. Bhagwan, R., Varghese, G., Voelker, G.: Cone: Augmenting DHTs to support distributed resource discovery. Technical Report CS2003-0755, UC, San Diego (2003)
8. Yalagandula, P., Dahlin, M.: A scalable distributed information management system. (2003) In submission.
9. Zhang, Z., Shi, S.M., Zhu, J.: SOMO: Self-Organized Metadata Overlay for resource management in p2p DHT. In: Proc. of the Second Int. Workshop on Peer-to-Peer Systems (IPTPS'03), Berkeley, CA (2003)
10. Huebsch, R., Hellerstein, J., Lanham, N., Loo, B., Shenker, S.: Querying the Internet with PIER. In: Proc. of the 19th Int. Conf. on Very Large Databases (VLDB). (2003)
11. Zhuang, S., Zhao, B., Joseph, A., Katz, R., Kubiatowicz, J.: Bayeux: An architecture for scalable and fault-tolerant wide-area data dissemination. In: Proc. of the 11th Int. Workshop on Network and Operating System Support for Digital Audio and Video, Port Jefferson, NY (2001)
12. Castro, M., Druschel, P., Kermarrec, A.M., Nandi, A., Rowstron, A., Singh, A.: SplitStream: High-bandwidth multicast in a cooperative environment. In: Proc. of the 19th ACM Symp. on Operating Systems Principles, Bolton Landing, NY (2003)

Friends Troubleshooting Network: Towards Privacy-Preserving, Automatic Troubleshooting

Helen J. Wang[1], Yih-Chun Hu[3], Chun Yuan[2], Zheng Zhang[2], and Yi-Min Wang[1]

[1] Microsoft Research, Redmond, WA, USA
[2] Microsoft Research Asia, Beijing, China
[3] University of California, Berkeley, CA, USA

Abstract. Content sharing is a popular usage of peer-to-peer systems for its inherent scalability and low cost of maintenance. In this paper, we leverage this nature of peer-to-peer systems to tackle a new problem: automatic misconfiguration troubleshooting. In this setting, machine configurations from the peers are "shared" to diagnose the misconfigurations on a sick machine. A key challenge for such a troubleshooting system is privacy preservation. To this end, we construct *Friends Troubleshooting Network* (FTN), a peer-to-peer overlay network, where the links between peer machines reflect the friendship of their owners. To preserve privacy, we use *historyless and futureless random-walk* in the FTN, during which search along with parameter aggregation are carried out for the purpose of troubleshooting. Many of our techniques can be applied to other application scenarios that require privacy-preserving distributed computing and information aggregation. We have also identified a number of open challenges that remain to be addressed.

1 Introduction

Today's desktop PCs have not only brought to their users an enormous and ever-increasing number of features and services, but also an increasing amount of troubleshooting cost and productivity losses. Studies [14][15] have shown that technical support contributes 17% of the total cost of ownership of today's desktop PCs. A large amount of technical support time is spent on troubleshooting.

In this paper, we tackle an important troubleshooting category in which application failures are due to misconfigurations on the troubled machine. In our prior work [16], we developed an effective algorithm called *PeerPressure* for diagnosing such misconfigurations. PeerPressure uses the *common* configurations from a set of helper machines to identify the anomalous misconfigurations on the sick one. *Searching* for the right set of helper machines and *aggregating* helper configurations is the topic of this paper. Maintaining helper configurations at a centralized server or database is expensive as it requires continuous update and maintenance. Further, such a solution places complete trust on a single entity. Hence, the privacy of both helpers and troubleshooting users are of great concern. These reasons lead us to explore the peer-to-peer approach where peers share their content at low cost of maintenance and with inherent scalability. In our setting, the "content" refers to the machine configurations of the peers. Further, the trust is distributed among the peers. There are two essential goals in designing a PeerPressure-based peer-to-peer troubleshooting system:

G.M. Voelker and S. Shenker (Eds.): IPTPS 2004, LNCS 3279, pp. 184–194, 2004.

– *Integrity*: We should preserve the integrity of the troubleshooting results.
– *Privacy*: We should protect privacy-sensitive configurations for both troubleshooting users and peer helpers during routing and information aggregation.

Ensuring *integrity* is challenging because malicious peers may lie about the applications they own and the configuration state they have, which can lead to incorrect troubleshooting results. A machine can be malicious either because its owner has ill intentions or because it is compromised by an attacker.

We cope with the ill-intentioned-user problem by designing well-established social trust into the troubleshooting framework. Today, when encountering computer problems, most people first seek help from their friends and neighbors. Based on this observation, we construct a *Friends Troubleshooting Network* (FTN), which is a peer-to-peer overlay network, where a link between two machines is due to the friendship of their owners. Here, we assume that a pair of friends intend to help each other out by contributing their own authentic, relevant non-privacy-compromising configuration information to each other for the purpose of troubleshooting. If the relevant configurations are privacy-sensitive, they will refuse to supply the information rather than giving false content. Further, just like in the real world, when Alice asks her friend Bob a question, if Bob only has a partial answer or does not know the answer, Bob can potentially ask his friend Carol *on Alice's behalf*, especially when Alice and Carol are not friends. This is exactly how a troubleshooting request recursively propagates in the FTN. One may quickly conclude that our system manifests *transitive trust*. However, in our example, because Carol and Alice are not friends, Carol may provide *untruthful* answers to Alice if Alice asks Carol *directly*. So, more precisely, FTN manifests *recursive trust* instead.

Coping with compromised FTN nodes is an open challenge. We provide a rough outline for integrity preservation under such conditions in Section 7.1.

Despite the friendship-based trust in the FTN, *privacy* remains a crucial goal in FTN since friends do maintain privacy from one another. In fact, much configuration state contains privacy-sensitive information, such as usernames, passwords, URLs visited, and applications installed. We achieve privacy through a *historyless and futureless random-walk* of an *ownerless* troubleshooting request, during which search as well as parameter aggregation are carried out for the purpose of PeerPressure troubleshooting. Unlike the traditional peer-to-peer search and routing protocols which are destination-driven, the historyless and futureless random-walk in FTN exhibits a new communication pattern which is *destination-free* searching and routing along with parameter aggregation.

For the rest of the paper, we first provide background on PeerPressure in Section 2. We state our privacy objectives in Section 3. In Section 4, we present our protocol design for privacy-preserving search and parameter aggregation. We discuss on how FTN achieves privacy objectives in Section 5. Then we discuss the overhead of our protocol in Section 6. In Section 7, we list the open challenges remaining in this work. We compare and constrast our work with the related work in Section 8 and finally summarize in Section 9.

2   Background: PeerPressure

PeerPressure [16] assumes that an application functions correctly on most machines and hence that most machines have healthy configurations. It uses the statistics from a set of sample machines to identify anomalous misconfigurations. The distinct feature of PeerPressure in contrast with other work in this area [17] is that it eliminates the need of manually identifying a healthy machine as a reference point for comparison. We have experimented with the PeerPressure algorithm and a corresponding troubleshooting toolkit on Windows systems where most of configuration data is stored at a centralized registry. Figure 1 illustrates the operations of our PeerPressure troubleshooter.

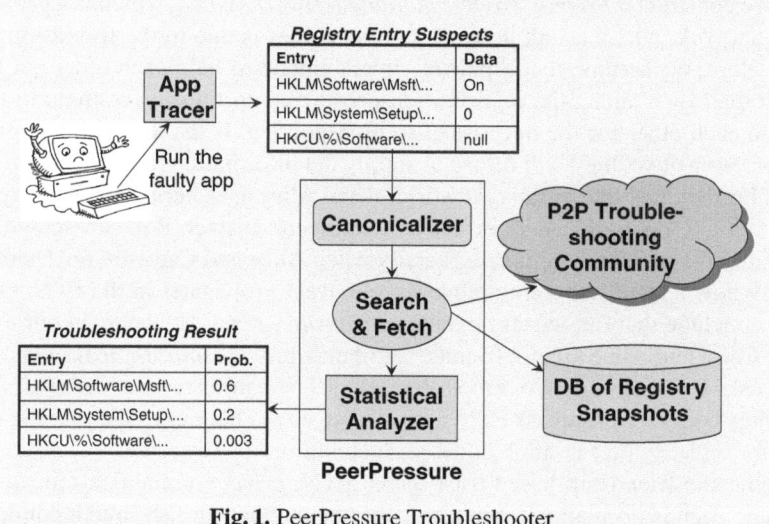

Fig. 1. PeerPressure Troubleshooter

PeerPressure first uses application tracing (with the "AppTracer") to capture the configuration entries and their values that are touched by the abnormal execution of the application under troubleshooting. These entries are misconfiguration *suspects*. Then, the canonicalizer turns any user- or machine-specific entries into a *canonicalized* form. For example, user names and machine names are all replaced with constant strings "USER_NAME" and "MACHINE_NAME", respectively. Next, from a sample set of helper machines, for each suspect entry, PeerPressure obtains the number of samples that match the value of the suspect entry, and the cardinality (the number of possible values this entry may have). PeerPressure uses these parameters along with the sample set size and the number of suspect entries to calculate the probability of a suspect entry being the cause of the symptom. The intuition behind this sick probability calculation is that the more conformant a suspect entry is with the samples, the more likely the entry is to be healthy. The top ranking entries with regard to the sick probability are diagnosed as the *root-cause candidates*. The sample set can be obtained either from a database of registry snapshots collected from a large number of user machines or from a peer-to-peer troubleshooting community such as the one described in this paper.

We have demonstrated PeerPressure [16] as an effective troubleshooting method: Our PeerPressure troubleshooter can pinpoint the root-cause misconfiguration accurately for 12 out of 20 real-world troubleshooting cases and for the remaining cases, it can narrow down the root-cause candidates by three orders of magnitude.

3 Privacy Model and Objectives

Before we dive into our protocol design, we first state our privacy model and objectives.

3.1 Private Information

The information being communicated in FTN is PC configuration data. We denote the complete set of configuration data on a machine as D. A subset of D is identity-revealing, such as usernames and cookies, which we denote as D_i. The remaining set $D_r = D - D_i$ may contain information that compromises privacy when *linked* with user identity. Some examples of such information are URLs visited and applications installed. Our privacy objective is to protect *all* peers' privacy by *anonymizing* such privacy-sensitive information in D_r. Of course, this forbids D_i to be revealed.

3.2 Attackers

We assume a friendly operational environment where attackers are simply curious friends. We address compromised nodes in Section 7.1, and not else where.

3.3 Attacks

The ways attackers attempt to obtain privacy-sensitive information include the following:

1. Message inspection attack: Infer privacy-sensitive information passively by inspecting the messages that are passing by.
2. Polling attack: Repeatedly send fake troubleshooting requests to a friend to obtain and infer his private information.
3. Eavesdrop on machines on the same LAN.
4. Known topology attack: Discover the FTN topology through side channels. This information may be used to deduce privacy-sensitive information.
5. Gossip attack: Friends may gossip (i.e., collude) and correlate pieces of information.

4 Privacy-Preserving Search and Parameter Aggregation Protocol in FTN

We assume that the FTN bootstraps and maintains its overlay links in the same way as Gnutella [8] or Kazaa [10] except that the neighbors are trusted friends' machines. We assume that each node and its immediate friends exchange their public keys through a secure out-of-band mechanism. The neighboring nodes use their public keys to establish secure channels for troubleshooting communications.

4.1   Basic Approaches

We take the following basic approaches to achieve our privacy objectives.

- **Integration of search and parameter aggregation in one transaction**: If the search is a separate step, which returns the IP addresses of helpers, then the querier can determine the applications running on the helpers' machines. Since application ownership could be private information, we integrate search and parameter gathering for PeerPressure into one step in such a way (next bullet point) that the parameter values at any point represents a collective state for a set of friends, and therefore does not reveal any individual state.
- **Historyless and futureless random-walk routing**: To preserve the privacy of the troubleshooting user as well as node owners on the path, we design the troubleshooting messages to be *ownerless*, and not to contain any routing history or future routing state such as the source and the nodes traversed or to be traversed. In addition, we make sure that the troubleshooting state gathered from the past is *aggregate* in nature so that individual state is disguised. Each node on the forwarding path of the random-walk is either a forwarder which simply proxies the request or a helper which contributes its own relevant configurations to the request and then proxies the request. Each node on the path keeps per-request state on the previous and next hop of the request. On the return path, the reply follows the same way back. The reply contains all the parameters needed by PeerPressure calculation at the sick machine.

4.2   Protocol Details

Figure 2 zooms into a segment of the random walk in FTN.

Creating a Request on the Sick Machine. A sick machine first filters out the identity-revealing entries from the suspects, for example by removing all entries that contain usernames. Then it creates a troubleshooting request as shown in Table 1.

The entry value distributions in field 3 are needed by the sick machine for determining the most popular values as legal values for root cause candidates as well as determining the cardinality of the entry (Section 2). The size of the value distribution depends on the cardinality of the entry. According to our study in [16], 87% of Windows registry entries have a cardinality of 1 and 94% have no more than 2. So, value distributions do not add significant overhead to our messaging.

Table 1. FTN Request

1	$H(app.exe)$ where H is a one-way hash function.
2	Remaining number of samples needed, R
3	For each suspect entry e, EntryName, SickEntryValue, the number of matches M_e, and the value distribution of e from the past samples

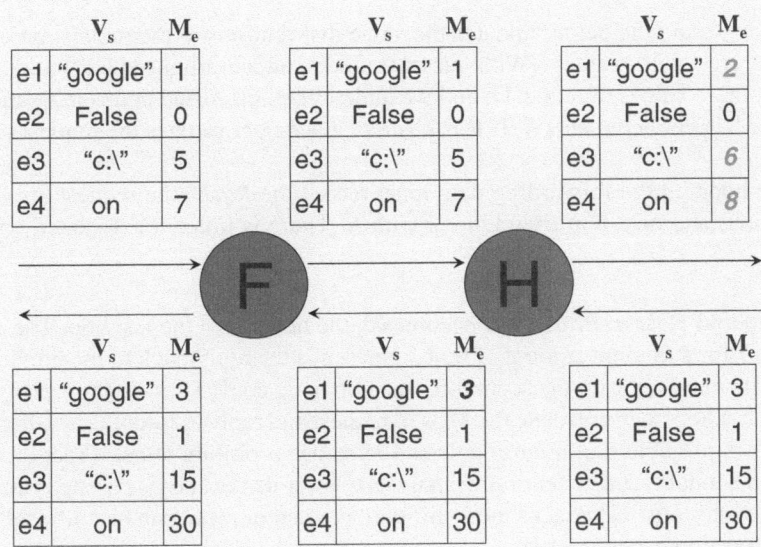

Fig. 2. FTN Search and Parameter Aggregation Protocol: in the forward path, H, the helper, updates value distribution (not shown) of each configuration entry e and the number of matches M_e if its value for e matches the sick value V_s. The forwarder only proxies the request. On the return trip, the complete PeerPressure parameter information is passed back to the sick machine following the same path. (The role of being a helper or a forwarder is only known to the node itself, and not anyone else)

To preserve anonymity, the requester initializes the value distribution with random values.

We identify each request with $RqID = H(n, AllEntryNames)$, where n is a nonce generated at the sick machine, and H is a one-way hash function.

Forward Path and Parameter Aggregation. The sick machine establishes a secure channel with an available friend chosen at random, then sends it the troubleshooting request. The friend sends an *ACK* if it can become either a forwarder or a helper for the request. If no *ACK* is received upon timeout, then the requester tries another friend chosen at random. To avoid routing loops, if a friend has seen the *RqID* of an arriving request in the past, the friend replies with a *NACK*.

If a node is involved in forwarding or helping and if it is capable to help because it also runs the application under troubleshooting, then the node becomes a helper with the probability of P_h. Without P_h, the second-to-last-hop node can potentially infer information about the last-hop-node. When the application under troubleshooting is very popular, with high probability, the last-hop node is capable to help. Then the second-to-last-hop node can correlate request and reply to infer the last-hop helper's configuration state. Nonetheless, even with P_h, a node can poll its next hop using fake requests with $R = 1$ to infer information statistically. We make such attacks more difficult with a bimodal P_h where P_h takes a smaller value for requests with small R's.

A helper needs to update the troubleshooting request accordingly. It increments M_e, the number of matches for each suspect entry e, when the helper's value matches that of the sick's. And the helper updates the value distributions in the request based on its own respective entry values. (With our trust model, uncompromised FTN nodes do not lie about these values (Section 1); and we address compromised nodes in Section 7.1). Then, the helper decrements R. If R is positive, the helper proxies the request to one of its friends.

Each node on the forwarding path must record the $RqID$, the request arrival time, the previous and next hop friend along with R. There is timeout associated with each request.

Last Hop and Return Path. If R becomes 0, the node is on the last hop. The last-hop node waits for a random amount of time, then sends the reply back to the previous hop. Without the random wait, the second-to-last hop node could know that the reply comes from the last hop, then correlate the M_e's in request and reply to infer the last-hop node's values. It is possible that a curious friend launches a polling attack (Section 3) with $R = 1$ and conducts statistical timing analysis to infer its next hop's private information. To make such statistical attacks more difficult, the random wait can be uniformly drawn from a large range, e.g., 15 hops.

The reply follows the request path back to the sick machine. The sick machine first subtracts the random initialization from the value distributions. Then it performs PeerPressure diagnosis.

5 Achieving Privacy Objectives

The historyless and futureless random-walk along with integrated search and parameter aggregation counters the message inspection attacks and polling attacks (see Section 3.3). The use of secure channel on each overlay link counters the eavesdropping attack. The use of P_h makes the potential inference in known topology attack difficult. We can mitigate most gossip attacks with the use of P_h along with historyless and futureless routing, except in one scenario: If a victim has two gossiping friends, whenever the victim "helps" with troubleshooting and is en route between the two, its information could be inferred by the two gossipers. A potential technique for reducing the impact of this attack is random perturbation which is discussed in Section 7.2.

6 Response Time and Bandwidth Overhead

In FTN, the troubleshooting response time is dictated by the number of hops a troubleshooting request and its reply traverse, which is $N/P_h * 2$ where N is the number of samples needed. When $N = 10$, PeerPressure is already effective; nonetheless, the larger the N is, the better the root-cause ranking becomes in general [16]. The response time can be improved with fan-outs and by gathering a fraction of samples on each branch.

In terms of bandwidth overhead, for the Windows applications we evaluated in [16], there is a median of 1171 suspect entries. So, according to Table 1, our troubleshooting messages are about 80 KB.

7   Open Challenges

7.1   Integrity in the Face of Compromised FTN Nodes

Though friends may be trustworthy, their computers' behaviors do not necessarily carry out their owners' intentions when they are compromised by attackers. To defend integrity when some FTN nodes may be compromised, all nodes on the request path remember the troubleshooting request (see Table 1) that they forward. Then, on the return trip, each node checks these invariants: the additional number of matches for each suspect does not exceed R, the recorded remaining number of samples needed; for each suspect, the count in value distributions in the reply did not decrease; and the sum of all counts in the reply minus the sum of all counts in the request equals to R. Only when these invariants are maintained, a node forwards on the reply. Ensuring absolute integrity here remains an open challenge.

Another serious attack is that *one* compromised node can bring in his gang of malicious friends which could all be himself in the form of the Sybil attack [5]. A large majority of "Sybils" impact the troubleshooting result without violating any integrity invariants mentioned above. One way to counter this attack is to initiate multiple troubleshooting requests, hoping that a majority of them will return with correct troubleshooting results, and therefore weed out the incorrect ones that have compromised nodes on the path. The earlier a compromised node appears on a path (i.e., the higher the R is), the more room the compromised node has to sway the final troubleshooting result. In such cases, using a high fan-out (Section 6) reduces R, and limits the compromised node's influence. Further analysis is needed on the number of requests needed given the positions of the compromised nodes.

7.2   Random Perturbation for Gossip Attack

In a gossip attack (Section 3), two common friends can collude to infer a third friend's private information by noticing the changes to M_e. To reduce the impact of this attack, it might be feasible for each node on the path to apply random perturbation [1] to R, the remaining number of samples required, M_e, the number of matches, and value distribution updates. For example, instead of incrementing M_e for Suspect e when a helper has a matching value, the helper adds a random noise to M_e to confuse the gossipers. Nonetheless, it is unclear how such random noise affect the final troubleshooting result especially when the total number of samples is small. We are investigating the applicability of this technique.

7.3   Ownerless Troubleshooting Request

Removing identity-revealing information from the original troubleshooting request is non-trivial since entries that are not identity-revealing individually could be combined to identify a user. Systematic recognition of all identity-revealing vectors of configuration entries is an open challenge.

8   Related Work

There is much related work in the arena of anonymization. Our chain style of historyless and futureless random-walk is similar in spirit to that of FreeNet [4] and Crowds [13]. FreeNet is a distributed anonymous information storage and retrieval system. Crowds is for anonymous web transactions. Chaum's approach to anonymization is based on the use of *mixes* [3] which serve as proxies to provide sender-receiver unlinkability through traffic mixing. Onion routing [9] extends the mixes with layers of onion-style pre-encryptions. Tarzan [6] implements the mix idea using a peer-to-peer overlay and provides sender anonymity and robustness to the mix entry point.

All of the above anonymization techniques address point-to-point communications. However, our protocol in FTN takes the form of one-to-many communications and is destination-free, since a sample set is drawn from the peers. As a result, nodes on the path must look into the packet content and potentially modify it before proxying it forward. Hence, our application additionaly requires user privacy not being compromised in this process of state aggregation.

Our problem of privacy-perserving parameter aggregation shares much similarity to the problem of secure and privacy-preserving voting [7][2] with four distinctions. First, voting requires voters to be authenticated by a centralized authority, such as the government. Second, our protocol requires participation privacy additionally; otherwise, the privacy of the application ownership is compromised. Third, unlike some voting scenarios where there are limited number of voting candidates, our problem scenario does not have such a limit. Lastly, while voting requires precise vote tallies, PeerPressure uses the statistics which allows small amount of inaccuracies; therefore, random perturbation could potentially be used for privacy in our scenario.

The authors of SIA[12] presented a set of techniques for secure information aggregation in sensor networks with the presence of malicious sensors and aggregators. The integrity of information aggregation is achieved essentially through authentication which is identity-revealing. In FTN, we cannot do the same because of the privacy concerns.

ACME [11] is a scalable, flexible infrastructure for monitoring, analyzing, and controlling Internet-scale systems. ACME collects, aggregates and reduces nodes' health data as the data is routed through a peer-to-peer network, but it does not address privacy or integrity.

9   Concluding Remarks

In this paper, we introduce automatic troubleshooting as an interesting application that can also benefit from the content-sharing nature of peer-to-peer systems while being legal at the same time. We leverage an automatic troubleshooting algorithm, PeerPressure [16], which uses statistics among the peers to diagnose the anomalous misconfigurations on a sick machine. For a privacy-preserving PeerPressure-based peer-to-peer system, we construct a Friends Troubleshooting Network (FTN) which is a peer-to-peer overlay network where the links between peer machines reflect the friendship of their owners. The FTN nodes manifest *recursive trust* rather than transitive trust. In

FTN, we use *historyless* and *futureless* random-walk for integrated search and parameter aggregation for PeerPressure. We believe these techniques can be applied to other application scenarios that require privacy-preserving distributed computing and information aggregation. There is much future work ahead of us in making FTN a reality. Integrity preservation in the face of compromised nodes, the feasibility of random perturbation in this setting, and recognizing identity-revealing configuration entries remain open challenges.

Acknowledgement

Josh Benaloh, John Docceur, John Dunagan, Jon Howell, David Oppenheimer and Alf Zugenmaier have given us invaluable discussions and critiques for numerous drafts of this paper from the technical content to the presentation. We are grateful to their generous help. We also thank the anonymous reviewers for their insightful comments and suggestions.

References

1. AGRAWAL, R., AND SRIKANT, R. Privacy Perserving Data Mining. In *Proceedings of SIGMOD* (2000).
2. BENALOH. *Verifiable Secret-Ballot Elections*. PhD thesis, Yale University, Sept. 1987.
3. CHAUM, D. L. Untraceable Electronic Mail, Return Addresses and Digital Pseudonyms. In *CACM* (1981).
4. CLARKE, I., SANDBERG, O., WILEY, B., AND HONG, T. W. Freenet: A distributed anonymous information storage and retrieval system. In Proc. International Workshop on Design Issues in Anonymity and Unobservability. In *Proceedings of International Workshop on Design Issues in Anonymity and Unobservability* (2001). Lecture Notes Computer Science Volume 2009.
5. DOUCEUR, J. R. The Sybil Attack. In *Proceedings of the 1st International Workshop on Peer-to-Peer Systems (IPTPS)* (2002).
6. FREEDMAN, M. J., SIT, E., GATES, J., AND MORRIS, R. Introducing Tarzan, a Peer-to-Peer Anonymizing Network Layer. In *IPTPS* (2002).
7. FUJIOKA, T., OKAMOTO, T., AND OHTA, K. A Practical Secret Voting Scheme for Large Scale Elections. In *Proceedings of Auscrypt* (Dec. 1992).
8. The Gnutella v0.6 Protocol, Gnutella Development Forum, 2001.
9. GOLDSCHLAG, D. M., REED, M. G., AND SYVERSON, P. F. Onion Routing for Anonymous and Private Internet Connections. In *CACM* (Feb 1999).
10. KaZaa. http://www.kazaa.com.
11. OPPENHEIMER, D., VATKOVSKIY, V., WEATHERSPOON, H., LEE, J., PATTERSON, D. A., AND KUBIATOWICZ, J. Monitoring, Analyzing, and Controlling Internet-Scale Systems with ACME. Tech. Rep. UCB/CSD-03-1276, U. C. Berkeley, October 2003.
12. PRZYDATEK, B., SONG, D., AND PERRIG, A. SIA: Secure Information Aggregation in Sensor Networks. In *Proceedings of ACM SenSys* (Nov 2003).
13. REITER, M. K., AND RUBIN, A. D. Crowds: Anonymity for Web Transactions. In *ACM Transactions on Information and System Security* (Nov 1998).
14. SILVER, M., AND FIERING, L. Desktop and Notebook TCO Updated for the 21st Century, September 2003.

15. Web-to-Host: Reducing the Total Cost of Ownership, The Tolly Group, May 2000.
16. WANG, H. J., CHEN, Y., PLATT, J., ZHANG, R., AND WANG, Y. M.   PeerPressure, A Statistical Method towards Automatic Troubleshooting. Tech. Rep. MSR-TR-2003-80, Microsoft Research, Redmond, WA, Nov 2003.
17. WANG, Y.-M., VERBOWSKI, C., DUNAGAN, J., CHEN, Y., WANG, H. J., YUAN, C., AND ZHANG, Z. STRIDER: A Black-box, State-based Approach to Change and Configuration Management and Support. In *Proceedings of LISA* (2003).

Spurring Adoption of DHTs with OpenHash, a Public DHT Service

Brad Karp[1,2], Sylvia Ratnasamy[3], Sean Rhea[3,4], and Scott Shenker[4,5]

[1] Intel Research Pittsburgh, Pittsburgh, PA 15213, USA
[2] Carnegie Mellon University, Pittsburgh, PA 15213, USA
[3] Intel Research Berkeley, Berkeley, CA 94704, USA
[4] UC Berkeley, Berkeley, CA 94720, USA
[5] ICSI, Berkeley, CA 94704, USA

1 Introduction

The past three years have seen intense research into Distributed Hash Tables (DHTs): both into algorithms for building them, and into applications built atop them. These applications have spanned a strikingly wide range, including file systems [1–3], event notification [4], content distribution [5], e-mail delivery [6], indirection services [7, 8], web caches [9], and relational query processors [10]. While this set of applications is impressively diverse, the vast majority of application building is done by a small community of DHT researchers. If DHTs are to have a positive impact on the design of distributed applications *used by real users outside this research community,* we believe that the community of DHT-based application developers should be as broad as possible.

Why, then, has this community of developers remained narrow? First, keeping a research prototype of a DHT running continually requires effort, and experience with DHT code. Second, significant testbed resources are required to deploy and test DHT-based applications. A hacker can download the code for Chord, but she cannot run that code alone; recall that only a tiny fraction of would-be developers has access to a testbed infrastructure like PlanetLab [11]. Consequently, most application developers would turn to ad hoc application-specific solutions rather than attempt to use a DHT.

Our central tenet is that we, as a community, need to harness the ingenuity and talents of the vast majority of application developers who reside outside the rarified but perhaps sterile air of the DHT research community. To that end, we issue a call-to-arms to deploy an *open, publicly accessible* DHT service that would allow new developers to experiment with DHT-based applications *without* the burden of deploying and maintaining a DHT. We believe that there are many simple applications that, individually, might not warrant the effort required to deploy a DHT but that would be trivial to build over a DHT service *were one available*. Many-to-many instant messaging and photo publication, where a user may share photos under a long-lived name even if the photos are served from a home machine with a dynamic IP address are but two of the many such applications. We term these *lite applications*, because they make only simple and often fleeting use of a DHT[1].

---

[1] Our claim is not that a DHT service is the *only* or *best* way to build these applications, but rather that a DHT service is a common building block that would be useful for a wide range of such applications, and would be far preferable to building one-off, special-purpose rendezvous or indirection mechanisms for each application (*e.g.,* dynamic DNS for photo publication).

G.M. Voelker and S. Shenker (Eds.): IPTPS 2004, LNCS 3279, pp. 195–205, 2004.
© Springer-Verlag Berlin Heidelberg 2004

To spur the development of these lite applications we propose *OpenHash*, an open, publicly accessible DHT service that runs on a set of infrastructure hosts and allows any application to execute put() and get() operations. Its presence would hopefully enable and encourage the development of a wide range of interesting and unexpected DHT applications[2].

However, we already know from our limited experience with DHT-based applications that some require application-specific processing and thus can't be limited to using the generic put()/get() interface. The technical contribution of this paper is an examination of what one can do to extend the functionality of a DHT service so that such application-specific requirements can be reasonably accommodated. That is, we seek to share a common DHT routing platform while allowing application-specific functionality to reside only on certain nodes. To meet this hybrid challenge of shared routing but application-specific processing we propose ReDiR, a distributed rendezvous scheme that removes the need in today's DHT systems to place application-specific code together with DHT code. The ReDiR algorithm itself requires only a put()/get() interface from a DHT, but allows a surprisingly wide range of applications to work over a DHT service.

2   DHT as Library *vs.* as Service

Implementing a DHT as a service that exports a narrow put()/get() interface is a departure from how present-day DHT-based applications are built. To illuminate the consequences of this design decision, we consider in turn the properties of the current approach and the service approach.

Many existing DHT applications (e.g. [5, 10, 3]) are built using a "bundled" model, where the application is able to read the local DHT state and receive upcalls from the DHT (as in [12]), either by being linked into the same process as the DHT code or through local RPC calls. For brevity, we will say these applications use the DHT as a *library* in either case. To support upcalls, the library model requires that code for the same set of applications be available at all DHT hosts. In practice, this limitation prevents sharing of a single DHT *deployment* by multiple applications – or even by different revisions of the same application – that require distinct upcall-invoked code on all DHT hosts. Instead, different applications only re-use the DHT *code*, amortizing the development of the DHT functionality over the set of applications that use it. A side effect of this is that every such application imposes the maintenance traffic associated with running a DHT on its underlying infrastructure.

The great strength of the library model is the flexibility it affords applications in functionality. By bundling arbitrary application code with DHT code, the model supports any operation at any overlay host on any data held at that host. However, this flexibility comes at the expense of synergy in deployment, and thus at the expense of ease of use of the DHT. We believe that these weaknesses in the library model are the primary reasons for the narrowness of the community of developers of DHT-based applications today. Most would-be DHT-using developers look elsewhere for rendezvous

---

[2] We are often reminded that the most successful peer-to-peer application was developed by a 19-year-old.

and indirection solutions, because the effort and resources required to deploy a DHT
are often greater than those required to hack up a more ad hoc solution.

In contrast, a DHT that provides a more limited interface, specifically only put()
and get(), does not need to be bundled with application code and can thus be deployed
as a common, openly accessible service. There are two principal weaknesses of this service model. First, a publicly accessible service is subject to attack[3]. We include a brief
discussion in Section 4 but defer a full exploration of the problem to later work. The second problem, which is the focus of this paper, is that the service model is far less flexible
in the functionality (and thus the applications) it supports. Intuitively the put()/get()
interface appears far more restrictive than the "any code, any node" approach of the
library model. We offer a detailed discussion of what the service model can and cannot support in the following section. The library model and service model are extremes
on a continuum between maximal flexibility without an easily adopted infrastructure,
and providing such an infrastructure with reduced flexibility. In the next section, we
explore the space between these extremes and the extent to which application-specific
functionality can live atop a DHT service.

3   Application-Specific Functionality in OpenHash

Existing, library-based DHT applications [3, 10, 8, 2] co-locate application-specific
functionality with the DHT. We distinguish between application functionality invoked
at the endpoint (*i.e.*, destination) of a DHT route versus functionality invoked at *every*
hop along a route and show that, surprisingly, the former is quite easily achievable over
a service while the latter is not.

3.1   Endpoint *vs.* Per-Hop Operators

We use illustrative examples drawn from existing applications, namely PIER and *i3*, to
expose the difference between endpoint and per-hop functionality.

The first system we consider is *i3*. In *i3*, packets are *forwarded* to identifiers called
triggers. To send a packet to x, a sender routes the packet to the DHT host responsible
for storing trigger entries for x. That DHT host then extracts the value I corresponding
to x and *forwards* the packet to I. There are two aspects to i3's support for packet
forwarding within a DHT. First, each DHT host in i3 must implement the forwarding
operation. Second, that forwarding code must read the (key, value) pair stored locally
at that DHT host.

Likewise, to execute a join operation in PIER [10], a DHT host iterates over all
the (key, value) pairs in its local store, and rehashes them by a portion of their value
fields. Here the code for a join operator resides at every DHT host and has full access
to the host's local store. The essence of the above behaviors is that the DHT routes
an operation request to a key within the keyspace, and the end DHT host responsible
for that key carries out an operation that typically accesses the key-value entries stored
locally. We term the combination of these behaviors an *endpoint operator.*

---

[3] Note, however, that almost any deployed DHT-based system is subject to attack, whether it
uses a DHT library or service.

A somewhat different example is PIER's computation of aggregates along a tree rooted at a particular key. Nodes route messages toward the root and each DHT host along the path aggregates data before forwarding them. Multicast forwarding within a DHT (as in Scribe, Bayeux, or M-CAN) also uses per-hop processing to set up and maintain dissemination trees. We term such behavior a *per-hop operator*, as it requires application-specific operations be executed at each hop along the path to a key (as opposed to at the final node that holds the key).

3.2 Endpoint Operators in OpenHash

Note that OpenHash cannot by itself support either endpoint or per-hop operators; code for these application-specific operators does not reside at the nodes that constitute OpenHash's DHT, as OpenHash is a shared service. However, we can allow application-specific code to live *outside* of OpenHash and use OpenHash to direct requests to hosts that do support the required operators. This approach allows developers to deploy application-specific code at will while still sharing OpenHash's common key-based routing infrastructure. We term hosts that run the OpenHash DHT *OpenHash hosts* and hosts outside OpenHash that run only application-specific endpoint operators *application hosts*. As with any DHT, application hosts must still divide ownership of their shared keyspace among themselves. In this paper, in the interest of requiring minimal application-specific support *within* OpenHash, we adopt an extreme point in the design space for endpoint operator support, in which application hosts are an entirely disjoint set of hosts from OpenHash hosts. However, the technique we present for supporting endpoint operators works equally well when these sets overlap, or even at the other extreme, where *only* OpenHash hosts implement endpoint operators, and each such host may support different sets of endpoint operators. These two extremes are both important: an application's popularity may warrant its endpoint operators' inclusion in the code at OpenHash hosts, whereas novel endpoint operators for fledgling applications may still be deployed on application hosts without modifying the code installed at OpenHash hosts.

To support endpoint operators, we introduce the notion of *namespaces*. Each application corresponds to a single, uniquely named namespace, and requires a particular set of endpoint operators be available for all keys in its keyspace. OpenHash must route requests destined for key k in application A's namespace (denoted $(A : k)$) to the application host that *both* runs application A *and* is responsible for key k in namespace A. Conventional DHTs consistently hash a set of keys over the hosts that run the DHT itself. We need to solve a different problem: to consistently hash a set of keys over a set of application hosts that may not run the DHT itself. This functionality is effectively the same as that of the `lookup()` interface first proposed in the Chord paper and adopted by the authors in [12] as the KBR or Key-Based Routing interface, with one important difference: our `lookup()` maps application keys to arbitrary application hosts, rather than only to the hosts that run the DHT.

In this section, we describe ReDiR (*Recursive Distributed Rendezvous*), a mechanism by which OpenHash can be used to achieve such application-specific lookup()s[4]. ReDiR requires hosts that support an endpoint operator for application A to register with OpenHash as application hosts in namespace A. Clients that wish to route to (namespace: key) destinations can then use OpenHash to route to the application host responsible for that key.

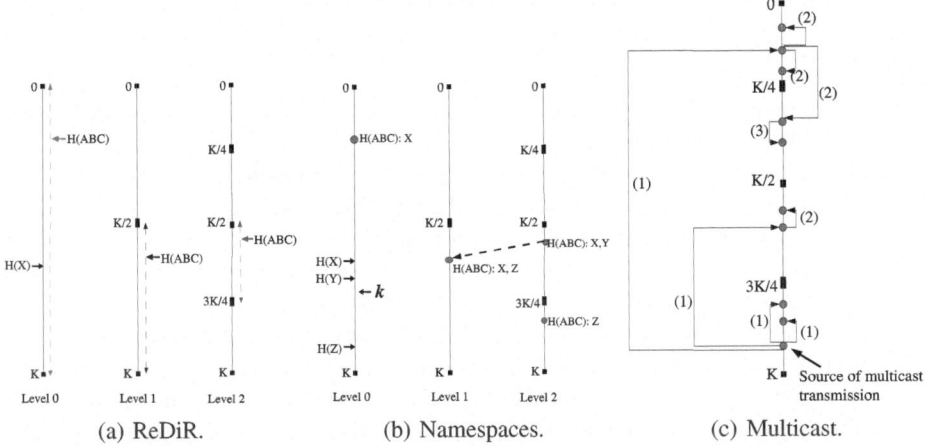

(a) ReDiR.   (b) Namespaces.   (c) Multicast.

Fig. 1. 1(a) ReDiR hierarchy and rendezvous points for a node X belonging to application ABC. Dashed lines denote enclosing partitions for X at each level. For clarity, the keyspace at each level is redrawn; in practice there is only one keyspace. 1(b) Using ReDiR to find the correct successor node for application ABC's key k: Node X joined first, then Y and Z. Each rendezvous point lists the nodes registered there. Node Z is key k's correct successor. Dashed lines denote rendezvous nodes contacted to locate k's successor. 1(c) Example of multicast forwarding: transmission links are labeled with their depth in forwarding hierarchy.

ReDiR. There are two interfaces to ReDiR. Application hosts use one interface to register as members of a namespace, and clients use the other interface to perform lookup()s of the form lookup(namespace: key), which return the IP address of the application host registered in namespace that is responsible for key. We describe each interface in turn, after first describing primitives used by both interfaces.

ReDiR hierarchically decomposes the OpenHash keyspace into nested binary partitions, as shown in Figure 1(a). Level 0 in the decomposition corresponds to the entire keyspace $[0, K-1]$, and generally, level i of the keyspace is decomposed into 2^i partitions, each of length $K/(2^i)$, to a depth of l levels, $i \in [0, l-1]$[5]. Thus, every point in the keyspace has a corresponding set of enclosing partitions, one at every level in the decomposition tree. We assume that all hosts have available the same

---

[4] Note that ReDiR solves a very different problem than bootstrapping multiple application-specific DHTs from a single DHT [13]; we propose a single DHT shared by multiple applications.

[5] In the interest of simplicity, we consider only base-2 decompositions and fixed depth l, though these need not be the same across applications, and could in fact be encoded into the rendezvous name.

hash function $H() \rightarrow [0, K-1]$ to map arbitrary data to keys. We define mapping a key $k \in [0, K-1]$ to k' within a narrower subrange of the keyspace $[P, Q]$ by scaling linearly: $k' = P + \lfloor k(Q-P)/K \rfloor$. For a key $k \in [0, K-1]$, when we write "get(k) or put(k) *over a subrange of the keyspace* $[P, Q]$," we invoke this mapping implicitly.

Each application that requires endpoint operators has its own namespace, identified by a unique string. Consider an application host X that runs endpoint operator code for application ABC. Essentially, host X registers in namespace ABC by walking up the ReDiR hierarchy, put$()$ting its own IP address as it goes, until it finds a predecessor. In detail:

- Host X computes $H(X)$. There is exactly one binary partition (keyspace subrange) at each level i that encloses $H(X)$.
- At each level i, starting at the deepest level (2 in the example in Figure 1(a)) and progressing up the tree toward its root (the partition including the entire keyspace), host X first executes put$(H(\text{ABC}), X)$ over the subrange of the keyspace in which $H(X)$ falls at that level. Figure 1(a) shows an example of where $H(\text{ABC})$ falls at each level, given a particular $H(X)$. Host X thus appends its IP address to the list of IP addresses (if any) previously put$()$ by other hosts within that partition that previously joined namespace ABC. Next, host X executes get$(H(\text{ABC}))$ over the same subrange of the keyspace. Host X then searches the one or more returned IP addresses I_j for a *predecessor* – for an I_j such that $H(I_j) < H(X)$ [6]. If for any j this condition is satisfied, and a predecessor has been found, host X has completed the registration process. If no predecessor was found, host X continues walking up the tree, and repeats this entire process at the level of the tree next closest to the root. If host X finds no predecessor at levels 1 or greater, the process terminates when it visits level 0 of the tree and stores its IP address there.

Because application hosts periodically refresh their ReDiR entries, as all put$()$s are timer-expired soft state (see Section 4.1), ReDiR converges to storing at most 2 IP addresses per namespace entry at levels $0 \ldots l-2$ of the hierarchy. At level $l-1$ of the hierarchy, ReDiR stores as many IPs per namespace entry as there are application hosts whose IP addresses fall within that portion of the keyspace; one must choose l commensurately.

A client performs lookup$(\text{ABC}: k)$ as follows:

- Note that k falls in one binary partition (keyspace subrange) at each level i of the hierarchy.
- As before, beginning at the deepest level of the tree, and proceeding upward, the client performs a get$(H(\text{ABC}))$ over the keyspace subrange at that level which encloses k. Among the IP addresses I_j returned, if any, the client searches for the successor to k; that is, for the I_j such that $H(I_j)$ is the smallest value satisfying $H(I_j) > k$, where modular wraparound at the high end of the *global* $[0, K-1]$ keyspace is used in the comparison, in the usual fashion when computing DHT keys' successors. When a successor I_j is found at one level of the tree, that I_j is the result of the lookup$()$. If no such successor is found, the search continues up the tree, at the next wider partition enclosing k.

---

[6] There is no modular wrapping here; the comparison is absolute.

Figure 1(b) shows an example of a client performing `lookup(ABC:` k`)` after the registration process has completed for hosts X, Y, and Z. In the worst case, ReDiR requires a client perform l `get()` operations to complete a `lookup(namespace: key)`; in practice, we expect client-side caching and other optimizations to reduce this cost significantly. We point out that the entire ReDiR mechanism builds exclusively over the simple DHT `put()`/`get()` interface. To OpenHash, the ReDiR-related (key, value) pairs appear as any others.

Even with ReDiR, OpenHash leaves developers with the burden of deploying application-specific operators. We imagine that over time OpenHash will grow to incorporate some of these more specialized operators, but we don't yet know what this subset should be. Moreover, expecting every node in the OpenHash infrastructure always to run exactly the same set of operators is unrealistically utopian. ReDiR enables a single routing layer to be shared by all services whether partially deployed or not. Without ReDiR, we are stuck with either utopia or bust.

3.3   Per-Hop Operators in OpenHash

Although a DHT service with ReDiR performs the route-to-key function for an application, there is no obvious way to support per-hop operators in OpenHash. However, in considering the various forms of per-hop operators described in the literature, we discovered that in most cases one could achieve similar functionality outside of the DHT service, essentially by converting per-hop operations into "scoped" endpoint operations (which ReDiR supports). While we do not claim to know whether all per-hop operators can be implemented using a service, we find this approach promising, and will explore it in greater detail in future work. In this section, we very briefly describe how three sample operations that typically use per-hop operations – multicast, aggregation and server selection (DOLR) – can be built over a DHT service.

Multicast. The following is a brief sketch of one possible solution to multicast in which OpenHash (using ReDiR) provides the rendezvous mechanism, while end nodes implement forwarding. To join group G, a node A inserts (G,A) within successively largely partitions enclosing $H(A)$ until it hits a partition in which there is already an entry for G. Let d be the maximum depth of the ReDiR hierarchy. Then, to multicast to all of group G, node A does a `get(`G`)` within its level d partition and unicasts the message to all the group members returned by the `get()`. A also does a `get(`G`)` within each of its "sibling" partitions from level $d - 1$ to 0 and unicasts a message to any *one* node at each level. A node, say B, that receives a message from A assumes that it is responsible for forwarding it on within its half of the smallest partition in the decomposition that contains both A and B; if that decomposition is at level d, B does nothing. Figure 1(c) shows an example of this forwarding. Note however, that unlike schemes like Scribe [5], the above solution need not result in trees optimized for low latency.

Aggregation. Aggregation along the path to a root R could be implemented similarly to multicast by having rendezvous nodes for R at level i aggregate messages before forwarding them on to level $i - 1$.

Server Selection Using DOLR. In systems such as OceanStore and PAST, a client's lookup returns the address of the node closest to the client that stores a copy of the requested object. These systems achieve this through a combination of proximity-sensitive DHT construction and by caching pointers along the path between a node storing a copy and the root node for that object's identifier. This mechanism (often called DOLR) serves two purposes: (1) server selection based on network latency and (2) fate sharing in the sense that if a closeby (*e.g.*, within the client's organization) server is available, the lookup will succeed even if a large fraction of the DHT is unavailable to the client. Both of the above can be achieved without explicitly embedding the supporting functionality into the DHT. For example, [7] and [6] use an org-store and local rings to achieve fate sharing, and [1, 8] use network coordinates to find close copies. In fact, such approaches frequently give applications more control over selection criteria (*e.g.*, server bandwidth or load could be used in place of or in addition to latency). Such flexibility is much harder to achieve using DOLR.

4   Architecture Details

In this section we discuss architectural issues in the design of OpenHash. We begin with the service model, then discuss issues of resource contention.

4.1   Basic Service Model

Figure 2 presents an overview of the OpenHash architecture. Each PlanetLab host runs the OpenHash code and maintains a local store of the (key, value) pairs for which it is responsible. These local stores are accessible to OpenHash clients only through the put()/get()interface. Lite applications use only the put()/get()interface, and

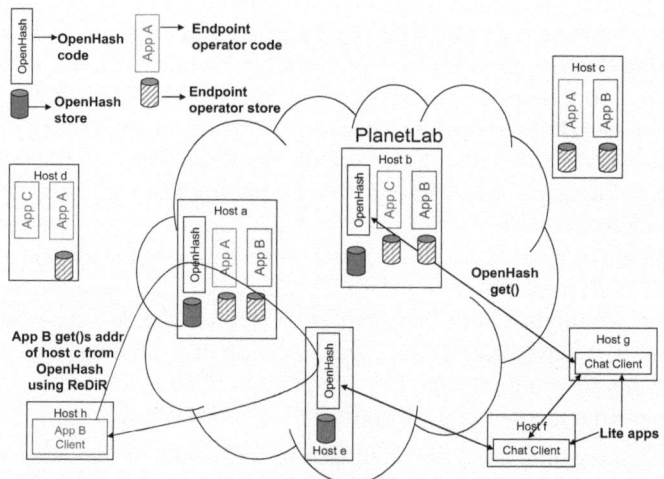

Fig. 2. Overview of the OpenHash architecture. Lite applications, such as instant messaging, use OpenHash only through its put()/get()interface, while more advanced applications deploy endpoint code and may be co-located with OpenHash servers.

are generally not co-located with OpenHash code and data. In the figure, two instant-messaging clients use OpenHash to discover each other, then communicate over IP. The endpoint operators of more advanced applications may run either by themselves on application hosts, or be co-located with OpenHash on OpenHash hosts. In the figure, endpoint operators for application *B* run on some of the PlanetLab hosts and on other hosts outside PlanetLab. Endpoint operator instances for *B* use ReDiR to coordinate amongst themselves. They may also maintain local data stores not managed by OpenHash.

An OpenHash put () consists of a client address, key, value, and time to live (TTL). Stored data are soft state; if a value is not refreshed before its TTL expires, OpenHash discards it. Consequently, stored entries do not consume resources indefinitely. put ()s are uniquely identified by client and key; a subsequent put () with the same client and key simply refreshes the TTL, and put ()s from separate clients do not overwrite each other. Additionally, a client may include a secret with a put (); a value thus stored may later be changed by resupplying the secret. We imagine using simple replication (*e.g.*, at *k* successor nodes) for availability and borrowing from the numerous proposals in the literature for caching and load balancing schemes [3, 14, 8]. An open question is the degree to which OpenHash should expose control over caching and load balancing to its users.

4.2   Resource Contention

A fundamental challenge in providing an open service is that of resource contention; under load, the service should provide each client with a "fair" share of the service's resources. In this section, we briefly put forth three different resource-management techniques as a starting point for discussion. The first approach is a best-effort service in which OpenHash makes no attempt to arbitrate between the needs of conflicting applications; excess requests are simply discarded and end hosts react to perceived losses by scaling back their rate of resource consumption, perhaps aided by stardardized end-host code as in TCP. This model is easy to implement but vulnerable to faulty or malicious clients that fail to scale back. A more sophisticated approach is to discourage selfish consumption by using fair queueing at every OpenHash node. One challenge with fair queueing is the need for secure identification of clients, though we believe such identification is achievable using SYN-cookie-like techniques [15]. A final approach to resource management is to charge for each use of a resource as has been previously proposed [16, 17], but using computational puzzles instead of micropayments as currency. Unlike with fair queuing, there is no need to securely identify clients in a charge-per-use model.

5   Future Work

Recasting OpenHash as an *active* service, in which DHT nodes download application-specific code, warrants future investigation. For an initial deployment, we believe the simple DHT model is appropriate because it avoids the complexity of downloadable code, yet still supports application-specific operators (with ReDiR), and is, in any case, a prerequisite for an active service.

We view our deployment plans (on PlanetLab, administered by the authors) as largely a bootstrap phase beyond which we imagine OpenHash will evolve to run on infrastructure hosts administered by different authorities. Ensuring robustness when service hosts are not mutually trusting is non-trivial, and the subject of future research.

Acknowledgements

We thank David Tennenhouse, Timothy Roscoe, Hans Mulder, Robert Morris, Frans Kaashoek, Kevin Fall, David Culler, David Mazières, Yatin Chawathe, Michael Walfish, Joe Hellerstein, Petros Maniatis, and John Kubiatowicz for insightful discussions and comments that improved this work.

References

1. Dabek, F., Kaashoek, M.F., Karger, D., Morris, R., Stoica, I.: Wide-area Cooperative Storage with CFS. In: Proceedings of the 18th ACM Symposium on Operating Systems Principles (SOSP 2001), Lake Louise, AB, Canada (2001)
2. Druschel, P., Rowstron, A.: Storage Management and Caching in PAST, a Large-scale, Persistent Peer-to-peer Storage Utility. In: Proceedings of the 18th ACM Symposium on Operating Systems Principles (SOSP 2001), Lake Louise, AB, Canada (2001)
3. Kubiatowicz, J.: Oceanstore: An Architecture for Global-Scalable Persistent Storage. In: Proceedings of the ASPLOS 2000, Cambridge, MA, USA (2000)
4. Luis Felipe Cabrera, M.B.J., Theimer, M.: Herald: Achieving a Global Event Notification Service. In: Proceedings of the HotOS VIII. (2001)
5. Castro, M., Druschel, P., Kermarrec, A.M., Nandi, A., Rowstron, A., Singh, A.: SplitStream: High-bandwidth content distribution in a cooperative environment. In: Proceedings of the IPTPS 2003. (2003)
6. Mislove, A., Post, A., Reis, C., Willmann, P., Druschel, P., Wallach, D., Bonnaire, X., Sens, P., Busca, J.M., Arantes-Bezerra, L.: POST: A Secure, Resilient, Cooperative Messaging System. In: Proceedings of the HotOS IX. (2003)
7. Walfish, M., Balakrishnan, H., Shenker, S.: Untangling the Web from DNS. In: Proceedings of the 1st Symposium on Networked Systems Design and Implementation (NSDI 2004), San Francisco (2004)
8. Stoica, I., Adkins, D., Zhuang, S., Shenker, S., Surana, S.: Internet Indirection Infrastructure. In: Proceedings of the ACM SIGCOMM 2002, Pittsburgh, PA, USA (2002)
9. Freedman, M.J., Freudenthal, E., Mazières, D.: Democratizing Content Publication with Coral. In: Proceedings of the 1st Symposium on Networked Systems Design and Implementation (NSDI 2004), San Francisco (2004)
10. Huebsch, R., Hellerstein, J.M., Lanham, N., Loo, B.T., Shenker, S., Stoica, I.: Querying the Internet with PIER. In: Proceedings of VLDB 2003, Berlin, Germany (2003)
11. Peterson, L., Anderson, T., Culler, D., Roscoe, T.: A Blueprint for Introducing Disruptive Technology into the Internet. In: Proceedings of the HotNets-I 2002, Princeton (2002)
12. Dabek, F., Zhao, B., Druschel, P., Kubiatowicz, J., Stoica, I.: Towards a Common API for Structured Peer-to-peer Overlays. In: Proceedings of the IPTPS 2003, Berkeley (2003)

13. Castro, M., Druschel, P., Kermarrec, A.M., Rowstron, A.: One Ring to Rule Them All: Service Discovery and Binding in Structured Peer-to-peer Overlay Networks. In: Proceedings of the 2002 SIGOPS European Workshop. (2002)
14. Rao, A., Lakshminarayanan, K., Surana, S., Karp, R., Stoica, I.: Load Balancing in Structured P2P Systems. In: Proceedings of the IPTPS 2003, Berkeley (2003)
15. Bernstein, D.: Syn cookies. http://cr.yp.to/syncookies.html (1996)
16. Hand, S., Roscoe, T.: Mnemosyne: Peer-to-Peer Steganographic Storage. In: Proceedings of the IPTPS 2002, Boston (2002)
17. Roscoe, T., Hand, S.: Palimpsest: Soft-capacity Storage for Planetary-Scale Services. In: Proceedings of the HotOS IX. (2003)

UsenetDHT: A Low Overhead Usenet Server[*]

Emil Sit[1], Frank Dabek[1], and James Robertson[1]

MIT Computer Science and Artificial Intelligence Laboratory, Cambridge, MA
{sit,fdabek,jsr}@mit.edu
http://pdos.lcs.mit.edu/

Abstract. UsenetDHT is a system that reduces the storage and bandwidth resources required to run a Usenet server by spreading the burden of data storage across participants. UsenetDHT distributes data using a distributed hash table. The amount of data that must be stored on each node participating in UsenetDHT scales inversely with the number of participating nodes. Each node's bandwidth requirements are proportional to the fraction of articles read rather than to the total number posted.

1 Introduction

Usenet is a large, distributed, messaging service that serves thousands of sites world wide. Since its introduction in 1981, the Usenet has been growing exponentially. The daily size of Usenet postings doubles approximately every ten months. In early 2004, users created approximately 1.4 TB of new Usenet data, corresponding to about 4 million articles, per day. Each server that wishes to carry the full content of Usenet (a "full feed") must replicate this amount of data each day, which is more than a 100 Mbps connection can support. To provide many days of articles for readers becomes an expensive proposition.

UsenetDHT provides a service that is substantially similar to Usenet but which reduces aggregate bandwidth and storage requirements by organizing the storage resources of servers into a shared distributed hash table (DHT) that stores all article data. This approach obviates the need for articles to be replicated to all participating servers. Instead of storing article data at each server, UsenetDHT stores article data on a small number of nodes in the DHT. The DHT distributes articles geographically, and can locate them quickly. It ensures high availability by re-replicating as necessary, maintaining the benefits of full replication without incurring the bandwidth and storage costs.

Using this approach, for an n-host system, each host will be able to offer a full Usenet feed while only storing $2/n$ as much data as it would have had to using a traditional system. Instead of using local storage to hold a large number of articles for a short period of time, UsenetDHT allows each server to hold fewer articles but retain them for longer periods of time.

---

[*] This research was conducted as part of the IRIS project http://project-iris.net/, supported by the National Science Foundation under Cooperative Agreement No. ANI-0225660. Emil Sit was supported by the Cambridge-MIT Institute.

G.M. Voelker and S. Shenker (Eds.): IPTPS 2004, LNCS 3279, pp. 206–216, 2004.
© Springer-Verlag Berlin Heidelberg 2004

The bandwidth required to host a Usenet feed using UsenetDHT is proportional to the percentage of articles that are read rather than to the total number of articles posted. Given the current size Usenet and known readership patterns, we expect this optimization to translate into a significant reduction in the bandwidth required to host a full feed.

2   Background

2.1   Usenet

Usenet is a distributed mesh of servers that are connected in a mostly ad-hoc topology that has evolved since its creation in 1981. Servers are distributed world-wide and traditionally serve readers located in the same administrative realm as the server. Each server peers with its neighbors in the topology to replicate all articles that are posted to Usenet.

The servers employ a flood-fill algorithm to ensure that all articles reach all parties: as a server receives new articles (either from local posters or from other feeds), it floods NNTP CHECK messages to all its other peers who have expressed interest in the newsgroup containing the article. If the remote peer does not have the message, the server feeds the new article to the peer with the TAKETHIS message. Because relationships are long-lived, one peer may batch articles for another when the other server is unavailable. RFC977 [10] and RFC2980 [1] describes the NetNews Transfer Protocol in more detail.

Articles are organized into a hierarchy of newsgroups. Upon receiving each article, each peer determines which newsgroups the article is in (based on metadata included in the article) and updates an index for the group. The group indices are sent to news reading software and is used to summarize and organize displays of messages.

Certain newsgroups are moderated to keep discussions on-topic and spam-free. Moderation is enforced by requiring a special header – articles posted without this header are sent to a pre-configured moderation address instead of being flood-filled as normal.

Special messages called *control* messages are distributed through the regular distribution channels but have special meaning to servers. Control messages can create or remove newsgroups, and cancel news postings (i.e. remove them from local indices and storage).

2.2   Server-Side Policies

Each Usenet site administrator has complete control over the other sites that it peers with, what groups it is interested in carrying and the particular articles in those groups that it chooses to keep. This flexibility is important as it allows administrators to utilize local storage capacity in a manner that best suits the needs of the site. For example, commercial Usenet providers will often invest in large amounts of storage in order to be able to retain articles over a longer period of time. Some Usenet providers will choose only to receive articles affiliated with text newsgroups in order to minimize the bandwidth and storage required. Most servers today will also filter incoming and outgoing articles with CleanFeed [13] to remove articles that are considered to be spam.

2.3   Usenet Data Characterization

The size of Usenet is a moving target; many estimates have shown growth by a factor of two in traffic volume every 10–12 months. Growth has largely been driven by increased postings of "binaries" – encoded versions of digital media, such as pictures, audio files, and movies. Users are increasingly taking advantage of Usenet as a distribution mechanism for large multi-media files. In 2001, there was an average of 300 GB of "binary" articles posted per day, but the volume in early 2004 is already approaching 2 TB [8]. In contrast, the volume of text articles has remained relatively stable for the past few years at approximately 1 GB of new text data, from approximately 400,000 articles [7].

2.4   Distributed Hash Tables

A distributed hash table (DHT) is a peer-to-peer storage system that offers a simple put and get interface to client applications for storing and retrieving data. DHTs are often built out of a robust self-organizing lookup system (such as Chord [16] or Tapestry [17]) and a storage layer (such as DHash [4]).

The lookup layer maintains state information about nodes and their identifiers while the storage layer automatically handles balancing storage load between the participants in the system. The storage layer automatically rebalances data as nodes join and leave the system. In order to keep data reliably available, DHTs will typically use replication or erasure codes to store data on geographically distributed machines. This strategy also allows DHTs to optimize reads by using nearby servers.

3   Architecture

In this section we present the high-level design of UsenetDHT, trace through the life of an article after it is posted, and discuss some tradeoffs of our design.

3.1   Design

The main goal of this system is to reduce the resources consumed by Usenet servers – specifically, the data transfer bandwidth and the on-disk storage requirements for articles – while mostly preserving the major features of Usenet. UsenetDHT accomplishes this goal by replacing the local article storage at each server with shared storage provided by a DHT. This approach saves storage since articles are no longer massively replicated; it also saves bandwidth since servers only download articles that their clients actually read.

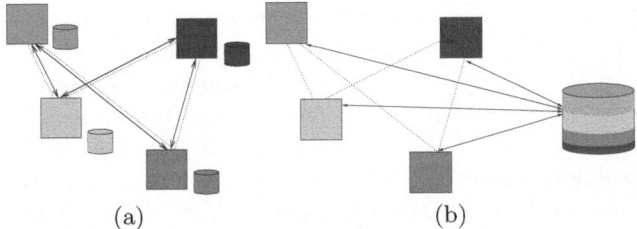

(a)   (b)

Fig. 1. The design of Usenet (a) and UsenetDHT (b). Usenet servers are connected to form a mesh network and exchange article data (solid lines) and meta-data such as article announcements and cancellations (dotted lines). Each Usenet server has enough local storage for all articles and meta-data. UsenetDHT servers are connected by the same mesh network to exchange meta-data, which is still stored locally. Articles are written to a a large, shared DHT (at right), with backing storage contributed by the peer servers. The colors associate each participant with the storage they provide.

All indexing of articles remains local to servers. In order to support this, UsenetDHT nodes exchange meta-data and control-data using the same flood-fill network as Usenet. In essence, the article bodies are elided from the news feed between servers. This approach allows cancellation and moderation of articles to work much as they do now; for example, cancellation simply updates the local group index to exclude the canceled article and no DHT storage needs to be touched. We considered using application-level broadcast to transmit meta-data. An efficient broadcast tree would reduce link stress by ensuring that data is transmitted over each link only once. However, Section 4 shows that the meta-data streams are relatively small, so the bandwidth reduction does not outweigh the complexities introduced by such a system. Further, the mesh network system is more robust, so we chose to leverage the existing infrastructure.

Figure 1 illustrates this design. Dotted-lines in the figure denote the transfer of meta-data, and solid lines denote article data. In the UsenetDHT design, each node donates storage capacity to form a DHT, which acts like virtual shared disk (right). Articles are stored in the DHT and fetched as required to satisfy read requests.

Servers will locally cache recently requested documents to avoid making multiple requests to the DHT for the same article. If servers cache locally, caching inside the DHT will be unnecessary. The main benefit of local caching is to reduce load on other servers in the system – if servers cache locally, no server is likely to experience more than n remote read requests for the DHT blocks corresponding to a given article. Each server will need to determine an appropriate cache size that will allow them to serve their readership efficiently.

3.2   ArtIcle Lifetime

Consider how an article is posted and eventually read using UsenetDHT. A newsreader in communication with a local server posts an article using the standard NNTP protocol. By design, the reader is unaware that the server is part of UsenetDHT, instead of a standard server. Upon receiving the posting, the server stores the article data in the DHT under the content-hash of an inode-like structure that points to fixed size chunks of the article [4]. As an optimization, if the article fits within a single 8KB DHT block, the body is stored directly in the inode [6]. The use of a secure hash function such as SHA-1 to produce the content-hash guarantees that articles will be evenly distributed through the nodes in the system. It also ensures that servers can verify the integrity of data received over the network.

After the block has been successfully stored in the DHT, the server sends an announcement with the article's header information and content-hash to its peers. This information is sufficient for the peer servers to insert the article into the appropriate group indices, provide a summary of the article to readers connecting to the server and retrieve the contents of the article when necessary. Each server, upon receiving the article, also shares the announcement with its other peers. In this manner, the article's existence is eventually flooded to all news servers.

When a reader wishes to read a newsgroup, he requests a list of new articles from his local news server. As is done in Usenet, the server responds with a summary of articles that it has accumulated from its peers. This summary is used by readers to construct a view of the newsgroup. When the client requests an article body, the server sends a get request to the DHT for the content-hash associated with the article. Once the server obtains the article data it can be returned to the reader. As with posting, the reader is not aware that the news server has been modified.

3.3   Tradeoffs

The primary drawback of UsenetDHT is a loss of control by individual administrators over what data (articles) are stored on and transit their machines. In a DHT-based storage system, article data will be evenly spread across all participating nodes. Similarly, all nodes must participate in processing DHT lookups for articles, even those in groups that they do not wish to carry. This sacrifice is inherent to the design as presented above.

From a resource standpoint, this drawback is probably not critical: each server in UsenetDHT need only provide a fraction of the space required to store a feed. Even if a traditional server only served a fraction of newsgroups, its storage requirements are not likely to rise if it participates in UsenetDHT. In addition, sites can run virtual nodes [4] to match DHT storage requirements with available capacity: each virtual node allows a physical node to claim responsibility for an additional fraction of the blocks stored in the DHT.

Article expiration must also be handled on a system-wide level. Blocks associated with articles can only be removed when the article has expired from the indices of all servers. This global parameter is set out-of-band.

More troubling are issues relating to content filtration. One common policy that UsenetDHT would like to support is the ability for servers to decide not to carry particular newsgroups, such as erotic newsgroups. Normally, such servers would request not to receive articles associated with unwanted groups from their upstream server. In UsenetDHT, a fraction of the articles from *all* groups will be randomly distributed to all servers. One possible solution may be to make use of recent work that enables a Chord ring to be organized into subrings such that a lookup could be targeted at an item's successor in a given subset of nodes [11]. Subrings could be used so that storage for content such as adult material would be limited to a single subring: lookups for articles in adult groups would be confined within the subring. We have not fully investigated this solution, but plan to do so in the future.

A different challenge is effectively filtering spam; the previous solution would not work since spam appears in all newsgroups. In total, the use of UsenetDHT should reduce the storage impact of spam since each spam message will only be stored once. However, administrators will still want to reduce the presence of spam in newsgroup indices – naively, any node wishing to do this would have to retrieve every complete article to determine if it is spam. This approach would lose all the bandwidth benefits of UsenetDHT. Fortunately, existing techniques such as spam cancellation can still work in UsenetDHT – a small number of sites determine what messages are spam (or are otherwise undesirable) and publish cancel messages. Other sites process the cancel messages to filter out spam locally. Sites would continue to filter local posts to prevent spam from originating locally as well.

4   Evaluation

We have implemented a prototype UsenetDHT server that can accept small news feeds, insert articles into the DHash DHT [4], and make them available to clients. However, the system has yet to be tested with a full feed. In this section, we quantify the potential bandwidth and storage requirements of a UsenetDHT server compared to a Usenet server based on available statistics about the current Usenet. We also describe what performance we require from the underlying DHT. We hope that a future deployment of our implementation running on the PlanetLab test bed will verify these calculations experimentally.

4.1   Analysis Model

The resource usage of a UsenetDHT server depends on the behavior of readers; we parameterize our analysis based on a simplistic model of the input rate to the system and estimated readership. Let n be the number of servers in the system. Let a represent the average number of articles injected into the system per second. Correspondingly, let b represent the average number of bytes injected per second. For example, based on recent statistics from a well-connected news server (newsfeed.wirehub.nl), $b \approx 21$ MB per second. Statistics from other large news servers are similar. When we examine the storage requirements of a UsenetDHT server it will be convenient to consider data stored per day: we will write $\bar{a}$ for the total number of articles injected on average each day ($\bar{a} = 86400a$) and $\bar{b}$ for total bytes injected per day.

To model the readership patterns of Usenet, we introduce r, the average percentage of unique articles read per site. Unfortunately, few studies have been done to measure how many articles are actually read on different servers. In 1998, Saito *et al.* observed that roughly 36% of all incoming articles were read on the server at Compaq [15]. Today, because of large traffic volume, many networks outsource their news service to large, well-connected providers, such as GigaNews. Byte-transfer statistics for the month of January 2004 from a small ISP that outsources news service to GigaNews suggest that the ISP's approximately 5000 customers read approximately 1% of the total monthly news. In fact, the trends from that ISP show that the number of bytes downloaded has remained relatively constant around 300 GB per month over the past year. This may mean that r will decrease over time if the growth of Usenet remains exponential.

For the purposes of this analysis, we will treat these parameters as constants, though of course, they will change over time.

Table 1. UsenetDHT reduces the bandwidth and storage requirements of hosting a Usenet feed in proportion to the fraction of articles read (r) and the number of servers in the network (n), respectively. This table compares the current transfer and storage requirements per day for a full Usenet feed in both systems, where $\bar{b}$ represents the total number of bytes for articles injected each day. A single peer is assumed.

	Total Bytes Transferred	Storage
Usenet	$2\bar{b}$	$\bar{b}$
UsenetDHT	$2\bar{b}r + 2 \cdot 512\bar{a}$	$2\bar{b}/n + 512\bar{a}$

4.2   Storage

UsenetDHT reduces system-wide storage by storing articles once in the DHT instead of copying them to each site. The storage requirements of a node are proportional to the amount of data in the system and the replication overhead of the underlying DHT and inversely proportional to the number of participating servers.

We assume that UsenetDHT is based on a low-overhead DHT that maintains and replicates data with a replication factor of 2 using some sort of erasure coding to ensure high availability. This assumption means that the system receives $2b$ bytes of new article data each second. This load is spread out over all n servers in the system instead of being replicated at all hosts, resulting in an overall per-host load that is $2/n$ times the load of traditional Usenet. If the number of servers participating in UsenetDHT increases and the number of articles posted remains constant, each server must bear less load. Because each server must dedicate a factor of n less storage, UsenetDHT should allow articles to be retained longer within the system.

There is also a small incremental cost required for local indexing. Suppose that each article requires about 512 bytes to store the overview data, which includes article author, subject, message-id, date, and references headers. This data adds an additional $512\bar{a}$ bytes per day to the cost of supporting a full feed. In early 2004, this corresponds to approximately 3.2 GB daily, which is barely 0.1% of the total data stored daily.

Sites must also provide some storage space for caching locally read articles. The sizing and effectiveness of this cache is dependent on the size of the reader population and the diversity of articles that they retrieve.

The total daily storage requirement for a UsenetDHT server is $2\bar{b}/n + C + 512\bar{a}$ where C is the size of the server's article cache. This differs from the cost of a traditional Usenet server by roughly a factor of $2/n$. A Usenet server requires $\bar{b} + 512\bar{a}$ bytes of storage daily.

4.3 Bandwidth

UsenetDHT servers save bandwidth by not downloading articles that are never going to be read at their site. Unlike Usenet, the bandwidth used by a UsenetDHT server is proportional to readership, not to the volume of the feed the server carries. In this evaluation, we are only interested in wide-area data transfer. When comparing UsenetDHT's bandwidth requirements to Usenet, we will not consider the cost of sending articles to readers for Usenet servers since these readers are likely to be on the same network as the server.

Servers must download articles from the DHT to satisfy requests by local readers. If the average actual fraction of read articles is r, each server will require roughly rb bytes per second of downstream bandwidth. In addition, each node is required to receive the header and DHT information for each article, which corresponds to $512a$ bytes per second. This header overhead may need to be multiplied by a small factor, corresponding to the overhead of communicating with multiple peers.

A server must also send data it stores in its role as part of the DHT. As we showed above, each server requests rb bytes per second from the DHT. This load will be spread out over all n servers. Correspondingly, each participating server must send rb/n bytes per second to satisfy read requests from each other server in the system. Thus, in aggregate, each site must have rb bytes per second of upstream bandwidth. Additionally, each site must have sufficient upstream bandwidth to inject locally-authored articles into the system.

A Usenet server's wide-area bandwidth requirements are equal simply to the size of the feed it serves. In our notation, a Usenet server is required to read b bytes per second from the network.

4.4 DHT Performance

The DHT used by UsenetDHT must provide sufficient read and write performance to support the aggregate load on the system. Because the news servers themselves will form the DHT, we expect that the membership of the DHT will be stable (more stable than, for instance, the membership of the Gnutella network). A stable membership makes it easier for the DHT to provide highly reliable storage [2].

Recent DHTs have demonstrated performance scaling properties that suggest they can meet the demands of UsenetDHT [5]. An improved version of the DHash DHT can locate and download an 8K block in approximately 100ms when run on the PlanetLab test bed [14]. The read latency of the DHT will be visible to end-users when they request an uncached article: reading a small text article requires the DHT to perform a single block download. The time required by the DHT to perform the fetch is likely to be significantly higher than the time to perform a similar operation on a local server. This delay can be partially masked by pre-fetching articles in a newsgroup when the indexing information is requested but before they are actually read. We believe that the bandwidth and storage savings of UsenetDHT are worth the delay imposed by the DHT.

The throughput requirement for a UsenetDHT node is rb. Thus, a full-feed deployment with $r = 0.01$ in early 2004 would require that each DHT node provide 200 KB/s of symmetric bandwidth. A node participating in the DHash DHT and located at MIT was able to read data at 1 MB/s from the DHT. Such performance should be sufficient to support a full feed for the near future. An experimental deployment of the system will allow us to verify that DHash is able to meet the performance requirements of the system.

5   Related Work

There have been some other proposals to reduce the resource consumption of Usenet. Newscaster [3] examined using IP multicast to transfer news articles to many Usenet servers at once. Each news article only has to travel over backbone links once, as long as no retransmissions are needed. In addition, news propagation times are reduced. However, Newscaster still requires that each Usenet server maintain its own local replica of all the newsgroups. Also, each news server still consumes the full news feed bandwidth across the network links closest to the server.

NewsCache [9] reduces resource consumption by caching news articles. It is designed to replace traditional Usenet servers that are leaf nodes in the news feed graph, allowing them to only retrieve and store articles that are requested by readers. In addition to filling the cache on demand, it can also pre-fetch articles for certain newsgroups. These features are also available as a mode of DNews [12], a commercial high-performance server, which adds the ability to dynamically determine the groups to pre-fetch. Thus, both NewsCache and DNews reduce local bandwidth requirements to be proportional to readership as well as more optimally using local storage. However, they only do this for servers that are leaf nodes and does not help reduce the requirements on upstream servers. By comparison, UsenetDHT also reduces resource requirements for those servers that are not leaf nodes. Also, standard caches will continue to work with Usenet-DHT servers.

6   Conclusion and Future Work

UsenetDHT has the potential to reduce the bandwidth and storage requirements of providing access to Usenet by storing article data in a DHT. UsenetDHT's bandwidth savings depend heavily on readership patterns, but UsenetDHT provides storage savings that scale with the number of participants. A planned deployment on PlanetLab will help to quantify the benefits of UsenetDHT.

Acknowledgments

We would like to thank Richard Clayton for his assistance in gathering statistics about Usenet's recent growth and status, and the anonymous reviewers and the members of the PDOS research group for their helpful comments.

References

1. BARBER, S. Common NNTP extensions. RFC 2980, Network Working Group, Oct. 2000.
2. BLAKE, C., AND RODRIGUES, R. High availability, scalable storage, dynamic peer networks: Pick two. In *Proc. of the 9th Workshop on Hot Topics in Operating Systems* (May 2003).
3. BORMANN, C. The Newscaster experiment: Distributing Usenet news via many-to-more multicast. http://citeseer.nj.nec.com/251970.html.
4. DABEK, F., KAASHOEK, M. F., KARGER, D., MORRIS, R., AND STOICA, I. Wide-area cooperative storage with CFS. In *Proc. of the 18th ACM Symposium on Operating Systems Principles* (Oct. 2001).
5. DABEK, F., SIT, E., LI, J., ROBERTSON, J., KAASHOEK, M. F., AND MORRIS, R. Designing a DHT for low latency and high throughput. In *Proc. of the 1st Symposium on Networked System Design and Implementation* (Mar. 2003).
6. GANGER, G. R., AND KAASHOEK, M. F. Embedded inodes and explicit grouping: exploiting disk bandwidth for small files. In *Proc. of the 1997 USENIX Annual Technical Conference* (Jan. 1997), pp. 1–17.
7. GRADWELL.COM. Diablo statistics for news-peer.gradwell.net. http://news-peer.gradwell.net/. Accessed 12 February 2004.
8. GRIMM, B. Diablo statistics for newsfeed.wirehub.nl (all feeders). http://informatie.wirehub.net/news/allfeeders/. Accessed 12 February 2004.
9. GSCHWIND, T., AND HAUSWIRTH, M. NewsCache: A high-performance cache implementation for Usenet news. In *Proc. of the 1999 USENIX Annual Technical Conference* (June 1999), pp. 213–224.
10. KANTOR, B., AND LAPSLEY, P. Network news transfer protocol. RFC 977, Network Working Group, Feb. 1986.
11. KARGER, D., AND RUHL, M. Diminished Chord: A protocol for heterogeneous subgroup formation in peer-to-peer networks. In *Proc. of the 3rd International Workshop on Peer-to-Peer Systems* (Feb. 2004).
12. NETWIN. DNews: Unix/Windows Usenet news server software. http://netwinsite.com/dnews.htm. Accessed 9 November 2003.
13. NIXON, J., AND D'ITRI, M. Cleanfeed: Spam filter for Usenet news servers. http://www.exit109.com/ jeremy/news/cleanfeed/. Accessed on 15 February 2004.

14. PlanetLab. http://www.planet-lab.org.
15. SAITO, Y., MOGUL, J. C., AND VERGHESE, B. A Usenet performance study. http://www.research.digital.com/wrl/projects/newsbench/usenet.ps, Nov. 1998.
16. STOICA, I., MORRIS, R., KARGER, D., KAASHOEK, M. F., AND BALAKRISHNAN, H. Chord: A scalable peer-to-peer lookup service for Internet applications. In *Proc. of the ACM SIGCOMM* (Aug. 2001). An extended version appears in ACM/IEEE Trans. on Networking.
17. ZHAO, B. Y., HUANG, L., STRIBLING, J., RHEA, S. C., JOSEPH, A. D., AND KU-BIATOWICZ, J. D. Tapestry: A resilient global-scale overlay for service deployment. *IEEE Journal on Selected Areas in Communications 22*, 1 (Jan. 2004).

Clustering in Peer-to-Peer
File Sharing Workloads

F. Le Fessant[1], S. Handurukande[2], A.-M. Kermarrec[3], and L. Massoulié[3]

[1] INRIA-Futurs and LIX, Palaiseau, France
[2] Distributed Programming Laboratory, EPFL, Switzerland
[3] Microsoft Research, Cambridge, UK

Abstract. Peer-to-peer file sharing systems now generate a significant portion of Internet traffic. A good understanding of their workloads is crucial in order to improve their scalability, robustness and performance. Previous measurement studies on Kazaa and Gnutella were based on monitoring peer requests, and mostly concerned with peer and file availability and network traffic. In this paper, we take different measurements: instead of passively recording requests, we actively probe peers to get their cache contents information. This provides us with a map of contents, that we use to evaluate the degree of clustering in the system[1], and that could be exploited to improve significantly the search process.

1 Introduction

File sharing using peer-to-peer (P2P) networks has gained wide popularity; some reports [10, 12] suggest that P2P traffic is the dominant consumer of bandwidth ahead of Web traffic. This popularity triggered a lot of research activity. While one research trend aims at improving the performance and features [11, 16, 5], another trend is concerned with analysing and modeling these networks.

In the last few years, many measurement analysis of P2P networks focusing on *Free-Riding* [2], peer connectivity and availability (e.g., [3, 14, 13]), peer distribution and locality within the network (in [14, 8]) were carried out. But to the best of our knowledge no detailed analysis has been done on the type of content shared on these networks.

Recent studies [8] show that locality-awareness in P2P networks can improve their efficiency significantly: by clustering users according to their *geographical* locality, file requests can be answered faster.

Similarly, clustering based on the types of files that peers have, also called *interest-based* locality, may improve search performance: it may reduce the duration of the search phase in general, and more specifically when searching for rare files [15]. Obviously, the performance gains obtained from exploiting either type of locality will depend on the corresponding degree of clustering. Our work investigates these issues.

---

[1] We define clustering here as the overlap between cache contents.

G.M. Voelker and S. Shenker (Eds.): IPTPS 2004, LNCS 3279, pp. 217–226, 2004.

Contribution. In this paper we present an analysis of contents (the type of files: music, video, documents etc) that peers offer to others in P2P file sharing networks. We used an active probing technique which allowed to capture the lists of files that peers offer. The community that we probed used eDonkey 2000, Kazaa's main competitor among all the P2P networks [9]. We then examine the clustering properties of the observed workload. Our preliminary findings show that both geographical and interest-based clustering are present and could thus be leveraged in order to yield significant performance improvements.

2   Experimental Setup

2.1   The eDonkey Network

The eDonkey 2000 network is one of the most advanced P2P file-sharing networks, providing features such as concurrent download of a file from multiple sources, detection of file corruption using hashing, partial sharing of files while being downloaded and expressive querying methods for file search. According to a recent study [19], in some European countries eDonkey is now ahead of Kazaa in terms of resulting traffic.

The eDonkey network is a hybrid two-layer network composed of clients and servers. The clients connect to a server and register the files that they are sharing, providing the meta-data describing the files. Once registered, the clients can either search by querying meta-data or request a particular file via its unique network identifier. Servers provide the locations of files when requested by clients, so that clients can download the files directly from the provided locations.

2.2   Methodology

Measurements reported in this paper have been obtained by crawling the eDonkey network during the first week of November 2003. 230,000 eDonkey clients were discovered; 55,000 of them were connected during a 3 days period. We kept 37,000 clients that could clearly be identified as distinct clients, among which 25,000 clients shared no files at all. Our study is based on the 923,000 different files shared by the remaining 12,000 clients.

Our crawler has been implemented by modifying an existing eDonkey client, namely MLdonkey [7]. Our modified client runs two concurrent tasks: discovering eDonkey clients and scanning their contents.

Client Discovery. Our crawler first connects to as many eDonkey servers as possible requesting their list of clients (server responses are limited to 200 clients). In order to obtain as many clients as possible from each server (servers may have up to 100,000 simultaneously connected users), we send requests for clients containing the strings "aa", "ab", "ac", ... and so on until "zz".

Client Content Scanning. Our crawler attempts to connect to every eDonkey client that is discovered. If it succeeds, it obtains the unique identifier of the client and requests its list of shared files. All these data are then stored in a file, named using a digest of the IP address and port of the client, so that the resulting trace is completely anonymised.

3   Workload Properties

Our crawler provides us with the content lists of each peer that replied with a non empty list of files. The first set of results presents the properties of the workload in terms of popularity, distribution between various types of files and sharing profiles of peers.

As opposed to previous studies which gathered requests from a particular location – such as a university [8]–, we gather a map of contents over a large number of countries (see Figure 1).

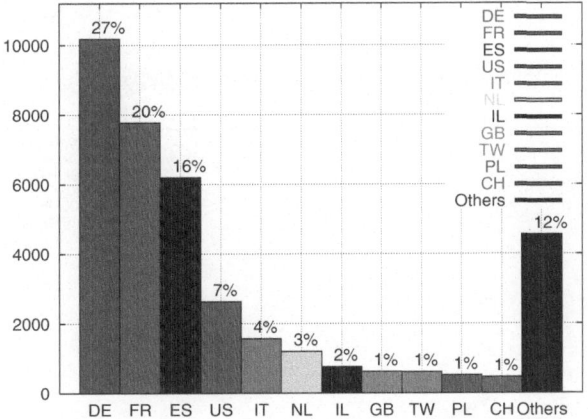

Fig. 1. Distribution of peers per country.

3.1   Replication Patterns

While previous studies evaluated the popularity as the number of requests per file, we measure a file's popularity by its replication degree. Results match former observations on file popularity; *i.e.*, a few files are extremely replicated while a large number is not replicated at all and approximately 100,000 files are present in two caches or more. Figures 2 and 3 respectively present the replica distribution of files for all files and for various types of files, per file rank. We observe similar properties between the eDonkey workloads and the Kazaa workloads presented in [8], and in particular after an initial flat region, the popularity distributions have a clear linear trend on log-log plots. Therefore, whether the popularity of a file is expressed in terms of number of requests or number of replicas, the observed patterns are similar.

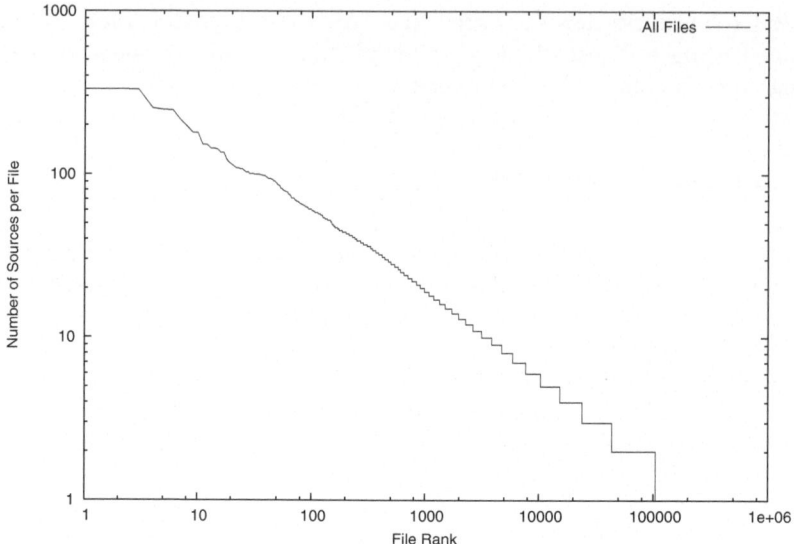

Fig. 2. Replica distribution of files (900,000 files).

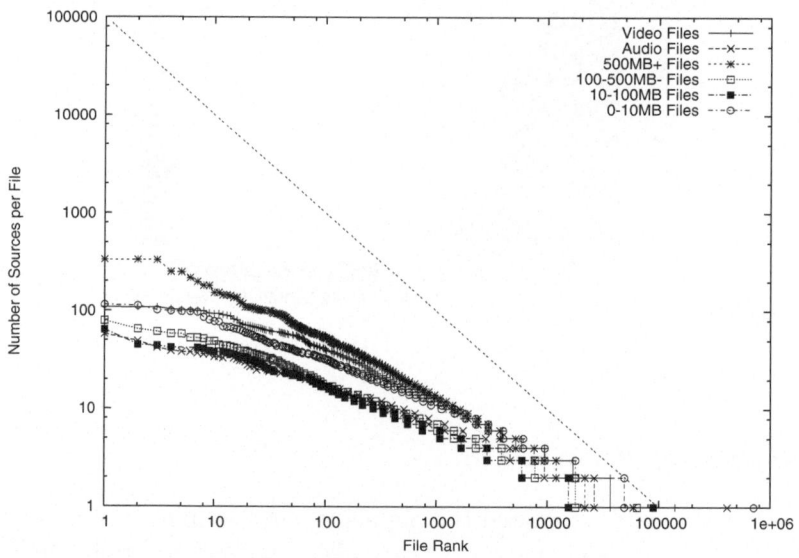

Fig. 3. Replica distribution of files depending of their type.

3.2 Sharing and Distribution

Figures 4 and 5 display respectively the CDF of number of files and the disk-space that each peer offers to the network. While the proportion of free-riding is still significant (68 %), most of the remaining clients share few files (between 10 and 100), but large files (between 1 and 50 GB of shared data, the protocol limit for file size is 4 GB).

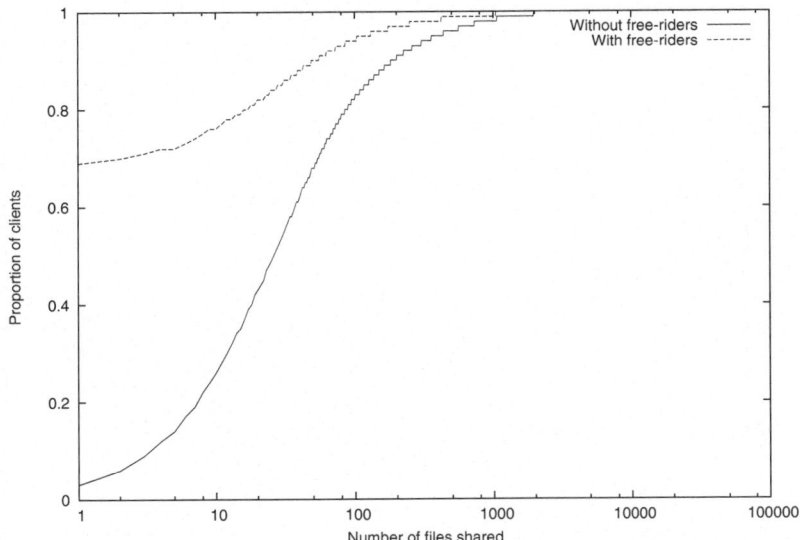

Fig. 4. Distribution of the number of files *offered* per client.

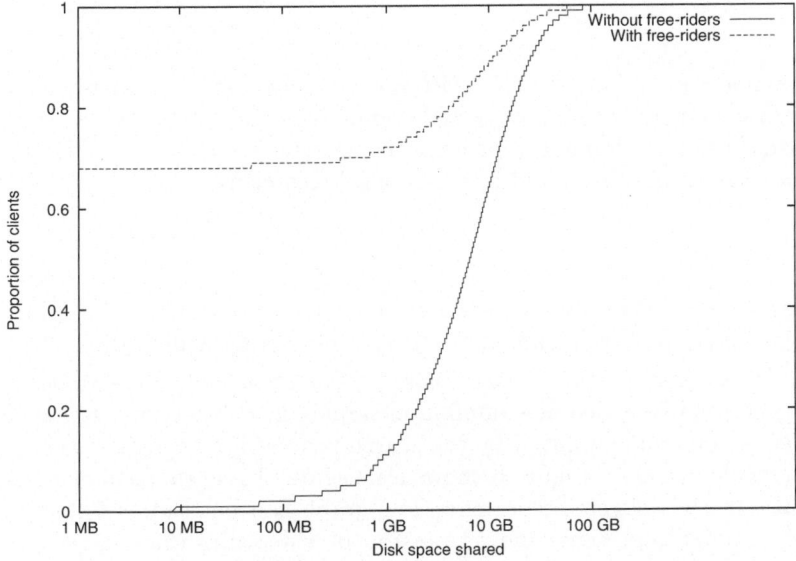

Fig. 5. Distribution of the disk-space shared per client.

We have also investigated the proportion of files of a given type share in the system, measured both in number of files and disk-space. We observe that multimedia files, audio and video, dominate: Audio files represent the largest number of files (48% against 16% for video), while in terms of size video files are dominant (67% against 16% for audio). Other measures show that *MP3*

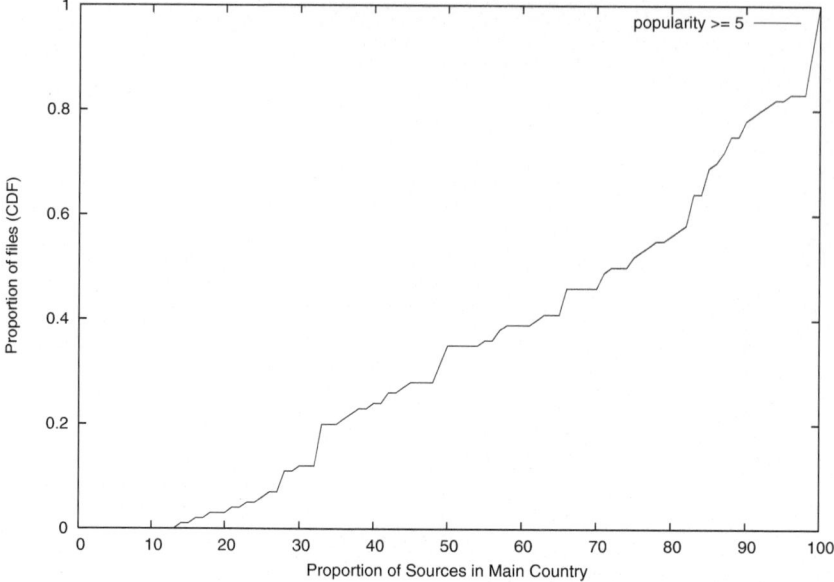

Fig. 6. Proportion of sources in one country (for video files with more than 5 sources).

files dominate in number, while *AVI* files largely dominate in terms of size. Although such distribution is expected and matches results obtained on different workloads, it is interesting since it leads to the exploitation of two different types of clustering: geographical and interest-based clustering.

3.3   Clustering

For clarity, we consider only the two major types of files, audio and video files, leading to different opportunities in terms of clustering exploitation.

Geographical Clustering and Video Files. It seems reasonable to assume that the traffic generated by video files dominates largely in the network. For such files, the latency and traffic induced by the search process are negligible as compared to the download phase. Figure 6 shows a measure of geographical clustering for video files in the collected workload. The graph can be read as follows: the y-value of a point represents the proportion of video files (having more than 5 replicas) for which x-value% of the sources are located in the main country of replication[2]. For example, the graph shows that, for 60 % of the files, more than 80% of the replicas are located in the main country. This definitively attests of the presence of geographical clustering, *i.e.*, peers requesting a given video file may in a large proportion of cases download it from peers in their own country, thus achieving low latency and network usage compared to downloading it from a randomly chosen peer.

---

[2] The main country is defined as the country where the majority of replicas are hosted.

Interest-Based Clustering and Audio Files. As 48 % of the shared files are audio files, it is reasonable to assume that most requests are for such files.

Performance of P2P search for such files can be greatly improved if we exploit interest-based locality [15, 6, 18]: if two peers share interests, (in other words if the contents of their cache overlap significantly) the search mechanism can be significantly improved by having these peers connect to one another and first send their requests to each other.

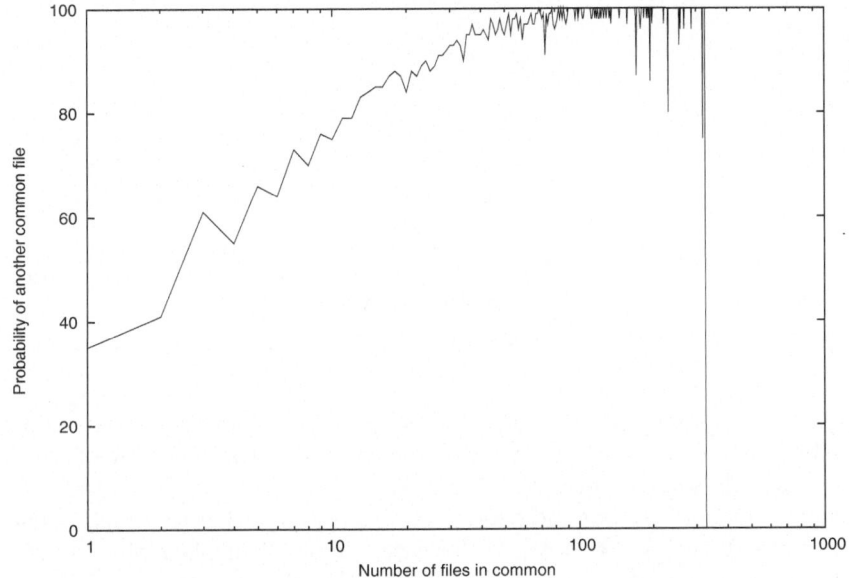

Fig. 7. Clustering between peers (for all files).

Clustering Measurements. Figure 7 displays the clustering between every pair of peers and is measured as the probability that any two clients having at least a given number of files in common share (at least) another one. We observe that this curve is increasing very quickly with the number of files in common, up to a certain point (here, 325) that reflects the maximal cache overlap in the observed trace. As soon as some peers have a small number of files in common (say 10), the probability is high (approximatively 0.8) that they will have another one in common. This probability is very close to 1 for peers sharing over 50 files in common.

Figure 8 presents the same clustering information, calculated for sub-classes of files, namely for audio files, and depending on their popularity. Results indicate that the clustering is pretty high for un-popular audio files (2-10 replicas) and in addition the maximal overlap between peers cache contents reach over 200 unpopular audio files. As the popularity increases, the overlap tends to decrease as well (30-40 replicas). However, the probability increases consistently and fairly quickly with the number of files in common.

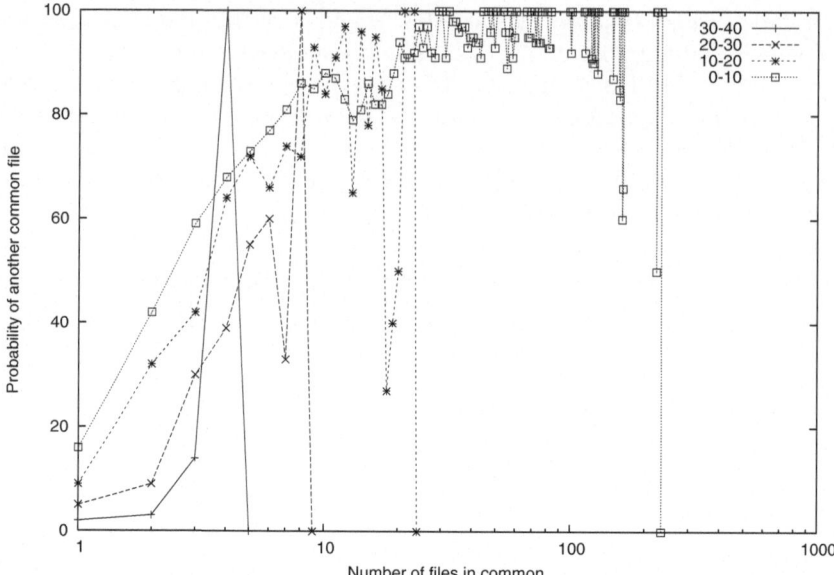

Fig. 8. Clustering between peers for audio files (according to popularity).

We also evaluated the correlation between files, rather than between peers. We define the correlation between two files as the correlation between the fact that a randomly selected peer has either file. More precisely, this is the correlation coefficient between the indicator variables equal to 1 if a randomly chosen peer has the document, and zero otherwise. Figure 9 displays the cumulative distribution function of the maximal correlation coefficients of files to other files. For example a correlation value of 60 % on the x-axis corresponds to a y-value of less than 70 % (for the curve of all files). Thus, at least 30 % of the files have a correlation larger than 60 % to some other file. This can be expected, as many files are cdrom images of programs or movies in several parts, sets of cracks for programs, and un-popular MP3 tracks of popular albums.

Further interpretation of the results, as well as processing of the data is needed to get a better characterization of interest-based clustering and how it might be exploited. Such extensions are currently under way.

4   Conclusion

Peer to peer file sharing is now the main component of Internet traffic. Yet, there have been only a few studies of workload measurements and even less consideration of clustering properties. In this paper, we presented the results of an evaluation we conducted on the most popular file sharing network in Europe, namely the eDonkey 2000 network, in an attempt to provide a map of the content shared by its peers. In particular, we focused on the geographical and the interest-based clustering properties for video and audio files respectively, of the observed

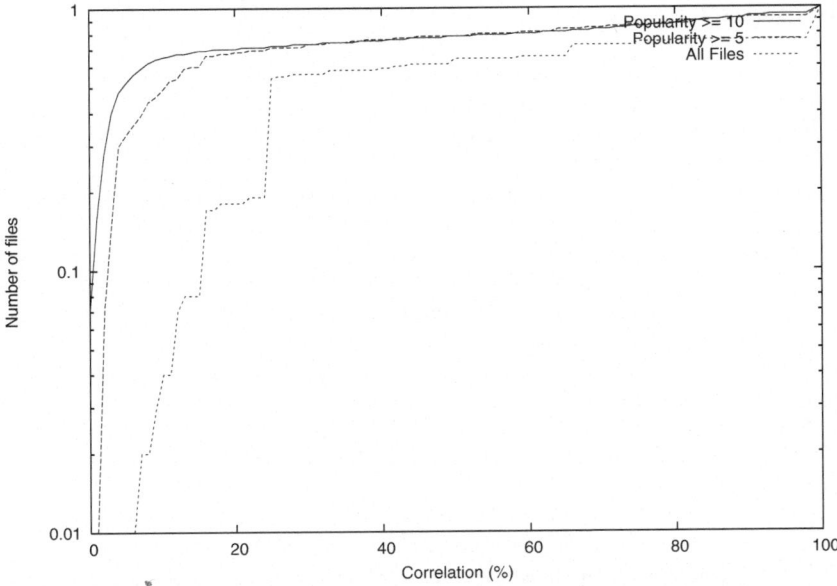

Fig. 9. The CDF of maximal correlation to other files (for distinct file popularities).

workload. We demonstrated that there is a significant locality of interest for audio files, that could be used to improve the search mechanisms without relying on servers. Interest-based locality can be exploited to create additional links to semantically related peers. These peers are contacted first before sending a request to the servers or to flood the request over the network. The advantage of implementing these additional links is that the technique is generic and can be applied to both flooding-based peer-to-peer networks, whether they are based on a structured [4] or unstructured network [17], and server-based [1, 7].

The interest of this measurement study is three fold: First, to the best of our knowledge, it represents the first evaluation study focusing on clustering properties and providing such a map of contents. Second, we also aim at doing a more comprehensive study by looking at a broader spectrum of users from different countries, and not limited to a particular community. Finally, the workloads we evaluated can be used as input to evaluate peer-to-peer file sharing systems and contribute to the improvement of such systems.

The trace collected demonstrates a certain degree of clustering between peers, we are currently investigating the impact of the generous peers (both in space and number of files) to evaluate their impact on the detected semantic relationships.

Analysing workloads of peer-to-peer file sharing system is crucial to understand and improve such systems and is very challenging as it depends on the cooperation of peers. Future work includes a similar study for the Kazaa network in order to study the similarities and differences between the two networks.

References

1. Kazaa (fasttrack network), sharman networks. http://www.kazaa.com/.
2. E. Adar and B. Huberman. Free riding on gnutella. *First Monday 5*, Oct. 2000.
3. R. Bhagwan, S. Savage, and G. Voelker. Understanding availability. In *IPTPS'03*, Feb. 2003.
4. M. Castro, M. Costa, and A. Rowstron. Should we build gnutella on a structured overlay? In *HotNets 2003*, Boston, MA, USA, Nov 2003.
5. Y. Chawathe, S. Ratnasamy, L. Breslau, N. Lanham, and S. Shenker. Making gnutella-like p2p systems scalable. In *SIGCOMM'03*, 2003.
6. A. Crespo and H. Garcia-Molina. Semantic overlay networks for p2p systems. Technical report, Stanford University, 2003.
7. F. L. Fessant. Mldonkey, a multi-network file-sharing client. http://www.mldonkey.net/, 2002.
8. K. P. Gummadi, R. J. Dunn, S. Saroiu, S. D. Gribble, H. M. Levy, and J. Zahorjan. Measurement, modeling, and analysis of a peer-to-peer file-sharing workload. In *SOSP'03*, 2003.
9. N. Leibowitza, A. Bergman, R. Ben-Shaul, and A. Shavit. Are file swapping networks cacheable? characterizing p2p traffic. In *WCW'02*, 2002.
10. D. Plonka. Napster traffic measurement. Technical report, University of Wisconsin-Madison, 2000.
11. A. Rowstron and P. Druschel. Pastry: Scalable, distributed object location and routing for large-scale peer-to-peer systems. In *Middleware*, 2001.
12. S. Saroiu, K. P. Gummadi, R. Dunn, S. D. Gribble, and H. M. Levy. An analysis of Internet content delivery systems. In *OSDI'02*, Dec. 2002.
13. S. Saroiu and S. G. P. Krishna Gummadi. A measurement study of peer-to-peer file sharing systems. In *MMCN'02*, Jan. 2002.
14. S. Sen and J. Wong. Analyzing peer-to-peer traffic across large networks. In *SIGCOMM'02 Workshop on Internet measurment*, 2002.
15. K. Sripanidkulchai, B. Maggs, and H. Zhang. Efficient content location using interest-based locality in peer-to-peer systems. In *INFOCOM'03*, 2003.
16. I. Stoica, R. Morris, D. Karger, F. Kaashoek, and H. Balakrishnan. Chord: A scalable peer-to-peer lookup service for internet applications. In *SIGCOMM 2001*, San Diego, USA, Aug. 2001.
17. Gnutella. http://www.gnutella.com/.
18. S. Voulgaris, A.-M. Kermarrec, L. Massoulié, and M. van Steen. Exploiting semantic proximity in peer-to-peer content searching. In *10th International Workshop on Future Trends in Distributed Computing Systems (FTDCS 2004)*, China, May 2004.
19. G. Wearden. eDonkey pulls ahead in European P2P race. http://news.com.com/2100-1025_3-5091230.html, 2003.

Cluster Computing on the Fly:
P2P Scheduling of Idle Cycles in the Internet

Virginia Lo, Daniel Zappala, Dayi Zhou, Yuhong Liu, and Shanyu Zhao[*]

Computer and Information Science, University of Oregon, Eugene, Oregon 97403-1202
{lo,zappala,dayizhou,liuyh,szhao}@cs.uoregon.edu

Abstract. Peer-to-peer computing, the harnessing of idle compute cycles throughout the Internet, offers exciting new research challenges in the converging domains of networking and distributed computing. Our system, *Cluster Computing on the Fly*, seeks to harvest cycles from ordinary users in an open access, non-institutional environment. CCOF encompasses all activities involved in the management of idle cycles: overlay construction for hosts donating cycles, resource discovery within the overlay, application-based scheduling, local scheduling on the host node, and meta-level scheduling among a community of application-level schedulers. In this paper, we identify four important classes of cycle-sharing applications, each requiring its own scheduling strategy: workpile, workpile with deadlines, tree-based search, and point-of-presence. We describe a Wave Scheduler for workpile tasks that exploits idle night-time cycles using a geographic-based overlay. The scheduler incorporates a quizzing mechanism to check the correctness of results and determine trust ratings for the hosts. We also propose a Point-of-Presence Scheduler to discover and schedule hosts that meet application-specific requirements for location, topological distribution, and available resources.

1 Introduction

Peer-to-peer computing, the harnessing of idle compute cycles throughout the Internet, offers an exciting new challenge for P2P networks beyond current information sharing applications. Experience has shown that not only are idle cycles widely available throughout the Internet, but in addition, many users are willing to share cycles [1–3]. This creates a compelling opportunity for research in this new juncture between the fields of networking and distributed computing.

Our research addresses the problem of *peer-to-peer computing*, which encompasses all of the activities involved with utilizing idle cycles from ordinary users in a distributed, open environment. In contrast to Grid computing [4,5] and other institution-based cycle-sharing systems [6], we are targeting an open environment, one that is accessible by the average citizen and does not require membership in any organization. Peer-to-peer computing represents the next step in distributed computing, providing potentially greater computing power

---

[*] This work was supported in part by the National Science Foundation under grant ANI-9977524.

G.M. Voelker and S. Shenker (Eds.): IPTPS 2004, LNCS 3279, pp. 227–236, 2004.

than institutional-based projects while also empowering ordinary users. This view of P2P computing is the focus of several other current research projects [7–9].

P2P computing in an open environment gives rise to a new generation of resource management problems that are dramatically different from those addressed by traditional scheduling systems, including issues of resource discovery, trust, incentives, fairness, security, and new criteria for evaluating performance. We use the term "P2P scheduling system" to encompass all activities involved in the management of idle cycles: overlay management for hosts donating cycles, resource discovery within the overlay, application-based scheduling, local scheduling on the host node, and meta-level scheduling which involves coordination of efforts among a community of application-based schedulers.

We believe that peer-to-peer scheduling solutions must be driven by the characteristics and goals of the specific applications to be scheduled. We identify four important classes of problems that are particularly well-suited to capturing idle cycles in the Internet: infinite workpile, deadline-driven workpile, tree-based search, and point-of-presence applications.

Popular applications for harvesting idle cycles from ordinary users, such as SETI@home [10], are limited to CPU-intensive workpile applications and require donors of cycles to manually coordinate through a centralized web site. More general cycle-sharing systems, such as Condor [6], provide automatic scheduling but require a centralized matchmaking service and are limited to members of participating institutions. *Our goal is the development of a scheduling infrastructure that supports automatic scheduling of these four broad classes of applications in an open environment.*

In this paper, we discuss the problems faced by P2P scheduling systems that presume an open and large scale environment. We first present a taxonomy of P2P cycle sharing applications and their specific requirements. We then describe the *Cluster Computing on the Fly* architecture and discusses issues and open problems involved in the design of an open P2P scheduling system. We conclude by illustrating how CCOF addresses some of these problems. In particular, we introduce CCOF's *Wave Scheduler*, which harvests night time idle cycles by using geographic timezones to organize the hosts, and CCOF's method for verification of results returned by the hosts. We also describe our *PoP Scheduler*, which utilizes scalable protocols to schedule point-of-presence applications by discovering strategically located hosts to meet application-specific requirements for location, topological distribution, and available resources.

2   P2P Scheduling Systems

2.1   P2P Cycle-Sharing Applications

We organize P2P cycle-sharing applications into four classes whose scheduling needs are starkly distinct, calling for individualized scheduling services that are tailored to those needs.

Infinite Workpile Applications. These applications consume huge amounts of compute time under a master-slave model in which the master delivers code to as many hosts as possible, over long periods of time. Each host computes intensively and then returns the results back to the master node. The workpile application is "embarrassingly parallel" in that there is no communication at all between slave nodes. Examples of infinite workpile applications include SETI@home [2], the Stanford Folding Project [11], and numerous mathematical applications ranging from number theory to cryptography [1].

Infinite workpile applications need scheduling that can (a) automatically identify large blocks of idle cycles and (b) support validation of results. Performance may be measured by some large-grained metric representing the *yield* of idle cycles, such as tasks completed per day or week. For the protection of the wider community, safeguards need to be installed to provide some notion of fairness among competing workpile jobs, as well as security against denial-of-service attacks from a malicious job that preys on the generosity of participating hosts.

Workpile Applications with Deadlines. Deadline-driven workpile applications are similar to infinite workpile applications, but their needs for compute cycles are more moderate. These applications are deadline-driven because they require that results be returned within a specified deadline (on the order of days or weeks). Examples of this class of application include compute intensive jobs: complex insurance analysis, simulation experiments with a large parameter space, 3D modeling and ray tracing code. These jobs needs to be completed to meet a business presentation deadline, research publication deadline, or school project deadline.

While many scheduling strategies are suitable for infinite workpile jobs with and without deadlines, the urgency of deadlines calls for more aggressive approaches for discovery and scheduling of cycles.

Tree-Based Search Applications. This class of applications requires substantial compute cycles, with loose coordination among subtasks requiring low communication overhead. Distributed branch-and-bound algorithms, alpha-beta search, and recursive backtracking algorithms are used for a wide range of optimization problems; these computationally intensive state-space search algorithms are ideal candidates for P2P scheduling.

Distributed branch-and-bound algorithms use a tree of slave processes rooted in a single master node. The tree dynamically grows as slave processes expand the search space and is dynamically pruned as subspaces leading to costly solutions are abandoned. There is a small amount of communication among slave nodes to inform other slaves of newly discovered lower bounds.

The scheduler manages the dynamic population of host nodes by continuously providing new hosts while the search tree is growing. It must also support communication among slave nodes, either indirectly through the master or directly from slave to slave.

Point-of-Presence Applications. PoP applications typically consume minimal cycles but require placement throughout the Internet (or throughout some subset of the Internet). The dispersement of tasks from a PoP application is driven by specific requirements of the job. For example, distributed monitoring applications (security monitoring, traffic analysis, etc.) require widely and evenly distributed placement as well as placement at strategic locations. Testing of distributed protocols requires placement of test-bots dispersed throughout the Internet in a manner that captures a variety of realistic conditions with respect to latency, bandwidth, and server performance. In addition, security concerns must be addressed by limiting communication only to the set of PoP tasks.

2.2   An Open P2P Cycle-Sharing Architecture

In the CCOF architecture, hosts join a variety of community-based overlay networks, depending on how they would like to donate their idle cycles. Clients then form a compute cluster on the fly by discovering and scheduling sets of machines from these overlays. The basic service offered by CCOF is best-effort in the sense that any host may preempt guest code at any time. Hosts retain local control and can thus offer a range of quality of service options.

The components of this architecture, as shown in Fig. 1, highlight the many complex research issues to be addressed in the design of an open P2P scheduling system which include the following:

Overlay Management of Host Communities. An important area of research for P2P computing lies in the organization of communities of hosts willing to share idle cycles. One way to organize such communities is through the creation of overlay networks based on factors such as interest, geography, performance, trust, institutional affiliation, or generic willingness to share cycles. Communities may span multiple organizations, such as a collaborative research project among several research groups. Chess enthusiasts, or participants in the Intel Philanthropic project [3] may form a community based on their hobbies or a spirit of volunteerism. Users may form nested communities based on trust, such as a group of family and friends, co-workers, and customers. We assume that it is possible to exclude untrusted hosts from the overlay using a central certificate-granting authority, as proposed by Pastry [12].

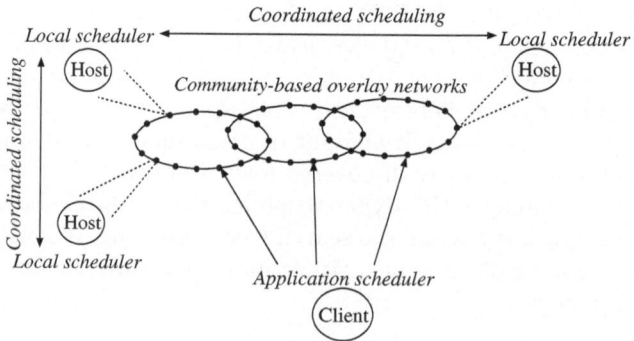

Fig. 1. CCOF architecture.

This arena of research exceeds the immediate bounds of scheduling research per se, but has a direct impact on it. Past work on overlay networks [13, 14, 12], trust and reputation systems, performance analysis and monitoring all serve as the foundations for new work in this direction.

Resource Discovery. The problem of resource discovery is extremely difficult in an open environment in which the set of participating hosts is potentially very large and highly dynamic. Resource discovery takes on new dimensions when the resource (compute cycles) is perishable, cannot be shared, and is dynamic. Moreover, the search for idle cycles may be coupled with the need for other resources such as memory and data. Work has already begun in this area, much of it focused towards institutional and Grid Computing environments.[15, 6, 16].

We conducted a comprehensive study of generic searching methods in a highly dynamic environment for workpile applications [17]. We compared four scalable search methods: expanding ring, advertisement-based, random walk and rendezvous point. We model a variety of workloads, simple scheduling strategies and stabilities of hosts. Our preliminary results show that under light workloads, rendezvous point performs best with respect to job completion, while under heavy workloads its performance falls below the other techniques. We expected rendezvous point to consistently outperform the other search techniques because of its inherent advantage in gathering knowledge about the idle cycles. However, in a peer-to-peer environment, which satisfies requests on-demand, large jobs may dominate, resulting in delays for scheduling smaller jobs. With respect to message-passing overhead, rendezvous point dramatically outperforms the other discovery strategies.

Application Scheduling. The application scheduler is responsible for selection of hosts for a P2P computation from a pool of candidates, for exporting the code to the hosts, and for managing and verifying returned results. Application scheduling requires an analysis of both the application's needs and the nature of the offered resources. The scheduler's decision about which hosts to select becomes very complex since trust, performance, and fairness all come into play. Strategies such as oversubscription and duplication scheduling, may be used for maximum flexibility. Furthermore, if coordination across a set of host nodes is required, it may be desirable to organize the selected hosts into a new overlay to support the interprocess communication needs of the application, further complicating the host selection process.

Local Scheduling. The local scheduler tracks idle cycles and negotiates with the application scheduler using local criteria for trust, fairness, and performance to decide which tasks to accept. It also interacts with its own native scheduler to inject those jobs into the scheduling queue.

Because each host may implement its own policies, we envision Quality of Service as an important feature of P2P computing. The job of a local scheduler can be viewed as an admission control problem, similar to that faced by integrated services networks [18]. Some hosts may provide guaranteed service by accepting only CCOF jobs – they have no local tasks that may preempt guest code. Likewise, a host may offer predictive service by providing a statistical performance estimate based on past behavior.

Incentives and Fairness. The choice of policies and mechanisms for fairness in a P2P scheduling system is a non-trivial decision since the notion of fairness is itself open to debate. Several current projects require *strict fairness*, fairly tightly controlled accounting of cycles and resources consumed through a variety of economic and social models (credit-based systems, bartering systems and auction-based systems, ticket-based systems) [7, 8, 19]. Our philosophy is much more open - we presume that the donors of idle cycles are more relaxed: they are concerned with immediate access to idle cycles but not cycle-for-cycle equality. Under this model of *long-term fairness*, it is still necessary to enforce some kind of accounting. In either case, interesting research questions arise with respect to what incentives work best, how to measure contributions and usage for fairness in a large scale and dynamic environment.

Trust and Reputation. Trust and reputation systems are needed throughout P2P scheduling for the formation of trust-based overlays as described above, for local hosts to use when deciding whether to accept or reject tasks from an application, and for applications to use to select host nodes from multiple candidates. Several new trust systems for P2P networks have recently been developed that can potentially be utilized in an open environment [20, 21]. However, several difficult problems remain: how to effectively utilize the trust values to make scheduling decisions and also how to determine whether the results returned by a host are correct or not. In Section 3 we describe how our CCOF application scheduler probes host nodes using undetectable quiz codes to develop a trust rating for each host, as well as to validate returned results.

Security. How can a host defend itself against denial of service attacks, such as when a malicious node occupies large numbers of hosts with useless code? Or worse yet uses hosts to launch a distributed denial of service attack or a worm?

We assume that hosts protect themselves from a variety of attacks by running guest code within a virtual machine monitor, creating a "sandbox" that protects the host and controls resource usage [22]. Despite this protection, hosts must still protect their resources from being misused. Preventing denial-of-service attacks, particularly those that are launched from the cluster itself, is a difficult problem. Likewise, the CCOF system itself can be abused if malicious users schedule large numbers of useless tasks.

One possibility for coping with these problems is for hosts to deny network access for untrusted clients, using the trust and reputation systems discussed above. Likewise, users can give priority to projects they have deemed trustworthy through any outside form of communication. In cases where a greater degree of openness is desired, it may be possible to use network monitors to detect and take action against attacks. We are working closely with fellow researchers at the University of Oregon who are working on distributed detection of worms and denial-of-service attacks.

Performance Monitoring. The P2P scheduling environment is radically different from traditional scheduling domains. Evaluation of scheduling performance is thus faced with several challenges. What are are the appropriate metrics, benchmarks, performance monitoring tools and techniques for an open P2P scheduler? What kinds of user interfaces, testing, simulation, and monitoring tools will be most effective?

3   Cluster Computing on the Fly

In this section we present CCOF's support for two classes of P2P applications: deadline-driven workpile applications and point-of-presence applications. Workpile jobs, with their heavy demand for free cycles, are scheduled using CCOF's Wave Scheduler, which captures available night time cycles in timezones from east to west. CCOF also provides a simple yet effective quiz system for verifying the results returned by hosts. CCOF scheduling of PoP applications involves fully distributed algorithms for careful placement of tasks according to topological or performance-based criteria.

3.1   Wave Scheduling for Workpile Applications

Wave scheduling seeks to capture cycles from the millions of machines that lie completely idle at night. By following night timezones around the globe, it continuously gives workpile tasks dedicated access to cycles without interruption from users reclaiming their machines. Wave scheduling is thus particularly useful for workpile applications with deadlines since it provides a higher guarantee of ongoing available cycles. Wave scheduling was motivated by the notion of prime time v. non-prime time scheduling regimes enforced by parallel job schedulers [23, 24] and by wave scheduling in systolic computing systems.

The CCOF Wave Scheduler uses a CAN-based DHT overlay to organize nodes located in different time zones. Our wave scheduling protocol functions as follows (see Fig. 2).

Timezones in the CAN Overlay. We select one dimension of the d-dimensional mesh to represent time zones. For example, a 1 x 24 CAN space could be divided into hourly zones 1 through 24 based on its second dimension.

Host Nodes Join the Overlay. A host node that wishes to offer its night time cycles knows which time zone it occupies, say zone 8. It randomly selects a node label in zone 8 such as (0.37, 7.12) and sends a join message to that node. According to the CAN protocol, the message will reach the physical node in charge of CAN node (0.37, 7.12) who will split the portion of the CAN space it owns, giving part of it to the new host node.

Application Scheduler Selects Initial Nightzone. The scheduler for a workpile application knows which timezones are currently nightzones. It selects one of these nightzones (based on some nightzone selection criteria) and decides

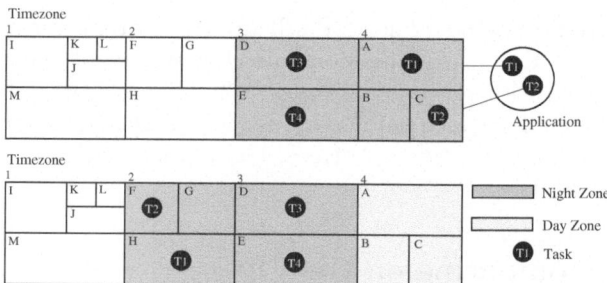

Fig. 2. Task initiation and migration in wave scheduling.

on the number H of hosts it would like to target. This number could be an over-estimation of the number it would ideally like to schedule in order to achieve more flexibility.

Application Scheduler Selects Set of Target Hosts. The scheduler randomly generates a collection of H node labels in the target nightzone. It sends a request message to each target host using CAN routing which finds the physical host managing that host node. After negotiations, the application scheduler selects a subset of those nodes to ship tasks to. It can make its selection based on trust or other criteria.

Migration to Next Timezone. When morning comes to a host node, it selects a new target nightzone, randomly selects a host node in that nightzone for migration, and after negotiating with that host, migrates the unfinished task to the new host.

Returning Results to the Application. Whenever a task finishes computing its results on a host node, it sends the results directly back to the application. If the application is offline, it can store the results in the CAN distributed file system. The application can later retrieve results using the DHT lookup.

We are investigating the use of wave scheduling for deadline-driven workpile tasks to see if it compares favorably with two other models: centralized master-slave approach and distributed master-slave approach. In both latter cases, idle nodes advertise their availability dynamically to the masters and the only option is to sleep when cycles are withdrawn. Our current evaluation includes application harvest yield (results returned per day); utilization (fraction of idle cycles being consumed relative to demand); host impact; and overlay traffic generated by the scheduler, by task migration, and return of results.

Our current implementation and evaluation is simulation-based, but in the future, we would like to do empirical experiments assuming we can find sufficient numbers and placements of volunteer nodes.

3.2   Trust-Based Verification for Workpile Applications

We validate the correctness of results returned by host nodes to the workpile application using a quiz mechanism. The application node sends a set of quizzes to the hosts whose solutions are known beforehand. Based on the hosts performance on the quizzes, the application can then decide whether to accept or reject the results. We are investigating two methods for quizzing hosts. One method uses quizzes that are distinct from the actual application code. These are packaged so that a (malicious) host cannot distinguish quiz code from genuine application code. If the host passes its quiz, it will then be sent another task, this one containing application code. The second method embeds simple short quizzes into the application code. Quiz and application results are periodically sent back from the host to the application. If the application node receives wrong quiz answers, it can immediately reschedule the task on another host. Note that for both methods, when a host does return correct (or incorrect) results, this information can be used to give that host an appropriate trust ranking. This information is stored in a reputation system such as Eigenrep [21] or TrustMe [20].

3.3   Scheduling Point-of-Presence Applications

Our investigation of scheduling PoP applications is motivated by collaborative work at the University of Oregon on distributed security monitoring systems and distributed massively multiplayer games.

Topological distribution of monitoring tasks involves placement of these tasks on selected hosts throughout the overlay such that ordinary nodes are within t hops of j host nodes. This problem has been proposed abstractly as leader election in distributed systems, and as the dominating set problem in graph theory.

This task is much more difficult in an open, large scale environment. One of our approaches uses a torus-based overlay similar to CAN [13] that provides its regular node labeling scheme and Lee distances [25] to elect leaders using only local computation in constant time. Another approach is a fully distributed protocol that uses gossiping in a tournament-style backoff algorithm. Initially, each node says hello to its k-hop neighbors. Nodes then gossip with its immediate neighbors and either persists as a leader or backs-off based on the information each neighbor provides on the number of non-leader nodes it covers. We have developed several versions of this algorithm that trade off communication overhead and latency for accuracy. We are also investigating placement of game-bots throughout the Internet that meet varying level of performance with respect to network bandwidth and computational power.

References

1. Hayes, B.: Computing Science – Collective Wisdom. American Scientist (1998)
2. D.Anderson, Cobb, J., Korpela, E., Lebofsky, M., Werthimer, D.: Seti@home: An experiment in public-resource computing. Communications of the ACM **45** (2002) 56–61
3. Intel: The Intel Philanthropic Peer-to-Peer Program (2003) http://www.intel.com/cure/.

4. F. Berman and G. Fox and A. Hey, ed.: Grid Computing Making the Global Infrastructure a Reality. John Wiley and Sons Ltd. (2002)
5. Foster, I., Kesselman, C., eds.: The GRID Blueprint for a New Computing Infrastructure. Morgan Kaufmann Publishers, Inc. (1999)
6. Litzkow, M., M.Livny, Mutka, M.: Condor – A Hunter of Idle Workstations. In: Eighth International Conference on Distributed Computing Systems. (1988)
7. Fu, Y., Chase, J., Chun, B., Schwab, S., Vahdat, A.: SHARP: An Architecture for Secure Resource Peering. In: SOSP. (2003)
8. Butt, A., Fang, X., Hu, Y., Midkiff, S., Vitek, J.: An Open Peer-to-Peer Infrastructure for Cycle-Sharing (2003) Poster, SOSP.
9. UC Berkeley: BOINC: Berkeley Open Infrastructure for Network Computing (2004) http://boinc.berkeley.edu.
10. D.Anderson, Cobb, J., Korpela, E., Lebofsky, M., Werthimer, D.: SETI@home: An Experiment in Public-Resource Computing. Communications of the ACM **45** (2002)
11. Stanford Folding Project: Folding@Home (2003) http://folding.stanford.edu/.
12. Rowstron, A., Druschel, P.: Pastry: Scalable, Decentralized Object Location, and Routing for Large-Scale Peer-to-Peer Systems. In: 18th IFIP/ACM Int'l Conf. on Distributed Systems Platforms. (2001)
13. Ratnasamy, S., Francis, P., Handley, M., Karp, R., Shenker, S.: A Scalable Content Addressable Network. In: ACM SIGCOMM. (2001)
14. Stoica, I., Morris, R., Karger, D., Kaashoek, F., Balakrishnan, H.: Chord: A Scalable Peer-to-Peer Lookup Service for Internet Applications. In: ACM SIGCOMM. (2001)
15. Iamnitchi, A., Foster, I., Nurmi, D.: A Peer-to-Peer Approach to Resource Location in Grid Environments. In: Symp. on High Performance Distributed Computing. (2002)
16. F. Berman: High-Performance Schedulers. In I. Foster and C. Kesselman, ed.: The GRID Blueprint for a New Computing Infrastructure. Morgan Kaufmann (1999)
17. Zhou, D., Lo, V.: Cluster Computing on the Fly: Resource Discovery in a Cycle Sharing Peer-to-Peer System. In: IEEE/ACM International Workshop on Global and Peer-to-Peer Computing. (2004)
18. Clark, D.D., Shenker, S., Zhang, L.: Supporting Real-Time Applications in an Integrated Services Packet Network: Architecture and Mechanism. In: ACM SIGCOMM. (1992)
19. Andrade, N., Cirne, W., Brasileiro, F., Roisenberg, P.: OurGrid: An Approach to Easily Assemble Grids with Equitable Resource Sharing. In: 9th Workshop on Job Scheduling Strategies for Parallel Processing. (2003)
20. Singh, A., Liu, L.: TrustMe: Anonymous Management of Trust Relationships in Decentralized P2P Systems. In: IEEE Intl. Conf. on Peer-to-Peer Computing. (2003)
21. S.Kamvar, Schlosser, M., Garcia-Molina, H.: The Eigentrust Algorithm for Reputation Management in P2P Networks. In: 12th International World Wide Web Conference 2003. (2003)
22. B. Dragovic, e.a.: Xen and the Art of Virtualization. In: ACM Symposium on Operating Systems Principles. (2003)
23. Veridian Systems: OpenPBS v2.3: The Portable Batch System Software (2000)
24. Lo, V., Mache, J.: Job Scheduling for Prime Time vs. Non-Prime time. In: 4th IEEE International Conference on Cluster Computing (CLUSTER 2002). (2002)
25. Lo, V., Bose, B., Broeg, B.: Lee Distance, Gray Codes and the Torus. Intl. Journal of Telecomm. Systems (1998)

Robust Distributed Name Service

Baruch Awerbuch[*] and Christian Scheideler[**]

Department of Computer Science, Johns Hopkins University,
3400 N. Charles Street, Baltimore, MD 21218, USA
{baruch,scheideler}@cs.jhu.edu

Abstract. This paper suggests a method called Trust-but-Verify that, under certain simplifying assumptions, provides robust distributed name service even under massive adversarial attacks.

1 Introduction

The Internet was originally designed for the purpose of being extremely robust against hardware attacks, such as natural disasters or wars. However, software attacks (such as viruses, worms, or denial-of-service attacks) have become increasingly severe over the past few years, whereas hardware attacks are negligible. Thus, for any distributed application to run reliably on the Internet, it is of utmost importance that it is robust against adversarial software attacks. This is especially important for critical applications such as name service, i.e. a service that translates names such as "machine.cs.school.edu" into IP addresses so that machines can communicate with each other.

The current way name service is provided in the Internet is server-based. However, server-based architectures are vulnerable to attacks. A much more robust alternative appears to be the recently emerged peer-to-peer paradigm with its strictly decentralized approach. Unfortunately, despite the appeal of a decentralized approach, it appears to be a daunting task to develop peer-to-peer networks that are robust against adversarial attacks. Obviously, in an open environment any attempt to keep adversarial peers out of the network is doomed to failure because a priori there are no trust relationships that would allow to distinguish adversarial peers from honest peers. So one approach has been to at least limit the number of identities adversarial peers can obtain. Here, the use of a certification authority was suggested that requires credentials, sensitive information, or a payment to obtain an identity that allows the peer to join the system [4]. However, being overly restrictive here would not only prevent adversarial peers but also many honest peers from joining the system, either because they cannot provide the necessary credentials or they are not willing to reveal sensitive information or to pay for their membership. Thus, it should be clear that without being overly restrictive, a certification authority will be ineffective in limiting the number of identities adversarial peers may obtain,

---

[*] Supported by NSF grant ANIR-0240551 and NSF grant CCR-0311795.
[**] Supported by NSF grant CCR-0311121 and NSF grant CCR-0311795.

allowing them to start so-called Sybil attacks [7] that can cause severe problems to all structured peer-to-peer systems that have been suggested so far. Hence, new designs are needed that provide reliability despite adversarial peers with a potentially unlimited number of identities.

The goal of this paper is to demonstrate that it is possible, under certain simplifying assumptions, to design *completely open* peer-to-peer systems that are *provably* robust against adversarial peers of *arbitrary behavior* with an *unlimited* number of identities, as long as the adversarial peers in the system (or more precisely, their currently active identities) are in the minority.

1.1   Distributed Name Service

A *peer* is defined as an entity with a unique identity, i.e. each peer p is uniquely identified by a tuple $(\mathsf{Name}(p), \mathsf{IP}(p))$ where $\mathsf{Name}(p)$ represents the name of p and $\mathsf{IP}(p)$ represents the IP address of p. In order to provide a distributed name service, the following operations have to be implemented:

- $\mathsf{Join}(p)$: peer p wants to join the system.
- $\mathsf{Leave}(p)$: peer p wants to leave the system.
- $\mathsf{Lookup}(\mathsf{Name})$: returns the IP address of the peer p in the system with $\mathsf{Name}(p) = \mathsf{Name}$, or NULL if there is no such peer.

These operations must be implemented so that they can be run *concurrently* and *reliably* in an *asynchronous* environment without any trust relationships in which adversarial peers have an unlimited number of identities at their disposal and behave in an arbitrary way (i.e. we allow Byzantine peers). To formalize this goal, we need a model.

1.2   Security Model

We consider a peer to be *adversarial* if it belongs to an adversary or it is simply unreliable. Otherwise, a peer is called *honest*. We do not assume any prior trust relationships between the peers. Hence, a priori honest peers cannot be distinguished from adversarial peers.

Certification Authority. A necessary requirement for a name service as defined above to work correctly is that every possible name x has at most one peer p with $\mathsf{Name}(p) = x$, i.e. the Lookup operation provides a unique peer for a given name (if such a peer is currently in the system). To guarantee this property, an authority is needed that resolves conflicts among the peers and that prevents peers from taking over names of other peers. Thus, we assume that a certification authority is available that issues certified names to peers that want to enter the system and that only provides such a name if no peer has registered under that name before. Certified names allow peers to prove that they are the rightful owner of a name, which prevents peers from taking over the identities of other peers. However, this does *not* prevent the adversary from registering a large number of adaptively chosen names that are different from names of the honest peers.

Notice that the certification authority does not need to be online during the operation of the peer-to-peer system if all peers have registered names with it before. Hence, it does not introduce a single point of failure for the operation of that system and therefore does not undermine the benefits of having a decentralized peer-to-peer system.

Semantics of Join, Leave, and Lookup. Recall that a peer p is defined as an entity with a unique, certified identity, i.e. $p = s(\mathsf{Name}, \mathsf{IP})$ where s is a signature scheme, Name is the name of p, and IP is the IP address of p. Join, Leave, and Lookup are operations acting on a name service relation $\mathsf{DNS} \subseteq \mathsf{Names} \times \mathsf{IPs}$ in the following way:

- Join(p): if this operation was initiated by $\mathsf{IP}(p)$ and p is correctly certified then $\mathsf{DNS} \leftarrow \mathsf{DNS} \cup \{(\mathsf{Name}(p), \mathsf{IP}(p))\}$
- Leave(p): if this operation was initiated by $\mathsf{IP}(p)$ then $\mathsf{DNS} \leftarrow \mathsf{DNS} \setminus \{(\mathsf{Name}(p), \mathsf{IP}(p))\}$
- Lookup(Name): if there is a peer q with $(\mathsf{Name}, \mathsf{IP}(q)) \in \mathsf{DNS}$ then return $\mathsf{IP}(q)$ and otherwise return NULL

Given that the certification authority maintains a mapping $\mathsf{CA} : \mathsf{Names} \to \mathsf{IPs}$ that is well-defined at any time (i.e. each name is associated with at most one IP address), also the lookup operation will be well-defined. Indeed, if the operations above are correctly implemented and executed, then $\mathsf{DNS} \subseteq \mathsf{CA}$ at any time and DNS consists of all identities currently present in the peer-to-peer system.

Notice, that there are many ways for adversarial peers to attack the correctness of DNS: adversarial peers may execute Join(p) for honest peers currently not in the system or Leave(p) for honest peers currently in the system, or may leave the system without notice. Also, adversarial peers may attempt to provide a wrong answer to a lookup operation. So countermeasures have to be taken to protect the system against these attacks.

Resources. We allow arbitrary adversaries with bounded presence, i.e. the number of adversarial identities or peers is at most an ϵ-fraction of the peers in the system at any time. Such adversaries are called ϵ-*bounded*.

We consider asynchronous systems in which every honest peer has roughly the same clock speed but there is no global time. Since honest peers are considered reliable, we assume that at any point in time, any message sent by an honest peer p to another honest peer q will arrive at q within a unit of time. (Other message transmissions may need any amount of time.) Furthermore, honest peers have unbounded bandwidth and computational power, i.e. an honest peer can receive, process, and send out an unbounded number of messages in a unit of time. The latter assumption allows us to ignore denial-of-service attacks, but it does *not* simplify the task of securing an overlay network against legal attacks (i.e. attacks exploiting security holes in its protocols). As long as adversarial peers do not transmit unnecessary packets, the number of messages an honest peer will have to deal with in a time unit will normally be low so that we believe that our protocols are practical despite this assumption. Designing provably secure overlay networks for honest peers with bounded bandwidth is very challenging and needs further research.

Bootstrap Peers. We assume that the certification authority provides a limited number of so-called *bootstrap peers* that are always part of the overlay network. This list of peers may be downloaded by a new peer when it registers its name so that it can contact one of the bootstrap peers without contacting the certification authority again. Bootstrap peers are like normal peers. For the Join protocol to work correctly we assume that at least one of the bootstrap peers is honest. Otherwise, there is no reliable way for a new peer to join the system. However, the Leave and Lookup protocols should *not* rely on the bootstrap peers so that the system is scalable and can work correctly under ϵ-bounded adversaries even if all bootstrap peers are adversarial.

To simplify the Join protocol in this extended abstract, we will assume that *all* bootstrap peers are honest.

Notice that the concept of bootstrap peers is necessary because somehow new peers have to be able to find out about peers already in the system. Assumptions like "peers contact random peers in the system" are not realistic because how should a peer find this random peer over the Internet? Furthermore, it is important to have peers that are permanently present in the overlay network because otherwise a server would have to be established that is always accessible and that provides a continuously updated list of peers currently in the system, which introduces a single point of failure.

Messages. Finally, we need some assumptions about how messages are passed. We assume that the (IP address of the) source of a message cannot be forged so that adversarial peers cannot forge messages from honest peers. Also, a message sent between honest peers cannot be deleted or altered by the adversary.

Notice that the source issue can actually be solved easily without cryptography as long as adversaries cannot hijack IP addresses or listen to communication between honest peers: if a message arrives from IP address x, then the receiver y asks x for a confirmation that contains a secret (for example, a random key). Only if y receives an acknowledgement from x containing the secret, y will accept the message. The assumption that messages cannot be deleted or altered by the adversary is realistic in our case because we assume the peers of our overlay network to sit at the edge of the Internet, and therefore peers cannot manipulate communication between other peers.

1.3   Security Goal

Recall that our security goal is to implement the Join, Leave, and Lookup operations so that they can be run concurrently and reliably in an asynchronous environment. More precisely, any of these operations executed by any of the honest peers in the system should be executed in a correct and efficient way. "In the system", "correct" and "efficient" require precise definitions.

A Join(p) (resp. Leave(p)) operation is called *completed* if any Lookup(Name(p)) operation executed afterwards by an honest peer in the system (and before another Join(p) or Leave(p) operation) returns IP(p) (resp. NULL). A peer p belongs to the system if Join(p) has been completed and Leave(p) has not been initiated yet. A Lookup(Name) operation is called *completed* once the peer initiating the request accepts the return value.

An overlay network operation is said to execute *correctly* if it completes within a finite amount of time. Furthermore, an overlay network operation is called

- *work-efficient* if it is completed using at most polylog(n) messages and
- *time-efficient* if it is completed using at most polylog(n) time,

where n be the current number of peers in the overlay network.

Finally, we call an overlay network *survivable* if it can guarantee the correct and (time and work) efficient execution of any overlay network operation initiated by an honest peer, with high probability, for at least 1/polylog(n)-bounded adversaries and a join/leave rate of at least 1/polylog(n), i.e. at least n/polylog(n) peers may join or leave the network in a time unit.

This definition implies that in a survivable network, any overlay network operation initiated by an honest peer can be executed correctly for at least poly(n) time units, with high probability, where n is the minimum number of peers in the system during that time.

Notice that we only require correct and efficient executions for honest peers, i.e. we do not care whether the semantics of Join, Leave, or Lookup are violated for adversarial peers. For example, a Lookup(Name) request for some Name owned by an adversarial peer q is allowed to give inconsistent answers, i.e. some honest peers may receive the answer IP(q) and others receive the answer NULL.

Also, notice that we have to add the term "with high probability" above, because we said that a priori, it is not possible to distinguish between honest and adversarial peers. So no absolute guarantees can be given, unless we completely interconnect all peers, which is highly inefficient and therefore out of question.

An overlay network is called *weakly survivable* if it can only guarantee correctness and time-efficiency, but no work-efficiency. In this paper we propose a design called Trust-but-Verify that provides weak survivability as long as the adversarial peers are in the minority. Recently, the authors also managed to design overlay networks that are survivable in the strong sense. See [1, 2] for details.

1.4   Existing Work

Classical distributed computing methods [13, 5, 14, 17] use Byzantine agreement and two-phase commit approaches with inherently *linear* redundancy and overhead to maintain a safe state.

The *proactive security* approach in [16, 12, 11, 3, 10] uses different coding techniques to protect unreliable data in *reliable* networks; applying these methods in our context still yields linear overhead.

Fixed topology networks as in [9], will work only for non-Byzantine peers, and only allow fail-stop faults; the construction cannot handle malicious behavior of even a few malicious players.

The reliability of *hash-based peer-to-peer overlays* (or DHT's) such as Chord [18], Pastry [8], and Tapestry [19] hinges on the assumption that the IDs given to the nodes are pseudo-random, so that they can cope with a constant fraction of the nodes failing concurrently, with only logarithmic overhead. While this may seem to perfectly defeat massive attacks under these randomness assumptions, DHT's cannot handle even small-scale adaptive adversarial attacks involving the selection of adversarial IP addresses (to get close to desired IDs). One such "Sybil" attack is described in [7]. Remarkably, the attackers do not need to do anything complex such as inverting the hash function; all that is needed is to get hold of a handful (actually, logarithmic) number of IP addresses so that IDs can be obtained that allow to disconnect some target from the rest of the system. This can be accomplished by a linear number (i.e. $O(n)$) of offline trial/errors. For similar attacks, see [6].

Random or unpredictable placement of data in a logarithmic size subset of locations (as in Freenet) ensures that data is difficult to attack, but also makes it *difficult to retrieve*. Specifically, data retrieval of randomly placed data requires a linear number of queries, which is definitely unscalable.

2   The Trust-but-Verify Approach

The basic approach of our Trust-but-Verify scheme is similar to previous hash-based overlay networks such as Chord [18]. All hash-based overlay networks are based on the concept of a virtual space. The basic idea underlying these systems is that peers are given virtual locations in some space, and the overlay network is constructed based on these virtual locations. That is, depending on its virtual location, a peer aims to maintain connections to other virtual locations and does this by establishing pointers to the peers closest to these locations. See, e.g. [15] for a general framework behind this approach. To illustrate this approach, we give the Chord network as an example.

2.1   The Chord Overlay Network

Suppose that we have a system currently consisting of a set V of n peers, and further suppose we have a (pseudo-)random hash function h : Names $\rightarrow [0, 1)$ that maps peers to real values in the interval $[0, 1)$. The real value a peer p is mapped to is called its *identification number* or ID and denoted by $\mathsf{ID}(p)$. The basic structure of Chord is a doubly-linked cycle, the so-called *Chord ring*, in which all peers are ordered according to their IDs. In addition to this, every peer p has edges to peers $f_i(p)$, called *fingers*, with $f_i(p) = \mathrm{argmin}\{q \in V \mid \mathsf{ID}(q) \geq \mathsf{ID}(p) + 1/2^i\}$ for every $i \geq 1$.

To avoid identity theft, h is usually assumed to be a one-way hash function so that it is hard to find a name Name $\neq$ Name(p) for some peer p so that $h(\text{Name}) = h(\text{Name}(p))$.

2.2 Problems with the Chord Overlay Network

Using a pseudo-random hash function allows to assume that IDs of honest peers are distributed uniformly at random in $[0, 1)$, but it does *not* allow to assume that also IDs of adversarial peers are distributed uniformly at random in $[0, 1)$. The problem is that adversarial peers may pick names deliberately for the purpose of getting very close to some values in $[0, 1)$.

For example, by generating a set A of adversarial peers with IDs in $[x - \epsilon, x]$, $[x, x + \epsilon]$, and $[x + 1/2^i, x + 1/2^i + \epsilon]$ for all relevant i with $\epsilon < 1/n^2$, peer p with $\text{ID}(p) = x$ will have no honest peer pointing to it any more, and all peers p is pointing to belong to A, with high probability. Hence, if the peers in A leave, p will be disconnected from the system, with high probability. Notice that even a relatively modest adversary can come up with such a set A, even if the hash function is not invertible. It just has to try enough names.

Once p is isolated, overlay network operations cannot be executed successfully any more, because p is not able to communicate with other honest peers in the system. Thus, the Chord overlay network is not survivable in our sense.

2.3 An Approach Robust Against Isolation Attacks

The Trust-but-Verify overlay network also uses a pseudo-random one-way hash function to map peers to IDs in $[0, 1)$. (Recall that the pseudo-randomness makes sure that IDs of honest peers are random, and the one-way property makes sure that if the name of a peer cannot be taken over, it is also hard to take over its ID.) However, peers are interconnected in a different way.

A *region* is an interval in $[0, 1)$ of size $1/2^r$ for some $r \in \mathbb{N}_0$ starting at an integer multiple of $1/2^r$. Imagine for a moment that every peer knew the current number of peers, n, in the system, and that every peer p aims to maintain connections to all peers in the system with IDs in the regions $R_i(p)$, $i \in \mathbb{Z}$, where $R_i(p)$ is the unique region of size closest from above to $(c \log n)/n$, for some fixed constant c, that contains $\text{ID}(p) + \text{sgn}(i)/2^{|i|} (\text{mod } 1)$.

Suppose now that the ID of every honest peer is like an independent, random value in $[0, 1)$ (but hash values of adversarial peers may be any values different from the values of honest peers). Then the well-known Chernoff bounds imply the following result:

Theorem 1. *For any $(1 - \epsilon)$-bounded adversary for some constant $\epsilon > 0$ there is a constant $c = O(1/\epsilon)$ so that in every region of size closest from above to $(c \log n)/n$ there are $\Omega(\log n)$ honest peers, with high probability.*

It follows from the theorem and the way the regions are selected that *no matter how the IDs of adversarial peers are distributed in $[0, 1)$*, the honest peers in the system will form a single connected component. However, just having connectivity among the honest peers does not seem to suffice to achieve the desired semantics of Join, Leave, and Lookup. The problem here is that in a Lookup(Name) execution adversarial peers may claim that a certain peer with that name is in the system, and there does not seem to be a reliable way for an honest peer to verify this claim because adversarial peers may represent the majority in the region containing $h(\text{Name})$. So a different approach is needed to achieve survivability.

2.4   Outline of Trust-but-Verify Approach

The main idea of our Trust-but-Verify approach is that honest peers will organize in regions $R \subseteq [0, 1)$ they consider to be safe (i.e. the honest peers are in the majority) and not just some regions of size $(c \log n)/n$. If an honest peer feels that one of its regions is no longer safe, it will change it to a larger region. On the other hand, if an honest peer feels that a subregion within one of its regions is now safe, it will move to the subregion. Each honest peer will continuously probe peers it knows in its regions. If some peer does not respond, the honest peer will drop its connection to it. Since we assume honest peers to be reliable, this will not happen to honest peers. Messages are routed along safe regions to make sure that adversarial peers cannot alter, delay, or delete them. Next we give a more detailed description of how to maintain regions, how to interconnect the peers, and how to join, leave, and search in the overlay network.

3   The Trust-but-Verify Scheme

3.1   Safe Regions

Recall that a region is an interval in $[0, 1)$ of size $1/2^r$ for some $r \in \mathbb{N}_0$ starting at an integer multiple of $1/2^r$. Suppose that every peer p knows the current number n of peers in the system. Given a peer p and a region R, let V_R^p denote p's *view* of R, i.e. the set of peers p knows in R. p considers R to be *safe* if, for some fixed constants $c > 1$ and $\epsilon \le 1/12$,

1. $|R| \ge (c \log n)/n$ and
2. $|V_R^p| \le (1 + \epsilon)|R| \cdot n$.

Safe regions have the following nice property when given an ϵ-bounded adversary:

Theorem 2. *Let $0 < \epsilon \le 1/12$ and $c > 0$ be constants. If for some peer p and region R, p considers R to be safe, V_R^p contains all honest peers in R, and c is sufficiently large compared to ϵ, then at least $3/4$ of the peers in V_R^p are honest, with high probability.*

The theorem directly follows from the well-known Chernoff bounds because if $|R| \ge (c \log n)/n$ for a sufficiently large c, then the number of honest peers in R is at least $(1 - 2\epsilon)|R| \cdot n$, with high probability. In this case, the fraction of adversarial peers in V_R^p can be at most $3\epsilon \le 1/4$ if $\epsilon \le 1/12$.

3.2 Maintaining Safe Regions

Since the membership of regions can change rapidly, each honest peer p will keep *safe snapshots* $(S_i(p), r_i^s(p))$ and *current versions* $(C_i(p), r_i^c(p))$ of regions containing $\mathsf{ID}(p) + \mathrm{sgn}(i)/2^{|i|}$, where $S_i(p)$ is the view and $1/2^{r_i^s(p)}$ is the size of the snapshot region $R_i^s(p)$ and $C_i(p)$ is the view and $1/2^{r_i^c(p)}$ is the size of the current region $R_i^c(p)$ of p. These regions are updated as follows.

1. A subregion $R \subseteq R_i^c(p)$ containing $\mathsf{ID}(p) + \mathrm{sgn}(i)/2^{|i|}$ is now safe: then p executes $(S_i(p), r_i^s(p)) \leftarrow (V_R^p, -\log|R|)$ and $(C_i(p), r_i^c(p)) \leftarrow (S_i(p), r_i^s(p))$, i.e. p updates its snapshot and current region to R.
2. $R_i^c(p)$ is unsafe: then p executes $C_i(p) \leftarrow C_i(p) \cup \mathsf{View}(R)$ and $r_i^c(p) \leftarrow r_i^c(p) - 1$, i.e. p doubles the size of its current region and extends its view by requesting a view of the unknown half, R, of the new region (the View command is specified below).
3. A new peer q joins $R_i^c(p)$: then p executes $C_i(p) \leftarrow C_i(p) \cup \{q\}$.
4. An old peer q leaves $R_i^c(p)$: then p executes $C_i(p) \leftarrow C_i(p) \setminus \{q\}$.
5. An old peer q leaves $R_i^s(p)$: then p executes $S_i(p) \leftarrow S_i(p) \setminus \{q\}$.

p maintains connections to all peers it knows of in every $R_i^c(p)$ and $R_i^s(p)$ (and some limited number of older versions of $R_i^s(p)$ to preserve the correctness of overlay network operations) and all peers q it knows of with p in $R_i^c(q)$ or $R_i^s(q)$.

Notice that there can be different values i_1 and i_2 with $R_{i_1}^c(p) \subseteq R_{i_2}^c(p)$, so regions may sometimes be contained in other regions, but for any two active regions R_1 and R_2 of a peer p it must hold that either $R_1 \subseteq R_2$ (resp. $R_2 \subseteq R_1$) or $R_1 \cap R_2 = \emptyset$. Those regions R_1 with $R_1 \subseteq R_2$ only have to be maintained implicitly, so that p only has to explicitly store $O(\log n)$ regions at any point in time.

Also, notice that $R_i^s(p) \subseteq R_i^c(p)$ at any time. New peers are only added to $C_i(p)$ because safe snapshots have to preserve the safeness condition at any time, and therefore new peers should not be added there. However, peers may still leave safe snapshots. Hence, they have to be updated quickly enough to make sure that honest peers always represent the majority. Fortunately, if the departure rate of honest peers is limited to $\epsilon/\log^2 n$ for some small constant $\epsilon > 0$, then the honest peers will be able to find new safe snapshots quickly enough. More precisely, the following result can be shown.

Theorem 3. *If the adversary is ϵ-bounded for some sufficiently small constant $\epsilon > 0$ and the arrival and departure rate of (honest and adversarial) peers is at most $\epsilon'/\log^2 n$ for some sufficiently small constant $\epsilon' > 0$, then our region update rules ensure that for every honest peer p and every i, at least $2/3$ of the peers in $R_i^s(p)$ are honest at any time, with high probability.*

To be able to verify this result, we describe below how to execute the $\mathsf{View}(R)$ operation. Notice that $R_i^s(p) \subseteq R_i^c(p)$ at any time. It is not difficult to check that this operation is well-defined and completes in $O(\log n)$ time.

View(R):
    // p: peer initiating the view request
    if $\exists i \in \mathbb{Z} : R \subseteq R_i^s(p)$ **then return** V_R^p (w.r.t. $C_i(p)$)
    else
        if $\text{ID}(p) \in R$ **then**
            // R_1, R_2: two halves of R, i.e. $R_1 \cup R_2 = R$
            for each $i \in \{1, 2\}$:
                if $\exists j \in \mathbb{Z} : R_i \subseteq R_j^s(p)$ **then** $V_i = V_{R_i}^p$ (w.r.t. $C_j(p)$)
                else
                    fix any $R_j^s(p) \subseteq R_i$
                    send to all peers in $S_j(p)$: (View, R_i)
                    wait until (View, $R_i, V_i(q)$) from $\geq 2/3$ of peers $q \in S_j(p)$
                    $V_i \leftarrow \{q' : |\{V_i(q) \mid q' \in V_i(q)\}| \geq |S_j(p)|/3\}$
            return $V_1 \cup V_2$
        else
            send to all peers in the $S_j(p)$ closest to R: (View, R)
            wait until receiving (View, $R, V(q)$) from $\geq 2/3$ of peers $q \in S_j(p)$
            $V \leftarrow \{q' : |\{V(q) \mid q' \in V(q)\}| \geq |S_j(p)|/3\}$
            return V

Upon receiving (View, R) from some peer p':
    // q: peer receiving the region request
    if $\exists i \in \mathbb{Z} : R \subseteq R_i^s(q)$ **then** send to p': (View, R, V_R^q)
    else
        if $\text{ID}(q) \in R$ **then**
            // use same strategy as above to compute V_1 and V_2
            send to p': (View, $R, V_1 \cup V_2$)
        else
            // use same strategy as above to compute V
            send to p': (View, R, V)

It remains to show how to execute Join, Leave, and Lookup operations and how to estimate n.

3.3 Join and Leave

If a new peer p wants to join via some bootstrap peer q, q starts with requesting views for regions of p of lowest possible size, i.e. $(c \log n)/n$. If this does not provide a safe region for some $S_i(p)$, q moves to a larger region for that i until it obtains views satisfying the requirements of a safe region for every relevant i (here, $i \in \{-\log n, \ldots, \log n\}$ is sufficient). Afterwards, q passes these views to p. p uses these views to integrate itself into the system.

The Leave(p) operation is straightforward: p just cuts all connections it has in the overlay network. Join takes $O(\log^2 n)$ time and Leave takes $O(1)$ time.

3.4   Lookup

Next we specify the **Lookup** operation. It is not difficult to check that it completes
in $O(\log n)$ time.

Lookup(Name):
  // *p: peer initiating the lookup request*
  if $\exists i :\ h(\mathsf{Name}) \in R_i^c(p)$ **then**
    if $\exists q \in C_i(p) :\ \mathsf{Name}(q) = \mathsf{Name}$ **then return** q
    else return NULL
  else
    send to all peers in the $S_i(p)$ closest to $h(\mathsf{Name})$: (Lookup, Name)
    wait until receiving (Lookup, Name, a) from $> 1/2$ of peers in $S_i(p)$
    return a

Upon receiving (Lookup, Name) from some peer p':
  // *q: peer receiving the lookup request*
  if $\exists i :\ h(\mathsf{Name}) \in R_i^c(q)$ **then**
    if $\exists q' \in C_i(q) :\ \mathsf{Name}(q') = \mathsf{Name}$ **then**
      send (Lookup, Name, q') to p'
    else send to p': (Lookup, Name,NULL)
  else
    send to all peers in the $S_i(q)$ closest to $h(\mathsf{Name})$: (Lookup, Name)
    wait until receiving (Lookup, Name, a) from $> 1/2$ of peers in $S_i(q)$
    send to p': (Lookup, Name, a)

3.5   Estimating n

Finally, we show how to estimate n. This is done recursively, starting with each
peer p executing $\mathsf{Size}(r_0)$ for $r_0 = \lfloor \log(\frac{n}{c \log n}) \rfloor$. $\mathsf{Size}(r_0)$ never has to wait for
incoming messages and therefore terminates for all honest peers. This will then

---

Size(r):
  // *p: peer executing the operation*
  $R \leftarrow$ unique region of size r containing ID(p)
  $(R_1, R_2) \leftarrow$ two halfs of R
  for each $i \in \{1, 2\}$:
    if $\exists j \in \mathbb{Z} :\ R_i \subseteq R_j^s(p)$ **then** $v_i = |V_{R_i}^p|$ (w.r.t. $C_j(p)$)
    else
      fix any $R_j^s(p) \subseteq R_i$
      wait until receiving (Size, $v_q, r + 1$) from $\geq 2/3$ of peers $q \in S_j(p)$
      $v_i \leftarrow$ median($\{v_q :\ q \in S_j(p)$ and q sent message$\}$)
  if $r = 0$ **then return** $v_1 + v_2$
  else
    $R' \leftarrow$ unique region of size $r - 1$ containing ID(p)
    send to all $q \in V_{R'}^p$: (Size, $v_1 + v_2, r$)

---

allow $\mathsf{Size}(r_0 - 1)$-calls to terminate, which allow $\mathsf{Size}(r_0 - 2)$-calls to terminate, and so on until an estimate of the number of peers in the system is returned by $\mathsf{Size}(0)$. To make sure that this estimates n sufficiently well, only estimates from honest peers are accepted by using the median rule in each stage.

It is not difficult to show that these operations make the Trust-but-Verify approach weakly survivable.

References

1. B. Awerbuch and C. Scheideler. Enforced Spreading: An improved protocol for provably secure distributed name service. Technical report, Johns Hopkins University, February 2004.
2. B. Awerbuch and C. Scheideler. Group Spreading: A protocol for provably secure distributed name service. In *Proc. of the 31st International Colloquium on Automata, Languages and Programming (ICALP)*, 2004.
3. R. Canetti, R. Gennaro, A. Herzberg, and D. Naor. Proactive security: Long-term protection against break-ins. *RSA CryptoBytes*, 3(1):1–8, 1997.
4. M. Castro, P. Druschel, A. Ganesh, A. Rowstron, and D. Wallach. Secure routing for structured peer-to-peer overlay networks. In *Proc. of the 5th Usenix Symp. on Operating Systems Design and Implementation (OSDI)*, 2002.
5. M. Castro and B. Liskov. Practical Byzantine fault tolerance. In *Proc. of the 2nd Usenix Symp. on Operating Systems Design and Implementation (OSDI)*, 1999.
6. S. Crosby and D. Wallach. Denial of service via algorithmic complexity attacks. In *Usenix Security*, 2003.
7. J. R. Douceur. The sybil attack. In *Proc. of the 1st International Workshop on Peer-to-Peer Systems (IPTPS)*, 2002.
8. P. Druschel and A. Rowstron. Pastry: Scalable, distributed object location and routing for large-scale peer-to-peer systems. In *Proc. of the 18th IFIP/ACM International Conference on Distributed Systems Platforms (Middleware 2001)*, 2001.
9. A. Fiat and J. Saia. Censorship resistant peer-to-peer content addressable networks. In *Proc. of the 13th ACM Symp. on Discrete Algorithms (SODA)*, 2002.
10. Y. Frankel, P. Gemmell, P. D. MacKenzie, and M. Yung. Optimal resilience proactive public-key cryptosystems. In *Proc. of the 38th IEEE Symp. on Foundations of Computer Science (FOCS)*, pages 384–393, 1997.
11. A. Herzberg, M. Jakobsson, S. Jarecki, H. Krawczyk, and M. Yung. Proactive public key and signature systems. In *Proc. of the ACM Conference on Computer and Communications Security (CCS)*, pages 100–110, 1997.
12. A. Herzberg, S. Jarecki, H. Krawczyk, and M. Yung. Proactive secret sharing or: How to cope with perpetual leakage. In *CRYPTO '95*, pages 339–352, 1995.
13. L. Lamport. The weak Byzantine generals problem. *Journal of the ACM*, 30(3):669–676, 1983.
14. L. Lamport and N. Lynch. Distributed computing. Chapter of Handbook on Theoretical Computer Science. Also, to be published as Technical Memo MIT/LCS/TM-384, Laboratory for Computer Science, Massachusetts Institute of Technology, Cambridge, MA, 1989.
15. M. Naor and U. Wieder. Novel architectures for P2P applications: the continuous-discrete approach. In *Proc. of the 15th ACM Symp. on Parallel Algorithms and Architectures (SPAA)*, 2003.

16. R. Ostrovsky and M. Yung. How to withstand mobile virus attacks. In *Proc. of the 10th ACM Symp. on Principles of Distributed Computing (PODC)*, pages 51–59, 1991.
17. R. De Prisco, B. W. Lampson, and N. Lynch. Revisiting the Paxos algorithm. In *Workshop on Distributed Algorithms*, pages 111–125, 1997.
18. I. Stoica, R. Morris, D. Karger, M.F. Kaashoek, and H. Balakrishnan. Chord: A scalable peer-to-peer lookup service for Internet applications. In *Proc. of the ACM SIGCOMM '01*, 2001.
19. B.Y. Zhao, J. Kubiatowicz, and A. Joseph. Tapestry: An infrastructure for fault-tolerant wide-area location and routing. Technical report, University of California at Berkeley, Computer Science Department, 2001.

Peer-to-Peer Authentication
with a Distributed Single Sign-On Service[*]

William K. Josephson, Emin Gün Sirer, and Fred B. Schneider

Department of Computer Science
Cornell University
Ithaca, New York 14853

Abstract. CorSSO is a distributed service for authentication in networks. It allows application servers to delegate client identity checking to combinations of authentication servers that reside in separate administrative domains. CorSSO authentication policies enable the system to tolerate expected classes of attacks and failures. A novel partitioning of the work associated with authentication of principals means that the system scales well with increases in the numbers of users and services.

1 Introduction

A central tenet of the peer-to-peer paradigm is relocation of work from servers to their clients. In the limit, the distinction between clients and servers becomes completely attenuated, resulting in a system of peers communicating with peers. CorSSO[1] (Cornell Single Sign-On), the subject of this paper, explores this peer-to-peer tenet in the design of a network-wide authentication service. In particular, authentication functionality is removed from *application servers* and relocated to their clients and to new *authentication servers*. This partitioning of functionality between clients and authentication servers is designed not only to support scalability but also to distribute trust, enabling the resulting service to tolerate attacks and failures.

When application servers outsource authentication, it becomes possible to support a single, persistent user identity. Users can now authenticate once and

---

[*] This work is supported in part by ARPA/RADC grant F30602-96-1-0317, AFOSR grant F49620-03-1-0156, Defense Advanced Research Projects Agency (DARPA) and Air Force Research Laboratory Air Force Material Command USAF under agreement number F30602-99-1-0533, National Science Foundation Grant 0205452, and grants from Intel Corporation and Microsoft Corporation. The views and conclusions contained herein are those of the authors and should not be interpreted as necessarily representing the official policies or endorsements, either expressed or implied, of these organizations or the U.S. Government. William Josephson is supported by a National Science Foundation graduate research fellowship.
[1] Pronounced as in the Italian *corso*, the past participle of the verb *correre* ("to run") which is broadly used in Italian to convey a sense of forward motion. The word *corso* variously could refer to a course at a University (a means of forward motion in learning) or to an avenue (a means for making forward motion in a city).

G.M. Voelker and S. Shenker (Eds.): IPTPS 2004, LNCS 3279, pp. 250–258, 2004.
© Springer-Verlag Berlin Heidelberg 2004

access any participating service. This so-called *single sign-on* service has several benefits:

- Users no longer need to keep track of multiple identities and associated secrets.
- The administrative burden required for running an application server is reduced, since expensive tasks, such as validating users, ensuring the confidentiality of per-user secrets, and recovering lost passwords, are delegated to authentication servers.
- The single user identity can be used to link actions performed by that user at different applications.

Microsoft's `passport.com` is an example of a single sign-on service. It has not been universally embraced, partly because users and developers of application servers are wary of having a single administrative entity in charge. CorSSO, by comparison, delegates authentication to a set of servers, each potentially managed by a separate administrative entity. An application server S, through its CorSSO *authentication policy*, specifies which subsets of the authentication servers must work together in checking a user's identity in order for S to trust the result. And a user U establishes an identity by visiting a subset of authentication servers that U selects; together, these must satisfy the authentication policies for application servers that U will visit.

Thus, the authentication policy for an application server (i) specifies which subsets of the authentication servers together make sufficient demands (e.g, by variously checking what the user knows, has, or is) to establish the identity of a user and (ii) embodies assumptions about independence with respect to failures and attacks of the authentication servers in those subsets. Authentication servers are more likely to exhibit independence when they are managed by separate entities, are physically separated, communicate over narrow-bandwidth channels, and execute diverse software.

2   The Authentication Problem

CorSSO is concerned with authenticating users, programs and services, which we henceforth refer to as *principals*. Each public key K_X and corresponding private key k_X is associated with a principal X; public key K_X is then said to *speak for* X, because K_X allows any principal to check the validity of signatures produced by X. A message m signed using k_X is denoted $\langle m \rangle_{k_X}$; a message m encrypted with key p is denoted $\{m\}_p$. We do not introduce distinct notations for symmetric versus assymetric encryption but instead rely on the type of the encryption key to disambiguate. We employ the (now common) locution "K_X *says* m" for the sending of $\langle m \rangle_{k_X}$.

The problem solved by CorSSO is – in a manner that an application server trusts – to establish a binding between a public key K_X and the principal X that asserts K_X speaks for X. Three kinds of name spaces are involved.

- Each application server S has a local name space $\mathcal{N}(S)$. The access control list at S associates privileges with names from $\mathcal{N}(S)$, and clients of S may refer to other clients of S using names from $\mathcal{N}(S)$.

- Each authentication server A has a local name space $\mathcal{N}(A)$. A implements one or more means to check whether a principal had previously registered with some given name from $\mathcal{N}(A)$.
- There is a single global name space $\mathcal{N}^*$. Each server H, be it an authentication server and or an application server, implements a correspondence between names from $\mathcal{N}^*$ and local name space $\mathcal{N}(H)$.

Global name space $\mathcal{N}^*$ is defined so that if $p_1 \in \mathcal{N}(A_1)$, $p_2 \in \mathcal{N}(A_2)$, ..., $p_r \in \mathcal{N}(A_r)$ hold then

$$p_1@A_1|p_2@A_2|\cdots|p_n@A_r \in \mathcal{N}^*$$

holds. Each application server S stores a mapping between names in $\mathcal{N}(S)$ and names in $\mathcal{N}^*$. But each authentication server A translates a request by a principal P to be authenticated as global name $p_1@A_1|p_2@A_2|\cdots|p_r@A_r$ into the task of checking whether P satisfies the identify requirements for every name p_i where $A = A_i$ holds, $1 \leq i \leq r$.

A single unstructured global name space would, in theory, have sufficed. But the richer structure of $\mathcal{N}^*$ grants a measure of naming autonomy to authentication servers and to application servers, which should prove useful for integrating legacy systems. Our structure also allows short human-readable names to be used for interacting with authentication servers and applications servers, yet at the same time enables principals at different application servers to be linked through a global name space.

2.1 Specifying Authentication Policies

A CorSSO authentication policy $\mathcal{P}$ is a disjunction $\aleph_1 \vee \aleph_2 \vee \cdots \vee \aleph_n$ of sub-policies; $\mathcal{P}$ is *satisfied* for a principal P provided some sub-policy $\aleph_i$ is satisfied. Each sub-policy $\aleph_i$ specifies a set $\hat{\aleph}_i$ of authentication servers $\{A_i^1, A_i^2, \ldots, A_i^m\}$ and a threshold constraint t_i; $\aleph_i$ is *satisfied* by a principal P provided t_i of the authentication servers in $\hat{\aleph}_i$ each certify their identity requirements for P.

Our language of authentication policies is equivalent to all positive Boolean formulas over authentication server outcomes, because $\hat{\aleph}_i$ with threshold constraint $|\hat{\aleph}_i|$ is equivalent to conjunction of authentication server outcomes. Consequently, CorSSO authentication policies range over surprisingly rich sets of requirements.

- The conjunction implicit in the meaning of a sub-policy allows an application server to stipulate that various different means be employed in certifying a principal's identity. For example, to implement what is known as 3-factor authentication, have every sub-policy $\aleph$ specify a threshold constraint of 3 and include in $\hat{\aleph}$ servers that each use a different identity check.
- The conjunction implicit in the meaning of a sub-policy also allows an application server to defend against compromised authentication servers and specify independence assumptions about those severs. For a sub-policy $\aleph$ involving threshold parameter t_i, a set of t_i or more authentication servers in $\hat{\aleph}_i$ must come under control of an adversary before that adversary can cause $\mathcal{P}$ to be satisfied.

- The disjunction used to form an authentication policy $\mathcal{P}$ from sub-policies and the threshold parameter in sub-policies supports fault-tolerance, since the failure of one or more authentication servers then won't necessarily render $\mathcal{P}$ unsatisfiable.

The disjunction and sub-policy threshold constraints implement a distribution of trust, since these constructs allow an authentication policy to specify that more trust is being placed in an ensemble than in any of its members. Finally, the absence of negation in authentication policies is worth noting. Without negation, the inability of a principal to be certified by some authentication server can never lead to a successful CorSSO authentication; with negation, it could. So, by omitting negation from our policy language, crashes and denial of service attacks cannot create bogus authentications.

3   Protocols for CorSSO Authentication

Three protocols are involved in authenticating a principal C to an application server S: a setup protocol for the application server, a client authentication protocol, and a protocol for client access to the application server. Throughout, let $\aleph_1 \vee \aleph_2 \vee \cdots \vee \aleph_n$ be the authorization policy $\mathcal{P}$ for application server S, and let sub-policy $\aleph_i$ have threshold constraint t_i.

Application Server Setup Protocol. This protocol (Figure 1) is used by an application server to enlist authentication servers in support of an authentication policy. For each sub-policy $\aleph_i$ in $\mathcal{P}$, if one does not already exist then the protocol creates (step 2) a fresh private key k_i that speaks for all collections of t_i servers in $\hat{\aleph}_i$. This is implemented by storing at each authentication server in $\hat{\aleph}_i$ a distinct share from an $(t_i, |\hat{\aleph}_i|)$ sharing[2] of k_i. Therefore, authentication servers in $\hat{\aleph}_i$ can create *partial signatures* that, only when t_i are combined using threshold cryptography, yield a statement signed by k_i. Moreover, that signature can be checked by application server S, because corresponding public key K_i is sent to S in step 3.

Client Authentication Protocol. This protocol (Figure 2) is used by a principal with name $C \in \mathcal{N}^*$ to acquire an *authentication token* for subsequent use in accessing application servers. Each authentication token corresponds to a sub-policy; the authentication token for $\aleph_i$ asserts: K_i says that K_C speaks for C. Any application server for which $\aleph_i$ is a sub-policy will, by definition of $\mathcal{P}$, trust what K_i says on matters of client authentication because K_i speaks for subsets containing t_i servers from $\hat{\aleph}_i$.

Validity of an authentication token can be checked by an application server S because the authentication token is signed by k_i; S was sent corresponding public key K_i (in step 3 of the Application Server Setup protocol). The authentication token itself is derived (step 5) using threshold cryptography from the partial

---

[2] A (t, n) sharing of a secret s comprises a set of n shares such that any t_i of the shares allow recovery of s but fewer than t_i reveal no information about s.

For $1 \leq i \leq n$:
1. For all $A \in \hat{\aleph}_i$:
   $S \rightarrow A$: Enlist A for $\aleph_i$
2. Authentication servers in $\hat{\aleph}_i$ create a
   $(t_i, |\hat{\aleph}_i|)$ sharing $k_i^1, k_i^2, \ldots, k_i^{|\hat{\aleph}_i|}$ for a fresh private key k_i, if one does not already exist.
3. For some $A \in \hat{\aleph}_i$:
   $A \rightarrow S$: Public key for $\aleph_i$ is: K_i

Fig. 1. Application Server Setup Protocol.

1. $C \rightarrow S$: Request authentication policy for S.
2. $S \rightarrow C$: $\mathcal{P}$
3. C: Select a sub-policy $\aleph_i$ and private key k_C.
4. For all $A_i^j \in \hat{\aleph}_i$:
   4.1 $C \rightarrow A_i^j$: Request partial certificate for:
            principal C,
            public key K_C,
            sub-policy $\aleph_i$,
            starting time st,
            ending time et
   4.2 A_i^j: If C satisfies identity checks then
            $A_i^j \rightarrow C$: $\langle C, K_C, \aleph_i, st, et \rangle_{k_i^j}$
5. C: Compute authentication token
        $\langle C, K_C, \aleph_i, st, et \rangle_{k_i}$
   from responses received in step 4.2 from servers in $\hat{\aleph}_i$.

Fig. 2. Client Authentication Protocol.

certificates obtained (in step 4) from t_i authentication servers in $\hat{\aleph}_i$. So the authentication token will be valid only if C satisfies the identity tests that t_i authentication servers $A_i^j \in \hat{\aleph}_i$ impose.

Client Access to Application Server. The preceding two protocols establish an authentication token and a corresponding public key that can be used to authenticate a client C to an application server S. The need for mutual authentication, the presence of trusted third parties, the trust placed in the integrity of the network, and the access patterns of clients, all impact the design of the Client Access to Application Server protocol. CorSSO deliberately leaves this protocol unspecified; applications choose a protocol that suits their assumptions and needs.

Figure 3 outlines a simple Client Access to Application Server protocol. In this protocol, C initiates a connection to S (step 1), and S replies (step 2) with a nonce n_S and a certificate $\langle S, K_S \rangle_{k_{CA}}$ signed by certification authority CA and containing public key K_S for server S. If C trusts K_{CA} (step 3) then C can provide the raw material for a symmetric session key for a mutually authenticated secure channel to S. This is done by C picking a random nonce n_C

1. $C \to S$: Initiate authentication.
2. $S \to C$: $n_S, \langle S, K_S \rangle_{k_{CA}}$ for a nonce n_S.
3. C: (i) Check signature $\langle S, K_S \rangle_{k_{CA}}$.
     (ii) Compute $k = \text{hash}(C, S, n_C, n_S)$ for a random nonce n_C.
4. $C \to S$: $\{n_C, n_S, \langle k \rangle_{k_C}\}_{K_S}, \langle C, K_C, \aleph_i, st, et \rangle_{k_i}$
5. S: (i) Extract $n_C, n_S, \langle k \rangle_{k_C}$ using k_S, reconstruct k
              using n_C, n_S and names C and S;
     (ii) Check validity of $\langle k \rangle_{k_C}$ using public key K_C from
              authentication token $\langle C, K_C, \aleph_i, st, et \rangle_{k_i}$;
     (iii) Check validity of the authentication token
              using K_i and the current time of day.

Fig. 3. Client Access to Application Server.

(step 3), computing $k = \text{hash}(C, S, n_C, n_S)$ (step 3), and sending $n_C, n_S, \langle k \rangle_{k_C}$ to S encrypted under K_S (step 4). Notice the signature in $\langle k \rangle_{k_C}$ associates k with client C; the presence of n_S rules out replay, names C and S rule out man-in-the-middle attacks, and n_C serves as a source of randomness for the symmetric key. C then establishes its identity to S by sending (step 4) an authentication token that asserts: K_i says K_C speaks for C. A valid such token (containing K_C) and a matching signature $\langle k \rangle_{k_C}$ allows S henceforth to conclude that messages K_C "says" do come from C. (The session key for the mutually authenticated secure channel is then derived from k.)

An actual deployment of CorSSO today in the Internet would likely build on SSL, now predominantly used only to authenticate application servers to clients. Here, to authenticate clients to application servers, it suffices for CorSSO sub-policy keys k_i to be installed in the SSL layer on application servers and for CorSSO authentication tokens to be used by SSL during session setup for client authentication.

Protocol Architecture Notes

In CorSSO, work associated with authentication is divided between application servers, authentication servers, and clients in a way that supports scalability in two dimensions: number of clients and number of application servers.

- In the Application Server Setup Protocol, the amount of work an application server must do is a function of how many sub-policies comprise its authentication policy $\mathcal{P}$; it is not a function how many application servers or clients use $\mathcal{P}$.
- In the Client Authentication Protocol, the amount of work a client must do is determined by what authentication policies it must satisfy; that is unrelated to the number of applications servers that client visits if, as we anticipate, application servers share authentication policies.
- The cost to an application server running the Client Access to Application Server protocol is independent of the number of authentication servers and of the complexity of the authentication policy.

Notice also that the size of an authentication token is unaffected by the number of application servers, the policy it is used to satisfy, and the number of authentication servers involved in constructing that token. This is in contrast to the naive implementation of single sign-on, which has the client obtain a separate certificate from each authentication server and then present all of those certificates to each application server for checking.

Implementation Status

To date, we have built the core cryptographic components of CorSSO. We implemented digital signatures based on threshold RSA using verifiable secret sharing [FGMY97,Rab98], and preliminary measurements indicate good performance and a favorable distribution of the computational burden. In particular, we benchmarked the performance-critical path consisting of the Client Authentication and Client Access to Application Server protocols on a 2.60GHz Pentium 4. For RSA signatures using a $(4, 5)$-threshold sharing of a 1024-bit RSA key, the Client Authentication protocol took 430 msec and the Client Access to Application Server protocol took 947 μsec.

The burden of the computation thus falls on the client, decreasing the chance that an authentication server would become a bottleneck. Time spent in the Client Access to Application Server protocol is evenly divided between partial signature generation at the authentication servers and the full signature construction at the client. So by performing communication with authentication servers in parallel, end-to-end latency for authentication is 431 msec, which is typically dwarfed by delays for the identity tests that authentication servers make.

4   Related Work

Prior work on decomposing network-wide authentication services has focused on delegation – but not distribution – of trust. Kerberos [SNS88] performs user authentication in wide-area networks, but ties user identity to a centralized authentication server. OASIS [Org04] and the Liberty Alliance Project [Lib03] are recent industry efforts aimed at supporting a federated network identity. OASIS provides a standard framework for exchange of authentication and authorization information; Liberty uses this framework to delegate authentication decisions and to enable linking accounts at different authentication servers. The authentication policy in these systems corresponds to a disjunction of sub-policies, each specifying a single authentication server.

PolicyMaker [BFL96] is a flexible system for securely expressing statements about principals in a networked setting. It supports a far broader class of authentication policies than CorSSO does. Besides authentication, PolicyMaker also implements a rich class of authorization schemes. But with PolicyMaker, an application server must check each certificate involved in authentication or authorization decisions. In contrast, with CorSSO, the check at an application server is constant-time, because work has been factored-out and relocated to set-up protocols at the authentication servers and clients.

CorSSO borrows from Gong's threshold implementation of Kerberos KDCs [Gon93] and from COCA [ZSvR02] the insights that proactive secret sharing and threshold cryptography can help defend distributed services against attacks by so-called mobile adversaries [OY91], which attack, compromise, and control a server for a limited period before moving on to the next. Ultimately, we expect to deploy in CorSSO protocols for proactive recovery of the $(t_i, |\hat{\aleph}_i|)$ sharing of k_i.

5   Discussion

If broadly deployed, CorSSO would enable a market where authentication servers specialize in various forms of identity checks and compete on price, functionality, performance, and security. And authentication servers comprising a CorSSO deployment could receive payment on a per-application server, per-principal, or per-authentication basis.

Markets work provided participants are not only rewarded for their efforts but also are discouraged from taking disruptive actions. The CorSSO protocols described above allow participants to subvert a market through various forms of free-riding. For instance, an unscrupulous application server S' can use the policy from, hence certificates issued for, an application server S that is paying for its authentication policy to be supported. So S is subsidizing S'. This problem could be avoided by restricting the dissemination of public keys for sub-policies, issuing them only to application servers that pay. Keys that have been leaked to third parties are simply revoked and reissued.

Acknowledgments

Lorenzo Alvisi provided prompt and informative answers to questions relating to some cultural aspects of CorSSO. Martin Abadi provided helpful comments on the Client Access to Application Server protocol.

References

[BFL96]   Matt Blaze, Joan Feigenbaum, and Jack Lacy. Decentralized trust management. In *Proceedings 1996 IEEE Symposium on Security and Privacy*, pages 164–173, May 1996.

[FGMY97] Y. Frankel, P. Gemmell, P. Mackenzie, and M. Yung. Proactive RSA. *Lecture Notes in Computer Science*, 1294:440–455, 1997.

[Gon93]   L. Gong. Increasing availability and security of an authentication service. *IEEE J. Select. Areas Commun.*, 11(5):657–662, June 1993.

[Lib03]   Liberty Alliance Project. Introduction to the liberty alliance identity architecture, March 2003.

[Org04]   Organization for the Advancement of Structured Information Standards. http://www.oasis-open.org, February 2004.

[OY91]   R. Ostrovsky and M. Yung. How to withstand mobile virus attacks. In *Proceedings of the 10th ACM Symposium on Principles of Distributed Computing*, pages 51–59, 1991.

[Rab98]   T. Rabin. A simplified approach to threshold and proactive RSA. *Lecture Notes in Computer Science*, 1462:89–104, 1998.

[SNS88]   J. G. Steiner, B. C. Neuman, and J. I. Schiller. Kerberos: An authentication service for open network systems. In *Proceedings of the Winter 1988 Usenix Conference*, February 1988.

[ZSvR02]   L. Zhou, F. B. Schneider, and R. van Renesse. COCA: A secure distributed on-line certification authority. *ACM Transactions on Computing Systems*, 20(4):329–368, November 2002.

Secure Acknowledgment of Multicast Messages in Open Peer-to-Peer Networks

Antonio Nicolosi and David Mazières

Courant Institute of Mathematical Sciences, New York University, NY, USA
{nicolosi,dm}@cs.nyu.edu

Abstract. We propose a new cryptographic technique, *Acknowledgment Compression*, permitting senders of multicast data to verify that all interested parties have either received the data or lost network connectivity. Joining the system and acknowledging messages both require bandwidth and computation logarithmic in the size of a multicast group. Thus, the technique is well-suited to large-scale, peer-to-peer multicast groups in which neither the source nor any single peer wishes to download a complete list of participants. In the event that sufficiently many nodes are malicious, a message may fail to verify. However, in such cases the source learns the real network address of a number of malicious nodes.

1 Introduction

Peer-to-peer (P2P) multicast systems are a promising technology for inexpensively distributing information to large numbers of nodes. Traditional, centralized distribution schemes consume prohibitive amounts bandwidth, transmiting data repeatedly from a handful of sources. In contrast, P2P schemes can exploit the high aggregate bandwidth of all peers to disseminate data without requiring any particularly high-bandwidth nodes. Indeed, several P2P multicast systems have already been built, based on trees [1], forests [2], meshes [3], and other topologies.

Unfortunately, current P2P multicast schemes provide no way to confirm the reliable delivery of information. Yet for many applications, a data source might like to know if all interested parties have received messages. For example, a publisher might wish to confirm the receipt of a multicast invalidation for widely-cached popular data before considering a modification operation complete. Alternatively, the maintainers of an operating system distribution might like to know that everyone who wants security-critical updates has received the latest one.

In the P2P setting, multicast message acknowledgment is complicated by the open nature of the systems. Not only might many of the nodes in a multicast group be malicious, but the source of a message has no way of even knowing precisely who wants to receive the data. In large-scale P2P systems, even just transmitting a complete list of all nodes in a multicast group might consume undesirable amounts of bandwidth. Fortunately, it is reasonable to assume malicious nodes cannot subvert the routing structure of the Internet itself. Thus,

G.M. Voelker and S. Shenker (Eds.): IPTPS 2004, LNCS 3279, pp. 259–268, 2004.

particularly given the number and diversity of participants that P2P systems are designed for, a good node is likely to be able to communicate with almost any other honest node given that node's network address.

In this paper, we propose a new cryptographic mechanism, *Acknowledgment Compression*, that enables confirmation of messages delivered to large numbers of participants in an open network. Using this new primitive, a node that joins a multicast group receives a signed receipt from the data source acknowledging its entry into the system. For efficiency, arbitrarily many such join operations can be aggregated; no matter how many people join, the maximum computation and bandwidth required at any node is logarithmic in the total size of the multicast group. In particular, a join receipt does not explicitly name each new node, as no single node may even wish to consume the bandwidth necessary to download such a list.

Once a node has joined the system, it must acknowledge any messages sent to the multicast group. When a node fails to produce an acknowledgment, the multicast source can likely uncover its network address and contact that node directly, or else delegate the task – for instance to a probabilistically chosen subset of another part of a multicast tree. If a multicast group fails unrecoverably, it may be impossible to recover the address of an unreachable participant, but then the multicast source will learn the network address of malicious or faulty nodes who are blocking proper operation of the system.

2   Our Scheme

In this section, we define a model for Acknowledgement Compression, and present an efficient instantiation based on the cryptographic properties of special algebraic groups. Our scheme provides cryptographic proof of message deliver at the cost of consuming a small (logarithmic in the number of users in the system) amount of storage, computing time, and upstream/downstream bandwidth at each node.

2.1   The Model

An Acknowledgment Compression scheme comprises four protocols – Init, Join, Leave and Collect – with the following operational semantics. The content provider (or *source*) uses the Init protocol to carry out an initialization phase, at the end of which a public key for a secure digital signature scheme is produced and made widely available as a public parameter of the just-created multicast group. After the initial setup, the system grows by allowing batches of multiple user additions at discrete time instants, handled by the Join protocol. Normally, users would leave gracefully by invoking the Leave protocol, but some robustness mechanism is provided to recover from unanticipated node departures (or *crashes*). The fundamental operation of our scheme is the Collect protocol, which allows the source to specify a payload message m (e.g., an acknowledgment for the last multicast message) and to obtain a compact proof that every unfailed user in the group saw and endorsed the message m. As a side-effect, Collect also purges the system of failed users.

2.2   A Cryptographic Construction

This Section presents a specific construction within the framework of Section 2.1, based on cryptographic groups known as *Gap Diffie-Hellman* (GDH) groups. We address the related cryptographic literature in Section 4. Briefly, a GDH group $G = \langle g \rangle$ is an algebraic group of prime order q for which no efficient algorithm can compute g^{ab} for random $g^a, g^b \in G$, but such that there exists an efficient algorithm $D(g^a, g^b, h)$ to decide whether $h = g^{ab}$.

Digital signatures can be obtained from such groups as follows. A user secret key is a random value $x \in \mathbb{Z}_q$; the corresponding public key is $y \leftarrow g^x$. The signature on a message m is computed as $\sigma \leftarrow H(m)^x$, where H is some cryptographic hash function (e.g., SHA-1 [4]). The validity of a putative signature σ on a message m under the public key y is tested by checking that $D(y, H(m), \sigma) = 1$. The key property of this signature scheme that we will exploit in our construction is that the product of two signatures of the same message m under two different public keys y_1, y_2 yields a signature of m under the combined public key $y \leftarrow y_1 y_2 = g^{(x_1+x_2)}$, since $H(m)^{x_1} H(m)^{x_2} = H(m)^{(x_1+x_2)}$.

We now describe an Acknowledgment Compression scheme for the case that nodes don't crash abruptly; in Section 2.3 we discuss how to make the construction robust against node failures.

For the sake of clarity, we detail the case in which the communication happens via an (almost) balanced multicast tree with bounded maximum branching factor k (which most P2P multicast schemes strive to achieve anyway); however, our techniques can easily be adapted to the case of multiple multicast trees [2, 5], or other application-level multicast schemes and information dispersal algorithms.

Notation. In describing the protocols, we will make use of the following notation. 1_G denotes the identity element in G. For a node i, let y_i denote its public key, Loc_i denote its location (e.g, its network address), and T_i denote the subtree rooted at i. We will refer to the quantity:

$$Y_i \stackrel{def}{=} \prod_{j \in T_i} y_j$$

as the *combined public key* for the subtree T_i. Furthermore, we will denote i's children with $i_1, \ldots, i_k$, and i's parent with i^1; more generally, let i^d denote node i's d^{th} ancestor – i.e., the node sitting d levels above i in the tree. Many of the quantities associated with the system (most notably, the combined public key Y_i associated with each subtree T_i) *evolve* during the lifetime of the system as a consequence of members joining and leaving the multicast tree. To distinguish between old and new values, we will use a prime notation for old values e.g., Y_i' refers to the value of the combined public key for T_i *before* the user additions of the current execution of Join.

The Init Protocol. Init starts by choosing a cryptographic hash function H and a GDH group $G = \langle g \rangle$, along with a secret key/public key pair $(x_s, y_s \leftarrow g^{x_s})$ for the source. It then initializes a variable $Y_s \leftarrow y_s$, which will always hold the value of the combined public key Y_s for the whole multicast tree, T_s. This will be guaranteed by the Join and Leave protocols, which will update Y_s in such a way that the source, as well as every user of the system, can verify that the new value of Y_s is indeed the product of the public keys of all the users in the multicast tree.

The Collect Protocol. Before detailing how the Join and Leave protocols each manage to fulfill their pledge, we show how, assuming that Y_s actually embodies the public keys of all users in the system, the Collect protocol can produce a compressed acknowledgment for a payload message m specified by the source[1]. First, the source prepares and signs a *collect request* message:

$$CollectReq \stackrel{def}{=} \{ \text{"CollectReq"}, m \}$$

and sends this signature to all its children. Internal nodes forward such signatures to their children; when the signed *CollectReq* message gets to a leaf j, node j verifies the source's signature, signs the payload message m as $\sigma_j \leftarrow H(m)^{x_j}$, and replies to its parent with a *collect* message:

$$CollectMsg_j \stackrel{def}{=} \{ \text{"CollectMsg"}, m, \sigma_j \}.$$

Upon receiving a reply from each of its k children $i_1, \ldots, i_k$, an internal node i combines its signature $\sigma_i \leftarrow H(m)^{x_i}$ with the multi-signatures $\Sigma_{i_1}, \ldots, \Sigma_{i_k}$ contributed by its children as:

$$\Sigma_i \leftarrow \sigma_i \cdot \prod_{l=1}^{k} \Sigma_{i_l}$$

and then it replies to its parent with the message:

$$CollectMsg_i \stackrel{def}{=} \{ \text{"CollectMsg"}, m, \Sigma_i \}.$$

Eventually, the source will get a collect message from each of its children. After combining their signatures with its own, the source obtains what should be a multi-signature Σ_s on the message m, bearing the endorsement of each user in the system. To check this, the source tests whether Σ_s verifies correctly as a signature of m under the current combined public key Y_s, at which point the Collect operation terminates. Since, under standard cryptographic assumptions [6], no adversary can forge a multi-signature for a fresh message m, the source can infer that all the users whose public keys have been included in Y_s must have signed m. Finally, by the correctness of the Join protocol, this guarantees that each user in the system endorses the message m, as required of the Collect protocol.

---

[1] For security, the payload message m should be different across all executions of Collect; it is up to the application to provide such a guarantee, for instance by including a sequence number in each message.

Messages exchanged in the Join protocol
$CertReq_i \overset{def}{=} \{\text{"CertReq"}, Y_i', Y_i, Loc_i, Loc_{i1}\}$
$\quad Cert_i \overset{def}{=} \{CertReq_i\}_{(Y_i)^{-1}}$
$\quad\quad C_{i,j} \overset{def}{=} \{CertReq_i\}_{(Y_j)^{-1}} \quad // j \ descendent \ of \ i$
$\quad\quad c_{i,j} \overset{def}{=} \{CertReq_i\}_{(y_j)^{-1}} \quad // j \ descendent \ of \ i$

State information stored at node i
$\mathbf{Cert}_i$ :: current self-certificate for T_i
$\mathbf{Cert}_i'$ :: previous self-certificate for T_i
for each ancestor i^d:
$\quad \mathbf{y}_{i^d}$ :: public key y_{i^d} of node i^d
$\quad \mathbf{Y}_{i^d}$ :: current value of combined public key Y_{i^d}
for each child i_l:
$\quad \mathbf{Cert}_{i_l}$ :: current self-certificate for T_{i_l}
$\quad \mathbf{Cert}_{i_l}'$ :: previous self-certificate for T_{i_l}

Fig. 1. Join protocol – Messages exchanged during the protocol and state information for node i.

The Join Protocol. We now describe the details of the Join protocol in terms of a distributed computation carried out by the source together with all the (unfailed) nodes in the multicast tree. Figure 1 defines the format of the messages that will be exchanged during the protocol, as well as the state information maintained at each node, which requires $O(k + \log n)$ space for a system with n users, assuming a (roughly) balanced multicast tree with fan-out factor at most k at each node.

The protocol starts with the source executing the distributed algorithm RE-PORTJOINS described in Figure 2. REPORTJOINS initiates a "parallelized" post-order traversal of the multicast tree that visits all the children of a given node *concurrently*, and in the process it gathers information about user additions since the last execution of Join.

The actual computation begins once the recursion has reached the leaves of the multicast tree. Pre-existing leaves simply report that they don't have any change, whereas a newcomer j finalizes its ingress into the system by returning to its parent a signed message containing its public key y_j and its location information Loc_j.

An internal node i whose children have all reported no changes reports to its parent that it has no changes. Otherwise, if at least one child i_l has reported changes (meaning that some user(s) just joined the subtree T_{i_l}), then i must update the combined public key Y_i to reflect the presence of the newcomers in the subtree T_i, as nodes in T_{i_l} belong to T_i, too. In order to report such a change to its parent, node i must construct a *self-certificate* $Cert_i$, cryptographically justifying the evolution of Y_i.

To obtain a self-certificate, node i has to get the signature on a *certificate request* $CertReq_i$ (cfr. Figure 1) from all its descendents – a self-certificate for a subtree is only valid if all nodes in that subtree endorse it. To achieve this

$i.\text{REPORTJOINS}()$
1. **if** i *is a pre-exisiting leaf* **return** $\perp$
2. **else if** i *is a new leaf* **then**
3. $\text{Cert}'_i \leftarrow 1_G$
4. $\text{Cert}_i \leftarrow c_{i,i}$
5.   **return** Cert_i
6. **else**
7.   **for** *each child* i_l *of* i $(l = 1, \ldots, k)$
8. $\text{Cert}'_{i_l} \leftarrow \text{Cert}_{i_l}$
9. $\text{Cert}_{i_l} \leftarrow i_l.\text{REPORTJOINS}()$
10. $A_{i_l} \leftarrow \langle \text{Cert}'_{i_l}, \text{Cert}_{i_l} \rangle$
11.   **if** $(\forall l = 1, \ldots, k)[\text{Cert}_{i_l} = \perp]$ **return** $\perp$
12. $\text{CheckCerts}(A_{i_1}, \ldots, A_{i_k})$
13. $Y'_i \leftarrow Y_i$
14.   *update* Y_i *according to* $A_{i_1}, \ldots, A_{i_k}$
15. $\text{Cert}'_i \leftarrow \text{Cert}_i$
16.   **for** *each child* i_l *of* i $(l = 1, \ldots, k)$
17. $C_{i,i_l} \leftarrow i_l.\text{SIGNCERT}(i, c_{i,i}, A_{i_1}, \ldots, A_{i_k})$
18. $\text{Cert}_i \leftarrow c_{i,i} \cdot C_{i,i_1} \cdot \ldots \cdot C_{i,i_k}$
19.   **return** Cert_i

$j.\text{SIGNCERT}(i, c_{i,i}, A_{i_1}, \ldots, A_{i_k})$
1. $\text{CheckCerts}(A_{i_1}, \ldots, A_{i_k})$
2. *look up* i *among* j*'s ancestors; let* $i = j^d$
3. *verify the signature on* $c_{i,i}$
4. *check that* $c_{i,i}$ *is consistent with* $A_{i_1}, \ldots, A_{i_k}$
5. *update* Y_{j^d} $(= Y_i)$ *according to* $A_{i_1}, \ldots, A_{i_k}$
6. **if** i *is a leaf* **then**
7. $C_{i,j} \leftarrow c_{i,j}$
8. **else**
9.   **for** *each child* j_l *of* j $(l = 1, \ldots, k)$
10. $C_{i,j_l} \leftarrow j_l.\text{SIGNCERT}(i, c_{i,i}, A_{i_1}, \ldots, A_{i_k})$
11. $C_{i,j} \leftarrow c_{i,j} \cdot C_{i,j_1} \cdot \ldots \cdot C_{i,j_k}$
12. **return** $C_{i,j}$

$\text{CheckCerts}(A_{i_1}, \ldots, A_{i_k})$
1. **for** $l = 1, \ldots, k$
2.   *parse* A_{i_l} *as* $\langle \text{Cert}'_{i_l}, \text{Cert}_{i_l} \rangle$
3.   **if** $\text{Cert}_{i_l} \neq \perp$ **then**
4.   *verify the signatures on* Cert'_{i_l} *and* Cert_{i_l}
5.   **if** *new PK in* $\text{Cert}'_{i_l} \neq$ *old PK in* Cert_{i_l} **then**
6.   **throw** $\text{InvalidCertsException}$

Fig. 2. Join protocol – Pseudo-code for the distributed algorithms REPORTJOINS (as run by node i) and SIGNCERT (as run by node j, a descendent of i). Exception handlers for consistency check failures are not shown.

goal, i puts its signature on $CertReq_i$, and invokes the SIGNCERT distributed algorithm (described in Figure 2), which recursively pushes the request down to all descendents.

Node i's descendents, however, do not blindly sign whichever message they get to see – they need to be convinced of the legitimacy of the certificate request $CertReq_i$. For this reason, node i attaches two self-certificates for each child i_l who has reported changes: a cached version $Cert'_{i_l}$ from the previous execution of Join, and the current version $Cert_{i_l}$ that i_l just provided.

Given such accompanying documentation, each descendent j of node i can test the legitimacy of the certificate request sent by node i (cfr. the CheckCerts() procedure, Figure 2); after this check, j affixes its signature on $CertReq_i$ and forwards the execution of the SIGNCERT invocation down to its own children $j_1, \ldots, j_k$.

Upon hearing back from its children, j will obtain the partial signatures $C_{i,j_1}, \ldots, C_{i,j_k}$ relative to their subtrees $T_{j_1}, \ldots, T_{j_k}$. Then, j will piece all the parts together as:

$$C_{i,j} = c_{i,j} \cdot \prod_{l=1}^{k} C_{i,j_l}$$

and will reply to its parent with the partial signature $C_{i,j}$ on $CertReq_i$ relative to subtree T_j.

Eventually, node i will obtain partial signatures from all its children, which will enable i to compute the actual self-certificate $Cert_i$. At this point, node i will have enough information to justify the evolution of the combined public key for subtree T_i from its old value Y'_i to the new value Y_i, thus being able to finally complete its part in the REPORTJOINS by sending $Cert_i$ to its parent.

As the recursion of REPORTJOINS climbs up the tree, it will eventually reach the source. Then, as part of the SIGNCERT call invoked by the source, every node in the tree will get the source's signature on the message:

$$CertReq_s \stackrel{def}{=} \{\text{"CertReq"}, Y'_s, Y_s, Loc_s, Loc_s\}.$$

This, together with all the consistency checks performed during each step of the protocol, guarantees each new user that its public key has been included into the new value Y_s of the system's combined public key, and each existing user that its public key has not been factored out.

The Leave Protocol. The Leave protocol proceeds similarly to the Join protocol. In particular, a distributed algorithm REPORTLEAVES (akin to the distributed algorithm REPORTJOINS from Figure 2; not shown) traverses the multicast tree in a concurrent, bottom-up fashion, collecting signed *leave messages* of the form:

$$\{\text{"LeaveMsg"}, y_j, 1_G, Loc_j, Loc_{j^1}\}_{(y_j)^{-1}}$$

for each departing user j.

Such messages are then forwarded up the tree, and in the process, the combined public key of each subtree that contained a departing node is updated, and the necessary self-certificates are constructed to provide evidence supporting the evolution of the affected combined public keys. We omit the details.

2.3 Dealing with Unanticipated Failures

During normal operation, the users of the system are often required to sign messages. Due to the cryptographic consistency checks performed by all the other users, a malicious user j cannot deviate from the protocol except by refusing to cooperate, thus preventing its ancestors from successfully completing subsequent Collects or Joins. However, a user j that crashes without executing the Leave protocol would cause its parent, node j^1, to experience a similar refusal, which creates a troublesome ambiguity.

Simply allowing node j^1 to drop its non-cooperating child, as is often done in multicast systems, would undermine the main goal of Acknowledgement Compression. Such a policy, in fact, would expose the system to a possible abuse, based on the difficulty of distinguishing the case that node j didn't want to release its signature from the case that j's parent, node j^1, pretended to have been unable to obtain a signature from j to make j look bad.

Instead, we deal with this problem by requiring j^1 to produce j's self-certificate, which contains j's network address. Thus, either j^1 can fail to cooperate and be ejected from the system, or else other nodes can obtain j's address and attempt to deliver the message to j directly. In this way, a list of unreachable network addresses can be compiled and forwarded up the tree. If none of the ancestors of these unreachable nodes can reach them to obtain the missing component of the acknowledgment, the source will obtain the list of network addresses.

3 Discussion

One limitation of Acknowledgment Compression is the bandwidth required to deal with crashes. As described in the previous section, the source node receives a list of network addresses of all nodes that have failed to acknowledge a message, so as either to deliver the message directly or to confirm each node's unreachability. Though the list could conceivably be partitioned between a small set of well-known, trusted nodes, if the churn is too high, it may simply require too much bandwidth for each trusted node to receive its portion of the list. Thus, the technique may be ill-suited to networks in which many nodes could exit ungracefully, unless the lifetime of a multicast group is considerably less than the half-life of nodes. For infrastructure nodes, however, such as news servers and routers, it seems reasonable to expect long uptimes and graceful exits.

There are two possible approaches to handling large numbers of crashed nodes, though the problem is future work – we do not have a complete solution along the lines of either approach. First, there may be ways of obtaining large numbers of effectively trusted nodes, so as to partition the work of downloading crashed nodes' locations and probing them. This might, for instance, be achieved through some PGP-like web-of-trust overlay. Second, verification could be probabilistically farmed out to large-enough subgroups of multicast peers that at least one of them is likely to be honest. Subgroups can confirm the results of their probes by supplying a product of missing acknowledgment components (for nodes they managed to deliver the message to), plus a compressed acknowledgment on the product of public keys of unreachable nodes.

A final, related issue is that while Acknowledgment Compression confirms reliable multicast, it is not in itself a multicast protocol. Much work exists on fault-resilient P2P infrastructures, but of course malicious nodes may still succeed in partitioning or otherwise subverting the P2P system, rendering honest nodes that are routable at the network layer unreachable in the overlay network. Acknowledgment Compression cannot prevent such attacks, but at least it exposes the network address of malicious nodes who can then potentially be excluded from the system. The reason is that any node unable to produce some necessary component of an acknowledgment signature must instead be able to show a signed *CertReq* containing the *Location* (e.g., network address) of the missing contact that is its child node. To avoid reporting the network address of an isolated honest node, all nodes through which the missing contact is supposed to be routable must fail to return the *CertReq* certificate, thereby exposing themselves as malicious or unreliable.

4 Related Work

4.1 Multicast in Peer-to-Peer Networks

Recently, there has been much promising work on P2P multicast and data distribution e.g., SCRIBE [1], SplitStream [2], P2PCAST [5] and Bullet [3].

SCRIBE is an application-level multicast infrastructure built upon the Pastry P2P routing scheme [7]. In Scribe, messages are multicast over a *single tree*, created as the union of the (reverse) Pastry routes from each group member to a group-specific rendez-vous key. SplitStream improves on this approach by employing a *forest* of multicast trees, thus shedding the forwarding load somewhat more evenly among the members. P2PCAST also operates on a forest of multicast trees, but departs from SplitStream's approach in that it sacrifices some freedom in the construction of the multicast forest so as to ensure a regular structure for the trees of the forest. Bullet advocates the use of a different topology, namely a *mesh*, to achieve more reliable and bandwidth-efficient data dissemination.

Although Section 2.2 focused on the case of a single multicast tree, we believe that our techniques can be adapted to the other topologies as well, so that current P2P multicast systems can be combined with Acknowledgment Compression to obtain confirmed message delivery.

4.2 Cryptography

GDH groups have been the focus of much cryptographic research [8–10]. The basic GDH signature scheme we use for a single-node signatures was proposed by Boneh et al. [11]. The idea of combining such signatures and public keys by multiplication was used by Boldyreva [6] to construct multi-signatures – a variation of digital signatures in which a group of users, each holding a unique signing key, can produce signed documents that can later be verified to bear the endorsement of every signer in the group.

5   Summary

Acknowledgment Compression is a new cryptographic primitive useful for verifying message delivery in open, P2P multicast systems. Acknowledgment Compression allows senders to learn the network address of nodes that fail to acknowledge messages, yet without ever having to download a complete list of all participants. We propose an instantiation based on Gap Diffie-Hellman groups, and briefly discuss some usage issues for the technique.

Acknowledgments

We are grateful to Victor Shoup for his help with this work, and to Nelly Fazio, Michael Freedman and the anonymous reviewers for their comments on earlier drafts. This research was conducted as part of project IRIS (http://project-iris.net/), supported by the NSF under cooperative agreement #ANI-0225660. David Mazières is supported by an Alfred P. Sloan Research Fellowship.

References

1. Castro, M., Druschel, P., Kermarrec, A., Rowstron, A.: SCRIBE: A large-scale and decentralized application-level multicast infrastructure. IEEE Journal on Selected Areas in communications (JSAC) **20** (2002) 1489–1499
2. Castro, M., Druschel, P., Kermarrec, A.M., Nandi, A., Rowstron, A., Singh, A.: Splitstream: High-bandwidth content distribution in a cooperative environment. In: SOSP '03, Bolton Landing, NY, USA (2003)
3. Kostić, D., Rodriguez, A., Albrecht, J., Vahdat, A.: Bullet: High bandwidth data dissemination using an overlay mesh. In: SOSP '03, Bolton Landing, NY, USA (2003)
4. FIPS 180-1: Secure Hash Standard. U.S. Department of Commerce/N.I.S.T., National Technical Information Service, Springfield, VA. (1995)
5. Nicolosi, A., Annapureddy, S.: P2PCAST: A peer-to-peer multicast scheme for streaming data. 1st IRIS Student Workshop (ISW'03). Available at: http://www.cs.nyu.edu/~nicolosi/P2PCast.ps (2003)
6. Boldyreva, A.: Efficient threshold signature, multisignature and blind signature schemes based on the gap-diffie-hellman-group signature scheme. Full length version of extended abstract in PKC'03, available at http://eprint.iacr.org/2002/118/ (2003)
7. Rowstron, A., Druschel, P.: Pastry: Scalable, distributed object location and routing for large-scale peer-to-peer systems. In: IFIP/ACM International Conference on Distributed Systems Platforms (Middleware). (2001) 329–350
8. Joux, A.: A one round protocol for tripartite diffie-hellman. In: Proceedings of ANTS IV. Volume 1838 of LNCS., Springer-Verlag (2000) 385–394
9. Joux, A., Nguyen, K.: Separating decision diffie-hellman from diffie-hellman in cryptographic groups. Available at http://eprint.iacr.org/2001/060/ (2001)
10. Boneh, D., Franklin, M.: Identity-based encryption from the Weil pairing. In: Advances in Cryptology - Crypto '01. Volume 2139 of LNCS., Springer-Verlag (2001) 213–229
11. Boneh, D., Lynn, B., Shacham, H.: Short signatures from the Weil pairing. In: Advances in Cryptology – AsiaCrypt'01. Volume 2248 of LNCS., Berlin, Springer-Verlag (2001) 514–532

Know Thy Neighbor's Neighbor: Better Routing for Skip-Graphs and Small Worlds*

Moni Naor** and Udi Wieder

Department of Computer Science and Applied Mathematics
The Weizmann Institute of Science
Rehovot 76100 Israel
{moni.naor,udi.wieder}@weizmann.ac.il

Abstract. We investigate an approach for routing in p2p networks called *neighbor-of-neighbor greedy*. We show that this approach may reduce significantly the number of hops used, when routing in skip graphs and small worlds. Furthermore we show that a simple variation of Chord is degree optimal. Our algorithm is implemented on top of the conventional greedy algorithms, thus it maintains the good properties of greedy routing. Implementing it may only improve the performance of the system.

1 Introduction

Our aim in this paper is to propose an approach for routing in DHT's which is better than greedy routing. Greedy routing is a common approach in many DHT constructions. Typically some metric is imposed on the key space and then routing is performed by moving the message to the closest neighbor to the target. Examples include Chord [15], Skip Graphs or Skip Nets [2, 6], Pastry [14], Tapestry [16] and more. We discuss constructions which do not employ greedy routing towards the end of this section. The greedy routing approach has many advantages, among which are the following:

Simplicity – Greedy routing is easy to understand and implement. The routing is oblivious in the sense that the link used depends only on the destination of the message.

Fault Tolerance – In greedy routing closer is better. So when nodes or links fail, as long as each node has some edge towards the target, it is guaranteed that the message would reach its destination. In many constructions (such as Chord and Tapestry) it is assumed that a ring like structure exists. It is clear that as long as the ring edges exist, greedy routing would eventually succeed.

Locality in the Key Space – Messages do not 'wander' in the key space. If the source and the target are close to each other in the key space, then during

---

* Research supported in part by the RAND/APX grant from the EU Program IST
** Incumbent of the Judith Kleeman Professorial Chair.

the routing, the message would stay between the source and the target, in a small portion of the key space. If the key of a resource is associated with its location in the physical world then greedy routing might have proximity preserving properties; i.e. it might minimize the physical distance a message travels. If keys have *semantic* meaning, such as file names and sizes, then greedy routing would supply prefix search (as in skip graphs, see Section 1.1).

If greedy routing is so good then why use something else? Greedy routing has one major disadvantage - it requires a large number of hops, at least larger than what is dictated by the degree. In the previous examples, the degree is logarithmic in the network size, while the number of hops used by greedy routing is $O(\log n)$. Logarithmic degree may permit theoretically path lengths of $O(\log n/ \log \log n)$, thus greedy routing is *not* degree optimal. Furthermore, there are lower bounds that show that under some general conditions, greedy routing uses $\Omega(\log n)$ hops, when the degree is logarithmic, see [1, 11]. The latter bounds any routing algorithm which uses the immediate neighbor only.

Recently constructions with optimal path length were suggested. De-Bruijn based DHT's [13, 8, 4] offer an optimal tradeoff between degree and path length for every degree, in particular logarithmic degree permits routing in $O(\log n/ \log \log n)$ hops. These routing algorithms however, are *not* greedy and rely on some arithmetic manipulation of the keys. Thus routing in these graphs is not local in the key space. Furthermore these algorithms assume keys are *random*, so there is no immediate way to make the keys carry semantic meaning.

Can We Have the Advantages of Greedy Routing Together with Optimal Path Length? In this paper we answer this question affirmatively. We show that a variation of the greedy algorithm called 'neighbor-of-neighbor (NoN) greedy' enjoys the advantages of greedy routing while being degree optimal in a large family of constructions. We show that our algorithm reduces substantially the latency of skip graphs and of small worlds. Furthermore while it is known that Chord is not degree optimal [5], we show that a variation of Chord is indeed degree optimal.

1.1 Small Worlds and Skip Graphs

The notion of 'small worlds' originated as a term to describe the high connectivity of social networks. Kleinberg [9] modelled social networks by taking a two dimensional grid and connecting each node u to q edges when edge (u, v) exists with probability proportional to $||u-v||^{-2}$. For simplicity, we remove the parameter q and assume that each edge (u, v) is connected with probability $||u-v||^{-2}$, thus creating a graph with average degree $\Theta(\log n)$. For any dimension $d > 1$, the small world graph of dimension d has n^d nodes associated with the points of a $d-$dimensional mesh, where edge (u, v) is occupied with probability $||u-v||^{-d}$. Small world graphs serve as a motivation for p2p networks. Indeed they were analyzed in this context by Aspnes *et al* [1] who proved that the one dimensional small world graph permits greedy routing of $O(\log n)$ even if nodes and links fail independently.

Skip-Graphs or Skip-Nets is a dynamic data structure meant to serve as a tool for locating resources in a dynamic setting. It was proposed independently by Aspnes and Shah in [2] and by Harvey *et al* in [6]. The main advantage of skip graphs is that they supply prefix search and proximity search. In a skip graph each nodes chooses randomly a string of bits called the *membership vectors*. The links are determined by the membership vectors, and therefore the keys could be arbitrary. In other words, there is no need for the keys to be randomized and they may maintain *semantic* meaning. It is therefore essential that routing algorithms remain local in the key space. This is achieved without compromising the complexity of the Insert and Delete operations, thus skip graphs(nets) are an especially attractive p2p construction. It is shown in [2, 6] that greedy routing takes $O(\log n)$ hops. It is shown in [11] that greedy routing takes $\Omega(\log n)$ hops.

2   The NoN-Greedy Llgorithm

The NoN approach originates from a work by Coppersmith *et al* [3], which used it to prove bounds on the diameter of the small world graph, though not in an algorithmic perspective. It was also used by Manku *et al* (under the name 'lookahead') as a heuristic for the 'Symphony' P2P construction [10] which is based upon small world graphs. We assume that each node holds its own routing table, and on top of that it holds its neighbors routing tables. Thus each node has knowledge of a neighborhood of radius 2 around it. The NoN algorithmis presented in Figure 1.

Algorithm for routing to node t.

1. Assume the message is currently at node $u \neq t$. Let $w_1, w_2, \ldots, w_k$ be the neighbors of u.
2. For each i, let $z_{i_1}, z_{i_2}, \ldots, z_{i_k}$ be the neighbors of w_i.
3. Among these k^2 nodes, assume z_{i_j} is the one closest to t.
4. Route the message from u via w_i to z_{i_j}.

Fig. 1. The NoN-Greedy Algorithm. It is assumed for simplicity that the degree of each node is k.

The NoN algorithmcould be thought of as greedy in two hops instead of just one. One might think that practically the NoN algorithm uses a routing table of size $O(\log^2 n)$. This however is not the case. In order to apply NoN, the *memory* allocated to hold the routing tables of the neighbors is $O(\log^2 n)$ instead of $O(\log n)$. The main cost of an entry in the routing table lies in its *maintenance* (pinging periodically etc.). The cost in terms of memory of simply holding the entry is marginal.

Step (2) of the algorithmis implemented internally by putting all the z in a search tree. Thus the time it takes to find the next link is the time it takes to find the correct link is the search time of the tree which is $O(\log(k^2))$. Assuming that $k = O(\log n)$, Step (2) takes $O(\log \log n)$ time, which is the same as in greedy routing.

NoN is not greedy since w_i might not be the closest node to t among the neighbors of u. While not being greedy per se it is clear that NoN enjoys the advantages of greedy. The following theorem is taken from a companion paper [11], and shows that asymptotically the NoN algorithm is optimal both for skip graphs and for small world graphs.

Theorem 1. *When using the NoN algorithm:*

(a) *The average number of hops it takes to route a message in a skip graph is* $O(\log n / \log \log n)$.

(b) *Using the NoN algorithm, the number of hops it takes to route a message in a small world graph of any dimension is* $O(\log n / \log \log n)$ *with high probability.*

2.1 An Interesting Phenomenon

A common approach when constructing p2p systems is to try and 'emulate' dynamically a good static network. Thus Chord, Pastry and Tapestry are 'inspired' by the hypercube. A perfect skip graph has a topology similar to that of Chord. A deterministic protocol that achieves it is presented by Harvey and Munro in [7]. The work of Ganesan and Manku [5] implies that the average diameter of a perfect skip graph is $\Omega(\log n)$, thus we conclude that the randomization of edges *reduces* the expected path length. See [11] for a discussion of this phenomena.

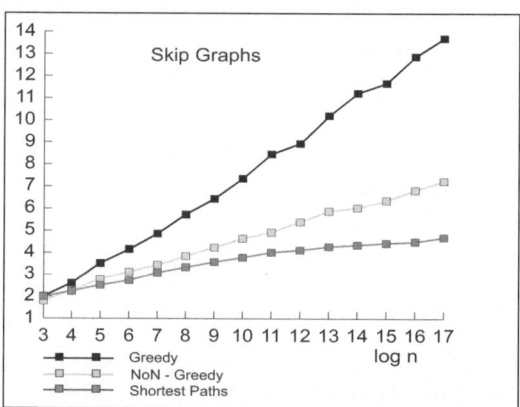

Fig. 2. The number of hops in skip graphs.

3   Simulation Results

We ran simulations in which we compared the performance of the greedy algorithm and the performance of the NoN greedy algorithm. We constructed a skip graph of up to 2^{17} nodes and a small world graph of up to 2^{24} nodes. In a small world graph it is not necessary to create the full graph in advance. Each time the message reached a node, we randomly created the neighborhood of radius 2 around the node. This is a negligible compromise over the definition of the model, since the edge in which the node was entered might not be sampled. This technique allowed us to run simulations on much larger graphs. For each graph size we ran 150 executions. A substantial improvement could be seen. Figures 2,3 demonstrate an improvement of about 48% for skip graphs of size 2^{17} and an improvement of 34% for small world graphs of size 2^{24}. Figure 2 also depicts the average shortest path in the graph. We see that the shortest paths may be 30% shorter than the paths found by NoN, yet even for moderate network sizes, the NoN algorithm performs substantially better than the Greedy one.

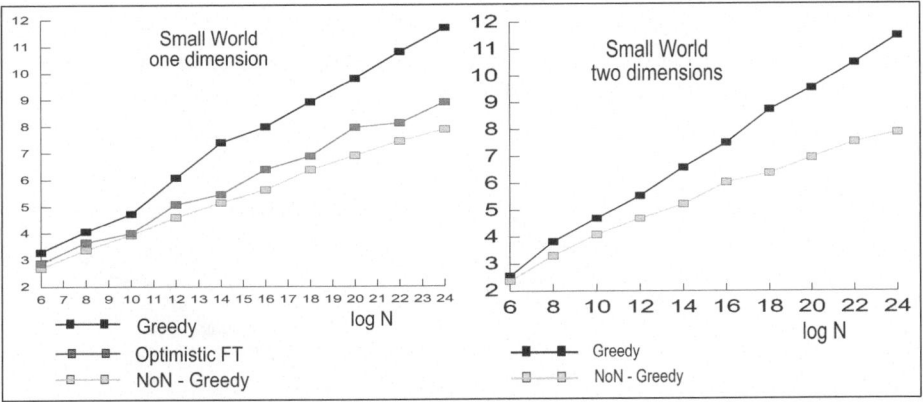

Fig. 3. The number of hops in a small world of dimensions $1, 2$.

An even more impressive improvement could be seen when the size of the graph is fixed and the average degree changes. We fixed a small world graph of size 2^{20}. After that we deleted each edge with a fixed probability which varied from 0 (the usual small world graph) to 0.9 (a graph with roughly one tenth of the edges). Figure 4 depicts the results of these simulations. It shows that the reduction in the number of hops is more or less independent from the number of edges. The latency achieved by the Greedy algorithmwhen the degree is 26 is achieved by the NoN algorithm when the degree is merely 12. In the case of skip graphs we ran the simulation for a graph of size 2^{17} and varied the size of the alphabet of the membership vectors. When the alphabet size is s the average degree is $O(\log_s n)$. We can see in Figure 4 that NoN with alphabet size 20 is better than Greedy with alphabet size 2, i.e. when the average degree is $\log_2 20 \simeq 4.3$ bigger.

3.1   A Different Implementation

The algorithm presented in Figure 1 is somewhat unnatural. Each NoN step has two phases. In the first phase the message is sent to a neighbor whose neighbor

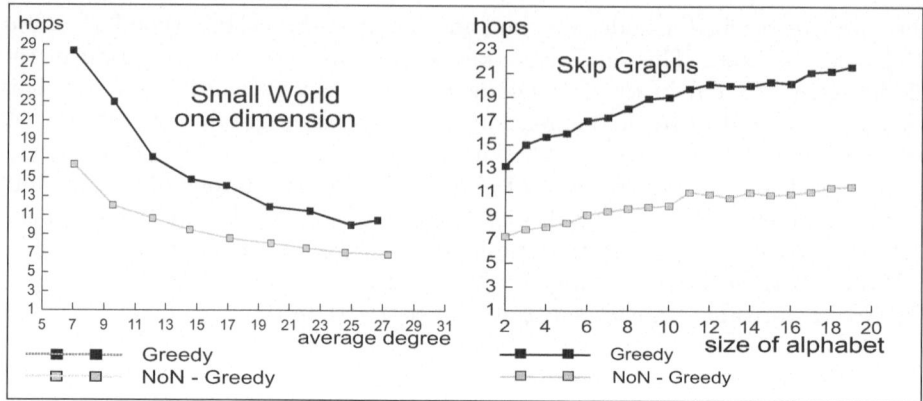

Fig. 4. The tradeoff between average degree and latency in a small world with 2^{20} nodes (left) and skip graphs of 2^{17} nodes (right).

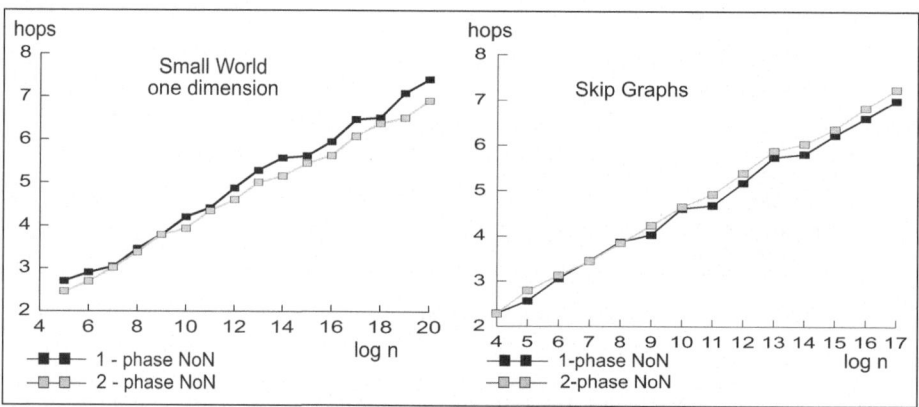

Fig. 5. Comparison between the two variants of NoN.

is close to the target. In the second phase a greedy step is taken (i.e. the message moves to the neighbor of neighbor). A 1−phase implementation would let each node initiate a NoN step again, i.e. each node upon receiving a message, finds the closest neighbor of neighbor, and passes the message on. This variant is harder to analyze, indeed Theorem 1 holds for the 2-phase version only. Yet, as Figure 5 shows, in practice the two variants have basically the same performance.

3.2   Fault Tolerance

The previous simulations assumed that the list of neighbor's neighbors each node holds is always correct. In reality this might not be the case. We examine two scenarios which capture the two extremes of this problem.

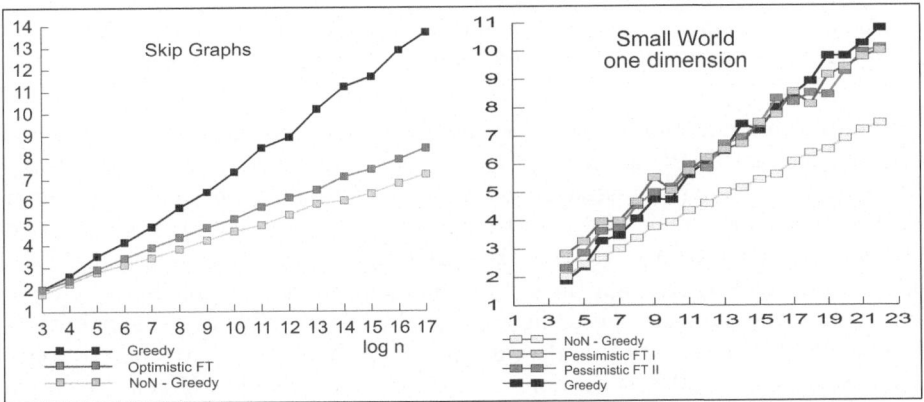

Fig. 6. Optimistic fault tolerance in Skip Graphs and pessimistic fault tolerance in Small Worlds.

Optimistic Scenario: In this case we assume that a node knows whether its neighbors of neighbors lists are up-to-date or not. Whenever a node has a stale list is performs a greedy step. If a node cannot perform the NoN step from any other reason, it performs the greedy step instead. We ran simulations in which each node performs with probability $\frac{1}{2}$ a NoN step, and with probability $\frac{1}{2}$ a greedy step. Whenever a NoN step is performed, both phases of it are performed correctly. Figures (3) and (6) show that the total performance is hardly compromised. A small world of size 2^{22} suffered a relative delay of less than one hop, A skip graph of size 2^{17} suffers a relative delay of 1.2 hops. But why is the optimistic scenario justified? Our suggestion is that each node would calculate a hash of its neighbors list. This hash would be sent to all its neighbors on top of the maintenance messages. Thus with a minuscule overhead in communication each node would know whether its lists are up-to-date. We discuss specific hash functions in Section 4.

Pessimistic Scenario: In this scenario we assume that a node is unaware that its neighbor's neighbors lists are not up-to-date. So when node u passes a message to node w expecting it to move on to node z, with probability $\frac{1}{2}$ the edge (w, z) no longer exists. We tested two variants: in the first one, whenever this occurs the intermediate node w performs a greedy step. In the second variant the intermediate node w initiates another NoN step. The results of the simulations appear in Figure 6. It could be seen that in the pessimistic scenario, the performance of NoN is approximately the same as the Greedy algorithm.

We conclude that even if we assume that the neighbor lists are error prone, still the use of the NoN algorithm may be beneficial.

4   Implementation Issues

The execution of a NoN hop requires a node to store the neighbor lists of its neighbors. This implies that nodes should update each other regarding their own lists of neighbors. Such an update occurs in two scenarios:

1. Each node upon entrance, must send its list of neighbors to its neighbors.
2. Whenever a node encounters a change in its neighbor list (due to the entrance or exit of a node), it should update its neighbors.

The extra communication imposed by these updates is not heavy due to the two following reasons. First, assume nodes u, v are neighbors. Node u periodically checks that v is alive (for instance by pinging it). Checking whether v's neighbor list has changed could be added to the maintenance protocol by letting v send a hash of its neighbor list on top of the maintenance protocol. A possible hash function may be MD5 (though the cryptographic properties of this hash function are not needed). Another possibility is simply to treat the id of neighbors as coefficients of a polynomial, and evaluate this polynomial at a random point. Either way the actual cost in communication is very small. When an actual update occurs there is no reason for v to send its entire neighbor list. It may only send the part of it which u misses. If it does not know which part it is then u, v may participate in a very fast and communication efficient protocol that reconciles the two sets, see e.g. [12] for details. The second reason the communication overhead is small is that the the actual updates are not urgent (as the simulations of the optimistic scenario show) and may be done when the system is not busy.

It is important to notice that the implementation of the NoN algorithmdoes not affect the Insert/Delete operations. Once a node enters, the needed updates should occur. We conclude that implementing NoN has very little cost both in communication complexity and in internal running time. It is almost a free tweak that may be implemented on top of the previous constructions.

5   Other Constructions – NoN-Chord

Does NoN-Greedy improve more p2p systems? In this section we show that a variation of Chord [15] is degree optimal. In Chord the key space is a ring $[0, 1, \ldots, n]$. A node whose i.d. is x is connected (more or less) to $x+1, x+2, x+4, \ldots, x + \frac{n}{2}$ mod n. It was shown by Manku [5] that the *average* diameter of Chord is $\Theta(\log n)$, thus no algorithm may significantly reduce the path length. We show a slight variation of Chord, (in search of a better name lets call it NoN-Chord). The idea is to make Chord resemble the Small-World graph. Now each node x is connected to $\log n$ nodes $y_0, y_1, y_2, \ldots$ such that y_i is a *random* point in the segment $[x + 2^i, x + 2^{i+1}]$. An easy adaptation of the proofs in [11, 3] shows that w.h.p the path length used by NoN is $O(\log n / \log \log n)$. The Insert operation now, would take $\log^2 n / \log \log n$ operations, in $\log n / \log \log n$ parallel time. So we have an interesting tradeoff of parameters. An increase in the communication complexity of the Insert operation (though not in the time complexity) reduces the latency of the paths.

Acknowledgments

We thank James Aspnes and Gauri Shah for supplying us with their implementation of skip graphs, and the anonymous referees for useful comments.

References

1. James Aspnes, Zoe Diamadi, and Gauri Shah. Fault-tolerant routing in peer-to-peer systems. In *Proceedings of the twenty-first symposium on Principles of distributed computing (PODC)*, pages 223–232, 2002.
2. James Aspnes and Gauri Shah. Skip graphs. In *fourteenth ACM SIAM Symposium on Discrete Algorithms (SODA)*, pages 384–393, 2003.
3. Don Coppersmith, David Gamarnik, and Maxim Sviridenko. The diameter of a long-range percolation graph. *Random Structures and Algorithms*, 21(1):1–13, 2002.
4. Pierre Fraigniaud and Philippe Gauron. The content-addressable network d2b. Technical Report LRI 1349, Univ. Paris-Sud, 2003.
5. Prasanna Ganesan and Gurmeet Singh Manku. Optimal routing in chord. In *fifteenth ACM SIAM Symposium on Discrete Algorithms (SODA)*, 2004.
6. Nicholas Harvey, John Dunagan, Michael B. Jones, Stefan Saroiu, Marvin Theimer, and Alec Wolman. Skipnet: A scalable overlay network with practical locality properties. In *4th USENIX Symposium on Internet Technologies and Systems, (USITS)*, 2003.
7. Nicholas Harvey and J. Ian Munro. Deterministic skipnet. In *Twenty Second Annual ACM Syposium on Priciples of Distributed Computing (PODC)*, pages 152–153, 2003.
8. Frans Kaashoek and David R. Karger. Koorde: A simple degree-optimal distributed hash table. In *Second International Workshop on Peer-to-peer Systems IPTPS*, 2003.
9. Jon Kleinberg. The Small-World phenomenon: An algorithmic perspective. In *Proceedings of the 32nd ACM Symposium on Theory of Computing (STOC)*, 2000.
10. Gurmeet Singh Manku, Mayank Bawa, and Prabhakar Raghavan. Symphony: Distributed hashing in a small world. In *4th USENIX Symposium on Internet Technologies and Systems, (USITS)*, 2003.
11. Gurmeet Singh Manku, Moni Naor, and Udi Wieder. Know thy neighbor's neighbor: the power of lookahead in randomized p2p networks. In *STOC*, 2004.
12. Yaron Minsky and Ari Trachtenberg. Practical set reconciliation. Technical Report 2002-03., Boston University, 2002.
13. Moni Naor and Udi Wieder. Novel architectures for p2p applications: the continuous-discrete approach. In *Proceedings of the fifteenth annual ACM symposium on Parallel algorithms and architectures SPAA*, pages 50–59, 2003.
14. Antony Rowstron and Peter Druschel. Pastry: Scalable, decentralized object location, and routing for large-scale peer-to-peer systems. *Lecture Notes in Computer Science*, 2218:329–350, 2001.
15. Ion Stoica, Robert Morris, David Karger, Frans Kaashoek, and Frank Dabek Hari Balakrishnan. Chord: A scalable Peer-To-Peer lookup service for internet applications. Technical Report TR-819, MIT LCS, 2001.
16. Ben Y. Zhao, John D. Kubiatowicz, and Anthony D. Joseph. Tapestry: An infrastructure for fault-tolerant wide-area location and routing. Technical Report UCB/CSD-01-1141, UC Berkeley, April 2001.

SmartBoa: Constructing p2p Overlay Network in the Heterogeneous Internet Using Irregular Routing Tables*

Jingfeng Hu, Ming Li, Weimin Zheng, Dongsheng Wang,
Ning Ning, and Haitao Dong

Computer Science and Technology Department,
Tsinghua University, Beijing, China
{hujinfeng00,lim01,nn02,dht02}@mails.tsinghua.edu.cn,
{zwm-dcs,wds}@tsinghua.edu.cn

Abstract. The high heterogeneity of large-scale p2p system leads us to the philosophy that the size of a node's routing table and its updating cost should correspond to the node's capacity. With this philosophy, we design a novel structured overlay: SmartBoa. SmartBoa categorizes nodes into different levels according to their capacities. A node at level k has a routing table with $N/2^k$ entries (N is the system scale). An efficient non-redundant multicast algorithm is introduced to distribute nodes' changing reports. With the multicast the routing table's updating cost is in proportion to its size. Node can change its level freely so as to adapt to fluctuation of the system. At the same cost as the $O(\log N)$ overlay, SmartBoa maintains with much larger routing tables and has much higher routing efficiency. A low-bandwidth (64 kbps) node can maintain 10,000 routing entries at the cost of only 10 percent of its bandwidth. Without the high bandwidth requirement of an one-hop overlay, SmartBoa is much more scalable.

1 Introduction

Observations in [5] show that there is great heterogeneity among p2p nodes: bandwidth of the most powerful node is $10^3 \sim 10^5$ times higher than the weakest one. However, there is no structured p2p overlay fully adapting to this heterogeneity. By far there are two types of structured overlay, i.e. O(logN) overlay (e.g. Pastry[4], Tapestry[7], Chord[6], and so on) and one-hop overlay[1]. Routing table's size of Pastry, Tapestry or Chord is $O(\log N)$. Very limited bandwidth is required to maintain their routing table. Therefore, the extra bandwidth of powerful nodes cannot be utilized. On the other hand, the one-hop overlay's routing table consumes too much bandwidth for updating, which may overburden weak nodes. Its scalability is somewhat poor. It is these realities that motivate us to design a new structured overlay, SmartBoa, in which each node's available bandwidth is adequately utilized. We consider an overlay of this kind more effective and scalable.

---

* This work is supported by The National High Technology Research and Development Program of China (G2001AA111010), Chinese National Basic Research Priority Program (G1999032702) and National Natural Science Foundation of China (G60273006).

G.M. Voelker and S. Shenker (Eds.): IPTPS 2004, LNCS 3279, pp. 278–287, 2004.

The fundamental idea of SmartBoa is that the size of a node's routing table should be in proportion to its available bandwidth. Nodes with higher bandwidth have larger routing table and consequently better routing efficiency. A direct approach to realize it is to control the routing table size of O(logN) overlay. This can be achieved by making different nodes have different b^1. Routing table is updated through periodical probing. In this manner, a weak node can handle no more than 2,000 routing entries at the cost of its entire bandwidth. In a p2p system having more than 1,000,000 nodes, this improvement is too trivial to make substantial sense.

A novel idea brought out by one-hop overlay is that a node can maintain a much larger routing table through event reporting than periodical probing. However, even with this effective mechanism, the maintaining cost of one-hop overlay is still too high to be handled by normal node. This greatly constrains its scalability. An applicable idea to improve the scalability is manipulating routing tables into different sizes according to nodes' capacities. The weaker the node is, the lower the maintaining cost is.

To manipulate routing tables of one-hop overlay into different sizes, designing an efficient report multicast algorithm is the key issue. It encounters the following challenges: 1) a node's changing report should be received only by nodes who care about its state change. (We call this set of nodes the report's "target group") 2) the report should be received by nodes in its target group once and once only. That is to say, the report algorithm should be non-redundant. Otherwise, the bandwidth used to update the routing table will not be in proportion to its size. 3) Not every node can maintain routing table covering the whole system. A node should not be required to send message to nodes outside its routing table 4) Powerful nodes should send out more reports than weak nodes in order to utilize powerful nodes' extra outgoing bandwidth. This can also enhance the robust of the multicast algorithm because the powerful nodes are more stable than weak nodes [5].

SmartBoa develops a novel multicast algorithm, which solves above problems successfully. Nodes in SmartBoa are categorized into different levels according to their capacities. The size and content of a node's routing table are related to its id and level. Reports flow from powerful nodes to weak nodes. When node M's state changes, whether node N should know about it is determined by M's id, N's id and N's level. No additional information is required to determine the target group. In the target group, the upper level nodes' routing tables contain those of the lower level nodes. This means that the upper level nodes know, and can control where the lower level nodes send the report. Therefore, if a report flows strictly from upper level nodes to lower level nodes, the multicast can be confined in the target group without redundancy.

Under current network environments, in SmartBoa even the weakest node (with a bandwidth of 64 kbps) can maintain thousands of routing entries at the cost of 10 percent of its bandwidth. Routing efficiency in SmartBoa is very high. On the other hand, when the system's scale or changing rate increases to a degree that a node cannot handle, the node can freely debase its level to decrease the maintenance cost. This gives SmartBoa great scalability. The long joining period, which is typical in one-hop

---

[1] In Pastry, the size of routing table is $(2^b - 1) \log_{2^b} N$. N is the system scale. b is a constant which is 4 typically.

overlay, can be hidden through *warm up*, a process in which the node's level rises gradually after joining.

2   Core Designs

In this section, we will discuss the core designs of SmartBoa. We will address the routing table structure, non-redundant multicast algorithm, the routing algorithm, and the joining process.

2.1   Routing Table

As in Pastry and Chord, each node in SmartBoa is assigned a 128-bit length node identifier, which indicates the node's position in a circular key space. The ids are generated randomly (for example, by SHA-1 hashing function) and supposed to scatter evenly in the id ring. A message with a 128-bit length key is sent to nodes whose id is closest to the key in the id ring. We call this node the key's *holder*.

SmartBoa's routing table consists of four components: routing entries, top entries, leaf set entries and finger entries. Figure 1 and Figure 2 illustrate an example of the routing table.

Routing entries. SmartBoa categorizes nodes into different levels (from level 0 to no more than level 127) according to their available bandwidth. A node in level k maintains routing entries whose id's k-bit length suffix is identical to local node. For example, a node in level 2 whose id is 101110 maintains routing entries whose id is xxxx10. A node in level k maintains approximately $N/2^k$ routing entries if all the nodes' id scatter evenly in the id ring (N is the system scale). Nodes in level 0 maintain routing entries covering the whole system, just like nodes in one-hop overlay. The lower the node's level is, the fewer routing entries it has to maintain.

We define the k-bit length suffix of a node M[2] in level k as the node's *"label"*, denoted by α_M. Labels of nodes in level 0 are empty, which is denoted by Φ. All nodes with the same label α form a set, which is denoted by $\{\alpha\}$.

Routing entries are maintained by report multicast. When a node joins into or departs from the system, a report about this event is multicast to all the nodes keeping the changing node in their routing entries.

A node may depart without notifying. Therefore, the first step of maintenance is to discover the node's silent departure. In SmartBoa, nodes are categorized into different sets according to their label. Nodes in the same set are fully connected to each other. Every node probes its right neighbor in the set periodically. When detecting its right neighbor's departure, the node will send a report to one of its top node. The top node will multicast the report. Similarly, when a node is joining into the system or changing its level, a report about this should also send to one of its top node by the node's bootstrap node or itself.

---

[2] In order to simplify discussion, we name a node with Id M as node M.

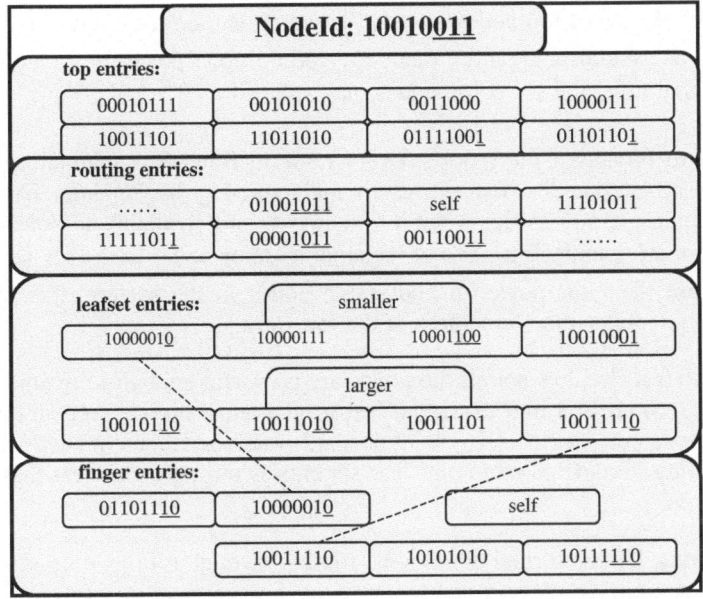

Fig. 1. An example of SmartBoa's routing table. Bits with underline is label.

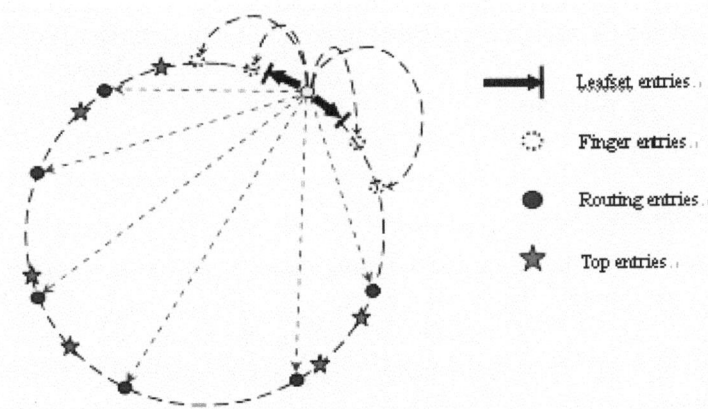

Fig. 2. Position of nodes in SmartBoa's routing table.

Top entries. Top entries are used in multicast. Firstly, we will give some definitions.

Definition 1. If node A's label α_A is a suffix of node B's label α_B, and $\alpha_A \neq \alpha_B$, then say A is superior to B, or A is B's super node, denoted as $A > B$. Obviously, B's routing table is a subset of A's.

Definition 2. If node A has no super node in the system, A is called a top node.

Definition 3. If $A > B$ or $\alpha_A = \alpha_B$, and A is a top node, then say A is B's top node.

Normally, the set of top nodes is set $\{\Phi\}$, which is the set of nodes in level 0. But if the scale of system is gigantic, there may be no node powerful enough to stay at level 0. At that time, the set of top nodes may split into $\{"0"\}$ and $\{"1"\}$ or sets in even lower level.

In order to broadcast the reports, every node in SmartBoa maintains top entries pointing to some top nodes. Top entries are maintained by lazy update, that is to say, a node only update its top entries when it find an entry not available any more. Then the node asks for a top entry from one of its super node or nodes in the set $\{\alpha\}$. Because top nodes are the most powerful and stable nodes in the system, this lazy update scheme can guarantee the correctness of the top entries.

Leaf set entries. Because not all the nodes are powerful enough to maintain one-hop routing table, SmartBoa introduces leaf set to guarantee the convergence of routing. Leaf set entries consist l (l is 16 or 32 normally) nearest nodes in each side of local node on id ring. SmartBoa maintains leaf set entries through heartbeat messages, just as Pastry does.

Finger entries. Under normal conditions, routing through routing entries and leaf set is efficient enough. However, when system scale is gigantic, there are too many nodes between neighbor entries of weak node's routing entries. Then after the first hop via routing entries, a message has to make several hops via leaf set. To accelerate routing, SmartBoa introduces finger entries. Finger entries are bi-search pointers between local node M and its right (left) neighbor node N in routing entries. They are pointers to node $(M+N)/2$, node $(M+(M+N)/2)/2$, ... (until overlapping with leaf set). Finger entries are maintained by heartbeat messages. Normally, the finger entries are quite few.

2.2 Multicast Algorithm

In SmartBoa, we call the set of nodes whose routing table contains pointer to node M as M's "target group", which is the union of $\{\Phi\}$, $\{"M_1"\}$, $\{"M_2M_1"\}$, ... , $\{"M_{128}M_{127}\cdots M_2M_1"\}$ (M_i denotes the i-th to last bit of M). Obviously, in the target group the upper-level nodes have routing tables entirely containing those of the lower-level nodes.

When a node joins into or departs from the system, a report about this event is generated and sent to a top node. After that, the report will be sent to all the nodes in the target group through a multicast tree. In the multicast tree, the higher level a node is, the more powerful it is and the more reports it will send out. All the nodes in the target group will receive the report once and only once.

The report is sent with a parameter S, which is the *step number*. S is zero when the report is firstly generated, and increases when the report traverses the multicast tree. A node receiving the report with step number S will updates its routing table according to this report. Then it enters into a multicast routine to propgate the report further. In the routine, the top node selects no more than (128-S) lower level nodes and sends the report to them. The selection is biased to higher level nodes. Following is the pseudo code of the multicast routine.

```
Routine Multicast (m, s):
//Receive report m at the step s.
  Rs = getTargetGroup(m)
  //Get target group of report m from local routing en-
tries
  For i := s+1 to 128 do
    Rn := getSuffix(Rs, i-1)
    //Get set of nodes in Rs whose ID's (i-1)-bit
length suffix is identical to local node, but the i-th
to last bit is different.
    If Rn = null then
      continue
    fi
    P := getHighestLevel(Rn)
    //Select one of the highest level nodes
    send_bcast(P, m, i)
    //Send the message to P, mark it as the i-th step.
  End do
```

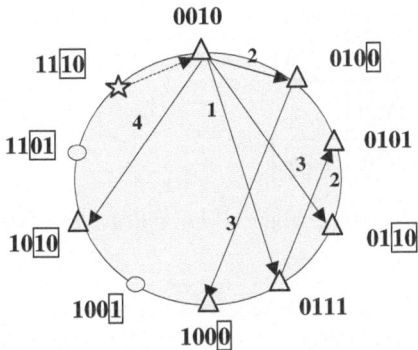

Fig. 3.1. Example of the multicast process. The star stands for the changing node. Triangles are nodes in the target group of the changing report. Arrows show the flow of report. Numbers besides the arrows are step numbers. Framed bits are labels.

Figure 3 is an example of the multicast process. Here we assume that something is happening to node 1110. Then a report is sent to one of its top node T, that is, node 0010. The multicast process is as following: 1) T selects a node T' from its routing entries and sends the report to T'. T' is in the target group is node 1110 and its id's last bit is different to T's. 2) T and T' both select a node whose id's last bit is same to theirs but the second to last bit is different, and send the report to them. And so on. In the n step, every node having received the report forwards it to another node whose id's last n-1 bits are identical to local node but the n-th to last bit is different. In every step, if there is no node satisfying the requirement, no action will be done. If there is more than one candidate node, the one in the highest level will be selected.

The report flows from powerful nodes to weak nodes, and the upper level nodes send more reports than lower level nodes. This makes the report lost rate low because powerful nodes are more stable and robust than weak nodes. Also, the powerful nodes' routing tables are fresher than weak nodes' because they receive the report earlier. This means that the correctness of powerful node's routing table is better than weak nodes, which can enhance routing efficiency.

Node	Routing Entries								
0010	0101	0111	1001	0100	1000	0110	1010	1101	1110
0100	0010	1000	0110	1010	1110				
0101	0010	0111	1001	0100	1000	0110	1010	1101	1110
0110	0010	1010	1110						
0111	0010	0101	1001	0100	1000	0110	1010	1101	1110
1000	0010	0100	0110	1010	1110				
1001	0101	0111	1101						
1010	0010	0110	1110						
1101	0101	1001							
1110	0010	0110	1010						

Fig. 3.2. Routing entries of nodes in Figure 1. Ids with green background are in the target group of node 1110.

Figure 4 shows nodes that have received the report after each step. The last S-bit length ids of nodes having received the report after step S are different to each other, which means that a node will only receive the report once.

Considering the limited space, formal proving of the completeness and non-redundancy of the multicast algorithm will not be presented in this paper (see [xx] for more details).

With the multicast algorithm, a weak node in SmartBoa can maintain a reasonably large routing table. For example, a modem-linked node whose bandwidth is only 64 kbps can maintain almost 15,000 routing entries. The result is drawn from following calculations. Assuming 10 percent of the node's bandwidth, i.e. 6.4 kbps, is used for updating its routing table. The size of a report is no more than 500 bits. Thus, the node can receive 12 reports per second. Assuming a node's average online period is one hour[5]. In one of its life circle, a node may cause 3 reports (joining, departure and level changing in warm up). Suppose the size of routing table is r. r nodes will trigger $3r / 3600 = r / 1200$ reports per second. A node can receive 12 reports per second. Then, $r / 1200 = 12$, $r = 14,400$. When the system scale is about 14,000, even the weak node can maintain routing table containing all the nodes in the system, and the routing can be done in one hop.

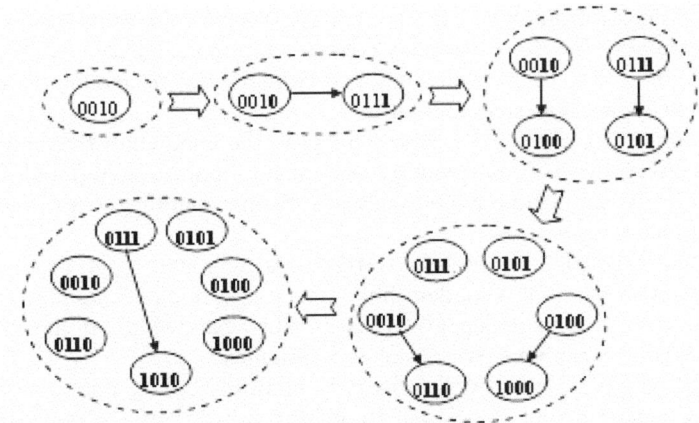

Fig. 4. Nodes having received report in step 0 to step 4. Bold bits of node Ids show that in step k the k-bit length suffix of any the nodes having received report is different from that of any others.

2.3 Routing

SmartBoa adopts greedy routing algorithm. A message with key M is sent to the closest (in ID space) node in local routing table in every routing step. The routing algorithm has no bias to powerful nodes, in order to not over burden them. From the following discussions we can see that even without bias to powerful nodes, the routing efficiency is good enough.

In a system with $r \times l / 2 = 14,400 \times 16 \approx 230,000$ nodes (r is number of routing entries, l is number of leaf set entries), generally a message can be route by weak node to its destination in two hops (first hop via routing entries, and second hop via leaf set).

When system scale is gigantic, the routing will be improved by finger entries. In a system having 1,000,000 weak nodes, the routing efficiency of SmartBoa is much better than Pastry. The first hop of routing is via routing entries. If ids are scattered evenly, after the first hop there are at most $N/2r$ nodes (averagely $N/4r$ nodes) between the message's current position and its target node. The following f hops are via finger entries. The last hop is via leaf set entries. Because each side of leaf set has $l/2$ entries, then $(N/4r)/2^f = l/2$, $f = \log_2(N/2rl)$. The total number of hops is $h = f + 2 = \log_2(2N/rl)$. When $N = 1,000,000$, $h \approx 2.12$. This is much fewer than that of typical 16-based Pastry ($\log_{16} N \approx 4.98$).

2.4 Joining and Warm up

A node X's joining process is as follows. 1) X contacts one existing node B, which is X's *bootstrap*. Suppose the level of B is k_B, and the bandwidth used to update B's routing table is W_B. X can determine its level as $k_{max} = \lceil k_B + \log_2(W_B / W_X) \rceil$. 2) X gets its k top entries from one of B's top nodes. 3) X downloads its own routing table from its top nodes. The download may consume too much bandwidth. To relieve the pressure on top nodes, the downloading can be redirected to another supper node or even different supper nodes concurrently.

A node can change its level freely to adapt to the bandwidth fluctuation. A node can debate its level by reducing routing entries and reporting to top nodes. Changing to an upper level requires the node to download some routing entries from its supper nodes additionally.

One serious drawback of one-hop overlay is its long starting up process. In a system having 100,000 nodes, a modem-linked node has to take 5 minutes to download its routing table even using up all of its 64 kbps bandwidth. If the system scale reaches 1,000,000, the above process takes 50 minutes.

SmartBoa adopts a "warm up" process to hide this boring period. When a node joins, it can select a lower level in which the downloading can be done in a few seconds. Then the node runs in this level temporarily with the downloading going on in background, which may take several minutes. After the downloading completes, the node elevates its level to normal.

3   Conclusion

The motivation of SmartBoa's design is the great heterogeneous between nodes in p2p systems. We want to enhance the routing efficiency by utilizing this heterogeneity, that is, making full utilize of every node's permitting bandwidth.

Generally, any structured overlay is a compromise of routing table's size (degree of peer) and routing efficiency (diameter of logical topology). In the two aspects, the routing efficiency deserves the premier consideration. The degree only affects the system cost and can be increased if user's normal operation is not disturbed.

There are some overlays utilizing the heterogeneity ([8], [9]). However, they category nodes into two kinds: weak node and powerful node. This category does not accord with the system well. They also relay on powerful node greatly, which brings heavy load to powerful nodes.

We think that there are two essential features in the ideal overlay: 1) routing table's size is determined by node's available bandwidth. 2) routing table is maintained by report multicast. These can fully utilize the powerful nodes. The key point is the design of multicast algorithm. Following problems are encountered: 1) not every node maintains routing table keeps and is kept by all the other nodes in the system. It is difficult to determine the set of nodes which should receive the report. 2) Even the target group is determined, the multicast should be confined in the target group. Otherwise we can not guarantee that the maintenance cost is in proportion to the size of routing table. 3) There may be weak nodes which do not keep all the nodes in the target group. They should not be required to send report to nodes outside their routing table. 4) The multicast algorithm should be non-redundant to decrease the maintenance cost.

SmartBoa solves above problems by categorizing nodes into different levels, relating routing table to node's id and level, designing an algorithm which multicast report level by level from powerful nodes to weak nodes. In SmartBoa, even the weakest node can maintain tens of thousand routing entries only utilizing 10% of its bandwidth. The node can also change its level freely, enhancing the adaptation of the system. This is also used in warm up and hides the boot up period typical in one-hop overlay.

Generally speaking, SmartBoa has following good qualities: a) fully utilize node's available bandwidth. b) without the uniform bandwidth requirement, any node can join the overlay. c) nodes can change their levels freely to adapt to the fluctuation of network condition. d) simple but effective routing algorithm. e) routing does not overburden any section of nodes. f) remarkable scalability. g) using warm up process to hide the long starting up period. h) can provide information about nodes' capabilities to upper applications.

There are still some open problems with SmartBoa: a) incentive mechanism. Without incentive, users tend to remain in lower level because of the high maintenance overhead in higher level. In fact, this is an open problem to the whole p2p realm. b) how to pack messages in multicast to decrease the overhead of IP address and UDP message head. c) relate routing entries to the network layer to increase the efficiency of every hop.

Acknowledgement

We thank all the anonymous reviewers for their valuable comments. We will consider these comments in our future work. We also acknowledge Dr. Zheng Zhang from MSR-Asia for his help.

References

1. Anjali Gupta, Barbara Liskov, Rodrigo Rodrigues. One Hop Lookups for Peer-to-Peer Overlays. HOTOS IX. May 2003.
2. Nicholas J.A. Harvey, Michael B. Jones, Stefan Saroiu, Marvin Theimer, Alec Wolman. SkipNet: A Scalable Overlay Network with Practical Locality Properties. USITS 2003. March 2003.
3. S. Ratnasamy, P. Francis, M. Handley, R. Karp, and S. Shenker. A Scalable Content-Addressable Network. In Proc. of ACM SIGCOMM, Aug. 2001.
4. A. Rowstron and P. Druschel. Pastry: Scalable, distributed object location and routing for large-scale peer-to-peer systems. In International Conference on Distributed Systems Platforms. (Middleware) November 2001.
5. SAROIU, S., GUMMADI, P. K., AND GRIBBLE, S. D. A Measurement Study of Peer-to-Peer File Sharing Systems. In Proceedings of MMCN'02. San Jose, CA, Jan. 2002.
6. I. Stoica, R. Morris, D. Karger, M. F. Kaashoek, and H. Balakrishnan. Chord: A scalable peer-to-peer lookup service for internet applications. In Proceedings of the ACM SIGCOMM '01 Conference, San Diego, California, August 2001.
7. Ben Zhao, John Kubiatowicz, and Anthony Joseph. Tapestry: An infrastructure for fault-tolerant wide-area location and routing. Technical Report UCB/CSD-01-1141, Computer Science Division, U. C. Berkeley. April 2001.
8. Zhichen Xu, Mallik Mahalingam, Magnus Karlsson. Turning Heterogeneity into an Advantage in Overlay Routing. The 22nd Annual Joint Conference of the IEEE Computer and Communications Societies (INFOCOM 2003). April 2003.
9. B. Y. Zhao, Y. Duan, L. Huang, A. Joseph, and J. Kubiatowicz. Brocade: Landmark Routing on Overlay Networks. 1st International Workshop on Peer-to-Peer Systems (IPTPS '02). March 2002.

Diminished Chord: A Protocol
for Heterogeneous Subgroup Formation
in Peer-to-Peer Networks

David R. Karger[1] and Matthias Ruhl[2]

[1] MIT Computer Science and Artificial Intelligence Laboratory
Cambridge, MA 02139, USA
karger@csail.mit.edu
[2] IBM Almaden Research Center
San Jose, CA 95120, USA
ruhl@almaden.ibm.com

Abstract. In most of the P2P systems developed so far, all nodes play essentially the same role. In some applications, however, different machine capabilities or owner preferences may mean that only a subset of nodes in the system should participate in offering a particular service. Arranging for each service to be supported by a different peer to peer network is, we argue here, a wasteful solution.

Instead, we propose a version of the Chord peer-to-peer protocol that allows any subset of nodes in the network to jointly offer a service *without* forming their own Chord ring. Our variant supports the same efficient join/leave/insert/delete operations that the subgroup would get if they did form their own separate peer to peer network, but requires significantly less resources than the separate network would.

For each subgroup of k machines, our protocol uses $O(k)$ additional storage in the primal Chord ring. The insertion or deletion of a node in the subgroup and the lookup of the next node of a subgroup all require $O(\log n)$ hops.

1 Introduction

In most of the P2P systems developed, all nodes play essentially the same role in the system. In many applications, however, this might not be appropriate: nodes might be heterogeneous either in their capabilities or their approved uses. From the capability perspective, a bandwidth-intensive application might wish to limit itself to the subset of nodes with high connectivity, a storage-intensive one might focus on nodes with large disks, a compute intensive one on fast machines. Socially, in an environment where many different P2P services can be offered, some users might be comfortable running only certain "nice" services on their machines, steering clear of music-piracy services, music piracy detection services, or code-cracking endeavors by hackers or the NSA.

One way to support such endeavors would be to form a separate P2P overlay for each service, and let nodes join all the overlays in which they wish to

G.M. Voelker and S. Shenker (Eds.): IPTPS 2004, LNCS 3279, pp. 288–297, 2004.

participate. This is inefficient, however, as the same routing infrastructure will have to be replicated repeatedly – a machine may find itself pointing at the same successors and fingers in an unlimited number of distinct P2P networks. Even worse, it might need to maintain *different* successors and fingers in each of its networks.

In this paper, we give an efficient mechanism for an arbitrary set of nodes to form "subgroups" without increasing their overhead. We augment the Chord protocol to allow queries of the following form: find the first node *in subgroup* X whose address follows a given address on the Chord ring. This query can be answered in the same $O(\log n)$ time as standard Chord queries. To join a given group, a machine performs $O(\log n)$ routing hops and deposits a tiny constant amount of additional information. In other words, within the larger Chord ring, we are able to simulate a Chord ring on the nodes in group X. The maintenance traffic a node uses to maintain its groups is negligible (per group) compared to the amount of traffic the node spends maintaining the underlying Chord infrastructure.

Besides the precisely measurable improvements in efficiency, our use of sub-rings instead of independent rings provides a less quantifiable reduction in complexity by delegating some of the most complex parts of the ring maintenance protocol to be performed only once, by the primal ring, instead of once per subring. For example, our approach simplifies the rendezvous problem. To join a Chord ring, a node needs to identify, using some out-of-band mechanism, at least one node already in the ring. This remains true for joining the base Chord ring in our protocol. But once a node is in the base Chord ring, it can easily join any existing subgroup in the ring, without any new out-of-band communication. Thus, if the primal join problem is solved once (for example, by making all nodes in the world part of a primal Chord ring) it never needs to be addressed again. As a second example, consider the use of numerous redundant successor pointers by Chord to provide fault tolerant routing in the presence of node failures. Since the subrings live inside of a ring that provides such fault tolerance, the subrings themselves do not have to do so.

Our protocol works by embedding in the base Chord ring, for each subgroup, a directory tree that lets a node find its own successor in the subgroup. We arrange for the edges of the directory tree to be fingers of the Chord ring so that traversing the directory tree is cheap. Finding the group-X successor of a given key is accomplished by finding the primal-ring successor s of the key and then finding the group-X successor of node s (from a practical perspective, this suggests that such subring lookups will take roughly twice as long as standard ones).

1.1   Chord

Our discussions below are in the context of the Chord system [1] but our ideas seem applicable to a broader range of P2P solutions. Since we are only interested in routing among subgroups of nodes, we can ignore item assignment issues and concentrate on the routing properties of the system.

Chord defines a routing protocol in which each node maintains a set of $O(\log n)$ carefully chosen neighbors called *fingers* that it uses to route lookups in $O(\log n)$ hops. To do so, it maps the nodes onto a ring which we shall consider to be the interval $[0, 1]$ (where the numbers 0 and 1 are identified). Every node receives as address some random (fractional) number in the interval (e.g. by hashing the node's name or IP-address). A node with address a then maintains *finger pointers* to all nodes with addresses of the form $succ(a+2^{-b})$, where $b \geq 1$ is an integer. By $succ(x)$ we refer to the first node succeeding address x in the address space. It can be shown that with high probability, only $O(\log n)$ of the pointers are distinct. Thus, each node has $O(\log n)$ neighbors.

For the purposes of this work, we will ignore the insertion and deletion of nodes into the (underlying) Chord system itself.

1.2   Our Results

The formal problem considered in this work is the following. We have a subset of nodes in the network which are associated with some identifier X. We want to efficiently (in terms of storage and communication) perform the following operations:

Insert(q, X): Inserts the node with address q into the subset with identifier X.

Lookup(q, X): Returns the first node succeeding address q that is a member of the subset with identifier X.

Note that our protocol has to handle an arbitrary number of subgroups in the P2P system simultaneously. Using the **Lookup**-function as a primitive, each node in a subgroup can determine its successor in the subgroup. Also, as with the base Chord protocol, we assume that deletions are handled just like node failures: nodes repeatedly insert themselves to stay in the system while alive, and are eventually expunged once they depart and stop inserting themselves.

We will give algorithms for **Insert** and **Lookup** that require $O(\log n)$ hops to execute. The protocol does not have to know the size of the subgroups to operate. For each subgroup of size k, we have to store $O(k)$ additional data in the network (i.e. at nodes that are not necessarily in the subgroup themselves), but at most $O(\log n)$ data per subgroup at any single node.

Moreover, our algorithms are load-balanced in the following sense. If random nodes call **Insert** and **Lookup**, then the access load will be equally distributed among $\Omega(k)$ nodes. This precludes, for example, storing the entire group membership list at a single node, since this node would get swamped with requests. If $k = 1$ the claimed load balance does not offer much help. While in this case we are already expecting the single member of X to cope with all requests to X, our approach does have the drawback of swamping a single non-member of X with routing requests. Presumably caching techniques can be used to address this issue.

The simplest version of our protocol relies on a minor technical modification of the Chord protocol. It requires that with every finger pointer $succ(a + 2^{-b})$

we also maintain a *prefinger* pointer to the immediate predecessor $pred(a + 2^{-b})$ of our finger. Here $pred(x)$ denotes the node preceding an address x. In Chord, fingers are actually found by finding prefingers and taking their immediate successors, so maintaining the additional prefinger information does not increase the processing requirements of the protocol.

For completeness we also give (more complicated) variants of our protocols that do without the prefinger pointers. These protocols require $O(\log n \log^* n)$ hops, however.

1.3   Related Work

An application where our subgroup protocol might be useful is a Usenet-caching application that runs on a P2P system [2]. The goal is to replace the current broadcast of Usenet news to all news servers with a more limited broadcast to an appropriate subset of servers from which news can be pulled by clients who want to read it. In this application, a given P2P node may wish to cache only certain newsgroups (e.g., those used by the node's owners). Our subgroup protocol can support this scheme by creating a single subgroup for each newsgroup.

Similar in spirit to our results, the OpenHash system [3] tries to separate the system layer in P2P system from the application layer. This allows several P2P applications to co-exist independently within the same P2P system.

In [4] subgroups within P2P systems are created, but the focus is on subgroups corresponding to regions of administrative control. To maintain this control, lookups are required to be resolved wholly within subgroups, not utilizing the rest of the network, as is done in our work.

2   The Subgroup Protocol

In this section, we state and analyze a Diminished Chord protocol for subgroup creation. For simplicity, we will just consider a single subgroup in the following discussion. We will refer to the nodes in the given subgroup as "green nodes." Later we will discuss the interactions between multiple groups.

2.1   A Tree-Based Solution

To provide some intuition, we outline a solution for the case where the nodes in our P2P network have somehow formed an ordered (by addresses) depth-$O(\log n)$ binary tree, such that each machine has a pointer to its parent machine in the tree. Some of the leaf nodes in the tree can become green, and we want any leaf node to be able to resolve a query of the form "what is the first green node following me in the tree?"

To support such queries, we augment the tree so that every node x stores the minimum address of a green node in the right subtree of x, if one exists. Note that this requires storing at most one value in any node. In fact, since each green node can be stored only in its ancestors, each green node will generate $O(\log n)$

storage in the tree. When a new node decides to become green, it takes $O(\log n)$ work for it to announce itself to its $O(\log n)$ ancestors.

Given such storage, we can easily answer a green-successor query. Let q be a leaf node and s the green successor of q. Consider the root-leaf paths to q and to s. These two paths diverge at some node a with the path to q going left and the path to s going right (since s is a successor of q). To be the green-successor of q, it must be that s is the first green node in the right subtree of a. It follows by the previous paragraph that a will hold s. This leads to the following algorithm for finding s in time $O(\log n)$. Walk up the path from q to the root. Each time we arrive at a node along a left-child pointer, inspect the contents of the node. This will ensure that we inspect node a and thus that we find s.

Since a green node may be stored in all of its ancestors, this scheme uses $O(\log n)$ space per green node. We can improve this bound by noticing that we only need to store s in the *highest* node in which it is stored in the scheme above. Since s is stored only at ancestors of s, any query that traverses *any* node storing s will necessarily, as it continues up to the root, traverse the highest node that stores s. This reduces the space usage to $O(1)$ per green node.

2.2 Embedding the Tree

We studied the tree because our approach using Chord is to embed just such a tree into the Chord ring. This can be explained most simply by assuming that all addresses in the Chord ring are occupied by nodes; once we have done so we will explain how to "simulate" the full-ring protocol on a ring with only a small number of nodes.

Our tree is actually built over a space of "address representations" in the Chord ring. For each subgroup, we have a *base address* a_0, which for example could be computed as a hash of the group's name X. Let $\langle a, b \rangle$ denote the address $(a_0 + b/2^a) \mod 1$ for $1 \le a$ and $0 \le b < 2^a$ (recall that we have defined the Chord ring to be the interval $[0, 1]$, so all addresses are fractions). Note that representations are not unique – in particular, $\langle a, b \rangle$ actually defines the same address as $\langle a + 1, 2b \rangle$ – but we will treat these as two distinct nodes in the tree. The work for a particular tree node will be done by the machine at the address the node represents; one machine thus does work for at most one tree node on each level of the tree.

We make the $\langle a, b \rangle$ into a tree by letting $\langle a, b \rangle$ be the parent of the two nodes $\langle a + 1, 2b - 1 \rangle$ and $\langle a + 1, 2b \rangle$ (where $\langle a, -1 \rangle := \langle a, 2^a - 1 \rangle$). Note that under this definition, one (the right) child of a node actually defines the same address as that node, while the left child is a (not immediate) predecessor of the node. Furthermore, given the full address space assumption, the address gap between a node and its parent is a (negative) power of two – meaning that there is a finger pointing from each node to its parent (see Figure 1).

Notice also that the tree thus defined is properly ordered with respect to the address space – that is, that the set of addresses represented in a node's subtree is a contiguous interval of the ring, and that the subtrees of the two children of a node divide the node's interval into two adjacent, equal-sized contiguous

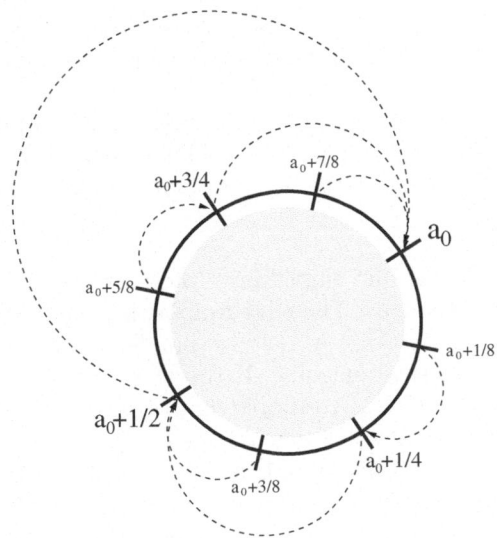

Fig. 1. The Chord address space shown as a loop. Nodes preceding the indicated addresses will be selected as nodes $p(a,b)$. The dashed lines show tree-pointers from left children to their parents.

segments. It follows that our tree-based green-successor algorithm can be applied to this tree, and will return the minimal green tree-successor, which by the consistent ordering is also the minimal green address successor, of any node in the tree. The depth of the tree is equal to the number of bits in the address space, and this determines the time to query or update the data structure.

The actual tree-structure of the addresses (i.e., which finger is the parent pointer of a given address) depends on the base addresses a_0. It would be prohibitively expensive to record the tree structure; however, this is unnecessary as the correct parent pointer can easily be determined as a function of the current address and the base address.

2.3   Sparser Rings

It remains to extend this scheme to sparsely populated rings. We use the same "simulation" approach as was used to simulate a de Bruijn network over the full address space in the Koorde protocol [5]. The work a given address $\langle a, b \rangle$ needs to do is simulated by the machine immediately *preceding* that address on the Chord ring. We will call that machine $p(a, b)$.

To implement both **Insert** and **Lookup**, we have to traverse a path through the (logical) tree from a leaf address q towards the root a_0 until we find an answer. To simulate this traversal, we need to visit all the nodes immediately preceding addresses on this path. We give two different algorithms for this. The first, simpler one takes $O(\log n)$ hops, but requires that with each finger to a node $succ(a + 2^{-b})$ in Chord we also maintain a prefinger to $pred(a + 2^{-b})$, the node preceding the address $a + 2^{-b}$. As discussed above, prefingers are already found by Chord when it looks up fingers [1]. Thus, this additional information comes "for free."

For completeness, we sketch a second algorithm that computes a node-to-root path without requiring prefinger pointers. This algorithm takes $O(\log n \log^* n)$ hops for **Insert** and **Lookup**, and is considerably more complicated to implement.

With Prefingers. Given our embedding, there are two kinds of edges on a (logical) path through the tree. The edge from a right child to its parent is easy to follow in simulation since $p(a + 1, 2b) = p(a, b)$, i.e. the two tree nodes are mapped to the same physical machine. It therefore suffices to show how to get from a left child $p(a + 1, 2b - 1)$ to its parent $p(a, b)$.

So assume that we are at some machine $q_1 = p(a + 1, 2b - 1)$ responsible for address $\langle a + 1, 2b - 1 \rangle$ and want to find the machine $q_2 = p(a, b)$ representing its parent $\langle a, b \rangle$. We know that q_1 precedes address $a_1 = a_0 + (2b - 1)/2^a$, while q_2 precedes address $a_2 = a_1 + 1/2^{a+1}$. First, we use the distance-$1/2^{a+1}$ prefinger from node q_1 to arrive at the node q preceding address $addr(q_1) + 1/2^{a+1}$. Then we repeatedly compute the successor of q until we pass the address a_2. This yields the last node before address a_2, i.e. node q_2.

To bound the running time, note that we perform one (prefinger) hop per move along the path. Since the tree has depth $O(\log n)$, this results in $O(\log n)$ hops. The prefinger from $p(a+1, 2b-1)$ may not point to exactly the node $p(a, b)$ that we want. For the node $p(a + 1, 2b - 1)$ is at an address slightly preceding $\langle a + 1, 2b - 1 \rangle$, so its prefinger may be at an address slightly preceding $\langle a, b \rangle$ and some nodes might end up in the gap. So we may have to follow some successor pointers to reach $p(a, b)$. Nonetheless, it can be shown [1] that over the whole path the number of successor computations is only $O(\log n)$ with high probability.

As with Koorde, it would seem that our simulation must perform a number of hops equal to the number of address bits. However all but the first few hops of the simulation are actually in the purview of the same node, so take no time to simulate. The number of actual hops performed in the simulation is $O(\log n)$ with high probability.

Without Prefingers. In the previous algorithm we crucially needed the fact that we had access to prefinger pointers. Had we used fingers, the uneven distribution of nodes on the ring could have made us "overshoot" the addresses we actually needed to traverse, without any option of backtracking to them. The intuition in the following algorithm is to leave some "buffer" between the visited machines and the addresses on the path to absorb the overshoot.

In this discussion, we use the word "distance" to denote the amount of the ring's address space traversed by a finger; i.e. a finger reaching halfway around the circle is said to traverse distance $1/2$.

In the previous algorithm, we simulated the traversal of a sequence of addresses on the ring by traversing the nodes immediately preceding those addresses, using prefinger pointers. The addresses we want to visit are separated by distances that are exact (negative) powers of two. Suppose that at each step, we instead traverse the finger corresponding to the desired power-of-two distance. This finger may traverse a slightly greater distance. But the random distribution of nodes on the ring means that the distance traversed by the ring is only $O(1/n)$ units greater than the intended power of two, and that over a sequence of $O(\log n)$ hops, the distance traversed is $O((\log n)/n)$ units greater than the sum of the intended powers of two (this analysis is similar to that used for Koorde [5]). In other words, even with the overshoots, we remain quite close to the intended path.

To cope with this overshoot, we arrange to begin the search at a node q' that is at distance $O((\log n)/n)$ *before* q (note that finding q' seems to require computing predecessors to move backward on the ring, which Chord does not support, but we will remove this technicality in a moment). From q' we use fingers to perform the same power-of-two hops that we would follow from q. By the previous paragraph, we will never overshoot the addresses we wanted to traverse from q. At the same time, those desired addresses will be only $O((\log n)/n)$ distance ahead of the nodes we visit; the random node distribution means that in such an interval there will be $O(\log n)$ nodes with high probability. To summarize, our finger-following path will traverse a sequence of $O(\log n)$ nodes, each only $O(\log n)$ nodes away from the address we actually want to traverse.

Chord actually proposes that each node keep pointers to its $\Theta(\log n)$ immediate successors for fault tolerance; these pointers let us reach the addresses we really want with one additional successor hop from each of the nodes we encounter on our path and thus accomplish the lookup in $O(\log n)$ time.

If we do not have the extra successor pointers, we can reach each desired address using $O(\log \log n)$ Chord routing hops from the addresses we actually traverse. By doing this separately for each address, we can find all the addresses on the leaf-to-root path of q in $O(\log n \log \log n)$ steps. This bound can be decreased to $O(\log n \log^* n)$ by computing not just one path starting $\Theta(\log n)$ nodes before q, but $\log^* n$ paths starting at distances $\log^{(k)} n$ before q. (Here $\log^{(k)}$ stands for the k-times iterated logarithm.) We omit the details in this paper, in particular since this algorithm is probably too complicated to be useful in practice.

It remains to explain how to get around the requirement of starting the search at a node q' which is $\Theta(\log n)$ nodes before q. Instead of going backward $\Theta(\log n)$ steps, we go forward $\Theta(\log n)$ steps using successor pointers. If we encounter a green node, we are done. If not, we end up at a node q'' with the same green successor as q. Since q is at distance $\Theta((\log n)/n)$ preceding q'', we can use q as the starting node to perform the green node lookup for q'', also providing the answer for q.

2.4   Load Balance

For a given subgroup, our protocol treats certain nodes (the ancestors of green nodes) as "special" nodes that carry information about the subgroup. These nodes attract query-answering work even though they are not part of the group, which may seem unfair. But much the same happens in the standard Chord protocol, where certain nodes "near" (immediately preceding) a given node become responsible for answering lookups of that node. And like the Chord protocol, our protocol exhibits a nice load balancing behavior when there are numerous subgroups. Recall that for a subgroup X, the "root" of the lookup tree for a subgroup named X is determined by a hash of the name, and is therefore effectively random. Thus, by symmetry, all addresses have the same probability of being on the lookup path for a given subgroup query. Since Chord distributes nodes almost-uniformly over the address space, we can conclude that the probability of any node being "hit" by a subgroup query is small. More precisely, since there are $O(\log n)$ steps per subgroup query, and each node is responsible for an $O(1/n)$ fraction of the address space in expectation, the probability a given node is hit by a subgroup query is $O((\log n)/n)$.

Of course, queries about the *same* subgroup tend to hit the same nodes. But suppose that many different subgroups are formed. The random (hashed) placement of query tree roots means that queries to *different* subgroups are *not* correlated to each other. This makes it very unlikely for any node to be involved in queries for many different subgroups. Space precludes fully formalizing this effect, but as one particular example, suppose that m different (possibly overlapping) subgroups are formed, and that one subgroup lookup is done for each group. Then with high probability, each node in the ring will be hit by $O(m(\log n)/n)$ subgroup queries.

3   Discussion

We stated and analyzed a protocol that allows for the creation of subgroups of nodes in the Chord P2P protocol. These subgroups are useful for efficiently carrying out computations or functions that do not require the involvement of all nodes. Our protocol utilizes the routing functionality of the existing Chord ring, so that subgroups can be implemented more efficiently than by creating a separate routing infrastructure for each subgroup.

Adding a node to the subgroup, or locating a node of the subgroup that follows a given address takes $O(\log n)$ hops. Although the algorithm is omitted for space reasons, the deletion of nodes from a subgroup can be performed in the same time bounds.

Our scheme requires only $O(k)$ storage per size-k subgroup, compared to the $O(k \log k)$ storage resulting from creating a new Chord ring for the subgroup. As opposed to the naive scheme, however, our protocol requires that information is stored at machines that are not part of the subgroup. We do not think that this is a significant problem however, as the protocol load is roughly equally distributed among at least $\Omega(k)$ machines in the network – the machines corresponding to the top k nodes in the embedded tree for a subgroup. A more complete analysis of the load distribution properties of our protocol will be in the full version of this paper.

Beyond the simple resource-usage metrics, our subring approach has an important complexity benefit over one using redundant, independent rings for each subgroup. The primal chord ring needs to handle complex correctness issues, keeping redundant successor pointers to preserve ring connectivity in the face of node failures, carefully maintaining successor pointers so as to avoid race conditions that would create artificial network partitions, and so on. Subrings can take all of this infrastructure for granted, using less robust but more efficient algorithms and relying on the primal chord ring to guarantee eventual correctness. Our approach thus parallels Chord's approach of layering efficient elements (such as proximity routing) atop a core that focuses on correctness issues (such as preserving connectivity).

Acknowledgments

We would like to thank the anonymous reviewers for their helpful comments.

References

1. Stoica, I., Morris, R., Karger, D., Kaashoek, F., Balakrishnan, H.: Chord: A Scalable Peer-to-peer Lookup Service for Internet Applications. In: Proceedings ACM SIGCOMM. (2001) 149–160
2. Sit, E., Dabek, F., Robertson, J.: UsenetDHT: A Low Overhead Usenet Server. In: Proceedings IPTPS. (2004)
3. Karp, B., Ratnasamy, S., Rhea, S., Shenker, S.: Spurring Adoption of DHTs with OpenHash, a Public DHT Service. In: Proceedings IPTPS. (2004)
4. Mislove, A., Druschel, P.: Providing Administrative Control and Autonomy in Peer-to-Peer Overlays. In: Proceedings IPTPS. (2004)
5. Kaashoek, F., Karger, D.R.: Koorde: A Simple Degree-optimal Hash Table. In: Proceedings IPTPS. (2003)

Author Index